CONSTRUCTION OF DATA PROCESSING SOFTWARE

John Elder

Queen's University of Belfast, Northern Ireland

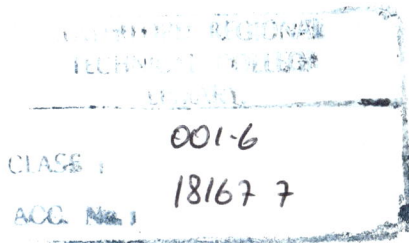

Prentice / Hall PHI International

Englewood Cliffs, NJ   London   New Delhi   Rio de Janeiro
Singapore   Sydney   Tokyo   Toronto   Wellington

Library of Congress Cataloging in Publication Data

Elder, John, 1949–
  Construction of data processing software.

  Bibliography: p.
  Includes index.
  1. Electronic digital computers — Programming.   2. File
organization (Computer science)   3. COBOL (Computer
program language)   I. Title.
QA76.6.E434   1984   001.64′2   83–24495
ISBN 0–13–168675–5 (pbk.)

British Library Cataloguing in Publication Data

Elder, John
  Construction of data processing software.
  1. Electronic data procesing
  I. Title
  001.6   QA76

  ISBN 0–13–168675–5

ISBN 0-13-168675 5

PRENTICE-HALL INTERNATIONAL, INC., *London*
PRENTICE-HALL OF AUSTRALIA PTY. LTD., *Sydney*
PRENTICE-HALL CANADA, INC., *Toronto*
PRENTICE-HALL OF INDIA PRIVATE LIMITED, *New Delhi*
PRENTICE-HALL OF JAPAN, INC., *Tokyo*
PRENTICE-HALL OF SOUTHEAST ASIA PTE. LTD., *Singapore*
PRENTICE-HALL INC., *Englewood Cliffs, New Jersey*
PRENTICE-HALL DO BRASIL LTDA., *Rio de Janeiro*
WHITEHALL BOOKS LIMITED, *Wellington, N.Z.*

Printed in the United States of America

10 9 8 7 6 5 4 3 2 1

CONSTRUCTION OF
DATA PROCESSING SOFTWARE

Prentice-Hall International
Series in Computer Science

C.A.R. Hoare, Series Editor

Published

BACKHOUSE, R.C., *Syntax of Programming Languages: Theory and Practice*

de BAKKER, J.W., *Mathematical Theory of Program Correctness*

BJORNER, D. and JONES, C., *Formal Specification and Software Development*

CLARK, K.L. and McCABE, F.G., *micro-PROLOG: Programming in Logic*

DROMEY, R.G., *How to Solve it by Computer*

DUNCAN, F., *Microprocessor Programming and Software Development*

ELDER, J., *Construction of Data Processing Software*

GOLDSCHLAGER, L. and LISTER, A., *Computer Science: A Modern Introduction*

HENDERSON, P., *Functional Programming: Application and Implementation*

INMOS, *The Occam Programming Manual*

JACKSON, M.A., *System Development*

JONES, C.B., *Software Development: A Rigorous Approach*

MACCALLUM, I., *Pascal for the Apple*

REYNOLDS, J.C., *The Craft of Programming*

TENNENT, R.D., *Principles of Programming Languages*

WELSH, J. and ELDER, J., *Introduction to Pascal*, 2nd Edition

WELSH, J. and McKEAG, M., *Structured System Programming*

CONTENTS

LISTINGS INCLUDED IN TEXT

PREFACE

This book is about the construction of programs for the implementation of data processing applications. It does not take the established pattern of most books in this area which typically use the treatment of a programming language, usually COBOL, as a means of introducing the various data processing activities together with the file structures and processing techniques to support these activities. Instead it examines the basic concepts, applications, and algorithms employed, as well as the different file organizations and their properties, before proceeding to considering their implementation in, and use of, particular programming languages.

The book is intended for use by computer science students who already have a knowledge of the basic properties of computer systems hardware, particularly input–output and mass-storage devices, and have taken an introductory programming course, preferably in Pascal or some similar language. The approach taken here is therefore to treat the particular application area of commercial data processing in the same way that computer scientists are taught about other applications areas such as compilers and operating systems, i.e., by the use of abstraction, the specification of appropriate abstract data types, and the use of concurrent processes. To this end the first programming notation employed is based upon an extended version of Pascal, known as Pascal Plus.

There are three main aims in writing this book:

1. to present the basic concepts and algorithms of commercial data processing;
2. to describe the properties of the main file organization methods, their associated access methods, the practical use of these file organizations, and their implementation;

3. to provide a sound basis for the introduction to programming in COBOL which forms the subject matter of the second part of the book.

The material of the book is split into two parts. Part 1 concentrates on introducing various file structures and algorithms for processing such files and using them in typical applications. Part 2 provides an introduction to a practical subset of American National Standard (ANSI) COBOL, as defined by the 1974 standard, and the use of COBOL to implement the algorithms and programs of Part 1.

A central feature of the book is the development and implementation of a case study suite of programs for a hypothetical savings bank application. These programs illustrate all of the major concepts presented in the text. Although the application itself is somewhat simplistic, and hence the programs developed are unrealistically small, the case study system nonetheless provides an appropriate illustration of the implementation of a set of typical file processing activities common to so many actual systems. Part 1 uses our Pascal-based language for implementing these programs; in Part 2 they are implemented in COBOL. The notations and design methods presented are appropriate as a basis for the implementation of file-processing applications not only in COBOL but also in other languages such as Pascal (and many languages based upon, or similar to Pascal) and Ada.

Part 1 begins with an introduction to typical data processing activities. It then introduces Pascal Plus, which is characterized by its provision of features to support the definition of abstract data types and concurrent processes. There then follows coverage of sequential, random, and indexed sequential file organizations (including the specification and implementation of abstract data types for such file structures), a definition of a file processing environment, and consideration of the algorithms associated with the processing of the various types of files. In particular, their use in master file updating, data validation, file sorting and report writing is considered in detail.

Part 2 begins with an introduction to the basic features of COBOL — its data structures, basic control structures, string-handling, and table-handling facilities. Individual chapters then describe the various file processing features provided by COBOL and their use in the application areas identified in Part 1. The COBOL subset described here is based upon the 1974 COBOL standard. This subset is sufficient to give a thorough introduction to the language and its use.

Where appropriate, each chapter has been augmented with a set of exercises, including both pen-and-paper and programming exercises.

My sincere thanks are due to Professor Tony Hoare for his
invaluable advice on the approach to be taken in writing the book, to
Damien McKeever for always being willing to discuss both the general ideas and the particular details, and to Henry Hirschberg of
Prentice-Hall International for his friendly and constant bullying
which resulted in the book reaching completion. The material has
been used in undergraduate courses at the Queen's University of
Belfast, and thanks must go to those students who endured the
various drafts and made constructive (and other!) suggestions. Some
of the exercises are taken from examination papers of the University.

The library modules and programs presented in Part 1 are
expressed in a non-executable program design notation based upon,
and almost identical to, the Pascal Plus programming language. However, readers with access to the VAX/VMS implementation of Pascal
Plus will find that practical versions of the file and data structures
developed herein have been implemented for that particular environment, and are available in standard Pascal Plus source form in the
system library.

JOHN ELDER
Belfast
January 1984

Part 1

FILES
AND
FILE PROCESSING

1 INTRODUCTION TO DATA PROCESSING

1.1 WHAT IS DATA PROCESSING?

The word *data* means facts that are known and from which inferences may be made; *processing* is any action that enables usable information to be derived from the data. Thus the term *data processing* is descriptive of computer-based systems in general, but is usually understood to refer to the class of computing activity which is involved with tasks such as financial accounting, stock and production control, maintenance of information on people, etc. Such applications typically involve the storage of large volumes of data in files, with this data periodically being updated, and reports generated summarizing certain aspects of the contents of the files. Essentially, data processing covers those computerized systems which are involved with recording the movement and control of data describing people, money, and goods — hence these applications are also commonly referred to as *business* or *commercial data processing*.

Typical data processing applications range across a wide spectrum. Nowadays most large organizations, and many smaller ones, have computerized accounting systems from which the familiar computer-printed statements and bills are produced ready to be sent to customers. If such an organization is, say, involved in wholesaling goods, it will almost certainly have a computerized stock control system which records the movement of stock in and out of its shops, depots, or warehouses, automatically sends invoices to its customers for goods purchased and produces reorder requests to be sent to its suppliers when in-stock quantities fall below some critical level, maintains details of all the financial transactions involved, and will generate management reports summarizing, e.g., the current stock

1

levels and sales statistics for given periods of time. A manufacturing company may well have a production control system which ensures that sufficient parts are always on hand for production purposes and generates production schedules so that the required products are manufactured in sufficient quantities. The raw data maintained by such systems also enables other information to be derived from it, e.g., from a stock control system's data it is possible to obtain sales statistics for particular products, as mentioned above.

Most organizations will use a computer system to maintain records containing details of all their employees so that staff information may be readily obtained — similarly many doctors now keep their patients' health records in a computer so that patient information may be obtained rapidly. Banks are among the very largest computer users and modern banking systems are among the most complex computer systems in existence — such systems have to maintain various types of financial information relating to customers in many branches, providing multi-branch banking facilities, ready-cash terminal facilities and automatic tellers, in locations that may be separated by very large distances.

Government agencies are also heavily involved in data processing activities — the Health Services, Inland Revenue, Education Boards, are all examples of public organizations which maintain and process large volumes of centralized data. Other common data processing applications that one meets in everyday life include reservation systems for hotels, theatres, and airlines; the production of mailing lists for advertising purposes; credit card accounting, and so on.

Data processing applications are characterized by the large amounts of data which they require to have stored. This data is usually held in files of records with each record containing detailed information relating to one of the objects of the system — e.g., people in a health records system; goods in stock control systems; money in accounting systems. These records are often held in some significant order, e.g., in alphabetical order for customer records, or account number order for banking records, in order to facilitate their location within the file concerned. From time to time these files will usually be *updated* — for example, on each occasion that goods are dispatched from a warehouse the stock control system must modify the records for the goods concerned to reflect the change in stock levels caused by the dispatch. The data describing the dispatch is known as *transaction data* — typically many such transactions will require to be processed, although the work involved in changing the file records concerned will normally require nothing more than some simple arithmetic.

The *accuracy* of all data entering a computer system in the form of transactions is essential as otherwise the information generated by the system will not be trustworthy — if a transaction states that 100 items of a given product were dispatched whereas 10 were actually dispatched then the stock levels for that product as recorded by the system will be inaccurate thereafter. Transactions entering a banking system must be correct as customers will obviously not tolerate mistakes in their accounts (except possibly in their favor, in which case the bank itself will not be too happy!).

From the files in a system periodical *reports* can be produced. In a banking system monthly statements can be produced to provide account holders and the bank with information about the state of their accounts; in a stock control system monthly reports could detail the current stock levels and give statistics about stock movement over the previous month (to enable management to take planning decisions). Such reports are usually printed but may also be provided for display on a video display unit.

A typical data processing system will thus consist, possibly, of many files of data and a larger number of applications programs which update and consult these files — a company's financial system might contain files recording details of all the goods it buys and supplies, the names and addresses of all its suppliers and customers, details of all goods currently on order from suppliers, details of goods to be sent to customers, personnel records, and taxation details — the programs which process these files would include production control, stock control, invoicing, billing, payment, and payroll programs.

For some of these programs the data required for a particular application might be gathered over a certain period of time and the program concerned run at regular intervals — for instance, in a stock control system details of all incoming supplies and outgoing dispatches might be accumulated over a period of, say, 24 hours, and the program which updates the master stock control file run once daily. Such a program is known as a *batch program*, since the transaction data is batched before being presented to the program. On the other hand, this same application could be implemented as a continuously running program to which details of a new transaction could be presented immediately they become available (possibly by a clerk typing in details through the keyboard of a terminal connected to the computer) and the master file records concerned updated at that point in time. The updating program in this case would be known as a *real-time program*, since the file updating is performed as soon as the transaction data becomes available. Similarly, a real-time program could be written to enable details of current stock levels to be made available upon demand and immediately displayed on a terminal screen.

The vast majority of commercial data processing activity is performed by small and medium-sized businesses, and hence the computers they use are small-to-medium size machines, although, of course, the large computer users still employ mainframe computers. The most important property required of whatever type of system is used is that it should provide a high rate of data transfer between the main memory of the computer and the peripheral devices, particularly magnetic tape and disk drives, on which the data files will be held. Since comparatively simple processing takes place on a file record once it has been retrieved from the file and read into memory but many such records are processed in a program run, it is important to use a computer system which enables fast record access and transfer rather than high-speed arithmetic facilities. In the early days of commercial data processing the peripheral devices used for transaction input were card readers and punched tape readers, and output was directed to line printers and card and tape punches. Nowadays more sophisticated devices are also employed — input may come from the keyboard of a video display unit (VDU), or a point-of-sale terminal, or from a magnetic ink character recognition device reading the data encoded in magnetic ink on a bank check, or from typed documents read by an optical character reader. Advances in both computer hardware (particularly the development of such input devices and random-access mass storage devices for holding files) and computer system design techniques, have led to a great increase in the scope and complexity of computer applications. Commercial data processing has now overlapped into the fields of application previously classified as real-time systems, communications systems, and even scientific computing, as the result of the introduction of on-line management information systems and national and worldwide networks of information systems, such as airline and hotel reservation systems, which many computer users have successfully integrated with their existing batch-processng and file-handling systems such as those described above.

1.2   STRUCTURE OF DATA PROCESSING SYSTEMS

As indicated in the previous section most data processing systems are based upon the existence of permanent files of semi-permanent data (such files are known as *master files*). The programs in a system typically include some *enquiry programs* which extract information from these master files (e.g., the current stock levels of goods in a warehouse), and also *updating programs* which modify the data in the master file records (e.g., details of receipt or dispatch of goods in the warehouse). Periodically *report programs* will also be run to produce summarized information from the master file data.

The transaction data coming into a system will require consultation of, or modification to, the data in some of the master file records. There is also incoming *amendment data* which causes changes to be made to the more static data held in the master file records, e.g., in an invoicing system any changes in the price of goods results in an amendment of the price recorded in the master file records for the goods concerned. Such transactions and amendments, which may be input on punched cards or keyed in directly by an operator, must be examined as they enter the system to ensure that the data they contain appears to be as correct as it is possible to determine. This process of rigorous examination of incoming data is known as *data validation* (and is discussed in greater detail in Chapter 6).

In the previous section we classified systems into two categories — batch systems and real-time systems. In a batch system

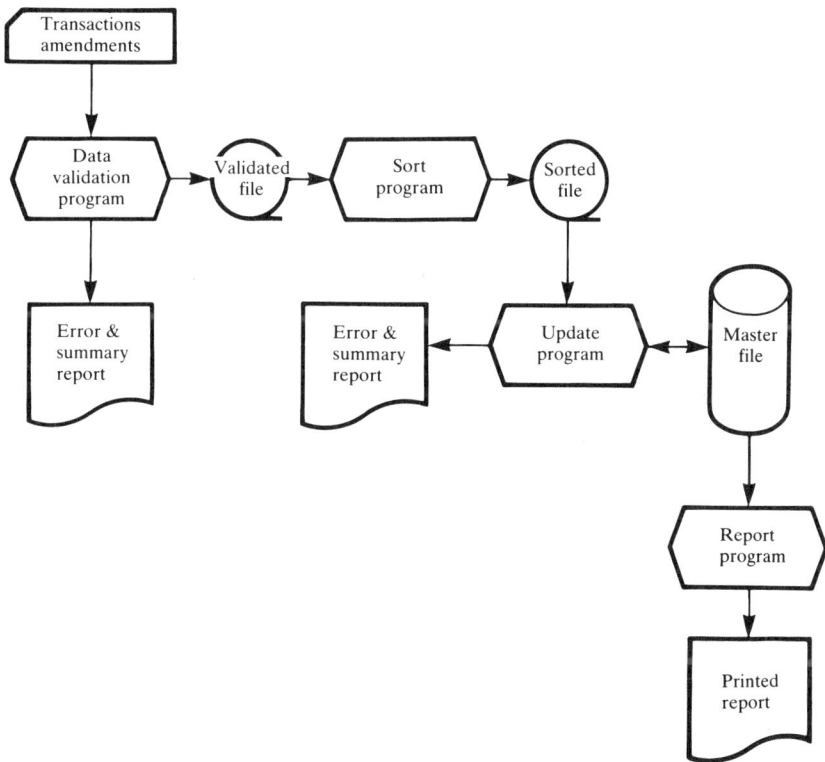

Figure 1.1   Typical batch processing system structure

an input file of (unvalidated) transaction and amendment data

a file held on a mass-storage device (magnetic tape or disk)

a file held on magnetic tape

a file held on magnetic disk

a human-readable report (produced on paper or a screen)

a file-processing program

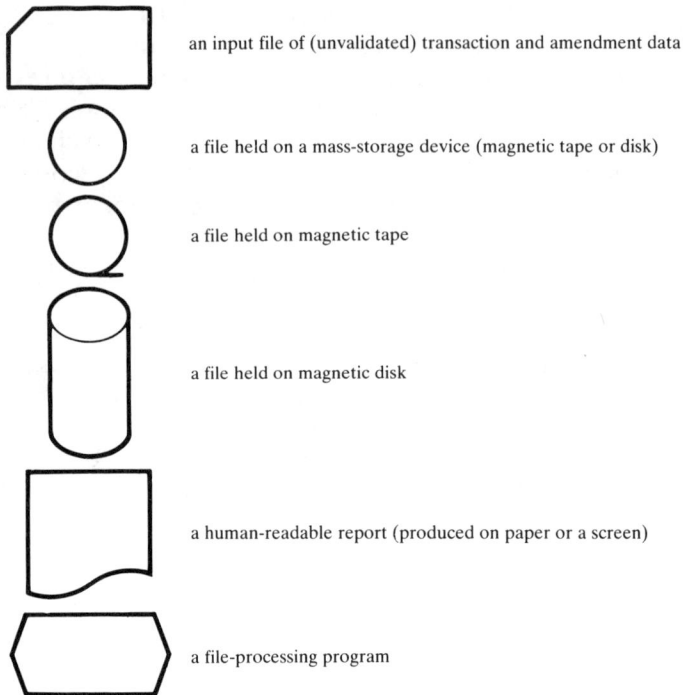

Figure 1.2   System diagram symbols

the file processing programs are scheduled to be run at fixed intervals of time (e.g., daily, weekly, monthly). All the transactions and amendments produced since the last run of the program concerned are batched together and initially processed by a data validation program which identifies any input records which appear to contain incorrect data. They are then (usually) sorted according to some key field in their data to produce a file of sorted transactions, which is then presented to the program that will be used to consult and update the master file. In this case the records in the master file are usually organized in the same sorted order as the records in the transaction and amendment batch and the file is stored on magnetic tape or disk. Figure 1.1 illustrates the structure of a typical batch processing system.

In this book we shall present various system diagrams such as that above. The symbols shown in Figure 1.2 will be used.

The system presented in Figure 1.1 might typically be a payroll system or stock inventory control system, in which cases the actual data might be as indicated in Figure 1.3.

	PAYROLL	INVENTORY CONTROL
Master files	employee records (name, address, works number, rate of pay and deductions) ordered by employee number	items in stock (item code, description, quantities in stock, reorder level and reorder quantity) ordered by item code
Transactions	time-cards	items received and dispatched
Amendments	new employees, pay rises	newly stocked items, deleted items no longer stocked, price changes
Reports	pay slips, credit transfers, payroll summaries	invoices, checks, stock reorders

Figure 1.3　Data files for payroll and inventory systems

In a payroll system the *key field* which would be used to order the master file records and determine the order into which a batch of time cards would be sorted would be the employee identification number (the company would allocate each newly employed worker a unique number and a master file record would then be created for him or her). In a stock control system the key data field would be the code number associated with each unique type of good stocked. Indeed, for a particular record type, the key field may be different according to the nature of the particular applications for which the records are used.

The various files in such batch processing systems might be stored on a variety of devices:

1. The batch of transactions and amendments might be held on punched cards.
2. The validated transactions and amendments records which pass the data validation stage might be written on to a magnetic tape or disk file.
3. The sorted transactions and amendments will probably also be written on to a magnetic tape or disk file.
4. The master files may be held on either magnetic tape (in which case the records will definitely be held in sorted order of the relevant key data field) or on magnetic disk (in which case, as we shall see, the records need not be ordered).
5. Outputs such as pay slips and bank credit transfers will be produced on line printer files, whereas details of current stock levels, say, might be produced on a terminal screen.

For a payroll system typical functions of the programs in the system would be:

1. the data validation program would verify that the employee number is legal and that the hours worked are realistic, as well as checking for general keying errors;
2. the sorting program would sort the validated time cards into ascending order of employee number;
3. the update program updates the details of the employees' total pay held on the master file, and uses the contents of the master file record for each employee (e.g., income tax code and details of other deductions) to produce pay slips and credit transfers;
4. various report programs might be run at different times including an annual program to give each employee details of his year's pay (for taxation confirmation purposes), or for management to be informed of the total salary paid to each employee, to (say) the employees in each department, and to the organization as a whole.

Although punched cards have been a primary means of inputting transaction data to computers for many years they are expensive, bulky to store and transport, and the input rate of punched card readers is quite slow. Nowadays transaction data is usually input directly to a system through a terminal (on-line input) or else by means of a secondary off-line *key-to-disk data entry system*. The equipment in a typical key-to-disk system consists of a number of terminals, or *keying stations* (e.g., 16 in Figure 1.4), a small computer, and disk drives. Operators at the keying stations input data which is edited and for-

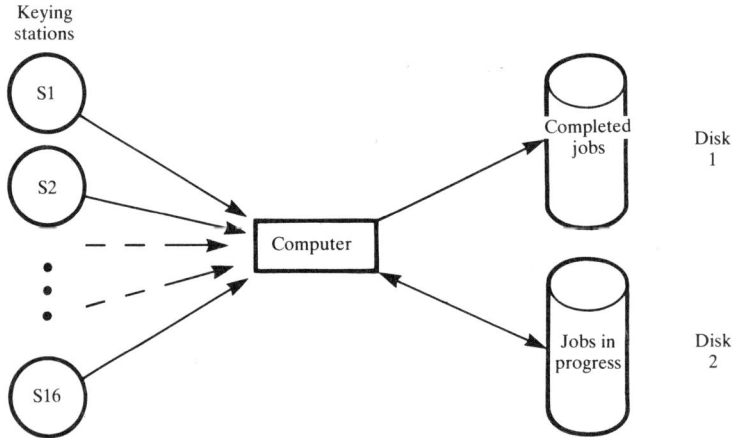

Figure 1.4   Key-to-disk data entry system

matted by the computer and written to a disk (disk 2, in Figure 1.4).
Completed jobs are transferred to another disk, whose contents are
then passed on to the main computer system for processing.

Enhanced key-to-disk systems often incorporate *intelligent terminals* which contain special software to perform tasks such as validation of the input data, error correction, editing, sorting of input data records, and collation of records so that the output produced by the key-to-disk system is immediately usable by the main data processing system.

A *real-time system* is one which receives inputs directly from its environment and transmits a reply quickly enough to influence that environment. An example of such a system would be an airline reservations system in which operators and travel agents at terminals enter enquiries and expect almost immediate responses from the system. Here fast access is required to the master files concerned as clients are only prepared to wait a short time for information, and so these files are held on random- (direct-) access devices such as magnetic drums and disks which enable rapid retrieval of the records required (in this case the records containing details of the flight in which the client is interested).

Additional problems in real-time systems arise from the fact that inputs to the system are usually random — terminal users (i.e., agents at different locations) can be simultaneously carrying out different enquiries which may even make use of different programs in the computer. Hence all the programs and files of the system must be immediately accessible. The orderliness of batch processing is sacrificed since the timing of events is no longer under the control of the system.

Thus if, in our example inventory system, we decide to extend the system to handle transactions on-line (i.e., transactions are generated at random time intervals from terminal inputs and require immediate processing) then the master file will have to be stored on disk or drum rather than magnetic tape to enable fast access to the relevant stock records (e.g., a customer may wish to know immediately if there is sufficient stock to fulfill his proposed order) and programs must be written to provide real-time file access and user communication.

1.3   THE MODEL SAVINGS BANK LIMITED

The case study programs presented in this book implement a model data processing system for the Model Savings Bank Limited — a mythical nation-wide savings organization which uses a central

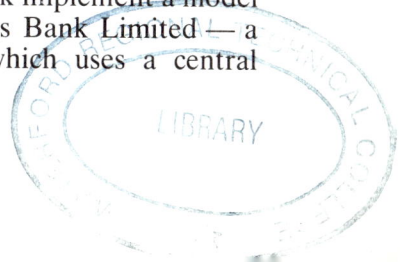

SUPER 2000 computer (a hypothetical machine with a standard COBOL compiler). Its branches are split up into a number of regional areas; there are six regions each having up to 50 branches at present. Each member of the bank, when he or she opens a new savings account, receives a passbook in which all transactions will be recorded for his own information and that of the bank tellers with whom he will deal, and is allocated a unique eight character account number (of which the first seven characters are digits) that also identifies the branch at which the member's account is held. This account number is structured as shown below, where X indicates a character and 9 a digit.

The first digit identifies the region in which the member's branch is located, the next two digits are the regional branch number, the next four digits are the member's local account number, and the final character is a so-called Modulus 11 check digit which enables the validity of a quoted account number to be determined.

Each time that a new account is opened or an existing account is closed, an appropriate form is submitted by the member, from which an amendment record is generated with the following format:

columns 1– 6 : date (in YYMMDD format, e.g., 830201 represents 1 February 1983)
columns 7–14 : account number
column   15 : transaction kind (N–new account, X– closed account)
columns 16–21 : amount deposited (in cents) — applies only to new accounts
columns 22–51 : client identity (used only for new accounts)
columns 52–80 : other information

For example, if William G. Smith had opened an account at branch number 17 in region 6 on 1 February 1983 (for which he had been allocated the local branch account number 12345), and deposited 200 dollars in this new account, the following string of characters would have been generated to record the opening of this new account:

```
83020161712345N020000WILLIAM G. SMITH
```

Whenever an existing account is credited or debited a particular amount a transaction record is generated with the same format as an amendment record, except that column 15 will contain either C (indicating a credit) or D (indicating a debit), and the amount concerned will appear in columns 16 to 21.

These transactions are assumed to be generated by means of a key-to-disk system of the type shown in Figure 1.4 where the keying stations are located in the various bank branches and each is connected to a centralized computer. No validation of the input transactions is performed by this data entry subsystem.

The rules of the bank are that there is an upper limit of $20 000 on the amount which a member may have in his account. No account is allowed to become overdrawn, and no one debit may exceed $2000. At the end of each month the savings bank pays monthly interest to its members, calculated as a percentage of their minimum balance

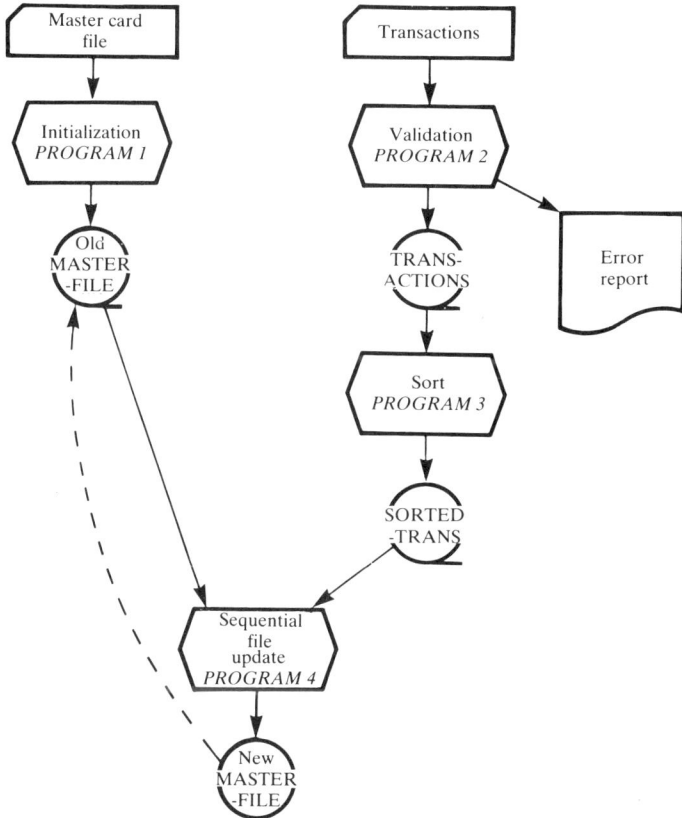

Figure 1.5   System based on magnetic tape master files

during the past month. The first $5000 of this minimum balance earns interest at a given lower rate, while the remainder earns interest at a higher rate.

Figure 1.5 indicates the structure of the original system used by the Model Savings Bank Limited to maintain its customer account records.

This initial system used magnetic tape master files to hold the account records with the records stored in the master files in ascending order of the account number in each account record. The records in these files had the following format (where X denotes an alphanumeric character and 9 a digit):

X(8)	X(30)	9999999	9999999
Account number	Client identity	Balance	Minimum Balance

For a given account such a record details the account number, the identity of the account holder, his current balance, and his minimum balance during the previous calendar month. The balances (which cannot be negative) are recorded as seven-digit integers representing amounts in cents.

Initially this file was created by a program (*PROGRAM1* in Figure 1.5) which read the customer account records organized as a punched card file of records in ascending account number order and wrote the initial version of the master file (known as the old MASTER-FILE). This punched card file will be used in Chapter 11 in an introductory demonstration COBOL program, and the implementation of *PROGRAM1* is fully described in Chapters 5 and 13.

Each day the transaction and amendment records keyed from the contents of the forms filled in by customers at each branch were formed (the past tense is used here since the system was subsequently changed, as will be described later) into a batch which was then forwarded down a communications line to a central site for processing in order to update the bank's master file of members' account records. At the central site all the batches arriving each day would be formed into a complete batch for the day concerned. Periodically (say every two or three days) the batches collected since the last file update would be submitted, in chronological order, to a data validation program *PROGRAM2* which rejected any records that appeared to contain errors (e.g., dates which were not possible such as 31 April; account numbers which appeared to be invalid; or transaction kinds which were not keyed as C or D or N or X; records which were out of chronological sequence; records in which amounts were non-numeric; or other errors resulting from the form being filled in incorrectly or mispunched by the key punch operator) All trans-action and amendment records which passed these validation checks were then written to a magnetic tape file of validated transaction and amendment records (TRANSACTIONS in Figure 1.5). *PROGRAM2* is presented in Chapters 6 and 14.

Since the valid transactions tape file TRANSACTIONS was not ordered by account number but by date it was not in a suitable form for immediate use in updating the sequential master file. Instead the valid transactions file was processed first by a sorting program *PROGRAM3* which sorted the valid transactions into ascending account number (with transactions for the same account ordered by date) and wrote them to another magnetic tape file SORTED-TRANS. Full details of *PROGRAM3* are given in Chapters 7 and 15.

Next the file SORTED-TRANS was used to update the latest version of the MASTER-FILE. The program *PROGRAM4* produced a new updated version of the master tape file, referred to as the new MASTER-FILE in Figure 1.5. This new master file would then be used as input to the next master file update run, and the old version of the master file retained as a security back-up in case any sub-sequent updates were affected by a hardware or software malfunc-tion. During the file update process any credit transactions which caused a current account balance to exceed the legal maximum, and any debits which would have resulted in an account balance becoming negative, were rejected and details of them reported so that remedial action could be taken by the bank. The implementation of *PRO-GRAM4* appears in Chapters 5 and 13.

The contents of the current master file were used to produce various reports for management purposes. At the end of each month the savings bank management required details of the total savings currently invested in the bank as a whole, in each of the regional areas, and in each branch. Since the first digit of each member's account number is the area number of his branch, and the next two digits are the branch number, the master file account records were already ordered by area number, and then by branch number within the account records for each area. Hence the file was suitably struc-tured for the immediate generation of such a report. The crediting of monthly interest to members was also incorporated in this process, but the consequent altering of the account balances and resetting of minimum balances required the generation of a new, updated, master file as shown in Figure 1.6. The production of a program *PRO-GRAM5* to implement this reporting and interest-payment process is described in Chapters 10 and 18. Other reports that could be pro-duced include a periodic print-out giving the current balance of each

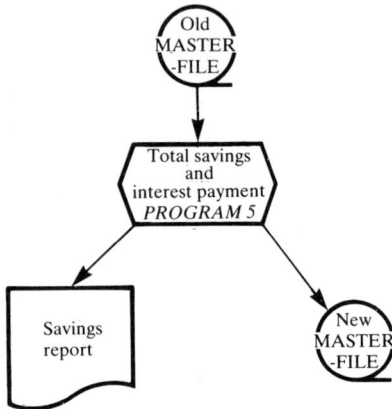

Figure 1.6 Savings report and interest payment process

member of the savings bank, ordered by account-number (for sending to the tax authorities, say).

The reader may well have noticed certain shortcomings in this particular system, resulting from the long delay between generation of a transaction record and its eventual processing as part of an accumulated batch of such records. This delay means that the account records are never quite up-to-date, and that accounts may become overdrawn, or the total balance exceed the legal maximum, without detection at the time the transaction is carried out (although this should not happen as the teller concerned will be able to determine the member's current balance from the member's passbook). In the event of a transaction form being completed incorrectly, it may be several days before the error is detected, which may even make it impossible to remedy the error.

Another problem in the system is the number of different versions of the master file that are created — a new version is constructed each time an update run is performed or the monthly interest payment report is run. In Chapters 8 and 9 we shall reconsider the design of the system using direct-access magnetic disk master files to overcome most of these problems.

1.4 COMMERCIAL PROGRAMMING LANGUAGES

The high-level languages used in commercial data processing fall into two groups, usually referred to as *procedural* and *non-procedural* languages. Programs written in a procedural language define how the processing is to be done, whereas programs written in a non-procedural language generally require the user to specify what is to be done and leave the language system to determine how to do it — they are sometimes called *fill-in-form* languages.

Procedural languages may be roughly subdivided into two sub-groups — those that offer a large number of standard features (e.g., PL/1, COBOL) and those that contain a few basic concepts upon which the user then builds (e.g., Pascal). The former category is generally preferred by programmers employed in commercial data processing since the use of these languages requires less effort on the part of the programmer, but this ease of use is offset by the problems caused by the size of such languages — the difficulty in fully learning and understanding the language, the effort that must be put into providing high-quality implementations, and the differing versions of the language that usually result.

COBOL is the traditional language for implementing commercial data processing software. PL/1 and RPGII (a non-procedural language) are becoming more popular. Part 1 of this book describes the properties of various types of files used in data processing, and develops various algorithms for use in performing the types of activities we have identified in this chapter. The notations we shall use in defining these properties and algorithms will be based upon those of the programming language Pascal, and the next chapter introduces the Pascal features that will be used as well as some necessary extensions to Pascal. In Part 2 the implementation of these algorithms, and of the programs employing the algorithms, using the facilities of COBOL, will be examined.

2 PROGRAM AND DATA ABSTRACTIONS

This book is primarily concerned with the design and implementation of programs to manipulate files of data. We will present various file processing algorithms that are commonly used in such programs and hence we require a notation in which to express these algorithms. It is assumed that the reader has some knowledge of the programming language Pascal — the algorithms, and also the design of various application programs employing the algorithms, will be expressed in an extended version of Pascal.

We shall find it necessary to extend the concepts provided by Pascal in two areas. Firstly, we shall be dealing with various types of file structures and will specify the properties of, and operations performable on, these file types. In order to separate the *logical* properties (upon which we wish to concentrate) from the actual *physical* representation of files (which will also be considered) we shall introduce the concept of an *abstract data type*, and develop notations for the description of such types. Secondly, when we come to the consideration of the problems of generating reports based upon the contents of data files (in Chapter 10) we will find that the report construction algorithm is most clearly expressed (and implemented) as a number of *concurrent activities*, i.e., as a number of *processes* which execute in parallel. Hence we shall extend the sequential programming notations of Pascal with additional notations to define concurrent processes and their interactions.

To summarize the approach we shall take, in Part 1 we will be using a language based on Pascal to specify various types of files and the operations provided for such files, and then to design algorithms and applications programs using various files in our case study system. Although we shall use this language as a design language, it is almost identical to the programming language Pascal Plus, except for a few minor differences. Those familiar with languages such as Ada, Concurrent Pascal, Modula, Pascal Plus, and Simula will recognize the similarities between the notations used here and those provided in such languages. The remainder of this chapter gives a very brief overview (for revision purposes) of those features of Pascal which we shall use, and introduces the additional notations for abstract data types and concurrent processes.

Most file processing programs in the commercial computing world are written in COBOL, and no text on the construction of such programs can ignore this fact. Hence in Part 2 all of our program designs are ultimately expressed in COBOL. Chapters 11 and 12 give an introduction to the basic features of COBOL and subsequent chapters of Part 2 describe the COBOL features necessary to implement the file-handling concepts presented in Part 1. However, by first using our Pascal-based language to specify the properties of the file types concerned and then to design the programs using these files, a greater appreciation can be gained of the nature of the operations that may be performed on the various types of files. Hopefully, it then becomes a less difficult task to understand the purpose and use of the COBOL features and thus to actually write the applications programs correctly in COBOL.

2.1 THE PROGRAMMING LANGUAGE PASCAL

The range of features provided by Pascal supports the stepwise refinement program design technique and is a balance of facilities for the description of data and performable operations on that data that is useful for the solution of a wide range of programming problems. These features reflect the strong correspondence between the structure of data and the structure of the processing required by the data.

Pascal provides four primitive scalar types

- The type *boolean* whose two values are denoted by the constant identifiers *true* and *false*, representing the logical truth values.
- The type *integer* defines an ordered set of whole numbers.
- The values of the type *char* are an ordered set of implementation-defined characters denoted by character literals, e.g., '*A*', '*#*'.
- The values of the type *real* are approximate representations of real numbers.

For any of these types constant values may be denoted by identifiers declared in constant definitions, e.g.

> **const**   *numberofcardreaders* = 3 ;
> *terminator* = ' . ' ;

The standard constant identifier *maxint* denotes the maximum positive integer value provided by the particular Pascal implementation.

In the Pascal if statement

> **if** *C* **then** *S1* **else** *S2*

the expression *C* must produce a boolean value that determines which of the alternative actions *S1* or *S2* is executed. The **else** limb may be omitted.

The repetitive control constructs

> **while** *C* **do** *S*
> **repeat** *S1* ; *S2* ; ... ; *Sn* **until** *C*

also involve the use of a controlling boolean expression *C* whose value determines whether execution of the repetitive loop is to continue.

Other types with two or more values may be defined by emunerating the identifiers that are to be used to denote these values, e.g.,

> **type** *sex* = (*male*, *female*) ;
> *transactiontype* = (*credit*, *debit*, *newaccount*, *deletion*) ;
> *dayofweek* =(*Sunday*,   *Monday*,   *Tuesday*,   *Wednesday*,
>   *Thursday*, *Friday*, *Saturday*) ;
> *peripheral* = (*cardreader*, *cardpunch*, *tape*, *disk*, *printer*) ;
> *month* =(*January*,   *February*,   *March*,   *April*,   *May*,   *June*,
>   *July*,   *August*,   *September*,   *October*,   *November*,
>   *December*) ;

Such enumerated values are considered to be ordered as determined by the order in which the identifiers are declared, viz.,

> *Monday* < *Tuesday*

is always true. For all ordered types (other than *real*) the ability to iterate through a range of values in order is provided by the for statement, e.g.,

> **for** *d* := *Monday* **to** *Friday* **do** *checkhoursworked*

to deal with each of the five days from Monday to Friday, in turn.

The ordering property shared by the above scalar types (other than *real*) enables the declaration of subrange types such as

```
type weekday = Monday .. Friday ;
     dayofmonth = 1..31 ;
     digit = '0'..'9' ;
     year = 1980..1989 ;
```

and variables of these types are constrained to take values only within the specified range — violations of this rule are automatically detected as programming errors.

For any type with N values, an N-way choice may be made by means of a case statement. Thus, if t is a variable of type *transaction-type*

```
case t of
   credit       : addamounttobalance ;
   debit        : subtractamountfrombalance ;
   newaccount   : createnewaccountrecord ;
   deletion     : closeaccount
end
```

Security against programming error is provided by the automatic error check that is applied whenever a case statement is executed in order to ensure that the chosen value is among the listed alternatives.

Structured types describe composite values that are built (ultimately) from scalar type values. The simplest composite data item is a *record* which consists of two or more components, perhaps of different types, e.g.,

```
type date = record
              m : month ;
              d : dayofmonth ;
              y : year
            end
```

Variables of such types may be assigned the values of other variables, e.g.,

$$date1 := date2$$

or individual components selected, e.g.,

if $(date1.m = February)$ **and** $(date1.d > 29)$ **then** *dateerror*

A record type groups a number of component items together to form a composite value. Similarly, a compound statement groups together a number of component actions that may be regarded as a single item, to be controlled by some control statement such as a while statement.

```
begin { New Year's Day }
   date1.m := January ;
   date1.d := 1 ;
   date1.y := 1983
end
```

When a record value is manipulated component by component the resulting compound statement often contains several references to the fields of the same record value. Pascal's *with* statement simplifies the expression of this, e.g.,

```
with date1 do { New Year's Day }
begin m := January ; d := 1 ; y := 1983 end
```

Variant records define the union of a number of types. Consider for example the register of all cars in a country. Cars are distinguished either as local cars owned by residents of the country, or as foreign cars currently visiting the country. For local cars the data recorded is as follows :

```
localcar =   record
                make : manufacturer ;
                regnumber : carnumber ;
                owner : person ;
                firstreg : date
             end
```

while, for foreign cars, the data recorded is :

```
foreigncar =   record
                  make : manufacturer ;
                  regnumber : carnumber ;
                  origin : country
               end
```

A data type *car* covering both kinds of car is the union of these two types and may be defined in Pascal by the following record type definition with variant parts :

```
carkind = (local, foreign);
car =   record
           make : manufacturer ;
           regnumber : carnumber ;
           case kind : carkind of
           local : (owner : person ;
                    firstreg : date) ;
           foreign : (origin : country)
        end
```

An *array* consists of a number of component items identical in nature and type, e.g., var *hoursworked* · **array** [*dayofweek*] **of** 0..24

with individual elements denoted as, e.g.,

hoursworked [*Wednesday*]

or

hoursworked [*d*]

where *d* is of type *dayofweek*.

Multi-dimensional arrays may also be defined, e.g.,

var *timecard* : **array** [*employeenumber*] **of**
array [*dayofweek*] **of** 0..24

Strings are defined in Pascal as packed arrays of characters, e.g.,

type *name* = **packed array** [1..20] **of** *char*

The string

'*EXAMPLE STRING*'

is a value of the type

packed array [1..14] **of** *char*

Strings of the same type may be assigned and compared, where the ordering depends upon the ordering of the type *char*.

A *powerset* type is the set of all subsets of some ordered scalar base type. Such powersets are defined as, e.g.,

type *daysworked* = **set of** *dayofweek* ;
deviceused = **set of** *peripheral* ;
var *mydays* : *daysworked* ;
inputdevices : *devicesused* ;

and the principal set operations include

1. construction, e.g.,

mydays:= [*Monday, Wednesday..Saturday*] ;
inputdevices := [*cardreader, tape, disk*]

2. membership testing, e.g.,

if *today* **in** *mydays* **then** *Iamofftowork*

Set types are often used in 'on-the-fly' tests such as

if not (*charvalue* **in** ['0'..'9', 'X']) **then** *charactererror*

to avoid the construction of complicated expressions.

Procedures in Pascal may take value parameters or variable parameters as well as procedure and function parameters. In the procedure

```
procedure increment (var i : integer ; by : integer) ;
  begin
    i := i + by
  end {increment}
```

the formal parameter i is a variable parameter and by is a value parameter. For a call of $increment$ the corresponding actual parameters must be a variable of type $integer$, and an expression yielding an integer value, respectively. Hence, given the call

$$increment \; (j, j*k+1)$$

the value of the expression $j*k+1$ is assigned to the actual parameter by, which then acts as a local variable of $increment$, while any value assigned to i within the procedure is actually assigned to the variable j, which must be an integer variable.

Pascal procedures may also take *conformant array* parameters. These allow different calls of a procedure or function to operate on array variables of different sizes, i.e., with different bounds. We shall be concerned mainly with conformant array parameters which are strings. Given a procedure with a heading such as

```
procedure openfile (filename : packed array [m..n : integer] of char) ;
```

filename is a conformant array, and m and n are known as its *bound identifiers*. When this procedure is called it may be supplied with the value of any string constant or variable as actual parameter. Within *openfile* the bound identifiers m and n may be used in expressions to obtain the lower and upper bounds of the actual string — the fact that the lower bound is always 1 for a string parameter cannot be represented in the formal parameter list. Hence, within the procedure, m is always equal to 1 and the value of n denotes the length of the actual string.

Functions in Pascal may take parameters as for procedures but may return only values of scalar types, e.g.,

```
function numberofdaysworked (mydays : daysworked) : integer ;
  var i : 0..7 ; d : dayofweek ;
  begin
    i := 0 ;
    for d := Sunday to Saturday do
      if d in mydays then i := i+1 ;
    numberofdaysworked := i
  end {numberofdaysworked}
```

We will assume the existence of a function which is not defined in standard Pascal. This function, *size*, given any type identifier as parameter, will return as its integer result the number of memory units occupied in the object program by a value of its parameter type, where it is assumed that the relation

$$size \,(integer) = 1$$

always holds, and hence defines the meaning of a memory unit as being the storage occupied at run-time by an integer value. Obviously the values produced by calls of *size* are implementation-dependent.

2.2 ABSTRACT DATA TYPES

In this book we are concerned with the construction of programs that create and process files of records. The programmer does not wish to have to be aware of how the records are actually represented on the physical file device and how they are read from and written to the device but, instead, wishes to be provided with a range of represent-ation-independent operators with which he may manipulate the records. Such files (and, in general, objects of any particular data type) may be considered as having two characteristic sets of proper-ties, or attributes. The first set, often known as the *specification attri-butes*, defines the operations which can be performed on objects of the type. The second set, the *representation attributes*, determines how such objects are represented by a particular implementation. The programmer, when using such objects, should ideally be un-aware of the representation attributes (i.e., the representational details of the objects) but should be concerned only with manipulat-ing them in terms of the specification attributes (i.e., the operators of the data type). Hence we define an *abstract data type* as a class of objects defined by means of a representation-independent specifi-cation — which will consist of a set of operators for creating such objects of the type, retrieving certain information from the objects, and updating the objects. Whatever operators are provided the form of these operators should in no way reflect how the objects are actually represented. They specify only what is to be done.

Consider, for example, a program which manipulates first-in, first-out queues of integer values — such queue structures occur fre-quently in computing applications but Pascal does not provide an explicit queue abstraction as it does for, say, sets and records. Irre-spective of how these queues are represented we will need to perform basic operations such as appending values to the back of a queue, removing values from the front of a queue, determining when a queue is full or empty, and determining the current length of a queue. All of these operations are best expressed in the form of procedures or functions whose specifications are independent of the representation chosen for queues, e.g.,

> **procedure** *append* (**var** *Q* : *integerqueue* ; *i* : *integer*) ;
> **function** *empty* (*Q* : *integerqueue*) : *boolean* ;

The programmer may use the operators specified without any knowledge of how the queues are actually represented. The implementation of the operators, i.e., the bodies of the specified procedures and functions, will reflect the representation involved, but their headings and calling sequences will not.

Since an abstract data type consists of a *set of operators* (visible to the user) and also an *implementation* (hidden from the user), the realization of such an abstract data type in a high-level language requires a language construct that enables both sets of attributes to be encapsulated in the same unit, such that the implementation details are invisible and inaccessible from the outside but the operators are accessible. We thus introduce the *class* structure (based upon similar structures provided in Simula, Concurrent Pascal, and Pascal Plus, among other languages) which permits the combination of the definition of the chosen data representation and operators (in the form of procedures and functions) in a single program unit. The designer of the abstract data type may select which operators he will make visible by starring their identifiers in their declarations. This has the effect also of hiding any unstarred identifiers (particularly those of the data structures forming the representation of the abstract objects defined by the class). For instance, the following skeletal class definition specifies the abstract data type *integerqueue* :

> **class** *integerqueue* ;
>   {... *definition of representation* ...}
>   **procedure** *append (*i* : *integer*) ; ... ;
>   **procedure** *remove (**var** *i* : *integer*) ; ... ;
>   **function** *full : *boolean* ; ... ;
>   **function** *empty : *boolean* ; ... ;
>   **function** *length : *integer* ; ... .
>   **begin**
>   { *initially the queue is empty* }
>   ***
>   { *finally recover any storage used by the representation* }
>   **end**

Since the data representing the implementation of the queue is unstarred it is invisible from outside the class, and the form of the starred operators is totally independent of the actual representation chosen. The body of the class also provides a default initialization of all the *integerqueue* data objects, as well as any finalization required. Thus a class definition consists of

1.   a data structure;
2.   a set of operators, some of which may be visible from the outside;
3.   initial and final actions to be applied to the data structure at the time of its creation and destruction — these initial and final actions are separated by the symbol ∗∗∗.

Instances of a class may be defined at the head of a block, viz.,

> **instance** *Q* : *integerqueue;*

This has the effect of creating the data structure which implements an *integerqueue* object, and the compound statement forming the body of the class is then executed as far as the ∗∗∗ separator. At completion of the execution of the block containing the instance declaration the rest of the compound statement, i.e., the part following the ∗∗∗ separator, is executed. Thus these two parts separated by the ∗∗∗ symbol act as initialization and finalization actions for the abstract objects, and the ∗∗∗ symbol effectively represents the execution of the block in which the class instance *Q* is declared.

Within the block containing the instance declaration the starred identifiers of the class are accessible using the normal record dot and with notations, e.g.,

> **if** *Q.full* **then** ...
> **with** *Q* **do begin** ... ; *append* (*j*) ; ... ; *remove* (*k*) ; ... **end**

It is possible to star not only the identifiers of procedures and functions declared within a class but indeed any identifiers declared therein, including variable and constant identifiers. Starred variables of a class may be accessed but not assigned values from outside, i.e., they are read-only variables outside the class definition.

Several instances of a class may of course be declared, thus

> **instance** *q1*, *q2* : *integerqueue;*

and also arrays of instances, thus

> **instance** *q* : **array** [1..5] **of** *integerqueue;*

Classes may also have formal parameters, in which case the actual parameters are supplied in the instance declarations. This allows minor variations in the details of the abstract objects created by the instance declarations, e.g., we might define the maximum size of a queue as a parameter of the *integerqueue* type:

```
class integerqueue (maximum : integer) ;
    ... definition of representation ...
    procedure *append (i : integer) ; ... ;
    procedure *remove (var i : integer) ; ... ;
    function *full : boolean ; ... ;
    function *empty : boolean ; ... ;
    function *length : integer ; ... .
    begin
        { initially the queue is empty }
        ***
        { finally recover any storage used by the representation }
    end ;
instance q1 : integerqueue (50) ;
         q2 : integerqueue (25) ;
```

For an array of instances a sequence of actual parameter lists, one for each element of the array, must be supplied

```
instance q : array [1..5] of integerqueue (20) (30) (50) (25) (10);
```

If just one instance of a class is required, the class definition and instance declaration may be combined into a single *module*, thus

```
class module Q ;
    ... definition of representation ...
    procedure *append (i : integer) ; ... ;
    procedure *remove (var i : integer) ; ... ;
    function *full : boolean ; ... ;
    function *empty : boolean ; ... ;
    function *length : integer ; ... .
    begin
        { initially the queue is empty }
        ***
        { finally recover any storage used by the representation }
    end
```

In addition to accepting actual parameters, class instances may themselves be passed as parameters to procedures, functions, or instances of other classes, using formal parameter declarations such as

```
procedure analysequeue (instance q : integerqueue)
```

Within the procedure *analysequeue* the formal parameter *q* may be manipulated like any other instance of the *integerqueue* class but the manipulation will of course apply to the actual *integerqueue* instance supplied as parameter at the point of call.

The use of the abstract type *integerqueue* in programs will be independent of its implementation, provided this implementation meets the requirements of the abstract type specification. The following implementation, using an array as a circular or *cyclic buffer* (Figure 2.1), illustrates this point.

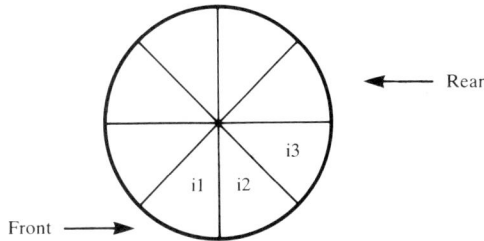

Figure 2.1   Cyclic buffer representation for queue

```
class integerqueue (maximum : integer) ;
    var buffer : array [1..maximum] of integer ;
        front, rear : 1..maximum ;
        *length : 0..maxitems ;

    procedure *append (i : integer) ;
        begin
            if length = maximum
            then writeln ('queue overflow')
            else begin
                    buffer [rear] := i ; rear := rear mod maximum + 1 ;
                    length := length + 1
                end
        end {append} ;

    procedure *remove (var i : integer) ;
        begin
            if length = 0
            then writeln ('queue empty')
            else begin
                    i := buffer [front]; front := front mod maximum + 1 ;
                    length := length − 1
                end
        end {remove} ;

    function *empty : boolean ;
        begin empty := (length=0) end ;

    function *full : boolean ;
        begin full := (length=maximum) end ;
```

begin
   length := 0 ; *front* := 1 ; *rear* := 1 ;
   ***
   { *no finalization required for array representation* }
end {*integerqueue*}

Note that the length function has actually been implemented by allowing external inspection of the value of the local variable *length* — externally such an inspection is syntactically indistinguishable from a function call.

Here our notation shows another divergence from Pascal in that we allow the bounds of an array to be determined using the value of a parameter of a class definition.

An alternative representation might maintain the queue as a linked list of records, using pointers. However, such a change in representation will not affect the outward specification of the *integerqueue* class in any way and hence the use of the abstract data type will also remain unaffected.

2.3   THE LIBRARY

It was mentioned previously that the concept of a queue is used frequently in programming — hence our abstraction of a queue of integers may be usable in many programs. We thus assume the existence of a *library* in which the text of such class definitions may be held and from which class definitions may be retrieved and included in a program — such a facility also assists in reducing the length of the overall program text. Thus a program requiring the use of an integer queue abstraction might have the form (assuming the text of *integerqueue* has previously been placed in the library)

program *user* ;
   ...
   class *integerqueue* **in library** ;
   instance *q1, q2* : *integerqueue* ;
   ...
end.

Thus a reader of the program text who is not interested in the details of the *integerqueue* implementation is not distracted by the text involved. If he does wish to see the details then he simply inspects the corresponding file in the library. This library mechanism encourages the development and use of a library of standard abstract data type definitions that are suitable for inclusion in a variety of programs. We shall be developing a range of such standard abstract data types for the various types of files that are used in commercial data processing. Indeed, not only data type definitions but also procedures and functions may be held in the library.

The usefulness of the queue abstraction may be enhanced if it can be extended to support the abstraction of queues of items of types other than just *integer*. The implementation of the *integerqueue* class given in the previous section implemented an abstract data type whose values are queues of integers. In doing so the implementation assumed the following:

1. that the global identifier *integer* denotes the type of the queue items involved;
2. that the operator := can be applied to operands of the type *integer*.

Apart from these, no other assumptions are made about the attributes of the type of the item values of the queue involved, and the logic used will work equally well for any item type that meets the above two requirements. Thus, by replacing appropriate occurrences of the identifier *integer* in the implementation given for *integerqueue* by a more general type identifier *itemtype* we obtain a library class called *queue*, say, which implements the queue concept for any *itemtype* meeting the above conditions. The specification of this class now becomes

```
class queue (maximum : integer) ;
    { assumes type itemtype = type of items   }
    { with operator := applicable to itemtype }
    ... definition of representation ...
    procedure *append (i : itemtype) ; ... ;
    procedure *remove (var i : itemtype) ; ... ;
    function *full : boolean ; ... ;
    function *empty : boolean ; ... ;
    function *length : integer ; ... .
    begin
        { initially the queue is empty }
        ***
        { finally recover any storage used by the representation }
    end ;
```

If this definition is held in a library it may be used by any program provided that the program specifies the type *itemtype* appropriate to its usage of the *queue* abstraction. Hence, the library retrieval mechanism is extended to allow the redefinition of the global identifiers assumed by a library class, in a way that does not disturb the use of identifiers in the surrounding program. Thus, if we require a queue of integers the queue abstraction is retrieved from the library using the form

class *queue* **in library (where type** *itemtype* = *integer*) ;

If a program requires two different types of queues, say a queue of characters and a queue of integers, then it is necessary to give each type a unique name and so the following alternative form of library retrieval specification is permitted

class *integerqueue* = *queue* **in library (where type** *itemtype* = *integer*) ;
class *charqueue* = *queue* **in library (where type** *itemtype* = *char*) ;

The where clause in a library retrieval can be used not only to re-map identifiers that denote global quantities but also to vary the nature of data manipulated by a library data type or procedure from one retrieval to the next. Assuming we have a library procedure for sorting an array, specified as

procedure *Sort* (**var** *A* : **array** [*i..j* : *integer*] **of** *element*)

this procedure may be retrieved for sorting arrays of integers as follows:

procedure *integersort* = *Sort* **in library (where type** *element* = *integer*)

or, for sorting arrays of characters, as

procedure *charsort* = *Sort* **in library (where type** *element* = *char*)

In general, this library sorting procedure can be used in this way to provide a means of sorting arrays of any element type for which the operations used within the procedure are applicable. Typically these will be assignment and an ordering operator, such as ≤. For element types on which the ≤ operator cannot be used (e.g., record types) a more general library sorting procedure can be written which requires an ordering function appropriate to the element type used. The library retrieval mechanism allows the global procedures and functions used in a library block to be re-mapped in the where clause. Thus, if we have a program that manipulates records of some type *recordtype* and in which a function

function *keyorder* (*rl, r2* : *recordtype*) : *boolean* ;

has been defined, then the sort procedure might be retrieved from the library as follows

procedure *recordsort* = *Generalsort* **in library**
                      (**where type** *element* = *recordtype* ;
                            function *lessthan* = *keyorder*)

assuming that the library procedure has the following heading

    procedure *Generalsort* (**var** *A* : **array** [*i..j* : *integer*] **of** *element*) ;

and that it expresses its ordering decisions in terms of calls to a global boolean function *lessthan*.

    Finally, when retrieving a class definition from a library for which only a single instance is required, the library retrieval mechanism allows its retrieval as a class module, thus

    class module *queue* **in library** (**where type** *itemtype* = *char*)

In practice, however, this can be done only for library classes without parameter lists (see Chapter 5 onwards for examples of such retrievals).

    The existence of a library is of great practical significance not only in providing a range of standard data abstractions (such as *queue*) for the programmer using a particular implementation of his chosen language, but also in the development of large programs and systems in general. For large systems in which groups of programmers develop individual modules, such modules, in the form of class definitions, procedures, and functions, may be held in the library, thus reducing the length of the overall program text and reducing the problems of putting together the complete program text. For systems consisting of files used by various programs, the file definitions may be held in the library and retrieved by those programs using them — such a facility is particularly useful in reducing the communication problems that invariably arise when a team of programmers is working on the implementation of a large system. Similarly, commonly used procedures and functions (such as file access routines) can also be held in a library. How the text of these program units is actually placed in the library will depend upon the particular language implementation but need not concern us further here.

2.4   CONCURRENT PROCESSES

Programs written in Pascal are sequential programs, i.e., a program describes the sequence of actions to be executed to perform a certain activity. However, many programs are more naturally described as a group of activities which proceed in parallel with each other and communicate in some way. Each of these activities is known as a *process* and such a program is said to consist of a number of *concurrent processes*.

    Such processes are not usually independent of each other but generally cooperate in order to perform the overall task. For example, in Chapter 10 we describe the construction of a report generation program — this program consists of two processes, one which produces the items of information to be displayed in the report (a *producer* process), and another which formats these items into physical pages ready for printing on some output device (a *consumer* process). Hence the two processes communicate as a result of the producer process making available to the consumer process the items of information which it is generating. These information items are usually stored in some global buffer data structure which is accessible by both processes (Figure 2.2).

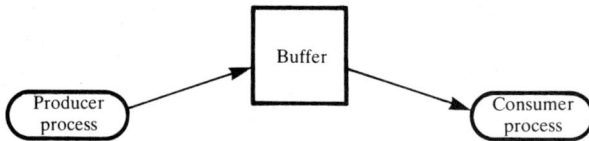

Figure 2.2   Producer – consumer communication

If both of the processes have access to the shared buffer this access must be regulated to ensure that both processes do not attempt to access the buffer simultaneously, for a chaotic situation could then arise. Thus we require this buffer to have the property of *mutual exclusion* associated with it, so that only one process at a time may attempt to access its contents.

It may also happen, since the producer and consumer processes may proceed at different rates, that the buffer becomes full or empty at different times. If the producer finds the buffer to be full, then it must wait before adding a new item to the buffer until the consumer enables it to proceed by removing an item from the buffer. Likewise the consumer process may find the buffer empty and therefore must be delayed until the producer adds an item to the buffer before it tries to remove any more items. Hence we also require a means of delaying processes when some condition occurs until such time as the delaying condition no longer holds.

Therefore, to extend our sequential programming notation to such concurrent activities we need three additional categories of notation:

1. a means of denoting concurrent processes;
2. a means of providing mutually exclusive access by processes to shared data structures;
3. a means of delaying processes until certain conditions no longer hold.

Processes are defined in a form similar to procedures, viz.,

```
process module producer ;
  var i : infotype ;
  begin
    repeat
      produce item value i ;
      add i into the buffer
    until programcompleted
  end
```

(the use of the word **module** again indicates the existence of just one such producer process), and the complete program structure then becomes

```
program concurrencyexample ;
  { declaration of a buffer which is a shared data structure }

process module producer ;
  var i : infotype ;
  begin
    repeat
      produce item value i ;
      add item i into the buffer
    until programcompleted
  end ;

process module consumer ;
  var i : infotype ;
  begin
    repeat
      remove item i from the buffer ;
      consume item
    until programcompleted
  end ;

  begin
    { program initialization }
    ***
    { program finalization }
  end.
```

The producer and consumer processes are assumed to be activated at the point indicated by the *** separator in the main program body. Their execution then proceeds in parallel until they have both terminated, at which point the finalization of the main program is performed.

The buffer, to which both processes require mutually exclusive access, is defined (together with access operators *add* and *obtain* and its initialization and finalization) in the form of a special class called a *monitor* which is assumed to enforce the mutual exclusion property on the use of the access operators (the starred procedures of the monitor). Thus any process calling an access procedure while another process is currently executing an access procedure is forced to wait until the other process has completed its access or relinquished its exclusive right of access.

```
monitor module buffer ;
   {  assumes size given by global integer constant N       }
   {            items are of type infotype                   }
   {                 with := defined                         }
   class queue in library (where type itemtype = infotype) ;
   instance Q : queue (N) ;
   procedure *add (j : infotype) ;
      begin
         if Q.full then wait until not full ;
         Q.append (j)
      end ;
   procedure *obtain (var j : infotype) ;
      begin
         if Q.empty then wait until not empty ;
         Q.remove (j)
      end ;
   begin *** end {buffer}
```

Here the buffer has been implemented as a queue of up to N items of type *infotype* where N is a global integer constant, using the library queue abstraction developed in the previous section and retrieved in a suitable form. Each time that a process calls *add* or *obtain* it is guaranteed to have exclusive access to the buffer until such time as it decides to relinquish this exclusion. In the producer process *add item i into the buffer* is now replaced by a call

$$buffer.add \ (i)$$

and likewise, in the consumer process *remove item i from buffer* is replaced by a call

$$buffer.obtain \ (i)$$

Hence a process can only access global data indirectly through an access operator of a monitor instance containing the data concerned.

For each condition (such as the buffer being full or empty) that may cause the delay of a process's execution before it can continue, a special queuing variable is introduced on which processes can wait until signalled by other processes that they may continue. These variables are declared to be of a predefined abstract data type *condition*, e.g.,

instance *notfull*, *notempty* : *condition* ;

for which access operators *wait* and *signal* are defined. The specification of *condition* takes the form

```
monitor condition ;
  procedure *wait ;
  procedure *signal ;
  begin *** end
```

Thus *wait until not full* is replaced by

notfull.wait

and *wait until not empty* is replaced by

notempty.wait

At the end of *buffer.add* (whose execution guarantees the buffer to be non-empty) we add

notempty.signal

to indicate to any process waiting for the buffer to become non-empty that it may proceed, and similarly add

notfull.signal

to the end of *buffer.obtain* (since its execution guarantees the buffer to be non-full).

When a process is delayed by a *wait* it is appended to the end of the appropriate condition queue and exclusion on the use of the buffer is released. A signalling process passes control to the process at the head of the condition queue concerned — the signalling process is itself then delayed until the reactivated process relinquishes use of the buffer. If no process is waiting on a condition, then a *signal* operation has no effect.

The complete form of the buffer data structure is thus

```
monitor module buffer ;
  {    assumes size given by global integer constant N     }
  {              items are of type infotype                }
  {                    with := defined                     }
  class queue in library (where type itemtype = infotype) ;
  instance Q : queue (N) ;
  instance notempty, notfull : condition ;
  procedure *add (j : infotype) ;
    begin
      if Q.full then notfull.wait ;
```

```
          Q.append (j) ;
          notempty.signal
      end ;
  procedure *obtain (var j : infotype) ;
      begin
          if Q.empty then notempty.wait ;
          Q.remove (j) ;
          notfull.signal
      end ;
  begin *** end {buffer}
```

This buffer monitor, which we will assume to be available in the library to buffer *N* items of an arbitrary type *infotype*, where *N* and *infotype* are to be specified in the retrieval, will be used again in Chapter 10.

3 FILES

3.1 INTRODUCTION

A *file* is a set of data values which is either presented to or produced by a computer under the control of a program. It is held on some auxiliary storage device, e.g., a punched card reader or a magnetic tape drive. In general a file contains a large volume of data in the form of a collection of many records, all containing information directed (usually) towards some purpose.

Files form the framework of a data processing system. The set of integrated files used in a data processing system is known as its *data base* and forms the foundation of the complete system. Given the size of most files it is obviously important that the data of the file is organized in such a way as to use as little storage space as possible but should, at the same time, also be capable of being processed as quickly as necessary.

A user of a file sees it as a collection of *records*, where a record is the unit of a file which is available for processing at any one time. A record consists of a number of data items known as *fields*. An *elementary* field is one which is not divided into subordinate fields, while a *group* field is one which is further subdivided into subordinate fields. Figure 3.1 illustrates the structure of a file of time cards generated for the employees who check in and out of a factory.

TIME-CARD-FILE is made up of many records (the asterisk denotes multiplicity) each named TIME-CARD. A TIME-CARD record consists of two group fields, EMPLOYEE-ID and WORK-DETAILS, where EMPLOYEE-ID is composed of two elementary fields (NUMBER and NAME) and WORK-DETAILS has three elementary subfields (HOURS, RATE, and DEDUCTIONS).

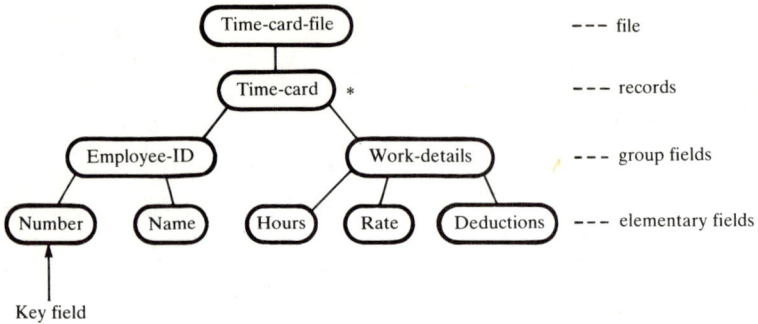

Figure 3.1   File structure

Although the records in a file consist of a number of fields, usually the value of one of those fields acts as a *key* field (known as the
primary key) by which the record is identified. For example, given a
file of time cards such as described above, obviously the primary key
in each record is the value of the employee number field, since each
employee in the company will have been assigned a unique reference
number. However, consider a file containing details of the sales of
products made by a retailing company to its customers. Here the
order number is the primary key by which a sales record is identified
(each individual order will have been assigned a unique order
number).

> *salesfile* : **file of record**
> > *order number* ;
> > *customer number* ;
> > *week number* ;
> > *product code* ;
> > *quantity sold*
> **end** ;

Each of the first four fields could be used as the key field by different
applications programs using *salesfile*. For instance, we may be
interested in the details of a particular order, or in all the orders
placed by a particular customer, or in all the orders placed in a particular week, or in all the orders for a certain product. In these latter
cases we refer to, e.g., the customer number, week number, and
product code fields as *secondary* keys. Note that these key field values
are not unique since, for example, there is almost certainly more than
one order placed in a given week, and a particular customer may
place more than one order.

Hence, although the records in such a file may be stored in order
of the values of a certain field (thus permitting sequential, i.e., key-

ordered processing involving that field), the organization of the file records may not be appropriate for applications involving sequential processing with respect to other fields. In such cases it is necessary to find a method of organizing the storage of the records in the file so that processing by any applications program using any of these possible key fields is equally efficient.

The data in a file is usually very important to the owner of the file, and often highly confidential. Hence the file must be protected against loss, accidental error, or deliberate misuse. For example, in the Model Savings Bank Limited system, there will be a file containing details of all the customers of the Bank and their accounts, one record per customer. Any permanent loss of the records in this file would be intolerable, likewise any errors which accidentally change, say, a customer's balance, or any deliberate alteration for fraudulent purposes. Thus the contents of a file must be protected against loss and error, while all data which is used in changing the contents of files must be closely vetted to ensure its correctness and legality.

Files may be used to hold various types of information ranging from character data to binary object code programs. Here we shall restrict ourselves to consideration of data files. Such files are usually classified according to five facets:

1. the *auxiliary storage medium* — a file may be stored on a *serial-access* storage device or a *direct-access* device. Serial-access devices (e.g., magnetic tape drives, paper tape and punched card readers) have physical characteristics that constrain records to be accessed strictly in the physical order in which they are stored, whereas direct-access devices (e.g., magnetic disk drives, magnetic drums) are such that each record has a physical address associated with it and a record may be directly accessed by presenting its address to the device concerned. Magnetic tape and disk are the media most commonly used for the long-term storage of files, and are often referred to as *mass storage* files.

2. the *contents* of the file — a file may be classified as
    *   a *master* file (which contains semi-static information that may be periodically referenced, updated, and amended, e.g., in the Model Savings Bank system there is a master file which contains records giving details of the accounts for each customer);
    *   a *transaction* file (which contains records created from source documents, e.g., the above sales file is a transaction file consisting of records giving details of each individual order placed);

- a *transition* file (which is a transaction file whose records have had information added to or deleted from them using information held in master files, e.g., the transaction sales file might be used to form a transition sales file in which the value of each order has been added to a sales record as a result of consulting a master file containing the prices of the various products ordered).

3. *storage mode (organization)* — this describes the way in which the records of a file are organized on the auxiliary storage medium. We shall consider four such methods of file organization:
    - *sequential* (in which the records are subsequently accessed in the order in which they were originally written to the file);
    - *random* (in which the position of a record in the file is determined by applying an addressing function to the record's primary key value);
    - *indexed* (in which the records are stored together with an index that enables, for each record, its position within the file to be determined from its primary key value);
    - *inverted* (a series of such indexes is maintained, one for each primary and secondary key).

4. *access mode* — the means by which the records of the file are accessed, including
    - *sequential* access (the records are accessed in the logical order in which they reside in the file);
    - *direct* access (for random files — a record is accessed using the same addressing function as was employed in organizing the records when the file was constructed);
    - via an *index* (for indexed organization and inverted files — a record key is used in a search of the appropriate index(es));
    - using a mixture of sequential and direct or indexed access — this is known as *dynamic* access.

5. *processing mode* — this defines the way in which the file is used by a particular applications program, i.e., as either an
    - *input* file (the file is only read by the program and hence its contents remain unchanged), or as an
    - *output* file (the program only adds new records to an initially empty file, thus creating the file contents), or as an
    - *input–output* file (a file which is used for both input and output by a program, i.e., the program not only reads existing records but may add new ones to the file as well as deleting records and replacing existing ones) — such a file must be stored on a direct-access device.

These last three characteristics of a file determine the auxiliary memory device to be used in storing a file. The serial-access characteristics of magnetic tape, punched card, and paper tape devices are such that these media can only be used for storing files of sequentially organized records which are going to be accessed sequentially and processed by programs which will use these files purely as input files or output files (but not for both input and output at the same time). Transaction files, which are sequences of records and usually processed solely as input files, normally reside on a serial-access medium.

The following two terms will be used in our subsequent discussions of files and their properties. The *volatility* of a file measures the expansion or contraction of a file, e.g., the Savings Bank master file might grow at an annual rate of about 15% due to the enrolment of new customers. The *hit ratio* (or *activity*) of a file with respect to a particular program using the file is the proportion of the records in the file which is accessed by that particular program — for instance, the processing of a batch of sales orders might access 15% of the customer records held in a master file of customer details but access 65% of the product records held in a master file of product details. For master files held on serial-access devices, such as magnetic tape files, the sequential access constraint gives rise to a 100% hit ratio since all the records will generally have to be accessed even though only a small percentage will actually require examination or updating.

3.2 CHARACTERISTICS OF MAGNETIC STORAGE MEDIA

In this section we describe some of the important physical characteristics of magnetic tape and disk storage devices so that the reader will be aware of the physical factors to be considered when attempting to obtain efficient processing of any files which he may create and use on these storage media.

3.2.1 Magnetic Tape

The usual length L of a reel of magnetic tape varies between about 250ft (76 m) and 2400ft (730 m). The normal *recording density P* is typically 1600 characters per inch (630 characters per centimeter), i.e., 1600 characters are encoded per inch of tape. Hence, in theory, a 2400 feet tape may hold as many as 46 million characters — the equivalent of 600 000 punched cards. However, in practice the effective capacity of a tape reel is much smaller.

Data is stored on a magnetic tape in *blocks* of characters, where we shall denote the number of characters by *B*. A block is the unit of transfer between the magnetic tape drive and the main store of the computer. Between blocks there is an unused piece of tape called the *inter-block gap*, or *IBG* (Figure 3.2). This is usually ⅝ inch (15.9 mm) long, or may be expressed in terms of the number of characters of space (which we denote by *G*) that are wasted (e.g., 1000 characters in the case of a ⅝ inch gap and a recording density of 1600 characters per inch).

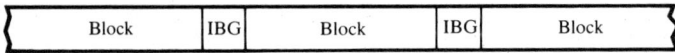

Figure 3.2   Layout of blocks in a file

In most cases more than one record is stored in a block (Figure 3.3). This is known as *blocking* records, and the number of records stored in a block is referred to as the *blocking factor*. Blocking of records is common practice because it increases the storage capacity of a tape as well as the speed at which records on the tape may be read and written (by reducing the number of inter-block gaps).

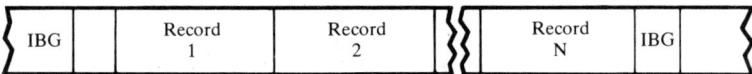

Figure 3.3   Blocking of records

If a block contains *B* characters, then the *effective capacity* of a tape reel is

$$LP \times \frac{B}{B + G} \quad \text{characters}$$

since, for every block of *B* characters, there is a wasted inter-block gap equivalent to *G* characters.

The length of tape required to hold a file of *N* characters is thus

$$\frac{N}{P} + \frac{NG}{BP}$$

since *N/B* gives the number of blocks (and hence inter-block gaps) in the file.

The *transfer rate R* of a tape drive is the speed at which data is transferred between the tape drive and main store, measured in characters per second. A typical value is 60K characters/second. However, the tape drive may actually stop and start at each inter-block gap, taking a time S seconds known as the *stop–start time* (typical values of which are about 10 milliseconds). Hence, although a tape may in theory be read in 10 minutes, it may actually take some 45 minutes to read the equivalent amount of blocked data. So the block size has a critical effect on the speed of processing of a data file.

The *effective transfer rate* is therefore

$$\frac{B}{B/R + S} \text{ characters/second}$$

since, to effectively transfer a block of B characters, the actual block transfer time is B/R plus the inter-block gap stop–start times. The time taken to transfer a file of N characters is thus

$$\frac{N}{R} + \frac{NS}{B} \text{ seconds}$$

The table in Figure 3.4 illustrates the effect of blocking for different block lengths, using $L = 2400$ feet (730 m) magnetic tapes for storage of a file of $N = 40$ million characters. Recording density P is 800 characters/inch (315 characters per centimeter); the inter-block gap is $G = 500$ characters long; stop–start time $S = 10$ milliseconds; transfer rate $R = 60$K characters per second.

Block size (chars)	Effective tape capacity (M chars)	File length (reels)	Effective transfer rate (K chars/s)	Total transfer time (minutes)
200	6.6	7	15.0	44.4
500	11.5	4	27.3	24.4
1000	15.4	3	37.5	17.8
2000	18.4	3	46.2	14.4
5000	20.9	2	53.6	12.4

Figure 3.4   Effect of various block sizes

Note how the efficiency gains become smaller once the block size reaches 1000 characters. This is because, for large block sizes, the effects of the inter-block gap length and stop–start time become dominated by the block size and block transfer time, respectively.

Thus, the larger the block size, the greater the effective capacity of the tape and the faster the effective transfer rate for a file. How large can the block size be? That depends upon the storage capacity of the computer. When a block of records is read, all of the data in the block is transferred into an area of main memory known as a *buffer* (Figure 3.5). The block size is therefore limited by the available buffer space.

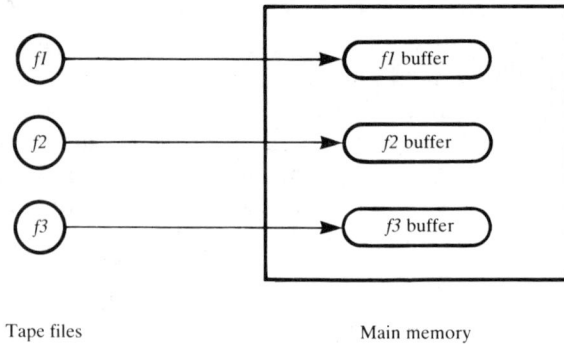

Figure 3.5 Use of file buffers

The choice of block size is important for a sequentially accessed file (i.e, one with a hit ratio of 100 per cent, implying that all of its records, and hence blocks, will be transferred) such as a magnetic tape file — if it is too small, then many transfers are required, processing time becomes excessive, and the inter-block gaps make the file very long. If it is too large, then too much main store may be used for its buffer. In practice many installations place a standard size on the blocks in magnetic tape files, so that such files may be processed by standard utility programs. For instance, in the Model Savings Bank system we shall use a standard block size of 1024 characters.

Without some form of *buffering* the entire program must wait while data is read or written since there is space in main memory for only one block of each file at a time. This may represent a considerable waste of time; it would be preferable for the program to process other data while data is being read or written. If *double buffering* is used, two blocks of a file can be accommodated in memory at a time — while one is being transferred the other is being processed, and so either the processing or the transfers may continue without interruption (i.e., the stop–start time may be eliminated as a component of the overall processing time). With double buffering, the data of one buffer is processed while the data of the other buffer is transferred. When the data in the first buffer has been processed and the data in the other buffer has been fully transferred, the roles of the two buffers are interchanged (Figure 3.6). Double buffering is normally used for files with large blocks since the transfer time will be greater than for small block files. The use of multiple buffering with three or more buffers is worthwhile only if the processing speed fluctuates.

The number of buffers that are used for a particular file thus

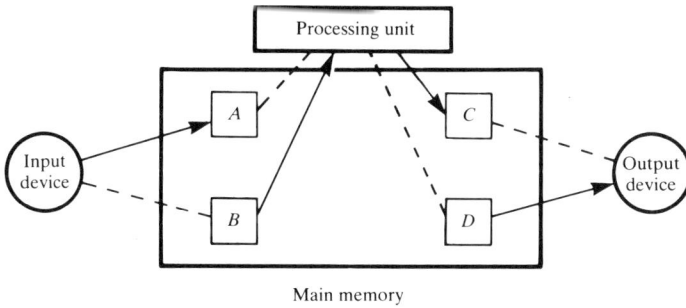

Figure 3.6   Double-buffered i/o devices

depends upon the total buffer space that can be made available for that file and the size of its blocks. In practice, a program must share the space available for its file buffers among a number of files which are being processed simultaneously (as in Figure 3.5), e.g., in a sequential file update program an old version of the master file, a new version, a transaction file, and an error report file might all be in use. The optimum allocation of available buffer space between files used concurrently by a program is determined using the square root theorem.

Square-root theorem: If a program uses N sequentially accessed files then it must share its available main memory buffer space between these files; to minimize the total number of transfers each file's share of the buffer space should be proportional to the square root of the number of characters to be transferred. For example, assuming that there is 15K of buffer space available and we have two files, F1 of length 1 million characters, and F2 of 4 million characters, and both files are to be completely read by a program:

File	Length	√length	Buffer size	Transfers
F1	1 M	1 K	5 K	200
F2	4 M	2 K	10 K	400
		totals	15 K	600

Proof for two files: Assume one file contains $r1$ characters, the other $r2$ and that the available buffer space S is shared in proportions k and $(1-k)$ respectively.
Total numbers of transfers $= r1/kS + r2/(1-k)/S$

Differentiate with respect to k and set to zero: this gives
$$\sqrt{(r1/r2)} = k/(1-k)$$
Differentiate again with respect to k: this shows this to be a minimum.

   Thus, having calculated the total buffer space for each file by the square-root rule, this space must be divided by the actual block size for the file to give the number of buffers that may be used (or alternatively, given the degree of buffering to be used, the maximum block size). If a file is used by a number of programs, then the block size for that file must be no larger than that which can be handled by all the programs.

3.2.2   File Labels

Most tape files contain special data blocks known as *labels*. Generally the data blocks on a magnetic tape reel (Figure 3.7) are preceded by a *volume* label identifying the reel and the files that it contains, and a header label at the start of each individual file on the tape will contain information such as the file name, creation date, and expiry date. The *trailer* label, which follows the data blocks of a file, is similar in content to the header label, but often contains a count of the number of data blocks in the file. These labels are usually processed by any programs using the tape file.

Volume label	File 1 header label	File 1 block 1	File 1 final block	File 1 trailer label	File n header label	File n block 1	File n final block	File n trailer label

Figure 3.7   File label blocks

3.2.3   Variable-length Records

If all the different types of records in a file occupy the same amount of storage, then they are known as fixed-length records. However, *variable-length* records sometimes occur, e.g., a record that is formed from a customer's complete order will contain a variable number of items. The variation in length may also be due to the variable length of the fields, e.g., in a name and address file. The computer system and applications programs usually require some means of determining the length of each record — often the first field in the physical implementation of a record is a special *record length count* which specifies the length of the record (Figure 3.8). It is of course possible to pad out the fields and make all the records the same length, but this has the disadvantage of wasting storage within many records and hence increasing the total length of the file.

Record length field	Actual information fields

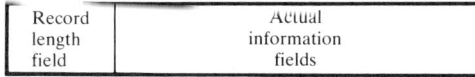

Figure 3.8   Physical record structure

3.2.4 Magnetic Disk

Magnetic tape files can only be used in a serial manner, i.e., new blocks may only be added to the end of a file but may not be inserted before, or replace, existing blocks. Hence, to modify a tape file, a completely new version must be constructed. This constraint may be overcome by using magnetic disk storage, which is the most common storage medium in use today.

There are various forms of magnetic disk stores — *exchangeable disk stores* (which may be loaded and unloaded from disk drives), *fixed disk stores, drum stores,* and *floppy disks.* Disks may be either fixed head disks or movable head disks (Figure 3.9). A fixed head disk is one which does not have a movable read/write assembly and hence there is a separate read/write head for every track. The discussion which follows relates to movable head disks, usually referred to as exchangeable disk stores (EDS).

The maximum capacity of one exchangeable disk pack is typically 8 to 40 million characters, structured as follows:

1. each track contains approximately 4000–8000 characters;
2. each disk surface contains 200–500 information tracks, i.e., 800 000–4 000 000 characters;

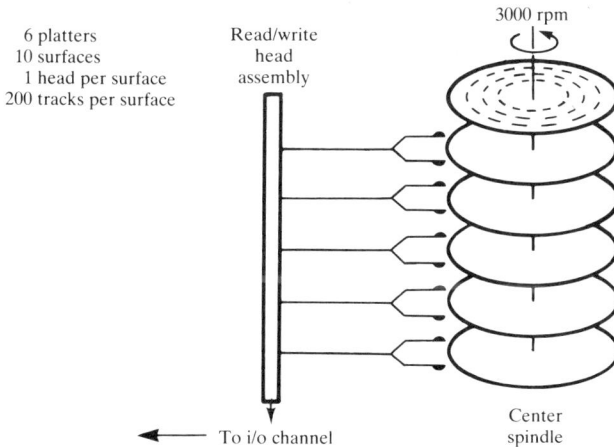

Figure 3.9   Exchangeable disk drive

3.   each pack contains 10 surfaces, i.e., 8–40 million characters.

For purposes of illustration we shall consider a disk pack of 10 surfaces, each with 200 tracks, and 4096 (4K) characters per track. The
rotation time is typically in the region of 20 milliseconds, i.e., the
disks rotate at 3000 revolutions per minute.

   The methods of storing and retrieving disk information are complex and vary between manufacturers, but the important elements
may be summarized as follows:

1.   In many disk systems a track is subdivided into a number of
     hardware *sectors*, between 2 and 16 per track, depending on the
     particular system. Figure 3.10 shows an eight sector, 4096 charac-
     ter track in which each sector is thus 512 characters long. A sector
     is the smallest addressable unit of a track. Block sizes in such disk
     systems must always be such that they are a multiple number of
     sectors in length, but not greater than one track, and such disk
     blocks are often referred to as *buckets*. Other disk systems use
     free format data storage in which the user chooses his own block
     size.

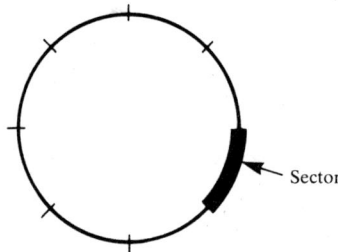

Figure 3.10   Sectors of a track

2.   All the arms move together such that all 10 read/write heads are
     in a vertical line. Thus the information that may be accessed with-
     out further arm movement forms a *cylinder* of 10 tracks (one per
     surface) — see Figure 3.11. If there are 200 tracks on each sur-
     face, then there are 200 such cylinders in the disk pack, each
     cylinder containing 40K characters (assuming each track to con-
     tain 4K characters). In practice files are stored cylinder-by-
     cylinder rather than surface-by-surface in order to minimize arm
     movements when processing the file. Hence a file is stored in
     cylinders 0, 1, 2, ... rather than on surfaces 1, 2, 3 ... .
3.   To access a block of information the program must define the

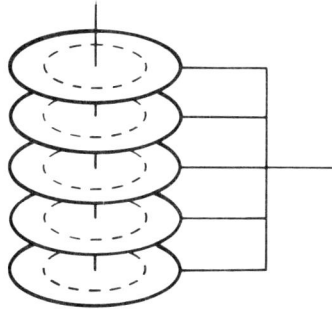

Figure 3.11   Cylinders of a disk pack

cylinder number (1 to 200) and track number (1 to 10) of the block. This address is used in a *seek* operation that moves the heads to the appropriate cylinder and then selects the appropriate head. A *search* operation then finds the required block on the track by comparing the keys for records held in the track against the required record key. Finally a data transfer (input or output) operation is specified.

4.   Records are blocked on disk to cut down rotational delays when successively processing records (however, if not processed successively, an entire block will still be transferred, although only one record of the block is required) and to cut down the overheads of inter-block gaps and control information (e.g., address, record keys, check characters) necessary for the disk hardware and software to function correctly. For direct-access files blocks should be as small as possible in order to minimize the transfer time and to permit the use of smaller buffers. For sequential-access blocks should be as large as possible, subject to the same considerations for magnetic tape files discussed in Section 3.2.1.

Hence the time components associated with transferring one block of information are:

1.   The *arm movement time*, or *seek time*, which depends on the number of cylinders the heads cross to reach the required cylinder from the previous cylinder. The heads move in either direction along a fixed path and remain positioned at a selected cylinder until another cylinder is selected. Arm movement time may vary between about 25 ms (single cylinder move) and 130 ms (full sweep across disk) typically, with an average of about 75 ms.

2.   The *head selection* or *switching* time, which is usually negligible.

3. The *rotational delay*, or *latency*, on average half a disk revolution, i.e., 10 ms, spent waiting for the required block to reach the head.
4. The *transfer time* for one block of information is the size of the block divided by the transfer rate, typically 200K characters per second (since it takes 20 ms to revolve round a 4K character track).

Example   estimate the disk usage time for the input from disk of a block of 2K characters which is amended and output back to its original position.

On average there will be:

(a)   one arm movement taking on average 75 ms (assume the arm does not move between input and output);
(b)   two half-revolutions of rotational delay (one each for input and output), i.e., 20 ms;
(c)   two half-revolutions of transfer time (since a 2K block occupies half a 4K track), i.e., 20 ms;

Hence a total disk usage time of 115 ms.

Exchangeable disk stores have the flexibility of allowing a disk pack to be removed from a disk drive and replaced with another disk pack. In contrast, a fixed-head disk store (FDS) consists of a disk permanently attached to its drive and typically has a recording surface of larger radius, more recording surfaces, and a higher recording density. There is a separate read/write head for each track, thereby eliminating the seek time component from a disk access.

A magnetic drum store is a cylindrical barrel which rotates abouts its axis. The surface of the barrel acts as the recording surface and the tracks are bands on this surface. Typically there are 200–800 tracks per drum. Each track holds about 10K characters and there is a read/write head for each track. Access time is typically one-third of that of an EDS.

Most minicomputer and microcomputer systems now make use of floppy disks — cheap, single- or double-sided surface, small capacity disks which individual users can retain for their own personal use.

3.2.5   Applications Appropriate to Tape and Disk

Tape files are used for files in applications which have a high hit ratio, i.e., most of the records will be accessed on any program run. Usually the records will be held in some significant sequential order and the references to the file (in the form of a transactions file referencing the magnetic tape file) will also have been pre-sorted into the same order, i.e., magnetic tape files are best suited to batch applications where it is possible to pre-batch and sort the transactions.

For certain types of application these limitations of batching and sequential access make tape files unsuitable and it is necessary instead to use a direct-access storage medium such as disk or drum. The type of application that may justify the higher cost of direct-access storage is any that has a very low hit ratio. Even though there is time to batch the transactions and the cost of sorting may not be excessive, it may still be unacceptably expensive in computer time to scan over all the tape records having zero activity.

Another type of application which demands the use of disk or drum storage is any in which the transactions must be processed as they arrive, i.e., where it is unacceptable to save the transactions until a sizeable batch has been accumulated. Typical of such a system would be an airline reservation system — since the master file must be accessed and action must be taken while the client waits, it is unacceptable to batch incoming transactions.

3.3   FILE ORGANIZATION METHODS

These define how the records of a file may be organized on the chosen storage medium for subsequent retrieval. We shall describe four types of file organization in this section
- *sequential*
- *random*
- *indexed*
- *inverted*

and, in the next section, shall describe the methods of accessing records organized in each of these four ways.

3.3.1   Sequential File Organization

Sequential files are organized such that each record in the file, except the first, has a unique predecessor, and each record except the last has a unique successor. This ordering relationship is established by the order in which records are written to the file during its creation but may be changed by the subsequent addition or deletion of records in the file.

Figure 3.12 illustrates the structure of a sequential organization file containing 10 records giving the details of students enrolled in courses at a college (in practice the file would of course be very much larger). Each record consists of five fields giving a student's identification number, name, age, faculty, and nationality.

number	name	age	subject	nationality
2293	Schmidt, P	20	Computing	German
5338	Sharma, P	22	Mathematics	Indian
7474	Fulton, H	21	Computing	British
5659	Hughes, W	21	Accountancy	British
1012	Browne, M	23	History	British
7487	Agnew, P	20	Mathematics	British
8836	Stewart, M	21	Mathematics	British
4992	Singh, Y	19	Accountancy	Indian
5660	Bird, R	23	History	British
2010	Neu, P	19	Computing	German

Figure 3.12 Sequential file organization

New records would usually be added to the end of the above sequence.

Sequential file organization is used for files held on both magnetic tape and disk (indeed it is the only form of file organization possible for files held on serial-access media such as magnetic tape, punched cards and printer devices). For efficiency of processing many sequential files are organized so that the records are in key field value order. For our student file the primary key field is the student identification number — Figure 3.13 shows the records of Figure 3.12 organized in ascending sequence of the student number field in each record.

New records must be inserted into this sequence at such positions as to maintain the key ordering of the sequence, e.g., a new record for

1012	Browne, M	23	History	British
2010	Neu, P	19	Computing	German
2293	Schmidt, P	20	Computing	German
4992	Singh, Y	19	Accountancy	Indian
5338	Sharma, P	22	Mathematics	Indian
5659	Hughes, W	21	Accountancy	British
5660	Bird, R	23	History	British
7474	Fulton, H	21	Computing	British
7487	Agnew, P	20	Mathematics	British
8836	Stewart, M	21	Mathematics	British

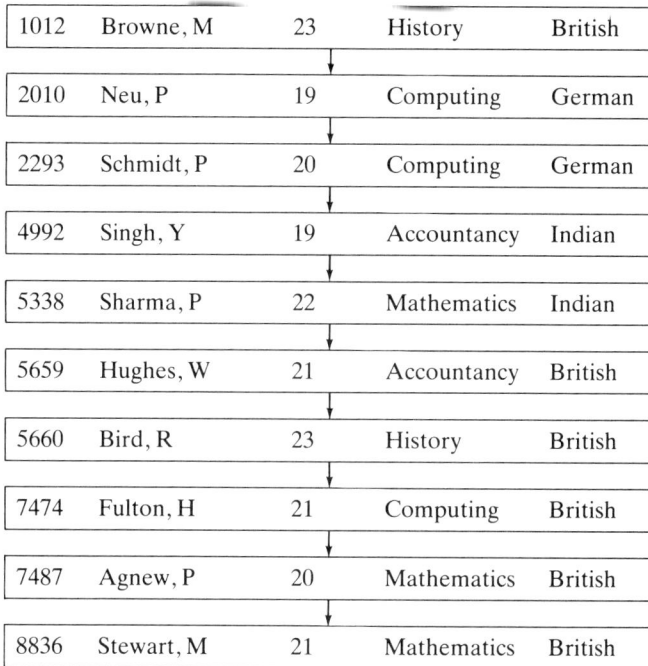

Figure 3.13   Ordered sequential file organization

a student with number 2264, say, must be inserted into the above sequence as the immediate predecessor of the record for student 2293, i.e., P Schmidt.

This file would be obtained by sorting the file of Figure 3.12. Chapter 5 gives detailed coverage of the processing of sequential organization files.

3.3.2   Random File Organization

The layout of records within a *random organization file* is determined by an *addressing algorithm* (commonly known as a *hashing function*) which calculates the physical address at which a particular record is to be stored in the file using the record's primary key value. This method of file organization is applicable only to files held on direct-access storage media and is used in applications for which speed of access to file records must be fast and the records are usually accessed in random order with respect to their primary key values, e.g., in real-time computer systems.

The structure of a random organization file is a sequence of record areas, each of which is capable of holding a record. Each record area in the sequence is identified by a *relative record number*, on the basis of which records are stored and retrieved. If there are N record areas in the file, then each record area is distinguished by a unique integer in the range $1..N$, as illustrated in Figure 3.14. *

Figure 3.14   Random file structure

Each record area may or may not contain a record value, hence the record areas for a file containing component values of type T might be defined by the following Pascal type definition:

```
type recordarea =  record
                       occupied : boolean ;
                       contents : T
                   end
```

or, more appropriately, as a variant record type

```
type recordarea =  record
                       case occupied : boolean of
                       true : (contents : T) ;
                       false : ( )
                   end
```

When a record is stored in a random organization file the record area which is to hold its value is determined by an addressing algorithm which transforms its primary key field value k into an integer in the range $1..N$, say j, where j is then known as the *preferred file position* for the record. When an attempt is subsequently made to retrieve this record from the file its key value will again be transformed into the same relative record number, by use of the same addressing algorithm.

The file is completely structured by the use of the addressing function and usually results in the records being organized in random key value sequence (however, some simple algorithms do produce key-ordered files). The function converts the key value into a relative record number within the range defined for the file, and this relative

0					
3	5338	Sharma, P	22	Mathematics	Indian
5	7474	Fulton, H	21	Computing	British
9	8836	Stewart, M	21	Mathematics	British
18	7487	Agnew, P	20	Mathematics	British
33	5659	Hughes, W	21	Accountancy	British
34	5660	Bird, R	23	History	British
42	1012	Browne, M	23	History	British
45	4992	Singh, Y	19	Accountancy	Indian
62	2293	Schmidt, P	20	Computing	German
70	2010	Neu, P	19	Computing	German
96					

Figure 3.15 Random organization of student file

record number is then transformed into the actual physical address of the record. Figure 3.15 shows the layout of the records of the student records in a random organization file structured using the following simple hashing function

relative record number = student-number **mod** 97

where the random organization file contains 97 record areas.

In practice each record area contains a boolean field *occupied* denoting whether a record is currently stored in that area. However, for simplicity, we have indicated only the occupied areas of the file in Figure 3.15 and omitted the *occupied* field from each record.

Note how the file consists of 97 record areas yet only ten of the areas are actually occupied and so the file contains large gaps (which will be used as new records are added to the file). Various other different types of addressing algorithm are commonly used for structuring random files and some of these are described in Chapter 9.

A problem arises with *synonyms*, i.e., primary keys which map onto the same relative record number, since once we have allocated

0					
3	5338	Sharma, P	22	Mathematics	Indian
5	7474	Fulton, H	21	Computing	British
9	8836	Stewart, M	21	Mathematics	British
18	7487	Agnew, P	20	Mathematics	British
33	5659	Hughes, W	21	Accountancy	British
34	5660	Bird, R	23	History	British
35	2264	Poirot, H	22	History	French
42	1012	Browne, M	23	History	British
45	4992	Singh, Y	19	Accountancy	Indian
62	2293	Schmidt, P	20	Computing	German
70	2010	Neu, P	19	Computing	German
96					

Figure 3.16 Insertion into a random organization file

a record to a certain record area in the file, other records which map onto the same record area have to be found alternative positions. For example, if a record with key 2264 is added to the above file it should be placed in record area 33, but this area is already occupied by the existing record with key 5659. In this case a *collision* is said to have occurred. A 'good' hashing function is one which produces a low number of such synonyms. Should a record area already be occupied by another record with a different key there are various strategies which may be chosen to find an alternative home for any record mapping onto that area. For example:

(a) use a so-called *re-hashing function* to calculate a step value *S* for the primary key value concerned; starting at the occupied record area with relative record number *X*, look at positions

$$(X + iS) \bmod N \qquad \text{for} \quad i = 1, 2, \ldots$$

(where *N* is the number of record areas in the file) until an empty record area is found and store the record in this area. The set of record areas thus inspected is known as the *probe sequence* generated by the re-hashing function. If this probe sequence arrives back at record area *X*, then, provided the table length *N* is prime, the file must be full and the new record cannot be added. An example of a very simple re-hashing algorithm is one which always returns the step value $S = 1$, i.e., which stores the record in the next unused record area of the file. Figure 3.16 shows the result of inserting a new record for a student with identification number 2264 into the file of Figure 3.15 using the same hashing function and a re-hashing function generating a constant step value 1.

(b) A second possibility is to increase the size of each record area so that it can contain not one record but a group of records, i.e., the definition of the record areas becomes

```
const maxrecordsinarea = ... ;
type recordarea =      record
                       numberofrecords : 0..maxrecordsinarea ;
                       contents : array [1..maxrecordsinarea] of T
                  end
```

New records can be added to the array contents in each record area until this array is filled. Subsequent records may then be added into specially reserved *overflow* record areas which hold all records which cannot be stored in their preferred record areas. Hence, in the insertion of the record with key 2264 above, it would become the second record held in record area 33. Usually these record areas (which are effectively blocks of records) are stored in disk buckets — the prefer-

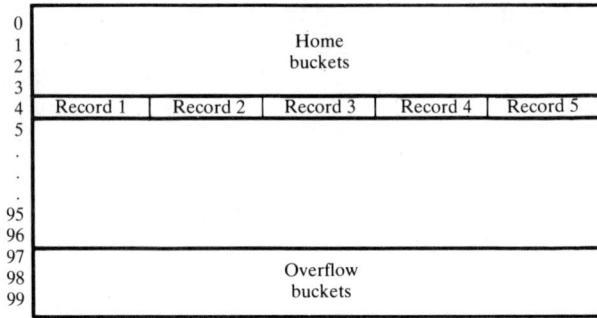

Figure 3.17   Random file organization to handle overflow

red record area is then known as the *home bucket*, and the record area used to hold overflows from home buckets is known as the *overflow bucket*.

A number of additional record areas are often reserved at the end of a file to act as overflow areas, as shown in Figure 3.17 (where each record area is assumed to be big enough to hold *maxrecordsin-area* = 5 records).

Retrieval of records from random organization files is discussed later in this chapter, and Chapter 9 gives detailed coverage of the processing of random files and also of their implementation.

INDEX

0	1012	42
1	2293	62
2	5338	3
3	7474	5
4	5659	33
5	5660	34
6	7487	18
7	8836	9
8	4992	45
9	2010	70

FILE

0					
3	5338	Sharma, P	22	Mathematics	Indian
5	7474	Fulton, H	21	Computing	British
9	8836	Stewart, M	21	Mathematics	British
18	7487	Agnew, P	20	Mathematics	British
33	5659	Hughes, W	21	Accountancy	British
34	5660	Bird, R	23	History	British
42	1012	Browne, M	23	History	British
45	4992	Singh, Y	19	Accountancy	Indian
62	2293	Schmidt, P	20	Computing	German
70	2010	Neu, P	19	Computing	German
96					

Figure 3.18   Indexed organization of student file

3.3.3 Indexed File Organization

The records of the file may be stored together with an index containing one entry for each record in the file, an entry consisting of a primary record key together with the file address or position of the record with that primary key value. *Indexed file organization* is used in practice only for files on direct-access media. Figure 3.18 shows the records of the file of Figure 3.15 and an associated index.

Note that the index is very much smaller than the file (since each index entry consists of just two fields) and so the index could be stored in main memory for fast access. In Figure 3.18 not only are the records of the file stored in random key field order but so also are the index entries. Indeed the records in the file need not be stored in a contiguous file area at all but may be stored in different areas of a disk pack provided that the index entries contain actual physical file addresses in that case. This allows more flexibility in the storage of a file. Access to the records can be made more efficient if the index entries are structured in some way. For instance, the index could be structured as a table using a suitable hashing function. Figure 3.19 shows the index of Figure 3.18 organized using a 47 entry table and the hashing function

index position = *student-number* **mod** 47

Now, to find the record with key 2010, say, the index hashing function is applied to this key value, leading to index entry 36, which

INDEX

0	8836	9
1	7474	5
10	4992	45
14	7487	18
19	5659	33
20	5660	34
25	1012	42
27	5338	3
36	2010	70
37	2293	62
46		

Figure 3.19 Index organization using hashing function

in turn Identifies record area 70 as the file position of the record. The problems of structuring such an index are exactly as for structuring a random file, i.e., the possibility of synonym keys has to be taken into consideration. Compared with random file organization on its own, such indexed access involves two accesses to storage (once to the record entry of the index, which is probably in main memory, and once to the record in the file). The extra storage of the index is offset by the faster access to synonym records since the search for such records involves repeated access to the index rather than to the actual records in the file.

It is of course possible to sort the entries of the index into key value order, as shown in Figure 3.20, and search the index using a *binary split search*.

INDEX

0	1012	42
1	2010	70
2	2293	62
3	4992	45
4	5338	3
5	5659	33
6	5660	34
7	7474	3
8	7487	18
9	8836	9

Figure 3.20   Sorted index

A binary split search operates by examining the mid-point entry in the index and comparing its key field value with the key of the record required. If this value is not the one required, then the process is repeated using either the upper half or lower half of the index (whichever is appropriate, remembering that the index entries are in key order) until either the key required is found, or it is certain that the key is not in fact in the index. This binary search technique can be implemented by the following Pascal procedure *locate*, which attempts to search an index of N entries in order to find the index entry with key value k, and assigns appropriate values to variable parameters *found* and *position*:

```
procedure locate (k : keytype ;  var found : boolean ;
                                 var position : fileaddress) ;
    var top, bottom, midway : integer ;
    begin
        found := false ; bottom := 1 ; top := N ;
        while not found and (bottom <= top) do
        begin
            midway := (bottom + top) div 2 ;
            if k = index [midway].key
            then found := true
            else if k < index[midway].key
                then top := midway − 1
                else bottom := midway + 1
        end ;
        if found then position := index[midway].address
    end ; { locate }
```

Since the size of the part of the index which can hold the required key is reduced by half at each iteration of the loop, the number of steps required will be at most $\log_2 N + 1$, where N is the number of entries currently in the index.

Holding the index in sorted key order enables the file records to be accessed in key order also, since the required ordering is provided by the order of the index entries. If not only the index is organized in sorted key order but also the file records themselves, we have what is known as an *indexed sequential file* (Figure 3.21). In each index entry the field value *ai* refers to the physical address of the record. This file organization techique is effectively a compromise between sequential and random file organization — an indexed sequential file may be processed as if it were an ordered sequential file (since the file records are in key order sequence) or its records may be accessed directly via the index. This flexibility makes such a file organization the most popular method of organizing record storage on magnetic disk. Although it is not necessary to store the records in a contiguous area, storing them in contiguous physical locations may mean that it is not actually necessary to hold the physical addresses in the index entries.

When a new record is assigned to an indexed file the new record must be located in the record storage area and its address recorded in a new entry of the index. In the case of an indexed sequential file this means that the new index entry must be inserted into the index at the appropriate point to maintain the ordering of the index entries.

Later in this chapter we shall show how this basic structure for an indexed sequential organization file is modified to provide more efficient access to the file records.

INDEX

0	1012	*a0*
1	2010	*a1*
2	2293	*a2*
3	4992	*a3*
4	5338	*a4*
5	5659	*a5*
6	5660	*a6*
7	7474	*a7*
8	7487	*a8*
9	8836	*a9*

FILE

a0	1012	Browne, M	23	History	British
a1	2010	Neu, P	19	Computing	German
a2	2293	Schmidt, P	20	Computing	German
a3	4992	Singh, Y	19	Accountancy	Indian
a4	5338	Sharma, P	22	Mathematics	Indian
a5	5659	Hughes, W	21	Accountancy	British
a6	5660	Bird, R	23	History	British
a7	7474	Fulton, H	21	Computing	British
a8	7487	Agnew, P	20	Mathematics	British
a9	8836	Stewart, M	21	Mathematics	British

Figure 3.21   Indexed sequential file organization

The category of application for which an indexed sequential organization is best-suited is any in which the file records may be processed randomly by some programs and in key order sequence by other programs. In such cases the availability of both direct and sequential access to the records in the file makes both types of processing convenient (and efficient). Chapter 8 describes the processing and implementation of indexed sequential files.

3.3.4   Inverted File Organization

Some applications which process files sometimes require records to be accessed in order of some key field other than the primary key, i.e., using one of the secondary key files. For example, consider our student file used in previous sections of this chapter. Assume it has been organized sequentially in order of the student number field, as in Figure 3.21. We might however wish to access the records in order of age, or subject by subject, or nationality by nationality. To provide this extra flexibility of access additional indexes may be established, one per secondary key, to give the addresses of records with given secondary keys. Since secondary keys are not usually unique, the entries in these additional indexes will consist of a key field and a list of record addresses. To avoid duplication of physical record addresses a *primary index* is set up containing the primary keys and physical addresses (as before), and the *secondary index* entries then contain the primary keys to enable reference to this primary index for the establishment of actual addresses. A file structured with such a set of indexes is known as an *inverted file*, and the set of indexes is referred to as an *inverted index*. Figure 3.22 shows an inverted file structure for our student file, where there are secondary indexes for age, subject, and nationality.

Such a file also allows the identification of groups of records, e.g., 'all the British students doing Computing and 21 years old'. By forming the intersection of the relevant entries in the nationality, subject, and age indexes we can deduce that the student with identification number 7474 is the only such student and his record, according to the primary index, is stored at address *a1*.

In some cases the information contained in the indexes is not held in the file records, e.g., the file records might be as shown in Figure 3.23. This form of inverted file structure is known as a *partially inverted* file.

FILE

a0	5338	Sharma, P	22	Mathematics	Indian
a1	7474	Fulton, H	21	Computing	British
a2	8836	Stewart, M	21	Mathematics	British
a3	7487	Agnew, P	20	Mathematics	British
a4	5659	Hughes, W	21	Accountancy	British
a5	5660	Bird, R	23	History	British
a6	1012	Browne, M	23	History	British
a7	4992	Singh, Y	19	Accountancy	Indian
a8	2293	Schmidt, P	20	Computing	German
a9	2010	Neu, P	21	Computing	German

AGE INDEX

19	2010
	4992
20	2293
	7487
21	5659
	7474
	8836
22	5338
23	1012
	5660

SUBJECT INDEX

Accountancy	4992
	5659
Computing	2010
	2293
	7474
Mathematics	5338
	7487
	8836
History	1012
	5660

NATIONALITY INDEX

British	1012
	5659
	5660
	7474
	7487
	8836
German	2010
	2293
Indian	4492
	5338

PRIMARY INDEX

1012	a6
2010	a9
2293	a8
4992	a7
5338	a0
5659	a4
5660	a5
7474	a1
7487	a3
8836	a2

Figure 3.22   Inverted file structure

FILE

a0	Sharma, P
a1	Fulton, H
a2	Stewart, M
a3	Agnew, P
a4	Hughes, W
a5	Bird, R
a6	Browne, M
a7	Singh, Y
a8	Schmidt, P
a9	Neu, P

Figure 3.23   Records in a partially inverted file

If all the fields of the records have indexes set up for them, then there is no need to hold the records at all, i.e., the file effectively becomes a set of indexes and is known as a *totally inverted file*. Inverted files are generally used for enquiry-type applications.

3.4 ACCESS METHODS

These describe the various ways in which records may be retrieved from a file.

3.4.1 Sequential Access

The records are simply accessed in the logical order in which they were written to the file. This method of access is applicable to any sort of file organization, although it is rarely used for random organization files (due to most addressing algorithms producing files in which the records are not in any key-order sequence). It is the usual access method for magnetic tape files since their records must be sequentially organized. If the records are in key sequence, then sequential access will result in the records being read in key order — this mode of access may also be used for indexed sequential files.

3.4.2   Direct Access

This is used to access records in a random organization file. Record addresses are determined using the same addressing algorithm (hashing function) as was used to locate new records in the file. Once again there is a problem in accessing records which are not stored in the preferred file position given by the addressing function. If the file stores single records in a record area and the preferred position is occupied by a record with a different key from that of the record required, then it is necessary to use the re-hashing function to determine the probe sequence of alternative positions at which the record may have been stored. Alternative positions are inspected until either the record is found, or an empty record area is inspected (in which case the record is not in the file) or the preferred position is revisited (in which case also the record is then known not to be in the file). The success of this method depends upon deleted records of the file not being physically removed but rather left in the file and flagged as obsolete prior to some subsequent reorganization of the file (otherwise a record placed at some position other than its preferred position may not be accessible due to the presence of an unoccupied record position in its probe sequence).

If the second collision strategy of Section 3.3.2 is employed, i.e., more than one record is stored in a record area (the home bucket), then a search is performed of the records in this home bucket. If the required record is not found but the home bucket is filled to maximum capacity, then it may be that the record was stored in an overflow record area when the record was assigned to the file — in which case a search of the records in the overflow bucket(s) must be performed before it can be assumed that the record is not in the file.

3.4.3   Indexed Access

An index defines the physical address of a record in the file given its key value. Depending upon how the index is structured an entry can be accessed by a serial search, use of a hashing function, or by a binary split search. Figure 3.24 shows a *single-level index* where the address of each record in the file is defined. The index is held in key sequence so that either a serial or binary search may be used to find an entry.

Single-level indexing is generally used for small files only, due to the lengthy search time involved in finding an entry in a long index. For an indexed sequential file of many records the index size will be such that even a binary split search may be expensive in terms of time.

For practical purposes the records of an indexed-sequential file are not stored in random key sequence (as in Figure 3.18) but instead

are organized in key-order sequence (as in Figure 3.21) and groups of key-ordered records are usually stored in disk buckets. Thus it is possible to set up a partial index for an indexed sequential file in which there is one entry for each bucket of the file giving the highest key stored in the bucket concerned.

	Address	
Key	Cylinder	Track
01005	1	2
01027	1	2
01193	1	2
20437	1	3
...		
98872	9	8
99943	9	9

Figure 3.24   Single-level index

The index search time can be further improved if a *multi-level* or *tree-structured* index is used — the index may be organized as a tree of up to three levels in practice. For a multi-cylinder file a first-level (*master*) index may be established giving the highest key in each cylinder of the file together with the address of the second-level (*cylinder*) index stored on each cylinder. These cylinder indexes will give the highest record key stored in each track of the cylinder together with the address of a third-level (*track*) index stored in each track of the cylinder. Each track index will give the highest key of the records stored in each bucket of the track. Figure 3.25 illustrates the structure of the entries in these indexes. The primary index will be held at the start of the file and be transferred into main memory as soon as processing of the file begins. The cylinder and track indexes will be read in from the disk as required. In practice two-level indexes are most frequently used with the primary index defining the highest key in each cylinder and the secondary indexes defining the highest key in each track. Figure 3.26 illustrates the search of a two-level index for an indexed sequential file, in which the records occupy seven cylinders of disk storage, to find a record with key 3072. The addresses of the indexes have been omitted for simplicity.

Hence the disk access normally involves just one single disk head movement, to the cylinder containing the required record. As was mentioned above, the primary index is usually transferred into main store at the beginning of the execution of the file access program and remains there; each secondary index is brought into main store and searched whenever necessary. All the index searches may be performed as binary searches.

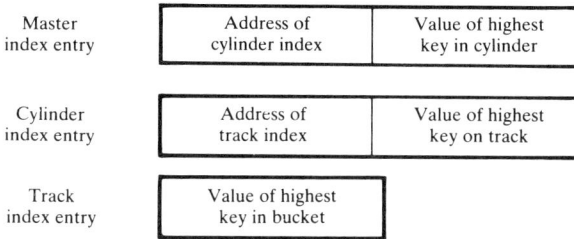

Figure 3.25   Index entry structures

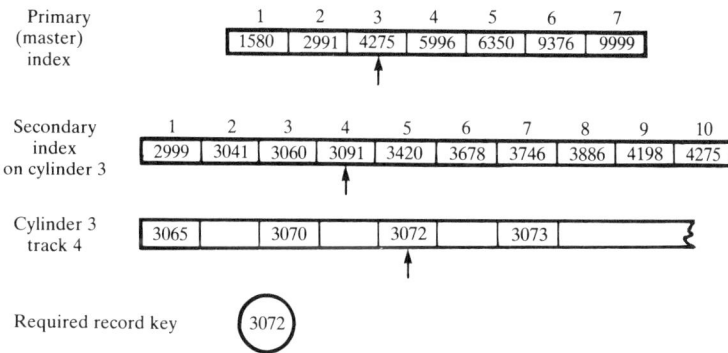

Figure 3.26   Two-level indexing

The reading of a record in an indexed sequential file with a two-level index such as in Figure 3.26 involves:

1. a search of the master index (already in main memory);
2. moving the read/write heads to the appropriate cylinder and selection of the first track;
3. a wait of an average half-revolution for the cylinder index to reach the head;
4. input of the cylinder index;
5. a search of the cylinder index;

6. selection of the required track and another half-revolution delay for the desired bucket to reach the head;·
7. input of the bucket.

Thus the total disk time is usually

> 1 arm movement
> + 1 revolution of delay
> + transfer time for 1 bucket and a cylinder index.

If the file access program is written in a high-level language such as COBOL, most of the above tasks are carried out by standard software — the user simply declares his file to be organized as an indexed sequential file and generates the appropriate transfer request for a record with a particular key.

If the file is processed randomly with accesses not being made in key sequence, there will be considerable arm movement. Hence, if possible, it is preferable to sort the file references into key sequence — in which case the heads move smoothly across the disk in just one sweep, and also the track index for each cylinder need be input only once in all instead of once per record, and buckets need only be transferred at most once.

Consider an indexed sequential file of 100 000 records of 50 characters each held on disk at 10 records per bucket and 8 buckets per track. Ignoring the possibility of overflow, and assuming the cylinder indexes to be small, the file uses

$$100\ 000 / (10 \text{ x } 10 \text{ x } 8) = 125 \text{ cylinders}$$

Assume that the file uses 125 adjacent cylinders of the disk pack and suppose a program run reads 5% of the records in the file with the records accessed in random order. The disk usage time is then

> arm movement $= 5000 \times 75$ ms (average arm movement time)
> rotational delays $= 5000 \times 20$ ms
> block transfers $= 5000 \times 1/8 \times 20$ ms
> total disk time $= 487.5$ s

However, suppose it is possible to access the records in key sequence. Then

> arm movement $= 125 \times 25$ ms (single cylinder movement time)
> rotational delays $= 125 \times 10$ ms (for cylinder indexes) plus
> $5000 \times 0.5 \times 20$ ms (before block transfers)
> block transfers $= 5000 \times 1/8 \times 20$ ms
> total disk time $= 66.875$ s

If each record is accessed by several transactions, then the savings become even greater. Hence, whenever possible, it pays to presort the file references into the same sequence as the file records.

3.4.4   Dynamic Access

Dynamic access involves switching between sequential access and non-sequential (direct or indexed) access, and vice versa. It may be used with indexed sequential files and random organization files. A particular record is first accessed randomly using indexed or direct access, after which subsequent records are accessed in the logical sequence in which they reside within the file. For example, in Figure 3.21, we might first access the record corresponding to student number 4992 using indexed access and then proceed to access the file records sequentially — the records accessed would then, in order, be those with keys 4992, 5338, 5659, 5660, 7474, 7487, and 8836 before the end of the file is reached. At any time sequential access may be discontinued and another record accessed directly. In Figure 3.15 direct access to the record with key 4992 followed by sequential access to the file records would lead to the records with keys 4992, 2293, and 2010 being processed before the end of the file was reached.

3.4.5   Choosing a Method of File Organization

The factors involved in making the choice of file organization (and file access method) are such as the storage media available, the file size, the volatility of the file, the hit ratio associated with the application, the response requirements, and the security of the file.

   If the only form of long-term magnetic storage is magnetic tape, then sequential organization will have to be employed. If the hit ratio is not very low and fast access to specific records is not necessary, then sequential file processing is usually appropriate and can be made efficient (see Chapters 4 and 5). Magnetic tape file updating, as we shall see in Chapter 4, also provides a back-up copy of the file for security purposes.

   Indexed sequential files have the significant capability for both sequential and direct access and are appropriate for applications where a file is to be processed both sequentially and randomly by the same, or different, programs. Indexed sequential file processing can, as we have seen, be made more efficient by batching the updating data into the same sorted sequence as the file records.

   Generally random organization using a simple addressing algorithm involves less processing time than the use of indexes in order to locate a direct access file record, but there is the loss of storage capacity in the file due to unused record positions — hence the use of random organization is primarily for applications where processing speed is critical (such as in on-line systems that provide enquiry facilities, e.g., reservations systems and library index interrogation systems).

Note that, for a language implementation which provides sequential access to a random organization file, sequential batch processing is made possible for such a file by sorting the transactions according to the transformed values of their key fields, i.e., in relative record number order (although this scheme will not work if any records are not stored in their preferred positions due to synonym collisions).

In Chapters 5, 8, and 9 we shall describe the various ways in which the records of files using the different organization methods may be processed, including the high-level language facilities provided to support these methods, and implement the various access methods discussed in this chapter.

3.5 BASIC FILE MANIPULATION OPERATIONS

When using a file in a program written in a high-level programming language it is first necessary to specify the characteristics of the file. These characteristics include

1. the *peripheral device* on which the file resides;
2. the *organization* and *access* methods used in creating the file and accessing its contents;
3. the *block* or *bucket size*, i.e., the size of the physical records which are stored in the file (as opposed to the logical records, in terms of which the programmer works);
4. the *number of buffers* required for the file;
5. the contents of the *labels* for the file;
6. the formats of the various *record types* in the file;
7. the *key fields* to be used in structuring and accessing direct-access files.

Having established these characteristics, various operations will then be performed on the file and its records, including

1. Initial *creation* of the file (as a file organized in a certain way and containing zero or more records).
2. *Opening* and *closing* of the file — all files must be opened before processing of them can begin, and closed when processing is com-

pleted. A file must be opened in a mode — e.g., input, output or input–output — appropriate to the manner in which it is to be processed. Files may be closed in various ways, e.g., simple closure (meaning that the file may be opened again later in the program execution), or closed 'locked' so that the file cannot be opened again during the program execution, or 'without rewind' (in the case of sequential access files) so that subsequent re-opening of a file will recommence processing at the record following the final one processed in the previous opening.

3. *Label-checking* — on opening an input file its header labels (if it has any) should be checked to ensure that it is the correct file, i.e., that its identity corresponds to that expected by the program; an output file may have header labels containing the required file identity written to it.

4. Record referencing operations — there are four operations which are normally used to retrieve records from the file, or change the state of the records in a file:
    (a) *reading* a record from a file;
    (b) *writing* a record to a file;
    (c) *deleting* a record from a direct-access file;
    (d) *overwriting* a record in a direct-access file.

5. *Blocking* and *deblocking routines* — when a program reads a block or bucket a number of logical records will be transferred into the input file's buffer area. Deblocking routines supply the individual records as the program needs them and so must keep track of which record in the block is currently being processed. Similar routines must assemble blocks of records in output buffer areas in preparation for output to files.

The facilities provided by most high-level commercial programming languages for opening, closing, and referencing files usually perform the label-checking, access, blocking and deblocking operations automatically, using relevant information supplied by the programmer.

Before beginning to describe the logical properties and ways of processing the various types of files whose physical organization and access methods we have described in this chapter, we shall attempt to define the environment in which such file processing will usually take place.

3.5.1 Abstraction of the File-processing Environment

Each file processing environment will define quantities such as the standard block size to be used for magnetic tape files, the size of a disk sector, and objects such as the form of a file identifier. It will also define the set of peripheral devices which are available to users, the modes in which files may be processed, and the modes in which files may be closed.

Additionally, we require this environment to provide the label-handling facilities, label-checking at file opening, and closing of files. It must also provide means of creating a file which did not previously exist, and to erase files which are no longer required.

For our Model Savings Bank system the standard magnetic tape block size and the disk sector size are both 512 characters; file identifiers are strings of up to 20 characters in length. The peripheral devices we shall assume to consist of four tape drives, four exchangeable disk drives, two card readers and one card punch (all using 80 column cards), and two line printers (with 120 character carriage widths).

Hence we may formulate an abstract data type to represent the environment in which our files will be processed. This environment will specify the various quantities, objects, and operations introduced above. Since only one instance of this type is required by any file processing program, we may define it as a class module of the form.

```
class module environment ;
    const *blocksize = 512 ;
          *sectorsize = 512 ;
          *maxbuffers = 2 ;
          *filenamelength = 20 ;
          *printerwidth = 120 ;
          *cardwidth = 80 ;
    type  *devices = ( *DA1, *DA2, *DA3, *DA4,
                       *MT1, *MT2, *MT3, *MT4,
                       *CR1, *CR2,
                       *CP1,
                       *LP1, *LP2 ) ;
          *massstoragedevices = DA1..MT4,
          *direct devices = DA1..DA4 ;
          *inputdevices = CR1..CR2 ;
          *outputdevices = CP1..LP2 ;
          *blockrange = 1..maxint ;
          *bufferrange = 1..maxbuffers ;
          *fileidentity = packed array [1..filenamelength] of char ;
          *fileprocessing modes = ( *input, *output, *inputoutput) ;
          *serialfileprocessingmodes = input..output ;
          *closingmodes = ( *simple, *locked, *norewind) ;
          *percentage = 1..100 ;
```

```
    var    *directaccessdevices : set of devices ;
    class  *fileinterface ( device : devices ; id : fileidentity ;
                              newfile : boolean ; blocksize : blockrange ;
                              numberofbuffers : bufferrange) ;
        begin
            if newfile then create a new file called id ;
            if file id on device exists
            then begin
                      construct a description of the file ;
                      physically attach the device to the program ;
                      *** ;
                      release the device from the program
                  end
            else error {report it or stop the program}
        end { fileinterface } ;
    begin
        directaccessdevices := [DA1..DA4] ;
        ***
    end { environment }
```

The class *fileinterface* provided by the environment allows the physical attributes of a file (its physical device, the file identity, block size, and degree of buffering required) to be indicated to the environment, which can then perform all the physical file manipulation operations automatically. This file interface will, if necessary, automatically create a new file (if the *newfile* parameter value is true) and its initialization actions will be to physically attach the device to the program (performing any label checking or writing, as required). Its finalization will involve releasing the physical device. Thus, before processing of a file by a program may begin, an interface of the class *environment.fileinterface* must be declared for the file. *fileinterface* will provide other operations (such as block retrieval and block writing operations), but these need not concern us here.

This environment definition will be used in later chapters which describe in detail the processing of files and hence we assume the availability of an actual implementation of the *environment* class in the library. The actual implementation will be dependent upon the actual environment, i.e., operating system, within which the processing will take place. In the next chapter we shall consider the problem of updating the records of master files held on both serial-access and direct-access media. In order to provide a definition of such file types suitable for use in these file updating algorithms, and also to illustrate how the environment specification may be used in practice, we shall now construct abstract data types for both serial-access and direct-access files.

3.5.2 Abstraction of a Serial-access File

Let us assume that a serial-access file contains values of some type *itemtype*. The four operations provided for a serial-access file are

1. *opening* the file (as an input or output file) ;
2. *closing* the file (in a certain closing mode) ;
3. *reading* the next record from an input file (which must be currently open) — this operation must also detect when the end of the file has been reached, i.e., when no next record exists to be read ;
4. *writing* a record to the end of a currently open output file.

The serial-access file type may be defined as an abstract data type, i.e., a class type, which is held in the library and for which the type *itemtype* will be specified upon retrieval of the class definition into a user program. The parameters of this class define the physical characteristics of the actual file. Hence the form of the serial-access file abstraction is given by the following class declaration :

```
class serialaccessfile ( device : devices ;
                         identity : environment.fileidentity ;
                         newfile : boolean ;
                         blocksize : environment.blockrange ;
                         numberofbuffers : environment.bufferrange) ;
    { requires type itemtype }
    procedure *open (mode : environment.serialfileprocessingmodes) ;
    procedure *close (mode : environment.closingmodes) ;
    procedure *read (var v : itemtype ; var atend : boolean) ;
    procedure *write (v : itemtype) ;
    begin
        ***
    end { serial-access file }
```

The parameters which define the physical file characteristics are, in turn, passed to the environment by declaring an instance of the class *environment.fileinterface* as a (hidden) object within this class, viz.,

```
instance interface : environment.fileinterface ( device, identity,
                                                 newfile, blocksize,
                                                 numberofbuffers);
```

This will enable the environment to handle correctly all operations associated with the physical file concerned.

To illustrate the use of this type in association with the environment specification consider the simple problem of copying the contents of an input file of records of type *T* held on magnetic tape drive 1 to an output file held on magnetic tape drive 2. The input file has an identity '*version1*' and the output file is to be given the identity '*version2*'. Both files use the standard *blocksize* defined by the environment and are to be double-buffered.

First of all we must define the required serial-access file type of which the input file and output file are to be instances (we shall denote this type by the name *fileofT*). This is achieved by retrieving the *serialaccessfile* class definition from the source library and supplying a retrieval specification for the file record type, viz.,

> **class** *fileofT* = *serialaccessfile* **in library**
> (**where type** *itemtype* = *T*)

Now we may declare two instances of our type *fileofT*, corresponding to the two files used. Each must be given the appropriate physical file description parameters.

> **instance** *f* : *fileofT* (*environment.MT1*, '*version1*', *false*,
> *environment.blocksize*, 2) ;
> **instance** *g* : *fileofT* (*environment.MT2*, '*version2*', *true*,
> *environment.blocksize*, 2) ;

Note that *g* is to be created and hence the *newfile* formal parameter value is *true*. The two files must then be opened in appropriate modes using the *open* operator of *fileofT*. Records are transferred one-by-one from the input file to the output file until an attempt to read a record from the input file *f* determines that the input file has been exhausted. Hence the copying procedure may be described by

```
var t : T ;
    endoffilef : boolean ;
begin
   with environment do
   begin
     f.open (input) ; g.open (output) ;
     f.read (t, endoffilef) ;
     while not endoffilef do
     begin
       g.write (t) ;
       f.read (t, endoffilef)
     end ;
     f.close (locked) ; g.close (locked)
   end
end { file copy }
```

3.5.3 Abstraction of a Direct-access File

The second file abstraction is that of a direct-access file of values of some type *itemtype*. For direct access the value of the key to be used in the access must be identified, thus the abstraction depends upon the key type, denoted by *keytype*. Specification of a direct-access file type is therefore characterized by two types, *itemtype* and *keytype*. The operations on a direct-access file are six in all – *open, close, read,* and *write,* as well as record deletion and replacement operators.

```
class directaccessfile ( device : environment.directdevices ;
                         identity : environment.fileidentity ;
                         newfile : boolean ;
                         blocksize : environment.blockrange) ;
              { requires type keytype }
              {          type itemtype }
      procedure *open (mode : environment.fileprocessingmodes) ;
      procedure *close (mode : environment.closingmodes) ;
      procedure *read (k : keytype ; var v : itemtype ; var found : boolean) ;
      procedure *write (k : keytype ; v : itemtype ; var found : boolean) ;
      procedure *delete (k : keytype ; var found : boolean) ;
      procedure *replace (k : keytype ; v : itemtype ; var found : boolean) ;
      begin
          ***
      end { direct-access file }
```

As before, declaration of an instance of this type will supply the necessary description of the physical file concerned. In this case, since direct access to the file records is being used, single buffering will be all that is required and the *numberofbuffers* parameter is not included.

Each record manipulation operation takes a value parameter of type *keytype*, denoting the key of the record concerned in the operation. Each also has a variable boolean parameter whose value is set by the operator to indicate the success or otherwise of the operation.

> **procedure** *read (k : keytype ; **var** v : itemtype ; **var** found : boolean)

This operator retrieves the record with key value k from the file and assigns its value to the variable parameter v. If such a record exists in the file then *found* is set to *true*, otherwise it will be assigned the value *false*.

> **procedure** *write (k : keytype ; v : itemtype ; **var** found : boolean)

attempts to add the record value v with key value k to the file. If a record with this key value already exists in the file then the addition will not be performed but, instead, the value of *found* will be set to *true*. For a successful addition *found* will be assigned *false*.

> **procedure** *delete (k : keytype ; **var** found : boolean)

attempts to remove the record with key k from the file — the value of *found* indicates whether such a record was actually in the file.

procedure **replace* (*k* : *keytype* ; *v* : *itemtype* ; **var** *found* : *boolean*)

attempts to replace the value of the record with key *k* with the new record value *v* (which should have the same key). Once again the value of *found* denotes the success of the operation.

The interface provided by this abstraction does not indicate how the direct-access file is structured and how the records are actually accessed – i.e., whether it is a random organization or indexed sequential organization file. This detail need not concern us as we can assume that it is dealt with in the implementation of the direct-access file abstraction. In Chapters 8 and 9 we shall develop separate and more complete abstractions for both indexed sequential and random organization files. We do not give an example of the use of the direct-access file abstraction at this point as a substantial example appears in the next chapter.

EXERCISES

In the exercises below assume the following characteristics of any magnetic tape and magnetic disk files:

Magnetic tapes
>2400 ft (730 m) long using a recording density of 800 characters per inch (315 characters per centimeter);
>inter-block gaps of 500 characters;
>transfer rate of 60 000 characters per second;
>inter-block start–stop time of 20 ms.

Magnetic disks
>exchangeable disks with ten surfaces per pack are used;
>the disk drive operates at 3000 r.p.m.;
>there are 200 tracks per surface;
>each track consists of eight sectors of 512 characters;
>arm movement time to move T cylinders $= 25 + (0.5*T)$ ms.

1. A medium-sized magnetic tape file contains 30 000 fixed-length records of 100 characters each. Ignoring loading and re-winding operations, what is the input time for this file using block sizes of
    (a)   100 characters;
    (b)   1000 characters;
    (c)   2000 characters;
    (d)   10 000 characters?

2. A program updates an old master file (which has 128 000 records of 500 characters) using a transaction file (with 90 000 records of 100 characters) to produce both a new master file (with 128 000 records of 500 characters) and a report file (with 10 000 records of 100 characters). Each file is stored on magnetic tape. Only single buffering is available and so the total run of the program is the sum of the processing time, the data transfer time, the inter-block stop/start time and the reel mounting/dismounting time. Calculate the total run time for each of the following cases:

(a) A blocking factor of 1 is used for each file;
(b) 10 000 characters of storage are available for blocking and are split equally among the four files;
(c) 20 000 characters of storage are available for blocking and are split equally among the four files;
(d) 10 000 characters of storage are available for blocking and are split optimally among the four files;
(e) 20 000 characters of storage are available for blocking and are split optimally among the four files.

What conclusions can you draw from these calculations regarding buffer size and the way in which it is apportioned between the files? What effect would the use of double-buffering have?

3. A program merges an old master file with a transaction file to produce a new master file. The approximate file lengths are 10 000 records, 3600 records and 10 000 records respectively, where each file has 512 character records. 13K characters of main memory are available for buffering. What block size would you recommend?

4. If bucket size is the maximum, i.e., equal to track size, how long will it take to:
(a) serially input the entire contents of a disk pack;
(b) randomly input the entire contents of a disk pack?

5. A program uses a transaction file (with 640 000 records of 100 characters) to update an old master file and produce a new master file (both master files containing 90 000 records of 400 characters). All three files are stored on magnetic tapes. Single-buffering is to be used and 8000 characters of storage are available for blocking.

(a) What block size would you recommend for each file?
(b) How many tape reels are required to hold each file?
(c) Ignoring processing time and reel mounting/dismounting time, what is the total time required to read the entire contents of the three files?

6. A program prices 20 000 customer orders, each containing on average quantities for five different products. A product file containing prices, etc., for 10 000 different products is held on exchangeable disk with five records per bucket and four buckets per track. Estimate the total disk reading time. (What would be the effect of sorting the product references for each customer?)

7. A large accounts file of 20 000 customers is stored on disk with five records/bucket and four buckets/track. Input transactions refer to this file (but do not update it) and the hit ratio is 5%; the hit records are randomly distributed over the file. What is the file input time if it is processed randomly?

8. An indexed-sequential file of 50 000 records of 50 characters is held on a disk pack with five records per bucket and eight buckets per track. If a program run updates 10% of the records in the file, and the updating transactions are presorted into key sequence, calculate the total disk access time of the program. Track indexes may be assumed to be small.

9. An indexed-sequential file of 40 000 records of 50 characters each is held on a disk pack at 10 records per bucket and four buckets per track. If a program run updates 10% of the records in the file in random order, calculate the total disk access time of the program. Track indexes may be assumed to be small.

10. Write a library procedure with the following heading

> **procedure** *binarysearch* (*A* : **array** [*m*..*n* : *integer*] **of** *elementtype* ;
>   *k* : *elementtype* ;
>   **var** *found* : *boolean* ;
>   **var** *position* : *integer*) ;
> { *assumes type elementtype with* <= *defined* }
> {   *by a function inorder*   }

that, given an ordered type *elementtype* (i.e., one for which the operator ≤ is defined), will perform a binary search of the array *A* (whose element values are assumed to be in ascending order) to find the position of the element of the array with value *k*. The parameter *found* is to be assigned an appropriate value indicating the success or otherwise of the search. Show how this procedure might be used in a program to search the array defined by

> **const** *N* = ... ;
> **type** *word* = **packed array** [1..*N*] **of** *char* ;
> **var** *wordspellings* : **array** [1..50] **of** *word* ;

to find the entry of *wordspellings* with value *w* (of type *word*).

4 FILE UPDATING

Much of the discussion that appears in this chapter on the problem of updating master files, and the algorithms developed, are based upon a paper by B.W. Dwyer entitled 'One more time — how to update a master file' which appeared in the *Communications of the A.C.M.* A reference to the paper appears in the Bibliography.

4.1 THE PROBLEM

The records of a master file define the status of objects of concern to the users and constructors of a system. In our Model Savings Bank case study system the master file records give details of the status of customers' savings accounts. The type of the records in these master files may be defined as:

> **type** *masterrecord =* **record**
> *key* : *accountnumber* ;
> *currentbalance,*
> *minimumbalance* : *money* ;
> *clientdetails* : *miscellaneous*
> **end**

where *key* is the primary field whose value uniquely identifies each such record, and *minimumbalance* is used to determine the interest to be paid to a customer for the current interest period.

These records change from time to time as the result of significant events (e.g., crediting or debiting an account) while at other times it is required merely to inspect the account details without changing them. In order to keep the master file in step with such events, transactions are created and used to update the master file.

With the savings accounts system, the following kinds of event may occur :

1. creation of an account;
2. debiting or crediting of an account;
3. deletion of an account.

In reality other events could be added to this list (such as inspecting an account record to determine its current balance, or to add interest to the account) but the above are sufficient for illustrative purposes. Only certain sequences of events can actually happen, e.g., an account may be credited and then debited, but it cannot be debited before it has been created. A sequence consisting only of debits and credits may be processed in any order — however, in general, sequence is important.

For purposes of efficiency, the status of each master record is not usually updated immediately after an event occurs. Instead transactions are collected into a batch and as many as possible processed at a time. In a given batch we may expect that

— the status of some master records will remain unchanged
— some may be affected by a single transaction and change status
— the status of others may change more than once in response to multiple transactions.

For batching to be efficient this last case should be relatively common. When two transactions are for the same master record their cumulative effect must be the same as for each taken separately.

The type of the records in a transactions batch may be defined as follows:

```
type transtype = (addition, deletion, credit, debit) ;
    transaction = record
                        key : accountnumber ;
                        kind : transtype ;
                        amount : money ;
                        details : miscellaneous
                  end ;
```

A file update program must preserve the logical order of the transactions. An account number might have the following history :

1. the account number is allocated to an account (an addition transaction);
2. the account is credited a certain amount;
3. the account is debited a certain amount;
4. the account number is deallocated (deletion);

5.   the account number is reallocated to a new account (an addition transaction);
6.   the account is credited a certain amount.

A batch update should achieve the same end result as a series of real-time updates. Thus a batch update program should handle such a sequence correctly, whether the transactions occur in the same batch or different batches. Hence any checks on transaction sequence need depend only on the status of the master file records. For example, if an account number is currently unallocated, it would be wrong to process a deletion transaction (or a credit or debit). This chapter describes the design of update programs which deal with batches containing any sequence of transactions.

Since the idea behind batching is to access each master record at most once during each execution of a file update program, the transactions must be sorted into master file primary key (i.e., account number in our case) order. For each key value, if there are multiple transactions, they must also be sorted appropriately. It should be clear from the above discussion of event sequences that the transaction type is not a suitable basis for sorting. The only suitable sequence is the order in which events actually occur. This can be done by assigning each transaction a unique serial number which represents the order in which the event took place, or more simply, to assume that the order in which transactions are presented for input is the order of events.

4.2   PROGRAM STRUCTURE

The basic framework of a master file update program follows the sequence of the sorted transactions. A loop processes a series of keys one at a time with each iteration carrying out the following actions:

1.   getting the initial status of the key;
2.   applying the group of transactions for that key in chronological order;
3.   recording the final status of the key.

In our savings system, if an account number is currently allocated, the status of the corresponding account record includes the current balance of the account and various other details. If the account number is not allocated, then the status of the account is simply 'unallocated'. This leads us to the accepted convention whereby no data is recorded in the master file for unallocated account numbers. Thus, if the update program is asked to find the status of an account number for which there is no account record in the file, it simply concludes that the account number is not currently allocated. Likewise, if the program is asked to record an account number as unallocated, it simply deletes, or omits to write, the associated master file record.

Thus addition and deletion transactions are not in any way special cases but merely change the account number status, just like any other kind of transaction. Although it is necessary to check the allocation status of an account number before applying a transaction of any kind, this is just one of several validation checks which are normally performed to ensure that a transaction can be correctly applied. Figure 4.1 gives the structure of the update algorithm.

```
begin {update algorithm}
    sort the transactions by time within primary key value ;
    open master and transaction files ;
    choose next key to process ;
    while keys remain to be processed on either file do
    begin
        get initial status of key ;
        while transactions remain for this key do
        begin
            process next transaction ;
            update status of the key
        end ;
        if status = unallocated
        then omit master record from file
        else record final status of key ;
        choose next key to process
    end ;
    close all files
end {update}
```

Figure 4.1   Update program structure

We have yet to determine how the master file records are organized. It happens that this makes no difference to the basic structure of the program but matters only at the detailed coding level where the exact means of accessing the master file records and the meanings of the '**while** *keys remain to be processed on either file* **do**' condition differ. Indeed the method of record organization is not of particular importance, but rather the access method which is used — this in turn depends basically upon whether the master file resides on a direct-access device or a serial-access device (e.g., on magnetic disk or on magnetic tape).

During the update of a direct-access file only those keys which are present in the transaction file need to be processed. However, in the update of a serial-access file, any master file records for which there are no transactions in the batch must be copied to a new version of the master file. Hence, for a serial-access master file, the update program must process each key which is in either or both of the transaction and master files. These differences between direct-access and serial-access file updating are hidden in a procedure *choosenextkeyto-process* which appears in all the update programs developed in this chapter.

The crucial part of the file update program, i.e., '*update status of the key*' does not differ in any way between the direct-access file and serial-access file update processes. This action consists of all the transaction processing logic, including that for addition and deletion transactions.

4.3 THE DIRECT-ACCESS FILE UPDATE

We will assume that the transactions file is actually a magnetic tape file containing transactions which have passed through a data validation phase in which validated transactions were copied to the tape file.

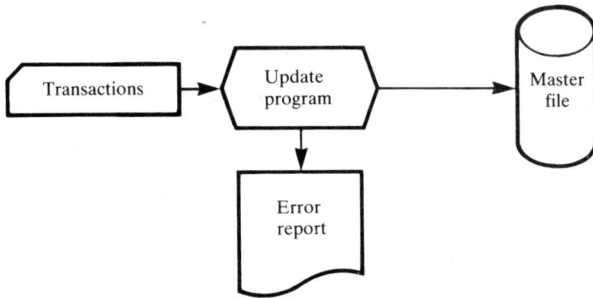

Figure 4.2 Direct-access file update

The direct-access master file may be organized as an indexed sequential or random file. We might declare such a file as an instance of a type *masterfile* (with suitable parameters defining the file's physical properties) based upon the direct-access file abstraction developed in Section 3.5.3, viz.,

class *masterfile* = *directaccessfile* **in library**
> (**where type** *itemtype* = *masterrecord* ;
> *keytype* = *accountnumber*) ;
instance *master* : *masterfile* (*environment.DA1*, *'DAmaster1983'*,
> *false*, *environment.sectorsize*) ;

This file is assumed to be loaded on disk drive 1 *(environment.DA1)*, have the file identity *'DAmaster1983'*, and use buckets equal in length to the standard sector size.

The transactions file may be similarly declared as an instance of another type based this time upon the *serialaccessfile* abstraction of Section 3.5.2, viz.,

class *transfile* = *serialaccessfile* **in library**
> (**where type** *itemtype* = *transaction*) ;
instance *trans* : *transfile* (*environment.MT1*, *'01FEB1983'*,
> *false*, *environment.blocksize*, 2) ;

Since it is a file of transaction records (each of which contains 80 characters), *trans* will have six such records in each standard 512 character block, and the file identity contained in the magnetic tape file label will contain the date on which the batch was written to the tape. This file will be double-buffered, since its records will be accessed sequentially.

The direct-access file update program is given in Figure 4.3.

```
begin {direct-access file update program}
  trans.open (environment.input) ;
  master.open (environment.inputoutput) ;
  getnexttransaction (transacnumber) ;
  choosenextkeytoprocess (currentacnumber) ;
  while currentacnumber <> sentinelacnumber do
  begin {process one key}
    getinitialstatus ;
    while currentacnumber = transacnumber do
    begin {process one transaction}
      applytransactiontomasterrecord ;
      getnexttransaction (transacnumber)
    end ;
    recordfinalstatus ;
    choosenextkeytoprocess (currentacnumber)
  end ;
  master.close (environment.locked) ;
  trans.close (environment.locked)
end {direct-access file update}
```

where

```
    const sentinelacnumber = ... ; {maximum account number + 1} ;
    var   currentacnumber, transacnumber : accountnumber ;
          newrecord : masterrecord ;
          transrecord : transaction ;
          originallyinfile, infile : boolean ;
    procedure getnexttransaction (var acnumber : accountnumber) ;
      var endoftransactions : boolean ;
      begin
        trans.read (transrecord, endoftransactions) ;
        if endoftransactions
        then acnumber := sentinelacnumber
        else acnumber := transrecord.key
      end ;
    procedure choosenextkeytoprocess (var acnumber : accountnumber) ;
      begin
        acnumber := transacnumber
      end ;
    procedure getinitialstatus ;
      begin
        master.read (currentacnumber, newrecord, originallyinfile) ;
        infile := originallyinfile
      end ;
    procedure applytransactiontomasterrecord ;
      begin
        with transrecord do
        case kind of
        addition :  if infile
                    then write (key, ' already in master file')
                    else  begin
                            infile := true ;
                            newrecord.key := key ;
                            newrecord.currentbalance := 0 ;
                            newrecord.minimumbalance := 0 ;
                            newrecord.clientdetails := details
                          end ;
        deletion :  if not infile
                    then write (key, ' not in master file')
                    else  if newrecord.currentbalance <> 0
                          then write ('balance not zero')
                          else infile := false ;
        debit    :  if not infile
                    then write (key, ' not in master file')
                    else  with newrecord do
                          if currentbalance < amount
                          then write ('not enough in account')
                          else begin
                                 currentbalance := currentbalance – amount ;
                                 if currentbalance < minimumbalance
                                 then minimumbalance := currentbalance
                               end ;
```

```
    credit    :  if not infile
                 then write (key, ' not in master file')
                 else with newrecord do
                      currentbalance := currentbalance + amount
       end
    end ; {apply transaction to master record}
procedure recordfinalstatus ;
    begin
      if infile
      then    if originally infile
              then master.replace (currentacnumber, newrecord, infile)
              else master.write (currentacnumber, newrecord, infile)
      else    if originally infile
              then master.delete (currentacnumber, infile)
    end ; {recordfinalstatus}
```

Figure 4.3   Direct-access file update logic

We assume that the records of the transaction file are already sorted in chronological order within account number order. The files are opened using the *open* operators of the respective file types, and subsequently closed (in *locked* mode) using the *close* operators. The transactions file is always read one record ahead, to simplify the program. The program of Figure 4.3 repeatedly processes one account number value at a time until a sentinel key value is found, indicating the end of the transaction file (see below for discussion of this sentinel key). The body of the {*process one key*} loop contains the details of updating the status of a particular account number. It processes one transaction iteratively until there are no more transactions for the current key. The body of this loop {*process one transaction*} first applies the transaction to the master record and then replaces it by the next transaction. *choosenextkeytoprocess* always chooses the account number of the current transaction as the next key. *getnexttransaction* reads the next record from the transaction file, by means of a call of the *read* operator of the *transfile* class, viz.,

trans.read (*transrecord*, *endoftransactions*)

which assigns the next record of the file *trans* to *transrecord* and sets *endoftransactions* to *false*, except if the end of the file is reached, when *endoftransactions* will be assigned the value *true*. At the end of the file *getnexttransaction* simulates the existence of a *sentinel record* — in this case a sentinel record has an account number value greater than any valid account number (i.e., an account number which cannot occur).

The procedure *getinitialstatus* attempts to read from the master file the record indicated by *currentacnumber*. This is performed by a call of the *masterfile* class direct-access operator

> *master.read* (*currentacnumber, newrecord, originallyinfile*)

If this operator finds such a master record, the boolean variable *originallyinfile* is set to *true* and the record read is assigned to the variable *newrecord*. If no record with account number value *currentacnumber* exists in the master file, then *originallyinfile* is set to *false*. The value of *originallyinfile* is then assigned to another boolean *infile* whose value always indicates whether the current account number being processed is currently allocated.

recordfinalstatus tests *infile*. If its value is *true* it either creates or replaces the record with key value *currentacnumber* (i.e., *newrecord.key*) on the master file with *newrecord*, otherwise it deletes the record with this key (if such a record exists in the master file). The saving of the original value of *infile* in *originallyinfile* (as assigned by *getinitialstatus*) simplifies the programming of *recordfinalstatus*. This procedure makes use of the direct-access file operators

> *master.replace* (…)
> *master.write* (…)
> *master.delete* (…)

The procedure *applytransactiontomasterrecord* is application-dependent. In Figure 4.3 we give the code for adding, deleting, crediting, and debiting the savings accounts. It uses the value of *infile* (i.e., the current status of the account number concerned) so that if, e.g., an account number is initially unallocated (i.e., *originallyinfile* is *false*) an addition transaction will set *infile* to true, thus eventually causing *recordfinalstatus* to write a new account record to the master file.

applytransactiontomasterrecord also checks that only accounts with zero balances are allowed to be closed, that no debit causes an account to become overdrawn, and checks debits to see if an account balance has reached a new low level for the current interest period. The error messages output by *applytransactiontomasterrecord* are very much simplified and, in practice, would have to contain more detail about the offending transaction and account records.

For a complete implementation of this direct-access file update applied to an indexed sequential master file, see Chapter 8. Chapter 9 gives the complete program coding for a random organization master file. The implementations of these updates in COBOL appear in Chapters 16 and 17.

4.4   THE SERIAL-ACCESS FILE UPDATE

A serial-access master file is usually updated by re-writing the complete file contents from one file to another, any unchanged records being copied — the old version of the master file is usually known as the *brought-forward* file and the new version as the *carried-forward* file (Figure 4.4). Such master files will be either magnetic tape files (as we shall use in this section) or magnetic disk files where the records are accessed purely sequentially. In either case the file records will be organized as a sequential file. Hence the terms serial-access master file and sequential organization master file are synonymous in the discussion below.

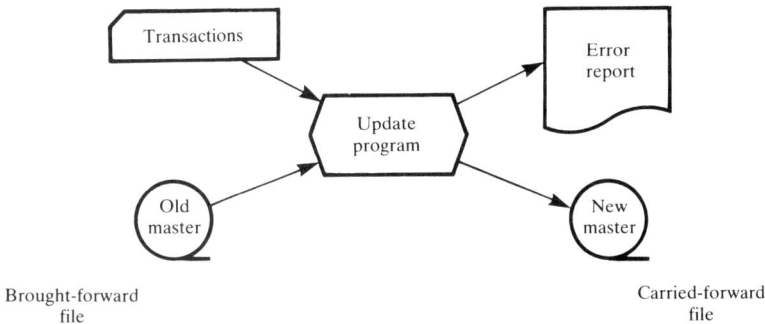

Figure 4.4   Serial-access file update

The serial-access master file records are assumed to be in ascending order of account number value and the transaction file has been sorted on the same key field. This permits the update to be performed by what is sometimes known as *unidirectional merging*.

The update program must merge the keys from the two input files correctly. It reads both the transaction and old master files one record ahead, i.e., as soon as a record has been used it is immediately overwritten by a newly read record. To avoid difficulties at the ends of the files sentinel account numbers are used. When the end of a file is reached the input procedures (*getnexttransaction* and *getnextoldmasterrecord*) return a sentinel record which in this case has an account number value higher than any valid data key, although such a record does not actually exist in the file. This allows the merge to terminate with a match on these sentinel account numbers.

This time the two master files are instances of a file type derived from the serial-access file abstraction developed in Section 3.5.2, viz.,

class *masterfile* = *serialaccessfile* **in library**
            (**where type** *itemtype* = *masterrecord*) ;
instance *oldmaster*: *masterfile*   (*environment.MT1*, *'MTmaster1'*, *false*,
                                  environment.blocksize, 2) ;
instance *newmaster* : *masterfile* (*environment.MT2*, *'MTmaster2'*, *true*,
                                  environment.blocksize, 2) ;

The transactions file is declared exactly as in the direct-access file update.

In the logic of Figure 4.5 the loop bodies {*process one key*} and {*process a transaction*}, also the procedure *getnexttransaction*, are exactly as in the direct-access file update logic of Figure 4.3. Indeed the two progams differ only in details. *choosenextkeytoprocess* now chooses the lesser of the transaction and oldmaster file keys. *getnextoldmasterrecord* uses the serial-access file type *masterfile*'s read operator to obtain the next record from the old master file or simulates a sentinel record when the end of the old master file has been reached. Full details can be given this time for *getinitialstatus* and *recordfinalstatus*.

getinitialstatus checks if there is an old master record for the current key and sets *infile* accordingly. Note the way that *getinitialstatus* stays one record ahead — if there is a master record for the current account number it copies the record into *newrecord* and performs another call of *getnextoldmasterrecord*; if there is not, then the master file is already one record ahead and no read is necessary. *recordfinalstatus* checks *infile* before writing a record to the new master file. Also note that when there are no transactions for the current account number the master file record is copied unchanged, since there will be zero iterations of the {*process one transaction*} loop body.

The procedure *applytransactiontomasterrecord* is exactly as for the direct-access file update, which is as it should be since the transaction processing logic is independent of the master file organization and access methods.

```
begin {serial-access update program}
    trans.open (environment.input) ;
    oldmaster.open (environment.input) ;
    newmaster.open (environment.output) ;
    getnexttransaction (transacnumber) ;
    getnextoldmasterrecord (masteracnumber) ;
    choosenextkeytoprocess (currentacnumber) ;
    while currentacnumber <> sentinelacnumber do
```

```
      begin  {process one key}
        getinitialstatus ;
        while currentacnumber = transacnumber do
        begin {process one transaction}
          applytransactiontomasterrecord ;
          getnexttransaction (transacnumber)
        end ;
        recordfinalstatus ;
        choosenextkeytoprocess (currentacnumber)
      end ;
      trans.close (environment.locked) ;
      oldmaster.close (environment.locked) ;
      newmaster.close (environment.locked)
    end ; {update}
```

where

```
    var transacnumber, masteracnumber, currentacnumber : accountnumber ;
      oldrecord, newrecord : masterrecord ;
      infile : boolean ;
    procedure getnexttransaction (var acnumber : accountnumber) ;
      { as in random file update }
    procedure getnextoldmasterrecord (var acnumber : accountnumber) ;
      var endofmasterfile : boolean ;
      begin
        oldmaster.read (oldrecord, endofmasterfile) ;
        if endofmasterfile
        then acnumber := sentinelacnumber
        else acnumber := oldrecord.key
      end ;
    procedure choosenextkeytoprocess (var acnumber : accountnumber) ;
      begin
        if transacnumber < masteracnumber
        then acnumber := transacnumber
        else acnumber := masteracnumber
      end ;
    procedure getinitialstatus ;
      begin
        if currentacnumber = masteracnumber
        then begin
            newrecord := oldrecord ;
            infile := true ;
            getnextoldmasterrecord (masteracnumber)
          end
        else infile := false
      end ;
    procedure applytransactiontomasterrecord ;
      { as in direct-access file update }
    procedure recordfinalstatus ;
      begin
        if infile then newmaster.write (newrecord)
      end ;
```

Figure 4.5   Serial-access file update logic

4.5   THE REAL-TIME FILE UPDATE

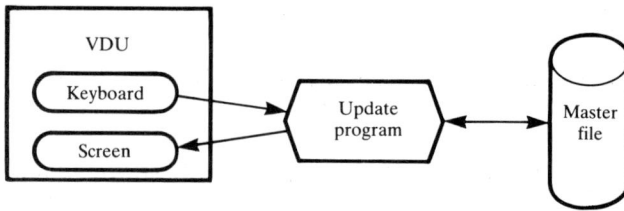

Figure 4.6   Real-time file update

Here the transactions arrive at random time intervals from (a number of) input/output devices (Figure 4.6). Hence the update program is a continually running program whose structure is based upon the direct-access file update program (since the master file will have to be a direct-access file for the updates to be performed quickly enough) but with a number of important modifications due to

1.   the fact that only one transaction is processed for each key pro-cessed (since the input is a series of individual transactions) ;

```
    begin {real time file update}
      master.open (environment.inputoutput);
      repeat {process an incoming transaction}
        waitforatransaction ;
        getinitialstatus ;
        applytransactiontomasterrecord ;
        recordfinalstatus
      until eternity ;
    99:master.close (environment.locked)
    end {update}
  where
    type messagekind = (closedown, data) ;
    var message : record
                    case kind : messagekind of
                    data : (content : transaction) ;
                    closedown : ( )
                  end
  and
    procedure waitforatransaction ;
      begin
        { await input message } ;
        if message.kind = closedown
        then goto 99
        else transrecord := message.content
      end ;
```

Figure 4.7   Real-time update logic

2.   the program having to wait for incoming transactions.

The real-time update program of Figure 4.7 is in the form of an infinite loop, each iteration of which waits for, and then processes, a single incoming transaction. The {*process one transaction*} loop of Figure 4.3 reduces to one and only one iteration. The procedure *wait-foratransaction* suspends the program awaiting some external event (i.e., a message containing a transaction or a command for the program to terminate). Otherwise the procedures *getinitialstatus*, *apply-transactiontomasterrecord*, *recordfinalstatus*, are exactly as in the direct-access file update program. The master file is assumed to have been declared as in section 4.3.

4.6   FILE SECURITY

Generally it is not a desirable practice to read and write to the same file during the updating process due to the danger of overwriting information that should be retained, or of replacing a record by one containing invalid data (although with direct-access file updates this risk has to be taken).

Hence, in the updating of serial-access master files, a new master file is always created from the contents of the old master and transactions files. Even though this practice significantly reduces the possibility of losing or corrupting correct data, there is always the danger of failure of either the hardware or software of a system with the consequent endangering of the integrity of any files open at the time of the failure. The solution to this problem is achieved by use of the 'grandfather system' (Figure 4.8).

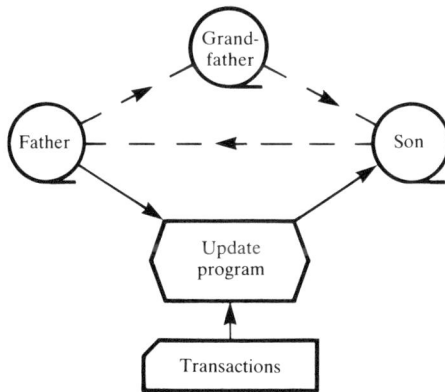

Figure 4.8   Grandfather system

For any serial-access master file there should always be three versions in existence, known as the *grandfather*, *father*, and *son* versions. During an update the transactions file is processed against the father file (i.e., old master) to produce a son version (i.e., new master); the grandfather file is the old master version used previously to produce the father file. In the next update the father file becomes the grandfather file and the son file becomes the father. The grandfather file is overwritten as the new son file. This cyclic life time of each file ensures that there is always one secure copy since the grandfather file is not attached to the machine.

If there is a hardware or software breakdown during an update and the father file is suspected of being corrupted then the grandfather file may be used to reconstruct the father file — provided, of course, that the previous transactions file has been retained and is available for the reconstruction. Therefore, after such a breakdown, the grandfather and old transactions file are used to reconstruct the father file and the current update can be rerun to create the son file.

For direct-access files (indexed sequential and direct organization files) file security is achieved by regular dumping, or by keeping a copy of all amendments on a magnetic tape file and dumping less regularly. File dumping involves regular writing of the entire contents of a file to magnetic tape for safe keeping. The regularity of this dumping depends upon the installation but the frequency is often of the order of four times a day. The retention period of the magnetic tapes containing the file dump is again installation-dependent.

Although hardware may have a very high degree of reliability it is very unwise not to take the precautions of retaining generations of a serial-access master file or regularly dumping direct-access files. The basic principle is to assume that a breakdown may occur at any time and to ensure that an effective recovery can always be made, i.e., without any loss of information.

5 PROCESSING SEQUENTIAL FILES

5.1 INTRODUCTION

Sequential file organization and access were introduced in Chapter 3 (see Sections 3.3.1 and 3.4.1). Sequential files are organized such that each record in the file, except the first, has a unique predecessor, and each record except the last has a unique successor. This ordering relationship is established by the order in which records are written to the file during its creation but may, as we shall see, be changed by the subsequent addition or deletion of records in the file.

If a sequential organization file is stored on a serial-access hardware medium (e.g., magnetic tape, punched cards, line printer), then the only method of access to the records is sequential. Indeed, for magnetic tape files the only method of both record organization and record access is sequential.

Suppose that we are given the key value of a record in a sequential file whose records are not in key field value order (Figure 5.1) and we wish to find the corresponding record. Since the records in the file are in random order with respect to the key field values each such record search must commence at the first record of the file and compare successive record keys with the required key until a match is found, or until all the record keys have been inspected (in which case it may be concluded that the record is not in the file). Hence, for a file of N records, each search involves inspection of $N/2$ record keys, on average. If R such sequential searches of the file are made, the total number of key comparisons is about $RN/2$.

Unordered file   Unordered requests
key

| 819 |
| 872 |
| 376 |
| 546 |
| 455 |
| 463 |
| 730 |
| 282 |
| 119 |
| 900 |

| 819 |
| 900 |
| 455 |

Figure 5.1   Searching an unordered sequential file

If a sequential file is held on disk with the records organized into ascending order of their key field values it is possible to search the file by a binary split search, provided that the records are all of fixed length and occupy contiguous positions in the file. In general this is not the case and we will be restricted to accessing the records sequentially — in which case the average number of comparisons is still $N/2$ per search. However, if the search requests can be batched together and also formed into a sequence ordered by value of the same key field (Figure 5.2) then each search begins from the previous file record examined and all the searches in the batch may be performed with just a single scan of the file, i.e., with at most N key comparisons altogether.

Consider a search for 50 records evenly distributed over a large file of 50 000 records; an unordered search requires an average of 1 250 000 comparisons in all, but searching for the keys in order through an ordered file requires at most 50 000 comparisons. Since the records of a magnetic tape file can only be accessed sequentially, processing of magnetic tape files, in particular, is made as efficient as possible by organizing the records on tape files in order of some significant key field and forming any search requests for the file into a batch which is then sorted according to the same key field values. This is the unidirectional matching technique previously described in Chapter 4 as the basis for sequential master file updating. Hence, for efficiency of processing, most sequential files are organized (where appropriate) with the records in key value order. To obtain a key-ordered file it may be necessary to sort the records of an existing unordered sequential file. Algorithms for performing such sorting are described in Chapter 7.

Ordered file   Ordered requests
key

119
282
376
455
463
546
730
819
872
900

455
819
900

Figure 5.2   Ordered search of an ordered sequential file

5.2   SPECIFICATION OF A SEQUENTIAL FILE ABSTRACTION

Sequential files may be processed in various modes, e.g., either as

1. *input* files, which are only read by a program;
2. *output* files, which are created for the first time by a program;
3. *input–output* files, which must reside on a direct-access medium and records of which may be read, inserted, deleted, or replaced by other records.

The operations which may be performed on a sequential file depend upon the mode in which it is being processed. This mode must be indicated when the file is opened. When the processing of a file in a particular mode has been completed it must always be closed. The operations applicable to a sequential file are

1. *reading* the next record of the sequence;
2. *writing* a new record to the sequence;
3. *deleting* a record from the sequence;
4. *replacing* a record of the sequence.

Figure 5.3 indicates which of these operations are permitted in each of the processing modes.

	PROCESSING MODE		
	input	output	input–output
read	X		X
write		X	X
delete			X
replace			X

Figure 5.3   Sequential file operations

Figure 5.4 illustrates a sequential file containing five records. Conceptually we assume that the first record is preceded by a special start-of-file marker (*SOF*) and the last record is followed by an end-of-file (*EOF*) marker.

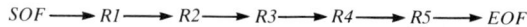

$$SOF \longrightarrow R1 \longrightarrow R2 \longrightarrow R3 \longrightarrow R4 \longrightarrow R5 \longrightarrow EOF$$

Figure 5.4   Sequential file organization

All of these operations involve manipulation of a conceptual file *window* which defines the currently accessible record in a sequential file. At any stage a program may process whichever record is currently in the window. The initial position of this window is determined by the mode in which the file is opened.

If a file is opened in input or input–output mode, the window is set so that it contains the start-of-file marker (Figure 5.5).

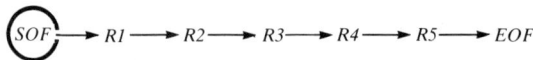

$$\bigcirc\!\!\!\!SOF \longrightarrow R1 \longrightarrow R2 \longrightarrow R3 \longrightarrow R4 \longrightarrow R5 \longrightarrow EOF$$

Figure 5.5   Opening an input or input–output file

An output file initially contains zero records (i.e., conceptually it consists of just start and end file markers) and the window initially contains the end-of-file marker (Figure 5.6).

SOF ——————→ EOF

Figure 5.6   Opening an output file

The effect of the read operation is to advance the file window to the next record of the sequence (Figure 5.7 shows the effect of the first read applied to the file of Figure 5.5), and hence the value of this record is made available. The read operation must not be applied when the end of file marker is in the window prior to its execution, and if a read operation moves the window so that it then contains the end-of-file marker, the end-of-file condition is said to be true (most programming languages provide a means of detecting this condition, e.g., the *eof* predicate in Pascal, the *AT END* clause in COBOL).

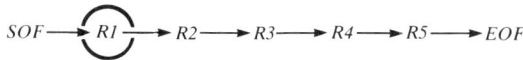

SOF ——→ R1 ——→ R2 ——→ R3 ——→ R4 ——→ R5 ——→ EOF

Figure 5.7   Read operation

For a write operation the record written to the file always becomes the predecessor of whatever record is presently in the file window, and the position of the window remains unchanged. For output files this means that new records are always appended to the file following its last record (i.e., as the predecessor of the end-of-file marker) and, for input–output files, a new record is inserted as the predecessor of whichever record is in the window — hence the write operation may not be applied when the window contains the start-of-file marker. Figure 5.8 shows the effect of writing the record value *R6* to an input–output file in the state shown in Figure 5.7.

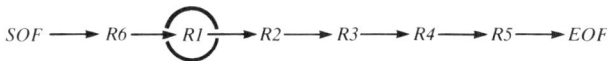

SOF ——→ R6 ——→ R1 ——→ R2 ——→ R3 ——→ R4 ——→ R5 ——→ EOF

Figure 5.8   Writing to an input–output file

A delete operation (which may only be performed on an input–output file) removes the record currently in the file window from the file. It may not be used when the start or end file marker is currently in the window — hence a delete operation must have been preceded by at least one read from the file. Figure 5.9 shows the effect of a delete operation on the file whose state is shown in Figure 5.8.

$$SOF \longrightarrow R6 \longrightarrow R2 \longrightarrow R3 \longrightarrow R4 \longrightarrow R5 \longrightarrow EOF$$

Figure 5.9   Deletion operation

The file window position becomes temporarily undefined following a deletion — it is reset by a subsequent read operation, in which case the window is positioned to contain the successor record of that record which was deleted. Figure 5.10 shows the effect of a read operation following upon the delete operation illustrated in Figure 5.9.

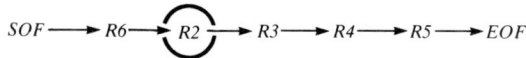

$$SOF \longrightarrow R6 \longrightarrow R2 \longrightarrow R3 \longrightarrow R4 \longrightarrow R5 \longrightarrow EOF$$

Figure 5.10   Read after deletion operation

Finally, the replace operator is used to replace the value of the record currently in the file window by a new value — it may only be used for input–output files and when neither the start nor end file marker is in the file window. Figure 5.11 shows the replacement of the current window contents of the file in Figure 5.10 by a new value $R7$. Note that the window position remains unmoved, i.e., before the next record value in the file can be replaced the file window will have to be moved forward by means of a read operation.

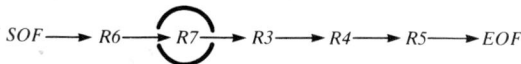

$$SOF \longrightarrow R6 \longrightarrow R7 \longrightarrow R3 \longrightarrow R4 \longrightarrow R5 \longrightarrow EOF$$

Figure 5.11   Replacing a file record

From the physical properties of sequential files as described in Chapter 3, and the above discussion of the sequential file processing modes and associated operations, we can now provide an abstract data type specification for a sequential file. This type *sequentialfile* will be characterized by the type, *itemtype*, of the file records and so a type, say *somefiletype*, defining a sequential file of records of some type T will be obtained by using the *sequentialfile* abstraction in a form such as

class *somefiletype* = *sequentialfile* **in library** (**where type** *itemtype* = T)

Any instance of such a file type must declare the physical properties of the file concerned and these physical properties, namely the device on which the file resides, its identity (given as a string of characters which will ultimately be converted into a label of the form used by the particular environment), whether or not it is a new file to be created, its block size, and the degree of buffering required for its processing, are described by the actual parameters supplied in a declaration of the file. We restrict ourselves here to the abstraction of files held on tape and disk (often referred to collectively as mass storage files). Card and printer files, which consist of sequences of characters organized into lines of text, have somewhat different and unique properties, and we shall consider such files in more detail later in this chapter. Hence the heading of the *sequentialfile* class becomes

> **class** *sequentialfile* (*device* : *environment.massstoragedevices* ;
> *identity* : **packed array** [*m..n* : *integer*] **of** *char* ;
> *newfile* : *boolean* ;
> *blocksize* : *environment.blockrange* ;
> *numberofbuffers* : *environment.bufferrange*) ;

where the file identity is now declared as a conformant array parameter, to allow file identities of any length to be passed.

The initialization of any instance of a type based upon this class will attach the device and thus the file to the program ready for processing (and have the environment perform any label-checking, etc.), and its finalization action will include releasing the device.

> **begin**
> { *attach file to program*}
> ***
> { *release file from program*}
> **end** {*sequentialfile*}

Hence a file *F* might be declared as

> *F* : *somefiletype* (*environment.MT1*, *'1983-data'*, *false*, 1024, 2)

This declares the file to be an existing magnetic tape file named *'1983-data'* which has 1024 character blocks, is held on magnetic tape unit 1, and double-buffering is to be used for its processing. Provided that sufficient buffer space is available it usually pays to double-buffer sequential files since their records will be processed strictly in sequential order.

Now we are interested in the logical processing of such a file. As we have already seen, there are different sets of operations applicable to a sequential file depending upon which processing mode — input, input–output, or output — is used. Thus we provide three starred abstract data types within the *sequentialfile* class to provide the required modes of processing and their defined operations.

```
class sequentialfile (...) ;
   class *input (...) ; ... ;
   class *output (...) ; ... ;
   class *inputoutput (...) ; ... ;
begin
   ...
end
```

To perform logical processing of a physical file *F* we must declare an instance of the required processing mode class of *F*, e.g.

inputfile : *F.input* (...)

The initialization of an instance of any of these processing mode types will open the file concerned ready for the required mode of processing, and the finalization will close the file. The required closing mode, as defined by a value of the *environment.closingmode* type, is indicated in the declaration of the processing mode instance, viz.,

inputfile : *F.input* (*environment.locked*)

For output to newly created disk files the degree to which buckets are to be initially filled with records (often we will wish to leave room for the subsequent insertion of new records) is defined by an additional parameter in the *output* processing mode class. This parameter denotes the percentage occupancy required for the file buckets when writing the file, e.g., if we wish to fill the buckets of a sequential disk file *Q* to half their capacity when creating the file, then the file processing mode instance required is of the form

outputfile : *Q.output* (..., 50)

For tape files this parameter should normally take the value *100*.

Hence the headings of the processing mode abstract data types are

```
class *input (closingmode : environment.closingmodes) ;
class *output (closingmode : environment.closingmodes ;
              bucketoccupancy : environment.percentage) ;
class *inputoutput (closingmode : environment.closingmodes) ;
```

Each of the processing mode classes provides a set of accessible operations as defined in Figure 5.3, i.e., the *input* class provides only a *read* operation, the *output* class provides a *write* operation, but the *inputoutput* class provides *read*, *write*, *delete*, and *replace* operators.

The full specification of the sequential file abstraction is therefore as given below.

```
class sequentialfile (device : environment.massstoragedevices ;
              identity : packed array [m..n : integer] of char ;
```

                        newfile : *boolean* ;
                        blocksize : *environment.blockrange* ;
                        numberofbuffers : *environment.bufferrange*) ;
   { *requires type itemtype* }
class **input* (*closingmode* : *environment.closingmodes*) ;
  procedure **read* (**var** *v* : *itemtype* ; **var** *eof* : *boolean*) ;
  begin
    { *open file and prepare to process as an input file* }
    ***
    { *close file* }
  end ; {*input*}
class **output* (*closingmode* : *environment.closingmodes* ;
                 bucketoccupancy : *environment.percentage*) ;
   { *bucketoccupancy refers to the extent to which* }
   { *buckets of a direct-access file should be*   }
   { *filled with records when initializing a file*   }
   { *** *for tape files this should be 100* ***   }
  procedure **write* (*v* : *itemtype*) ;
  begin
    { *open file and prepare to process as an output file* }
    ***
    { *close file* }
  end ; {*output*}
class **inputoutput* (*closingmode* : *environment.closingmodes*) ;
  procedure **read* (**var** *v* : *itemtype* ; **var** *eof* : *boolean*) ;
  procedure **write* (*v* : *itemtype*) ;
  procedure **replace* (*v* : *itemtype*) ;
  procedure **delete* ;
  begin
    { *check device is in environment.directaccessdevices* }
    { *open file and prepare to process as an input-output file* }
    ***
    { *close file* }
  end ; {*inputoutput*}
begin
  { *attach file to program*}
  ***
  { *release file from program*}
end {*sequentialfile*}

    Note that the *inputoutput* class ensures that the file is a direct-access file (i.e., a disk file in our environment) since input–output processing is not applicable to tape files.

The *sequentialfile* class, together with other file abstractions developed in later chapters, is now assumed to be available in the library.

As an example of the use of this abstraction in practice, consider the design of the following simple program. A stream of text is to be read in from the standard input stream (represented by the Pascal text file *input*) and stored in a sequential organization disk file. This file of text is then to be edited so that all vowels are removed, all asterisks replaced by spaces, and any question mark is to be replaced by two question marks. Finally, the edited text is to be sent to the standard output stream (i.e., the Pascal file *output*) for printing.

The outline of the program is thus

```
program texteditor (input, output) ;
   class module environment in library ;
   {declare a suitable file to hold the text}
   begin
      constructfile ;
      editfile ;
      printfile
   end.
```

This program design, in common with all of our program designs in this and subsequent chapters, will require the use of the *environment* class, and hence its inclusion at the start of the program text.

Firstly, consider the declaration of the file. It is to be a sequential file containing text and so a type *textfile* may be declared using the *sequentialfile* abstraction, viz.,

```
class textfile = sequentialfile in library
   (where type itemtype = char)
```

and an instance *F* of this file type declared as

```
instance F : textfile ( environment.DA1, 'editfile', true,
                        environment.sectorsize, 2)
```

where we have indicated that this is to be a new disk file, held on disk drive 1. We give it the name *'editfile'*, it uses the standard disk sector size (as defined by the environment) and, being sequentially processed, it uses double-buffering. This file will then be automatically attached to the program at the start of execution and released immediately before execution is completed.

The *constructfile*, *editfile*, and *printfile* procedures process this file *F* as an output, inputoutput, and input file, respectively. The *constructfile* procedure, for example, then contains a local declaration of an instance *f* of the *output* processing mode class provided by the file object *F*

$$f : F.output\ (environment.simple, 90)$$

where the parameters indicate that simple file closure is required and the file buckets are to be 90% filled when the file is constructed, to allow for later insertions. The *inputoutput* instance required by the *editfile* procedure is another local instance

$$f : F.inputoutput\ (environment.simple)$$

and the final *printfile* procedure uses an *input* instance which also causes the file to be locked upon closing

$$f : F.input\ (environment.locked)$$

Since these declarations are local to the three procedures, their lifetimes (i.e., the time between their associated opening and closing actions) are entirely disjoint — it would not be permissible to have a file being processed in two modes at the same time (and the implementation of the sequential file abstraction must guard against this possibility). The complete program design thus becomes

```
program texteditor (input, output) ;
  class module environment in library ;
  class textfile = sequentialfile in library
    (where type itemtype = char) ;
  instance F : textfile (environment.DA1, 'editfile', true,
                          environment.sectorsize, 2) ;
  procedure constructfile ;
    instance f : F.output (environment.simple, 90) ;
    var ch : char ;
    begin
      while not eof (input) do
      begin read (ch) ; f.write (ch) end
    end ;
  procedure editfile ;
    instance f : F.inputoutput (environment.simple) ;
    var ch : char ; atend : boolean ;
    begin
      with f do
      begin
        read (ch, atend) ;
        while not atend do
        begin
          if ch in ['A','E','I','O','U']
          then delete
          else if ch = '*'
               then replace (' ')
               else if ch = '?'
```

```
                        then write ('?') ;
                  read (ch, atend)
              end
            end
          end ;
       procedure printfile ;
          instance f : F.input (environment.locked) ;
            var ch : char ; atend : boolean ;
            begin
              f.read (ch, atend) ;
              while not atend do
              begin write (ch) ; f.read (ch, atend) end
            end ;
          begin
            constructfile ; editfile ; printfile
          end.
```

Further examples of the use of this sequential file abstraction will be given in the design of two programs from our Model Savings Bank system later in this chapter.

5.3   MERGING SEQUENTIAL FILES

Most sorting algorithms involve the merging of two or more sorted sequences of records to produce single, longer, sorted sequences. The procedure given below implements the merging of two disk files *F* and *G*, both containing records of the same type *datatype* which are ordered in ascending sequence of values of a field *key*, to produce a single ordered file of records *H* (Figure 5.12).

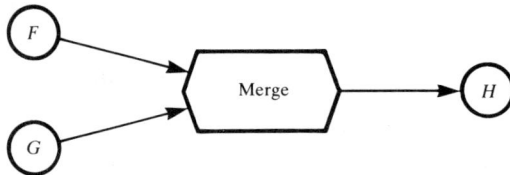

Figure 5.12   Merging of two files

Once again we start by defining the file type concerned.

```
class datafile = sequentialfile in library
                (where type itemtype = datatype)
```

and then declare the three files with their physical parameters

> **instance** *F* : *datafile* (*environment.DA1* , *'file1'* , *false* ,
>   *environment.sectorsize* , 2) ;
> **instance** *G* : *datafile* (*environment.DA2* , *'file2'* , *false* ,
>   *environment.sectorsize* , 2) ;
> **instance** *H* : *datafile* (*environment.DA3* , *'file3'* , *true* ,
>   *environment.sectorsize* , 2) ;

Here we assume that all three files are double-buffered disk files which use the standard disk bucket size (i.e., one sector). The merge procedure then declares an appropriate logical processing instance for each of the three files *F*, *G*, and *H*. Note that the output file buckets are three-quarter filled.

```
procedure merge ;
    instance f : F.input (environment.locked) ;
    instance g : G.input (environment.locked) ;
    instance h : H.output (environment.locked, 75) ;
    var Frecord, Grecord, Hrecord : datatype ;
        endofF, endofG : boolean ;
    begin {merge F and G into H}
    f.read (Frecord, endofF) ; g.read (Grecord, endofG) ;
    endofForG := endofF or endofG ;
    while not endofForG do
    begin {choose record with lower key value}
        if Frecord.key < Grecord.key
        then begin
                Hrecord := Frecord ; f.read (Frecord, endofF) ;
                endofForG := endofF
            end
        else  begin
                Hrecord := Grecord ; g.read (Grecord, endofG) ;
                endofForG := endofG
            end ;
        h.write (Hrecord)
    end ;
    {copy tail of unfinished file}
    while not endofF do
    begin
        Hrecord := Frecord ; h.write (Hrecord) ;
        f.read (Frecord, endofF)
    end ;
    while not endofG do
    begin
        Hrecord := Grecord ; h.write (Hrecord) ;
        g.read (Grecord, endofG)
    end
  end {merge}
```

This procedure may be simplified if both of the input files contain a final and suitable sentinel record. The consequent rewriting of the procedure is left as an exercise for the reader.

5.4 CASE STUDY: SEQUENTIAL MASTER FILE INITIALIZATION

Figure 1.5 gave details of the programs making up the Model Savings Bank system. The program *PROGRAM1* serves to create an initial version of the magnetic tape master file used by various other programs of the system. It reads a deck of punched cards one at a time, each card containing details of a customer's account and, for each card read, writes a corresponding record to the magnetic tape file. The format of the card file is as shown below

1	8 9	38 39	45 46	52 53	80
account number	*client identity*	*current balance*	*minimum balance*	*other details*	

Since these card records are in ascending order of account number, so also will be the records written to the tape file. This file initialization process is shown in Figure 5.13 — we will also produce a print out of the customers' account records on a line printer file.

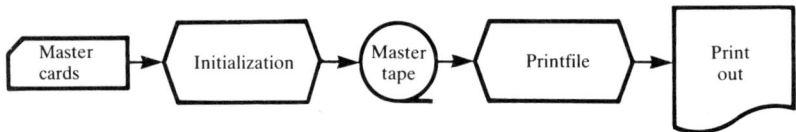

Figure 5.13 Master file initialization

If we consider the design of this initialization process in our Pascal-based notation, its outline becomes

```
begin
    read a card ;
    while not end of cards do
    begin
        transfer card contents to tape record ;
        write out tape record ;
        read a card
    end
end
```

The *read a card* process might be expressed abstractly as

begin
    read account number ;
    read client identity ;
    read current balance ;
    read minimum balance ;
    read remainder of card
end

However, this approach illustrates some of the problems which arise when we wish to process fixed-format data in a language such as Pascal which employs a so-called stream method for input and output:

1. it is not possible to specify the reading of a fixed-length string directly into a suitable variable (indeed, string manipulation in Pascal is generally difficult);
2. if the current balance and minimum balance are declared as integer fields it is not possible to read them directly as separate integer values using the standard integer input facility since they occupy immediately adjacent character positions in the input stream — even an attempt to read them as a combined integer value and then split this into two parts by division will almost certainly fail since most Pascal implementations will not handle 14-digit integer values. Thus, in general, we cannot read fixed-length numeric values unless the fields they occupy are surrounded by suitable non-numeric characters, and a special procedure must be written to read the field contents character by character;
3. there will always be a problem of reading integer input values which exceed the maximum value permitted by an implementation;
4. if a numeric field contains an illegal character (which does not happen in this case since we may assume that the master card file contents are entirely valid) then the effect of the attempted input operation becomes unpredictable, which is not tolerable in a real-world situation;
5. it is only possible to read the input stream once, i.e., we cannot back up in the input of a line from a terminal, say, to re-read a field or read the data again in a different format.

Problems also arise in the use of the Pascal output facilities, especially in the generation of tabular output. To remove our dependency on these restricted input–output facilities we shall define suitable abstractions for textual input and output files, such as those held on card, VDU and printer devices. Before describing these text file abstractions we shall introduce two new types which will allow us to work independent of the integer-handling and string-handling facilities of Pascal. We extend the facilities provided by the *environment* module to include two new types, *numeric* and *string*.

5.4.1   Specification of Numeric and String Abstractions

The type *numeric* is an abstraction of the concept of a signed number whose value may have a maximum number of significant digits in its representation (as defined by the constant *environment.maxdigits*), and is represented precisely to a certain number of decimal places. Its range of values will certainly exceed the range of integer values provided. The implementation of this type is determined by the *environment* module and hidden entirely from the user. A number of operators are provided by the *environment* module to enable manipulation of such values.

The *zeroize* operator

procedure **zeroize* (**var** *d* : *numeric* ; *length*, *fracdigits* : *numericdigits*)

where

type *numericdigits* = 1..*maxdigits* ;

is used to specify the maximum value of the numeric variable *d* and the number of significant and fractional digits required, as well as to set its value to zero, e.g.,

zeroize (*n1*, 10, 4)

specifies that *n1* takes values in the range -999999.9999 to $+999999.9999$ and its value (initially zero) is always to be represented correct to at least four decimal places.

Other operators provide arithmetic operations, viz.,

procedure **addnumeric* (**var** *d1* : *numeric* ; *d2* : *numeric*) ;
procedure **subtractnumeric* (**var** *d1* : *numeric* ; *d2* : *numeric*) ;
procedure **multiplynumeric* (**var** *d1* : *numeric* ; *d2* : *numeric*) ;
procedure **dividenumeric* (**var** d1 : *numeric* ; *d2* : *numeric*) ;

where the result is assigned to the first parameter; and a set of transfer procedures is provided to enable conversions of values between the *numeric* type and the *integer* or *real* types, and vice versa:

procedure **integertonumeric* (*i* : *integer* ; **var** *d* : *numeric*) ;
procedure **numerictointeger* (*d* : *numeric* ; **var** *i* : *integer*) ;
procedure **realtonumeric* (*r* : *real* ; **var** *d* : *numeric*) ;
procedure **numerictoreal* (*d* : *numeric* ; **var** *r* : *real*) ;

Six functions enable numeric values to be compared

> **function** **positive* (*d* : *numeric*) : *boolean* ;
> **function** **negative* (*d* : *numeric*) : *boolean* ;
> **function** **zero* (*d* : *numeric*) : *boolean* ;
> **function** **numequals* (*d1*, *d2* : *numeric*) : *boolean* ;
> **function** **numlessthan* (*d1*, *d2* : *numeric*) : *boolean* ;
> **function** **numgreaterthan* (*d1*, *d2* : *numeric*) : *boolean* ;

The second new type provided in the *environment* module is the abstraction of a string of characters, defined by the type *string* and associated operators. The maximum length of a string is defined by the constant *environment.maxstringlength*. Such strings may be constructed using two operators

> **procedure** **setall* (**var** *s* : *string* ; *l* : *stringlength* ; *ch* : *char*) ;

which specifies that the string *s* is to be of length *l* and its value is to be a string of *l* characters, all of value *ch*.

> **procedure** **construct* (**var** *s* : *string* ;
> $\qquad\qquad\qquad\qquad$ *p* : **packed array** [*m..n* : *integer*] **of** *char*) ;

is a transfer function which allows a string variable to be assigned the value of any Pascal packed array of characters (note the use of a conformant array parameter to enable the value of any such string to be passed as parameter), e.g.,

> **var** *s* : *environment.string* ;
> ...
> *environment.construct* (*s*, *'an example string'*)

assigns *s* a 17 character string.

String comparisons are provided by functions

> **function** **equals* (*s1*, *s2* : *string*) : *boolean* ;
> **function** **lessthan* (*s1*, *s2* : *string*) : *boolean* ;
> **function** **greater* (*s1*, *s2* : *string*) : *boolean* ;

Other operators enable the length of a string to be determined

> **function** **length* (*s* : *string*) : *stringposition* ;

where

> **type** *stringposition* = 0..*maxstringlength* ;

as well as access to particular data fields within a string, viz.,

> **procedure** **getchar* (*s* : *string* ;
> $\qquad\qquad\qquad\qquad$ *at* : *stringposition* ; **var** *ch* : *char*) ;

procedure *_getstring_ (_s_ : _string_ ;
 _at_, _length_ : _stringposition_ ;
 var _t_ : _string_) ;
procedure *_getinteger_ (_s_ : _string_ ;
 _at_, _length_ : _stringposition_ ;
 var _i_ : _integer_ ; **var** _ok_ : _boolean_) ;
procedure *_getnumeric_ (_s_ : _string_ ;
 _at_, _length_, _fracdigits_ : _stringposition_ ;
 var _d_ : _numeric_ ; **var** _ok_ : _boolean_) ;

These last four operators provide access to

1. a character at a certain position in a string _s_ ;
2. a string value in a certain region of a string _s_ ;
3. an integer value of a certain length at a given starting position in a string _s_ ;
4. a numeric value of a certain length at a given starting position in _s_, with a certain number of digits representing its fractional part (i.e., the string does not contain an explicit decimal point).

Given the 15 character string _s_ with the value shown below

XJOHN 47356789

the procedure calls

 getchar (_s_, 1, _ch_) ;
 getstring (_s_, 2, 6, _name_) ;
 getinteger (_s_, 8, 3, _i_, _ok_) ;
 getnumeric (_s_, 11, 5, 2, _n_, _ok_)

assign the values _'X'_, _'JOHN '_, _473_, and _567.89_ to the variables _ch_, _name_, _i_, and _n_, respectively.

The _getinteger_ and _getnumeric_ operators both contain a variable parameter _ok_ in their headings — this parameter is assigned the value _true_ if a suitable value can be obtained from the specified field of the input line. However, if the field contains non-numeric characters, then this parameter will be assigned _false_ to indicate that a value of the required type could not be obtained.

Other operators provide for assignment of new values to parts of a string variable, viz.,

procedure *_putchar_ (**var** _s_ : _string_ ;
 _ch_ : _char_ ; _at_ : _stringposition_) ;
procedure *_putstring_ (**var** _s_ : _string_ ;
 _t_ : _string_ ;
 _at_, _length_ : _stringposition_) ;

procedure *puttext* (**var** *s* : *string* ;
                p : **packed array** [*m..n* : *integer*] **of** *char* ;
                at, *length* : *stringposition*) ;
procedure *putall* (**var** *s* : *string* ;
                ch : *char* ; *at*, *length* : *stringposition*) ;
procedure *putnumeric* (**var** *s* : *string* ;
                d : *numeric* ;
                at, *length*, *fracdigits* : *stringposition*) ;
procedure *putinteger* (**var** *s* : *string* ;
                i : *integer* ; *at*, *length* : *stringposition*) ;
procedure *putreal* (**var** *s* : *string* ;
                r : *real* ;
                at, *length*, *fracdigits* : *stringposition*) ;

enable values of various types to be placed at required positions in a string s. The procedure *putnumeric* places its value at the required position in the string in the specified format with a decimal point inserted at the appropriate point, e.g.,

$$putnumeric\ (s, n, 40, 7, 2)$$

causes the string ' 567.89' to be output to positions 40–46 of the string s assuming the value of n is obtained as above, and provided that the string is at least 46 characters long — otherwise the assignment will not take place. The procedures *putnumeric*, *putinteger*, and *putreal* all perform replacement of leading zeroes by spaces in the receiving string s. The procedure *putstring* is used for assigning values of type *environment.string*, and *puttext* for assigning packed character arrays, e.g.,

$$puttext\ (s, 'hello', 20, 10)$$

places the five characters of the string *'hello'* in positions 20–24 of the string s followed by five spaces. The effect of *putstring* is similar. If the receiving field width is shorter than the string to be output, then the string is truncated at the right, e.g.,

$$puttext\ (s, 'hello', 20, j)$$

if j has the value 2, places *'he'* in positions 20 and 21 of s. If the receiving field is longer, then the string being assigned to it is padded out to the required length with spaces.

A particular field of a string may be set to a sequence of values of a certain character by a call of *putall*.

The full form of the *environment* module now becomes as shown below. We have omitted some of the facilities defined in Chapter 3 for handling serial-access devices since the serial-access abstraction has now been superseded by the various file abstractions of this chapter.

```
class module environment ;
    { environment parameters and description }
    const *blocksize = 512 ;
          *sectorsize = 512 ;
          *maxbuffers = 2 ;
          *filenamelength = 20 ;
          *printerwidth = 120 ;
          *cardwidth = 80 ;
    type *devices = ( *CR1, *CR2,
                      *DA1, *DA2, *DA3, *DA4,
                      *MT1, *MT2, *MT3, *MT4,
                      *CP1,
                      *LP1, *LP2 ) ;
          *massstoragedevices = DA1..MT4 ;
          *directdevices = DA1..DA4 ;
          *inputdevices = CR1..MT4 ;
          *outputdevices = DA1..LP2 ;
          *blockrange = 1..maxint ;
          *bufferrange = 1..maxbuffers ;
          *fileidentity = packed array [1..filenamelength] of char ;
          *closingmodes = ( *simple, *locked, *norewind) ;
          *percentage = 1..100 ;
    var *directaccessdevices : set of devices ;
    class *fileinterface ( device : devices ; id : fileidentity ;
                           newfile : boolean ; blocksize : blockrange ;
                           numberofbuffers : bufferrange) ;
        begin ... end ;
            { numeric type facilities }
    const   *maxdigits = ... ;
    type  numericdigits = 1..maxdigits ;
    type  *numeric = ... ;
    procedure *zeroize (var d : numeric ; length, fracdigits : numericdigits)
    procedure *addnumeric (var d1 : numeric ; d2 : numeric) ;
    procedure *subtractnumeric (var d1 : numeric ; d2 : numeric) ;
    procedure *multiplynumeric (var d1 : numeric ; d2 : numeric) ;
    procedure *dividenumeric (var d1 : numeric ; d2 : numeric) ;
    procedure *integertonumeric (i : integer ; var d : numeric) ;
    procedure *numerictointeger (d : numeric ; var i : integer) ;
    procedure *realtonumeric (r : real ; var d : numeric) ;
    procedure *numerictoreal (d : numeric ; var r : real) ;
    function  *positive (d : numeric) : boolean ;
    function  *negative (d : numeric) : boolean ;
    function  *zero (d : numeric) : boolean ;
    function  *numequals (d1, d2 : numeric) : boolean ;
    function  *numlessthan (d1, d2 : numeric) : boolean ;
    function  *numgreaterthan (d1, d2 : numeric) : boolean ;
            { string handling facilities }
```

```
const *maxstringlength = ... ;
type  stringposition = 0..maxstringlength ;
type  *string = ... ;
procedure *setall (var s : string ; 1 : stringposition ; ch : char) ;
procedure *construct ( var s : string ;
                              p : packed array [m..n : integer] of char) ;
function   *equals (s1, s2 : string) : boolean ;
function   *lessthan (s1, s2 : string) : boolean ;
function   *greater (s1, s2 : string) : boolean ;
function   *length (s : string) : stringposition ;
procedure *getchar ( s : string ;
                              at : stringposition ; var ch : char) ;
procedure *getstring ( s : string ;
                              at, length : stringposition ;
                              var t : string) ;
procedure *getinteger ( s : string ;
                              at, length : stringposition ;
                              var i : integer ; var ok : boolean) ;
procedure *getnumeric ( s : string ;
                              at, length, fracdigits : stringposition ;
                              var d : numeric ; var ok : boolean) ;
procedure *putchar ( var s : string ;
                              ch : char ; at : stringposition) ;
procedure *putstring ( var s : string ;
                              t : string ;
                              at, length : stringposition) ;
procedure *puttext ( var s : string ;
                              p : packed array [m..n : integer] of char ;
                              at, length : stringposition) ;
procedure *putall ( var s : string ;
                              ch : char ; at, length : stringposition) ;
procedure *putnumeric ( var s : string ;
                              d : numeric ;
                              at, length, fracdigits : stringposition) ;
procedure *putinteger ( var s : string ;
                              i : integer ; at, length : stringposition) ;
procedure *putreal ( var s : string ;
                              r : real ;
                              at, length, fracdigits : stringposition) ;
begin
  directaccessdevices := [DA1..DA4] ;
  ***
end { environment }
```

The *string* and *numeric* abstractions now assist us in defining more powerful and flexible abstractions of sequential textual input and output files.

5.4.2   Specification of Text File Abstractions

The abstraction we define for a text file is that of a sequence of pages, each consisting of a sequence of lines of characters (considered to be strings) residing on some input device. The device concerned together with the degree of buffering are defined as parameters when declaring particular file instances. Hence we define a standard library class to represent an input text file

> **class** *inputtextfile* (*device* : *environment.inputdevices* ;
> $\qquad\qquad$ *numberofbuffers* : *environment.bufferrange*) ;
>
> $\quad$ **begin**
> $\qquad$ { *open file* } ;
> $\qquad$ *** ;
> $\qquad$ { *close file* }
> $\quad$ **end** { *inputtextfile* }

Hence

> **class** *cardfile* = *inputtextfile* **in library**

and a particular file is declared as, e.g.,

> **instance** *timecards* : *cardfile* (*environment.CR1*, 2) ;

as residing on a particular card reader and using double-buffered input. In this case each card is considered as a line of input (but the card file has a single page structure).

$\qquad$ This class *inputtextfile* provides sequential access to the pages and lines of an input text file — an operator

> **procedure** *readline (**var** *line* : *environment.string* ;
> $\qquad\qquad\qquad$ **var** *endoffile* : *boolean*)

is used to obtain the next line as the value of the string variable *line* from the input device. To obtain the next line from the input file a call of *readline* is made, where the value of the parameter *endoffile* after the call indicates whether or not a next line was obtainable from the file.

> **procedure** *skiplines (*i* : *integer* ; **var** *endoffile* : *boolean*)

causes the next *i* lines of the input file to be read but without assignment to any string variables. If skipping over these *i* lines is not possible because insufficient lines remain in the file, then *endoffile* will be assigned *true*.

> **procedure** *readpage (**var** *endoffile* : *boolean*)

causes the lines of the input file to be read until the last line of the current page has been read — *endoffile* is set to *true* however if this is the last page of the file, otherwise *endoffile* is assigned *false* and the next line that will be available from the input file will be the first of the next page.

function **endofpage : boolean*

returns the value *true* if and only if the last line read from the input file was the last line of a page.

The full specification of the input text file abstract data type is given below.

```
class inputtextfile ( device : environment.inputdevices ;
                     numberofbuffers : environment.bufferrange) ;
  procedure *readline ( var line : environment.string ;
                       var endoffile : boolean) ;
  procedure *skiplines (i : integer ; var endoffile : boolean) ;
  procedure *readpage (var endoffile : boolean) ;
  function *endofpage : boolean ;
  begin
    { open file } ;
    { initially endofpage is false }
    *** ;
    { close file }
  end { inputtextfile }
```

The output text file abstraction again requires each instance to provide the appropriate device and parameter characteristics, viz.,

```
class outputtextfile ( device : environment.outputdevices ;
                      numberofbuffers : environment.bufferrange) ;
  begin
    { open file }
    *** ;
    { close file }
  end { outputtextfile } ;
```

and hence we might define a printer file type

```
class printerfile = outputtextfile in library
```

and

```
instance report : printerfile (environment.LP2, 2) ;
```

is an actual instance of this printer class. Initialization of any instance of this class causes a new page to be taken automatically on the printer file concerned.

To deliver a string to the output file as its next line the starred procedure *writeline* is called. The procedure *newpage* is used to cause a new page to be taken in the output of the file, while a number of blank lines may be generated by a call of the procedure *newlines*.

The complete output text file abstraction is thus:

```
class outputtextfile ( device : environment.outputdevices ;
                       numberofbuffers : environment.bufferrange) ;
    procedure *writeline (var line : environment.string) ;
    procedure *newpage ;
    procedure *newlines (i : integer) ;
    begin
        { open file }
        newpage ;
        *** ;
        { close file }
    end { outputtextfile } ;
```

5.4.3   Program Implementation

With these abstractions of string and numeric types, and also those for input and output sequential files of lines of characters, we may proceed to design the sequential master file initialization program. We will assume that the magnetic tape master file will be held on magnetic tape unit 1, the card input file on card reader unit 1, and the output listing of the master records will be printed on line printer unit 1.

The master file records may now be defined using the environment types *numeric* and *string* as

```
type accountnumber = environment.string ;
     money = environment.numeric ;
     masterrecord = record
                         key : accountnumber ;
                         clientidentity : environment.string ;
                         currentbalance, minimumbalance : money
                    end ;
```

and the master file itself is then declared by the series of definitions

```
class masterfile = sequentialfile in library
                   (where type itemtype = masterrecord) ;
instance MT : masterfile ( environment.MT1, 'master-file', true,
                           environment.blocksize, 2) ;
```

The card input file is an instance of

```
class inputtextfile in library
```

and the output file is an instance of

```
class outputtextfile in library
```

The main program calls procedures *createmasterfile* and *list masterfile*. *createmasterfile* declares an output instance of the file *MT* together with a card reader text file instance, named *clientdata*

> **instance** *newmaster* : *MT.output* (*environment.simple*, 100) ;
> **instance** *clientdata*   : *inputtextfile* (*environment.CR1*, 2) ;

New card records are then obtained as the values of a string variable *inputline* by means of calls of

$$clientdata.readline\ (inputline,\ endofinput)$$

The various fields of these input lines are obtained by appropriate calls of the *getstring* and *getnumeric* operators, viz.,

> *getstring* (*inputline*, 1, 8, *key*) ;
> *getstring* (*inputline*, 9, 30, *clientidentity*) ;
> *getnumeric* (*inputline*, 39, 7, 2, *currentbalance*, *ok*) ;
> *getnumeric* (*inputline*, 46, 7, 2, *minimumbalance*, *ok*) ;

For the listing of the master file records, a printer file instance (*printfile*) and an input instance of the master file are required. Initially a new page is taken on the printer and the output line filled with as many spaces as there are printing columns on the line printer (defined by *environment.printerwidth*). For each tape record read the required fields have their values placed in a string *outputline* by calls of the operators *putstring* and *putnumeric*, and this string is sent as the next line to the printer by a call of

$$printfile.writeline\ (outputline)$$

Listing 1 gives the full coding of this program.

```
                    LISTING 1 : PROGRAM1


program PROGRAM1 {initialize sequential master file} ;

    class module environment in library ;

    type accountnumber = environment.string ;
         money = environment.numeric ;
         masterrecord = record
                           key : accountnumber ;
                           clientidentity : environment.string ;
                           currentbalance, minimumbalance : money
                        end ;

    class inputtextfile in library ;

    class outputtextfile in library ;

    class masterfile = sequentialfile in library
                          (where type itemtype = masterrecord) ;

    instance MT : masterfile (environment.MT1, 'MASTER-FILE', true,
                          environment.blocksize, 2) ;
```

```
procedure createmasterfile ;

    instance clientdata : inputtextfile (environment.CR1, 2) ;
    instance newmaster  : MT.output (environment.simple, 100) ;

    var newrecord : masterrecord ;
        endofinput, ok : boolean ;
        inputline : environment.string ;

    begin
       clientdata.readline (inputline, endofinput) ;
       while not endofinput do
          with environment, newrecord do
          begin
             getstring (inputline, 1, 8, key) ;
             getstring (inputline, 9, 30, clientidentity) ;
             getnumeric (inputline, 39, 7, 2, currentbalance, ok) ;
             getnumeric (inputline, 46, 7, 2, minimumbalance, ok) ;
             newmaster.write (newrecord) ;
             clientdata.readline (inputline, endofinput)
          end
    end [createmasterfile} ;

procedure listmasterfile ;

    instance printfile : outputtextfile (environment.LP1, 2) ;
    instance newmaster : MT.input (environment.locked) ;

    var newrecord : masterrecord ;
        endofnewmaster : boolean ;
        outputline : environment.string ;

    begin
       setall (outputline, environment.printerwidth, ' ') ;
       newmaster.read (newrecord, endofnewmaster) ;
       while not endofnewmaster do
          with environment, newrecord do
          begin
             putstring (outputline, key, 6, 8) ;
             putstring (outputline, clientidentity, 19, 30) ;
             putnumeric (outputline, currentbalance, 54, 8, 2) ;
             putnumeric (outputline, minimumbalance, 67, 8, 2) ;
             printfile.writeline (outputline) ;
             newmaster.read (newrecord, endofnewmaster)
          end
    end {listmasterfile} ;

begin
   createmasterfile ;
   listmasterfile
end.
```

Listing 3 illustrates the resultant contents of the master tape file when the card file, parts of whose contents are given in Listing 2, is used as input to a run of *PROGRAM1*. The implementation of this program in COBOL is given in Chapter 13.

LISTING 2 : MASTER CARD FILE

account number	client-identity		currentminimum balancebalance
10118632J.ADAIR			07054370000000
10124268T.ADAIR			06802580580258

```
10111103F.ADAMSON              07705430570543
10175229G.ADDISON              07680250468025
10182047B.AICKEN               08770540477054
10182446M.AIKEN                03768020056802
10183272E.ALCORN               05877050077705
10192247A.ALEXANDER            04376800006680
10214534C.ALLEN                02587700007770
10223983F.ALLEN                05437680003768
10232486J.ANDERSON             00258770025877
10253866C.ANDESON              00543760044376
10263101W.BEST                 08025870602587
10264663J.BLAKE                07054370405437
10272569L.BROWN                06802580280258
10282270T.CLYDE                07705430270543
10315225M.CRAIG                07680250168025
10326960M.MOLLOY               08770540177054
10352422S.RAMSEY               03768020026802
10354603R.LONGMORE             05877050047705
10362916F.SNOW                 04376800004680
10363122H.MOODY                02587700258760
10363130A.GRAHAM               05437680543568
10388354T.IMTIAZ               00258770013877
10422609D.LUCAS                00543760032376

                       .
                       .
                       .

60254181P.KYLE                 05877050350000
6026439XN.SHERMAN              04376800258770
60316527W.MCQUEEN              02587700200000
60326441R.CARSWELL             05437680015000
60332271L.CHURMS               00258770015000
60336544V.CONEY                00543760005000
60336927J.DUNLEA               08025870543568
60343249W.FOYE                 07054370326570
60347198C.HILL                 06802580550000
60356855G.LATIMER              07705430455000
60414359M.NIXON                07680250350000
60415223M.QUIGG                08770540258770
60422246F.GORMAN               03768020300000
60424265D.LEITCH               05877050300000
60434333H.MCVEIGH              04376800350000
60436581L.SHIVERS              02587700258770
60444053S.LIDSTER              05437680258770
60453389R.TAYLOR               00258770005000
60517743U.BAYER                00543760010000
60524545F.BREEN                08025870543568
6055438XM.CALDWELL             07054370326570
60581840R.CARLISLE             06802580550000
60584033R.COURTNEY             07705430455000
60587652B.HANNA                07680250600000
60588381B.LIVINGSTONE          08770540543568
60598409L.MAGEE                03768020326570
```

LISTING 3 : MASTER FILE CONTENTS

account number	client-identity	current balance	minimum balance
10118632	J.ADAIR	7054.37	0.00
10124268	T.ADAIR	6802.58	5802.58

```
10141103     F.ADAMSON                 7705.43      5705.43
10175229     G.ADDISON                 7680.25      4680.25
10182047     B.AICKEN                  8770.54      4770.54
10182446     M.AIKEN                   3768.02       568.02
10183272     E.ALCORN                  5877.05       777.05
10192247     A.ALEXANDER               4376.80        66.80
10214534     C.ALLEN                   2587.70        77.70
10223983     F.ALLEN                   5437.68        37.68
10232486     J.ANDERSON                 258.77       258.77
10253866     C.ANDESON                  543.76       443.76
10263101     W.BEST                    8025.87      6025.87
10264663     J.BLAKE                   7054.37      4054.37
10272569     L.BROWN                   6802.58      2802.58
10282270     T.CLYDE                   7705.43      2705.43
10315225     M.CRAIG                   7680.25      1680.25
10326960     M.MOLLOY                  8770.54      1770.54
10352422     S.RAMSEY                  3768.02       268.02
10354603     R.LONGMORE                5877.05       477.05
10362916     F.SNOW                    4376.80        46.80
10363122     H.MOODY                   2587.70      2587.60
10363130     A.GRAHAM                  5437.68      5435.68
10388354     T.IMTIAZ                   258.77       138.77
10422609     D.LUCAS                    543.76       323.76
10439153     I.NORTH                   8025.87      5004.87
10457410     E.THOMPSON                7054.37      4024.37
10464182     M.LYONS                   6802.58      6702.58
10488219     P.MOORE                   7705.43      7505.43
1049653X     W.ANDREWS                 7680.25      7380.25
10497323     N.BELL                    8770.54      8370.54
10498613     J.COYLE                   3768.02      3268.02
10516670     E.DICKSON                 5877.05      5277.05
10517588     F.ELMORE                  4376.80      4046.80
10528121     J.GILBERT                 2587.70      2067.70
                                  .
                                  .
                                  .

20594984     R.MCCOMB                  6802.58      5435.68
30011985     K.JAMES                   7705.43      2000.00
30124123     T.JOHNSON                 7680.25      2000.00
30137624     J.RAWE                    8770.54      3500.00
30146542     R.ROSE                    3768.02      2587.70
30156904     J.MCCOOK                  5877.05         0.00
30168945     B.NEESON                  4376.80         0.00
3017614X     S.STEVENSON               2587.70      2587.70
30184983     N.ATALLI                  5437.68      3368.02
30214122     W.BEATTIE                  258.77         0.00
30227623     M.BOYCE                    543.76       100.00
30236541     J.BRIGGS                  8025.87      3265.70
30246903     G.BUNN                    7054.37      5435.68
3026894X     R.CAMERSON                6802.58      2000.00
30276144     M.CONNOLLY                7705.43      4550.00
30283175     A.HAWTHORNE               7680.25      3500.00
30298830     W.MCCOURT                 8770.54      7000.00
30318610     M.OWENS                   3768.02      2000.00
30328233     S.ROBERTS                 5877.05      3000.00
30337321     A.MCCROSSAN               4376.80      3500.00
30342678     F.MAGUIRE                 2587.70      2587.70
30356199     M.SINNAMON                5437.68      3368.02
30365716     J.CASSIDY                  258.77        50.00
30373344     G.CLAKE                    543.76         0.00
30374413     E.CRAWFORD                8025.87      3265.70
30414164     J.CURRY                   7054.37      5435.68
3042433X     P.DONAGHY                 6802.58      2000.00
30436168     C.FENTON                  7705.43      4550.00
30448611     W.FULTON                  7680.25      3368.02
30452376     J.HOLOHAN                 8770.54      7770.54
30468515     P.MCDALD                  3768.02      3500.00
30478561     W.GREEN                   5877.05      2000.00
30484936     S.ROBINSON                4376.80      2587.70
30515467     G.MALONE                  2587.70         0.00
30527473     H.MCDOWELL                5437.68      3265.70
```

30528232	L.PATIENCE	350.77	50.00
30534070	F.TURNER	543.76	100.00
30546524	W.AYTON	8025.87	3368.02
30552346	S.BEGGS	7054.37	2000.00
30566053	M.BOYD	6802.58	5435.68
30572525	D.BRITTON	7705.43	4550.00
40113124	D.BURNS	7680.25	3500.00
40128407	C.CAMPBELL	8770.54	0.00
40138372	P.CONVERY	3768.02	2000.00
40141624	L.HECTOR	5877.05	3265.70
40158225	E.MCEVOY	4376.80	3000.00
40167259	T.MARSHALL	2587.70	2587.70
4017445X	H.ROONEY	5437.68	3500.00
40187187	C.MCGERTY	258.77	0.00
40216640	R.SMEETH	543.76	100.00
40224392	W.MARTIN	8025.87	2000.00
40236927	R.CATNEY	7054.37	7000.00
40246183	W.CLARKE	6802.58	3368.02
	.		
	.		
	.		
60336927	J.DUNLEA	8025.87	5435.68
60343249	W.FOYE	7054.37	3265.70
60347198	C.HILL	6802.58	5500.00
60356855	G.LATIMER	7705.43	4550.00
60414359	M.NIXON	7680.25	3500.00
60415223	M.QUIGG	8770.54	2587.70
60422246	F.GORMAN	3768.02	3000.00
60424265	D.LEITCH	5877.05	3000.00
60434333	H.MCVEIGH	4376.80	3500.00
60436581	L.SHIVERS	2587.70	2587.70
60444053	S.LIDSTER	5437.68	2587.70
60453389	R.TAYLOR	258.77	50.00
60517743	U.BAYER	543.76	100.00
60524545	F.BREEN	8025.87	5435.68
6055438X	M.CALDWELL	7054.37	3265.70
60581840	R.CARLISLE	6802.58	5500.00
60584033	R.COURTNEY	7705.43	4550.00
60587652	B.HANNA	7680.25	6000.00
60588381	B.LIVINGSTONE	8770.54	5435.68
60598409	L.MAGEE	3768.02	3265.70

5.5   CASE STUDY: SEQUENTIAL MASTER FILE UPDATE

We now present the second case study program from our Model Savings Bank system. This is the sequential file update program, *PROGRAM4* of Figure 1.5. A file SORTED-TRANS of valid transactions sorted by date within account number (the production of this file is given as a case study in Chapter 7) is used to update the sequentially organized master file MASTER-FILE (also ordered by account number) in order to produce a new master file (Figure 5.14). This is also called MASTER-FILE and will then be used as input to the next update run, with the old master file retained as a security back-up (the grandfather version).

Note again that only accounts with zero balances may be deleted, that accounts may not be overdrawn nor exceed an upper balance limit (currently $20 000), and minimum balances must also be recorded.

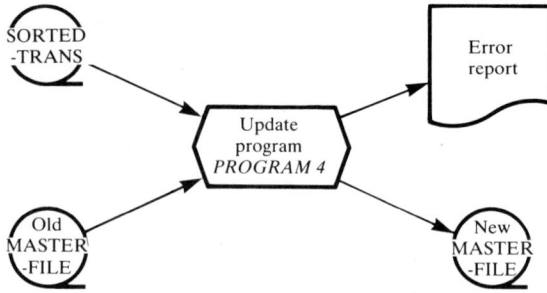

Figure 5.14   Sequential file update

The design of this sequential master file update program is based upon the algorithm developed in Section 4.4, except that we now have available a sequential file abstraction rather than the serial-access file abstraction.

We assume that the old master file is held on tape unit 1, the new master file on tape unit 2, the sorted transactions file on tape unit 3. All three are sequential files, which will use double buffering to allow processing and data transfers to overlap and all employ the standard 512 character block size used throughout the Model Savings Bank Ltd. system.

The sorted transactions file is assumed to have been processed previously by programs which validated the transactions and sorted them into the required order. The records of this file have the form

```
type transaction = record
                date : environment.string ;
                key : accountnumber ;
                kind : transtype ;
                amount : money ;
                clientidentity : environment.string ;
                other : environment.string
           end
```

where

```
accountnumber = environment.string ;
transtype = (addition, deletion, credit, debit) ;
money = environment.numeric ;
```

and the master file records have the form

```
type masterrecord = record
                key : accountnumber ;
                clientidentity : environment.string ;
```

$$currentbalance, minimumbalance : money$$
end ;

Hence, the three mass storage files may be declared as follows:

class *transfile* = *sequentialfile* **in library**
              (**where type** *itemtype* = *transaction*) ;
class *masterfile* = *sequentialfile* **in library**
              (**where type** *itemtype* = *masterrecord*) ;
instance *TF* : *transfile* (*environment.MT3*, '*SORTED-TRANS*', *false*,
              environment.blocksize, 2) ;
instance *OM* : *masterfile* (*environment.MT1*, '*MASTER-FILE*', *false*,
              environment.blocksize, 2) ;
instance *NM* : *masterfile* (*environment.MT2*, '*MASTER-FILE*', *true*,
              environment.blocksize, 2) ;

and the printer file is defined by

class *outputtextfile* **in library** ;
instance *errorreport* : *outputtextfile* (*environment.LP1*,2)

The file update procedure (see below) then follows closely the form of the program in Figure 4.5. A processing instance of each mass storage file is declared local to the *update* procedure, viz.,

instance *oldmaster* : *OM.input* (*environment.locked*) ;
instance *newmaster* : *NM.output* (*environment.simple*, 100) ;
instance *transfile* : *TF.input* (*environment.locked*) ;

The new master file is not locked on closure since the program then goes on to list its contents after the update has been completed. Use of the *sequentialfile* and *outputtextfile* abstract data types makes it unnecessary to open and close the files explicitly since the initialization and finalization are performed by the respective file processing instances. The error reporting generated by the *applytransaction-tomaster* procedure is somewhat simplistic and would normally require further details of the offending transactions to be displayed. Listing 4 gives the full implementation of this update process.

```
                    LISTING 4 : PROGRAM4


program PROGRAM4 {sequential file update} ;

    class module environment in library ;

    const maxsavings = 20000 ;

    type  accountnumber = environment.string ;
          transtype = (addition, deletion, credit, debit) ;
          money = environment.numeric ;
          transaction = record
```

```
                              date : environment.string ;
                              key : accountnumber ;
                              kind : transtype ;
                              amount : money ;
                              clientidentity : environment.string ;
                              other : environment.string
                          end ;
         masterrecord = record
                              key : accountnumber ;
                              clientidentity : environment.string ;
                              currentbalance, minimumbalance : money
                          end ;

   class transfile = sequentialfile in library
                     (where type itemtype = transaction) ;

   class masterfile = sequentialfile in library
                     (where type itemtype = masterrecord) ;

   class outputtextfile in library ;

   instance TF : transfile (environment.MT1, 'SORTED-TRANS', false,
                             environment.blocksize, 2) ;
   instance OM : masterfile (environment.MT1, 'MASTER-FILE', false,
                             environment.blocksize, 2) ;
   instance NM : masterfile (environment.MT2, 'MASTER-FILE', true,
                             environment.blocksize, 2) ;
   instance errorreport : outputtextfile (environment.LP1, 2) ;


   procedure update ;

      instance oldmaster : OM.input (environment.locked) ;
      instance newmaster : NM.output (environment.simple, 100) ;
      instance transfile : TF.input (environment.locked) ;

      var sentinelacnumber, transacnumber, masteracnumber,
          currentacnumber : accountnumber ;
          transrecord : transaction ;
          oldrecord, newrecord : masterrecord ;
          infile : boolean ;
          savingslimit : money ;

      procedure getnexttransaction (var acnumber : accountnumber) ;
         var endoftransactions : boolean ;
         begin
            transfile.read (transrecord, endoftransactions) ;
            if endoftransactions
            then acnumber := sentinelacnumber
            else acnumber := transrecord.key
         end ;

      procedure getnextoldmasterrecord (var acnumber : accountnumber) ;
         var endofmasterfile : boolean ;
         begin
            oldmaster.read (oldrecord, endofmasterfile) ;
            if endofmasterfile
            then acnumber := sentinelacnumber
            else acnumber := oldrecord.key
         end ;

      procedure choosenextkeytoprocess (var acnumber : accountnumber) ;
         begin
            if environment.lessthan (transacnumber, masteracnumber)
            then acnumber := transacnumber
            else acnumber := masteracnumber
         end ;

      procedure getinitialstatus ;
         begin
```

```
        if environment.equals (currentacnumber, masteracnumber)
        then begin
                newrecord := oldrecord ;
                infile := true ;
                getnextoldmasterrecord (masteracnumber)
             end
        else infile := false
    end ;

procedure applytransactiontomasterrecord ;
    var outputline : environment.string ;
    begin
        with environment, transrecord do
        begin
            setall (outputline, printerwidth, ' ') ;
            case kind of
            addition :
                if infile
                then begin
                        putstring (outputline, key, 10, 8) ;
                        puttext(outputline,
                                ' already in master file', 25, 25) ;
                        errorreport.writeline (outputline)
                     end
                else begin
                        infile := true ;
                        newrecord.key := key ;
                        zeroize (newrecord.currentbalance, 7, 2) ;
                        zeroize (newrecord.minimumbalance, 7, 2) ;
                        newrecord.clientidentity := clientidentity
                     end ;
            deletion :
                if not infile
                then begin
                        putstring (outputline, key, 10, 8) ;
                        puttext(outputline,
                                ' not in master file', 25, 25) ;
                        errorreport.writeline (outputline)
                     end
                else if not zero(newrecord.currentbalance)
                    then begin
                            putstring (outputline, key, 10, 8) ;
                            puttext(outputline,
                                    ' balance not zero', 25, 25) ;
                            errorreport.writeline (outputline)
                         end
                    else infile := false ;
            debit    :
                if not infile
                then begin
                        putstring (outputline, key, 10, 8) ;
                        puttext(outputline,
                                ' not in master file', 25, 25) ;
                        errorreport.writeline (outputline)
                     end
                else with newrecord do
                    begin
                        newbalance := currentbalance ;
                        subtractnumeric (newbalance, amount) ;
                        if negative (newbalance)
                        then begin
                                putstring (outputline, key, 10, 8) ;
                                puttext(outputline,
                                        ' not enough in account',
                                        25, 25) ;
                                errorreport.writeline (outputline)
                             end
                        else begin
                                currentbalance := newbalance ;
                                if numlessthan (newbalance,
                                                minimumbalance)
```

```
                                                  then minimumbalance := newbalance
                                         end
                         end ;
                 credit   :
                     if not infile
                     then begin
                              putstring (outputline, key, 10, 8) ;
                              puttext(outputline,
                                      ' not in master file', 25, 25) ;
                              errorreport.writeline (outputline)
                         end
                     else with newrecord do
                         begin
                              newbalance := currentbalance ;
                              addnumeric (newbalance, amount) ;
                              if numgreater (newbalance, savingslimit)
                              then begin
                                       putstring (outputline, key, 10, 8) ;
                                       puttext (outputline,
                                               ' savings exceed limit', 25, 25) ;
                                       errorreport.writeline (outputline)
                                   end
                              else currentbalance := newbalance
                         end
                 end
             end
        end ; {applytransactiontomasterrecord}

    procedure recordfinalstatus ;
        begin
            if infile then newmaster.write (newrecord)
        end ;

begin { update }
    with environment do
    begin
        construct (sentinelacnumber, 'XXXXXXXX') ;
        zeroize (savingslimit, 7, 2) ;
        integertonumeric (maxsavings, savingslimit) ;
        getnexttransaction (transacnumber) ;
        getnextoldmasterrecord (masteracnumber) ;
        choosenextkeytoprocess (currentacnumber) ;
        while not equals (currentacnumber, sentinelacnumber) do
        begin {process one item number}
            getinitialstatus ;
            while equals (currentacnumber, transacnumber) do
            begin {process one transaction}
                applytransactiontomasterrecord ;
                getnexttransaction (transacnumber)
            end ;
            recordfinalstatus ;
            choosenextkeytoprocess (currentacnumber)
        end
    end
end ; { update }

procedure printmasterfile (instance M : masterfile) ;
    const printerwidth = environment.printerwidth ;
    instance master : M.input (environment.simple) ;
    var nextrecord : masterrecord ;
        eof : boolean ;
        outputline : environment.string ;
    begin
        with environment, errorreport do
        begin
            newpage ;
            setall (outputline, printerwidth, ' ') ;
            puttext (outputline, 'master file contents', 30, 20) ;
            writeline (outputline) ;
            setall (outputline, printerwidth, ' ') ;
            master.read (nextrecord, eof) ;
```

```
        with nextrecord do
        while not eof do
        begin
           putstring (outputline, key, 1, 8) ;
           putstring (outputline, clientidentity, 14, 30) ;
           putnumeric (outputline, currentbalance, 48, 8, 2) ;
           putnumeric (outputline, minimumbalance, 60, 8, 2) ;
           writeline (outputline) ;
           master.read (nextrecord, eof)
        end
     end
  end ; { printmasterfile }

begin
  printmasterfile (OM) ;
  update ;
  printmasterfile (NM)
end.
```

The printing of the master file contents is performed by a call of the procedure

procedure *printmasterfile* (**instance** *M* : *masterfile*) ;

Given an instance *M* of a master file as parameter, this procedure declares a local input processing instance for the file concerned and sends its details to the output stream. The main program then calls

printmasterfile (*OM*)

before the update, and

printmasterfile (*NM*)

after the update to produce listings of the master files involved.

The implementation of this program in COBOL appears in Chapter 13.

Listing 5 shows a print-out of the contents of an actual file of sorted transactions used as input to a run of *PROGRAM4*. Listing 6 gives the new master file contents that result from the program execution using as input the old master file whose contents appeared in Listing 3. The error messages produced during the update process are shown in Listing 7.

```
          LISTING  5  :   SORTED TRANSACTIONS FILE CONTENTS


     date        account    kind   amount       client-identity

    820201      10118632     C     005000
    820201      10182047     C     010000
    820201      10182446     D     010000
    820201      10223983     D     020000
    820202      10253866     C     010000
    820201      10272569     C     010000
    820202      10326960     D     010000
    820201      10354603     D     020000
```

820202	10388354	C	010000	
820201	10422609	C	010000	
820201	10464182	D	300000	
820201	10464182	C	800000	
820202	10464182	C	300000	
820202	10464182	C	400000	
820202	10464182	C	400000	
820202	10497323	D	010000	
820202	10498613	D	100000	
820202	10543937	C	010000	
820203	10586563	C	010000	
820203	1058725X	D	010000	
820203	2011690X	D	010000	
820203	20165919	C	010000	
820201	20174462	D	010000	
820201	20260156	C	010000	
820203	20266170	D	010000	
820201	2028277X	N		W.COEY
820202	20346387	D	010000	
820202	20393342	C	010000	
820202	20436831	D	010000	
820202	20473648	C	010000	
820201	20564880	D	030000	
820201	20575629	D	010000	
820201	30111110	N		J.FRAZER
820201	30124123	D	068025	
820202	30124123	D	100000	
820201	30146542	C	010000	
820201	30214122	D	025877	
820201	30214122	X		
820202	30214122	X		
820202	30214122	D	000500	
820201	30227623	C	010000	
820201	30283175	D	010000	
820202	30342678	C	010000	
820202	30414164	C	010000	
820202	30468515	D	010000	
820203	30528232	X		
820202	30534070	C	010000	
820201	40111113	N		H.WILSON
820201	40111113	C	100000	
820202	40111113	D	010000	
820202	40113124	D	010000	
820202	40167259	C	010000	
820201	40216640	D	054376	
820202	40216640	X		
820202	40216640	X		
820203	40216640	N		T.PATTERSON
820203	40216640	C	100000	
820203	40246183	D	010000	
820203	40316432	C	010000	
820203	40345815	D	010000	
820203	40443914	C	010000	
820201	40495647	C	010000	
820201	4055872X	D	010000	
820201	50111116	N		D.FLYNN
820201	50111116	C	050000	
820202	50111116	D	050000	
820203	50111116	X		
820203	50111116	C	100000	
820201	50118730	C	010000	

```
820202   50154257   C   010000
820201   50227327   D   105437
820202   50238825   D   010000
820202   50324462   C   010000
820202   50347756   D   010000
820203   50427091   C   010000
820203   50518305   D   010000
820201   50553755   C   010000
820201   60134666   D   010000
820202   60168145   C   010000
820202   60236604   D   010000
820202   60326441   C   010000
820203   60347198   D   010000
820201   60424265   C   010000
820201   60517743   D   010000
820202   60587652   C   010000
820201   60598409   C   012345
820201   60598409   D   001234
820202   60598409   D   000123
820202   60598409   C   010000
820203   60598409   C   005000
```

LISTING 6 :   NEW MASTER FILE CONTENTS

account number	client-identity	current balance	minimum balance
10118632	J.ADAIR	7104.37	0.00
10124268	T.ADAIR	6802.58	5802.58
10141103	F.ADAMSON	7705.43	5705.43
10175229	G.ADDISON	7680.25	4680.25
10182047	B.AICKEN	8870.54	4770.54
10182446	M.AIKEN	3668.02	568.02
10183272	E.ALCORN	5877.05	777.05
10192247	A.ALEXANDER	4376.80	66.80
10214534	C.ALLEN	2587.70	77.70
10223983	F.ALLEN	5237.68	37.68
10232486	J.ANDERSON	258.77	258.77
10253866	C.ANDESON	643.76	443.76
10263101	W.BEST	8025.87	6025.87
10264663	J.BLAKE	7054.37	4054.37
10272569	L.BROWN	6902.58	2802.58
10282270	T.CLYDE	7705.43	2705.43
10315225	M.CRAIG	7680.25	1680.25
10326960	M.MOLLOY	8670.54	1770.54
10352422	S.RAMSEY	3768.02	268.02
10354603	R.LONGMORE	5677.05	477.05
10362916	F.SNOW	4376.80	46.80
10363122	H.MOODY	2587.70	2587.60
10363130	A.GRAHAM	5437.68	5435.68
10388354	T.IMTIAZ	358.77	138.77
10422609	D.LUCAS	643.76	323.76
10439153	I.NORTH	8025.87	5004.87
10457410	E.THOMPSON	7054.37	4024.37
10464182	M.LYONS	18802.58	3802.58
10488219	P.MOORE	7705.43	7505.43
1049653X	W.ANDREWS	7680.25	7380.25
10497323	N.BELL	8670.54	8370.54
10498613	J.COYLE	2768.02	2768.02
10516670	E.DICKSON	5877.05	5277.05
10517588	F.ELMORE	4376.80	4046.80
10528121	J.GILBERT	2587.70	2067.70

.
.
.

20594984	R.MCCOMB	6802.58	5435.68
30111110	J.FRAZER	0.00	0.00
30114985	K.JAMES	7705.43	2000.00
30124123	T.JOHNSON	6000.00	2000.00
30137624	J.RAWE	8770.54	3500.00
30146542	R.ROSE	3868.02	2587.70
30156904	J.MCCOOK	5877.05	0.00
30168945	B.NEESON	4376.80	0.00
3017614X	S.STEVENSON	2587.70	2587.70
30184983	N.ATALLI	5437.68	3368.02
30227623	M.BOYCE	643.76	100.00
30236541	J.BRIGGS	8025.87	3265.70
30246903	G.BUNN	7054.37	5435.68
3026894X	R.CAMERSON	6802.58	2000.00
30276144	M.CONNOLLY	7705.43	4550.00
30283175	A.HAWTHORNE	7580.25	3500.00
30298830	W.MCCOURT	8770.54	7000.00
30318610	M.OWENS	3768.02	2000.00
30328233	S.ROBERTS	5877.05	3000.00
30337321	A.MCCROSSAN	4376.80	3500.00
30342678	F.MAGUIRE	2687.70	2587.70
30356199	M.SINNAMON	5437.68	3368.02
30365716	J.CASSIDY	258.77	50.00
30373344	G.CLAKE	543.76	0.00
30374413	E.CRAWFORD	8025.87	3265.70
30414164	J.CURRY	7154.37	5435.68
3042433X	P.DONAGHY	6802.58	2000.00
30436168	C.FENTON	7705.43	4550.00
30448611	W.FULTON	7680.25	3368.02
30452376	J.HOLOHAN	8770.54	7770.54
30468515	P.MCDALD	3668.02	3500.00
30478561	W.GREEN	5877.05	2000.00
30484936	S.ROBINSON	4376.80	2587.70
30515467	G.MALONE	2587.70	0.00
30527473	H.MCDOWELL	5437.68	3265.70
30528232	L.PATIENCE	258.77	50.00
30534070	F.TURNER	643.76	100.00
30546524	W.AYTON	8025.87	3368.02
30552346	S.BEGGS	7054.37	2000.00
30566053	M.BOYD	6802.58	5435.68
30572525	D.BRITTON	7705.43	4550.00
40111113	H.WILSON	900.00	0.00
40113124	D.BURNS	7580.25	3500.00
40128407	C.CAMPBELL	8770.54	0.00
40138372	P.CONVERY	3768.02	2000.00
40141624	L.HECTOR	5877.05	3265.70
40158225	E.MCEVOY	4376.80	3000.00
40167259	T.MARSHALL	2687.70	2587.70
4017445X	H.ROONEY	5437.68	3500.00
40187187	C.MCGERTY	258.77	0.00
40216640	T.PATTERSON	1000.00	0.00
40224392	W.MARTIN	8025.87	2000.00
40236927	R.CATNEY	7054.37	7000.00

```
LISTING  7  :  FILE UPDATE ERROR REPORT


10464182          savings exceed limit
2028277X          already in master file
20564880          not enough in account
30214122          not in master file
30214122          not in master file
30528232          balance not zero
40216640          not in master file
50111116          not in master file
```

5.6 IMPLEMENTATION OF SEQUENTIAL FILES

In this section we give a high level description of a possible implementation of the sequential file abstraction. We shall restrict our description to files containing fixed length records.

5.6.1 The Environment

The *fileinterface* abstract data type defined by the environment looks after the creation of files and the physical attachment of their associated peripheral devices to a program. Since access to records of a file will involve the transfer of blocks between a device and the program, we extend *fileinterface* to define blocks of a file as

type *block* = **array** [1..*blocksize*] **of** *integer*

where *blocksize* is one of the parameters of a *fileinterface* declaration, measured in memory units, and one memory unit is defined as the amount of storage occupied by the representation of an integer value in the particular environment. A file is considered to be a sequence of such blocks numbered *1* to *N*, where *N* is the total number of blocks in the file (Figure 5.15). The file interface is also augmented with operators

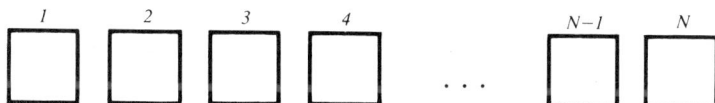

Figure 5.15   Abstract structure of a file

> **procedure** **getblock* (*blocknumber* : *integer* ; **var** *B* : *block* ;
>   **var** *exists* : *boolean*) ;

and

> **procedure** **putblock* (*blocknumber* : *integer* ; *B* : *block*) ;

which provide for the transfer of blocks between the file and the program. *getblock* obtains a particular block and assigns its value to a block variable *B*. The boolean variable parameter *exists* in *getblock* is used to indicate when the required block is actually in the file. *putblock* places a block *B* into the file at a certain block position, possibly overwriting an existing block. The full form of the *fileinterface* specification is thus

> **class** **fileinterface* (*device* : *devices* ;
>   *id* : **packed array** [*m..n* : *integer*] **of** *char* ;
>   *newfile* : *boolean* ; *blocksize* : *blockrange* ;
>   *numberofbuffers* : *bufferrange*) ;
>   **type** **block* = **array** [1..*blocksize*] **of** *integer* ;
>   **procedure** **getblock* (*blocknumber* : *integer* ; **var** *B* : *block* ;
>   **var** *exists* : *boolean*) ;
>   **procedure** **putblock* (*blocknumber* : *integer* ; *B* : *block*) ;
>   **begin**
>   **if** *newfile* **then** *create a new file called id* ;
>   **if** *file id on device exists*
>   **then begin**
>   *construct a description of the file* ;
>   *attach the device to the program* ;
>   *** ;
>   *release the device from the program*
>   **end**
>   **else** *error* {*report it or stop the program*}
>   **end** { *fileinterface* }

The implementation of these operations will usually depend on the facilities provided by the local operating system.

5.6.2   Abstraction of a File Block

We require to be able to perform operations such as reading records from a given block, deleting records, replacing records, and inserting new records. These operations may involve obtaining a new block from the file or writing a block out to the file. Thus we define an abstraction of a file block as a sequence of records (of some type *recordtype*) numbered *1* to *M*, where *M* is the number of records in the block (Figure 5.16).

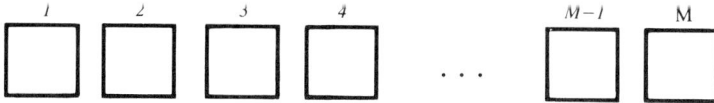

Figure 5.16   Abstract structure of a block

Associated with this abstraction we define seven operations

1. getting a numbered block from the file as the current block (in the case of a sequential file, the next non-empty block, if there is one);
2. writing the current block out to a certain block position in the file ;
3. obtaining the *j*th record of the current block, and assigning its value to a record variable *v* ;
4. replacing the *j*th record of the current block by a new record value *v* ;
5. deleting the *j*th record of the current block ;
6. inserting a new record value *v* as the *j*th record of the current block ;
7. defining the current block to be an empty block ;
8. obtaining the length (in records) of the current block.

Thus we define the following abstract data type *blockcontrol* (which is characterized by the file record type) to provide access to, and manipulation of, the currently processed file block.

```
class blockcontrol ( device : environment.devices ;
                     id : packed array [m..n : integer] of char ;
                     newfile : boolean ;
                     blocksize : environment.blockrange ;
                     numberofbuffers : environment.bufferrange) ;
{ requires type recordtype }
instance interface : environment.fileinterface ( device, id, newfile,
                                                 blocksize,
                                                 numberofbuffers) ;
var *length : integer ;
procedure *get ( var blocknumber : integer ; sequential : boolean ;
            var found : boolean) ;
procedure *put (blocknumber : integer) ;
procedure *getrecord (j : integer ; var v : recordtype) ;
procedure *replacerecord (j : integer ; v : recordtype) ;
procedure *deleterecord (j : integer) ;
procedure *putrecord (j : integer ; v : recordtype) ;
procedure *clear ;
```

begin

***

end { *blockcontrol* }

Declaration of an instance of this class will be assumed to deal with the physical file opening and closing actions, i.e., the *blockcontrol* abstraction will interface to the environment by means of the *fileinterface* class provided by the environment.

This abstraction of a block will be used not only in the implementation of sequential files, but also in the descriptions of the implementations of indexed sequential and random files in subsequent chapters.

5.6.3 Implementation Details

Now we are in a position to consider the detailed implementation of the *sequentialfile* class. It will declare an instance, named *block*, of the *blockcontrol* class to represent the file block currently being processed, with the element type defined for the file being supplied as the block record type, viz.,

class *blockcontrol* **in library** (**where type** *recordtype = elementtype*) ;
instance *block : blockcontrol* (*device, identity, newfile,*
                              blocksize, numberofbuffers) ;

Local procedures are provided to handle logical file opening and closing, as well as error diagnostics. The initialization of the *sequentialfile* class determines the blocking factor for the file using the type storage size function, *size*.

The *input* class begins by opening the file, and finally closes it. It maintains a variable *currentrecord* to denote the record to be read from the current block. Successive record values *v* are obtained by the sequential file *read* operator by means of calls of

block.getrecord (*currentrecord, v*)

and, whenever all the records of a block have been read, the next block is obtained from the file by a call of

block.get (*currentblock, true, ok*)

which attempts to obtain the block numbered *currentblock* (or, if it is empty, the first non-empty predecessor — the second parameter value indicates that the file is a sequentially processed file). The parameter *ok* is set to *false* if and only if no more non-empty blocks exist in the file, i.e., the end of the file has been reached. *currentblock* is used to record the number of the file block currently being processed.

The *output* class checks the value of the *bucketoccupancy* parameter — for tape files its value must be 100. The initial occupancy of a disk file should reflect the expected volatility of the file so as to allow for the later insertion of new records. The *write* operator fills the current block to the required extent by appending records to the end of the block, via calls of

$$block.putrecord\ (block.length + 1)$$

and sends blocks to the file by calls of

$$block.put\ (currentblock)$$

When the file is about to be closed any unfilled last block is also sent to the file.

The *inputoutput* class checks that the file is a disk file. Records are deleted by calls of *block.removerecord*. Deletions complicate the read operation in that the meaning of the value of *currentrecord* now depends on whether the last record read was also deleted (since a deletion will have resulted in the record numbers of its successor records in the block being reduced by one). The replacement of records is effected by calls of *block.replacerecord* and insertion of new records requires a check that the current block (bucket) is not full — if it is then the new record cannot be inserted. Any altered blocks must be written back to the file in their original position whenever processing is complete, hence the use of the variable *blockchanged*.

LISTING 8 : SEQUENTIAL FILE IMPLEMENTATION

```
class *sequentialfile
        (device : environment.massstoragedevices ;
         identity : packed array [m..n : integer] of char ;
         newfile : boolean ;
         blocksize : environment.blockrange ;
         numberofbuffers : environment.bufferrange) ;

   { assumes type elementtype }

   class blockcontrol in library
      (where type recordtype = elementtype) ;

   instance block : blockcontrol (device, identity, newfile,
                                  blocksize, numberofbuffers) ;

   type filestatus  = (opened, closed, locked) ;

   var status : filestatus ;
       blockingfactor : integer ;

   procedure error (message : packed array [m..n : integer] of char) ;
      begin
         writeln (identity, ' - ', message) ;
         halt
      end { error } ;
```

```
procedure openfile ;
   begin
      case status of
      opened : error ('file already in use') ;
      closed : status := opened ;
      locked : error ('file closed in lock mode')
      end
   end { openfile } ;

procedure closefile (closingmode : environment.closingmodes) ;
   begin
      case closingmode of
      environment.simple : status := closed ;
      environment.locked : status := locked ;
      environment.norewind : status := closed
      end
   end { closefile } ;


class *input (closingmode : environment.closingmodes) ;
   var atend : boolean ;
       currentblock, currentrecord : recordrange ;

   procedure *read (var v : elementtype ; var eof : boolean) ;
      var ok : boolean ;
      begin
         if atend
         then error ('attempt to read beyond end of file')
         else begin
                 if currentrecord = block.length
                 then begin
                         currentblock := currentblock + 1 ;
                         block.get (currentblock, true, ok) ;
                         if ok
                         then currentrecord := 1
                         else atend := true
                      end
                 else currentrecord := currentrecord + 1 ;
                 eof := atend ;
                 if not atend
                 then block.getrecord (currentrecord, v)
              end
      end ; {read}

   begin
      openfile ;
      currentblock := 0 ; block.clear ; currentrecord := 0 ;
      atend := false ;
      *** ;
      closefile (closingmode)
   end ; {input}


class *output (closingmode : environment.closingmodes ;
               bucketoccupancy : environment.percentage) ;
   var currentblock, loadingfactor : integer ;

   procedure *write (v : elementtype) ;
      begin
         with block do
         begin
            if length = loadingfactor
            then begin
                    put (currentblock) ;
                    currentblock := currentblock + 1 ;
                    clear
                 end ;
            putrecord (length + 1, v)
         end
      end ; {write}
```

```
    begin
       if not (device in environment.directaccessdevices)
          and (bucketoccupancy <> 100)
       then error ('incorrect occupancy for tape device')
       else begin
                openfile ;
                loadingfactor :=
                   round (blockingfactor*bucketoccupancy/100) ;
                currentblock := 1 ; block.clear ;
                *** ;
                if block.length > 0 then block.put (currentblock) ;
                closefile (closingmode)
             end
    end ; {output}


class *inputoutput (closingmode : environment.closingmodes) ;
    var atend, blockchanged, lastwasdeleted : boolean ;
        currentblock, currentrecord : integer ;

    procedure *read (var v : elementtype ; var eof : boolean) ;
       var ok : boolean ;
       begin
          if atend
          then error ('attempt to read beyond end of file')
          else with block do
                 begin
                    if (currentrecord = length
                        and not lastwasdeleted) or
                       (currentrecord > length)
                    then begin
                            if blockchanged then put (currentblock) ;
                            currentblock := currentblock + 1 ;
                            get (currentblock, true, ok) ;
                            blockchanged := false ;
                            if ok
                            then currentrecord := 1
                            else atend := true
                         end
                    else if not lastwasdeleted
                         then currentrecord := currentrecord + 1 ;
                    eof := atend ;
                    if not atend
                    then begin
                            getrecord (currentrecord, v) ;
                            lastwasdeleted := false
                         end
                 end
       end ; {read}

    procedure *delete ;
       begin
          if lastwasdeleted or atend
          then error ('no value to delete')
          else begin
                  lastwasdeleted := true ; blockchanged := true ;
                  block.deleterecord (currentrecord)
               end
       end ; {delete}

    procedure *replace (v : elementtype) ;
       begin
          if lastwasdeleted or atend
          then error ('no value to replace')
          else begin
                  block.replacerecord (currentrecord, v) ;
                  blockchanged := true
               end
       end ; {replace}
```

```
procedure *write (v : elementtype) ;
    begin
        if lastwasdeleted or atend
        then error ('no value to insert before')
        else if block.length = blockingfactor
            then error ('block overflow')
            else begin {insert in block}
                    blockchanged := true ;
                    block.putrecord (currentrecord, v) ;
                    currentrecord := currentrecord + 1
                end
    end ; {write}


begin
    if not (device in environment.directaccessdevices)
    then error ('not a disc file')
    else begin
            openfile ;
            currentblock := 0 ; currentrecord := 1 ;
            block.clear ; atend := false ;
            lastwasdeleted := true ; blockchanged := false ;
            *** ;
            if blockchanged then block.put (currentblock) ;
            closefile (closingmode)
        end
    end ; {inputoutput}
begin
    status := closed ;
    blockingfactor := (blocksize - 1) div size (elementtype) ;
    ***
end {sequentialfile}
```

Finally, we look briefly at the implementation of the block control abstraction. It defines an instance *interface* of the *environment.fileinterface* class to deal with the physical file handling. A variable

$$\textbf{var } block : interface.block ;$$

is used to hold the contents of the current block. This is assumed to be structured as shown in Figure 5.17, i.e., as a sequence of memory units, the first of which contains the record count for the block and the remainder the records of the block, organized as groups of X memory units, where X is the storage size required for one record.

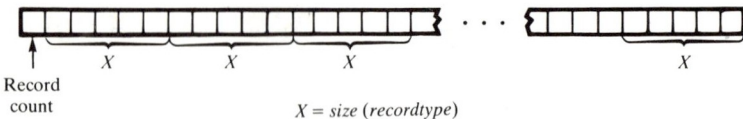

$X = size\ (recordtype)$

Figure 5.17   Physical block structure

Block transfer involves the use of the operators *interface.getblock* and *interface.putblock*. The implementation of the

EXERCISES

1. Extend the merge algorithm of Section 5.3 to merge records from three input files. Three sorted input files are to be merged to produce a fourth sorted file. Each file record consists of a six letter key followed by a further thirty characters. The records of each file are sorted into ascending key order. Use the above algorithm in a program to perform this merge.

2. Implement the serial and ordered search algorithms described in Section 5.1 using the *sequentialfile* abstraction.

3. Rewrite the merge algorithm using sentinel records.

4. Re-implement the file editor program using the input and output text file abstractions.

5. Three card readers and three line printers are available. A program is to read and compare three card files which are supposed to be identical; each file has its cards sorted into ascending order but several cards are missing from each file. The program is to list on one printer all the cards that are missing from the first file, on another printer all those that are missing from the second file, and on the remaining printer all the cards that are missing from the third file.

    Write the program using the file abstractions developed in this chapter.

6. Extend the sequential file implementation to allow closing of files with 'no rewind', i.e., so that processing of a file when it is reopened begins at the record at which the file was previously closed.

7. Implement the *numeric* and *string* abstract data types specified in this chapter.

8. Implement the input and output text file abstractions using the block control abstraction. Hint: assume that text files contain special control characters denoting the ends of lines, pages, and files — the values of these could be defined by the *environment* abstraction.

6 VALIDATION OF INPUT DATA FILES

A data processing system must obviously guard against the possibility of erroneous data entering it — the probability of such data occurring is very high and the effect of not discovering errors is normally very expensive and detrimental to the quality and reliability of the system. In this chapter we examine how the input of data can be made as efficient and error-free as possible, and how the contents of input data files can be checked to ensure their correctness.

6.1 DATA INPUT

Data enters a system from a wide variety of possible source devices which may however be classified into two groups — *off-line* input devices and *on-line* input devices.

Off-line data entry devices include punched card readers and paper tape readers as well as key-to-tape and key-to-disk systems. The data records in this case are lines of textual characters which have been generated by a keying operator who transcribes the contents of source documents (usually forms) onto the particular computer-readable medium. These forms are typically filled in by people who are possibly unaware of the subsequent use of the form and the problems involved in a computer reading it and checking the correctness of its contents.

Carefully designed source documents can reduce the chances of erroneous data entering a computer system by making it easier for a person to fill in the form correctly, and also by making it simple for the keying operator to read the document and extract the information to be keyed. The data capture process can be made more efficient and accurate if the source documents (usually forms) are designed with the following points in mind:

1. the forms should be well laid out with headings above all entry positions, instructions where appropriate, and the information should be entered in a logical sequence;
2. the forms should be easy for the keying operator to read;
3. standard formats (such as *dd/mm/yy* for dates, and the 24 hour clock for times) should be used;
4. layout should be as uniform as possible with equal length numbers as far as possible — gaps should be avoided within fields;
5. the contents of different fields should be meaningful and dissimilar from each other;
6. any coding schemes involved should use brief numbers (as well as meaningful ones, where possible — see Section 6.2);
7. standard character representations should be employed in order to avoid confusion between similar characters (e.g., I and 1, Z and 2, O and 0);
8. different forms might be printed on different colors of paper to assist in ensuring that the correct form is actually being completed.

When a batch of such forms has been gathered together they are usually passed to a keying operator for the preparation of a batch of computer-readable records. To avoid the possibility of errors arising during this off-line data preparation phase, it is normal practice to have an operator key only one type of document at a time (so that he or she has to deal with a single form layout only), and for all keyed data to be *verified*. Verification involves re-keying of the input data and the keying device will indicate (either mechanically or electronically, depending on the device) any discrepancies between the characters entered in the two keying passes. This does not guarantee full protection against keying errors since the operator may of course make the same mistake both times.

All source documents and keyed records should be sequence-numbered, to guard against the possibility of some documents or records becoming lost. *Batch* and *control totals* should also be set up for all batches of source documents — a batch total is computed by summing the values of some field in each document, and the program which reads in the batch of keyed records will form its own batch total. Any discrepancy between the two totals indicates that some error has occurred, e.g., one or more of the field values may have been miskeyed, or one or more of the records have been lost. The data must then be inspected to find the error. Control totals include the total number of documents in the batch, and other control information that might be useful could include the legal range of values of certain record fields (e.g., if the documents contain dates, then the first and last legal dates would be significant). Often the keyed file of data records is preceded by a special batch header record containing batch totals and control information. This batch header should also contain identification and date information which enables the program reading the input data into the system to ensure that it has the correct file.

The data entry devices mentioned above are all unidirectional, with data flowing from the operator to a computer-readable recording medium. The use of video terminals as input devices allows interactive communication between the operator and the computer system, which can check the data coming in and inform the operator if the data appears to be invalid in any way.

Input can either be in the form of a *dialogue* between the operator and the system — the user is prompted for input and his replies are immediately checked and acknowledged, or the *format* method is used. Basically this consists of the system displaying a form on the VDU screen and the operator filling in certain fields. The terminals used often require special function keys, e.g., cursor controls, backspace, erase, field erase, screen clear, etc. Upon completion of the form it is transmitted to the computer which vets the filled-in contents and sends suitable responses. In this case it is most important that the user be given specific and helpful error responses in the event of the input data being incorrect in some way — this is usually a difficult exercise in man–machine interfacing. Many of the comments made concerning forms design also apply to the design of man–machine dialogues.

6.2   CODING SCHEMES

One way of reducing the possibility of erroneous data entering a system is to reduce the amount of data that has to be entered onto a source document, and hence reduce the amount of data that has to be keyed by an operator. Thus objects in a computer system are usually denoted by code numbers rather than by lengthy textual descriptions, e.g., instead of entering on a form that the product ordered was a 'size 16, men's blue cotton shirt, regular fitting', a suitable shorter and equivalent coded description might be entered. The use of coding schemes produces not only a reduction in data input, but can also reduce the likelihood of erroneous data entering the computer system, make it simpler to analyse the data, serve as a basis to sort it, and also facilitate the addressing of records in a file.

Code numbers are designed to provide a brief and unique identi-fication of an object. Any coding scheme should also be designed with the possibility of future expansion in mind. To facilitate the use of the coding scheme by humans the code numbers should obviously be as brief, simple, and meaningful as possible. A *significant* code is one which reflects the characteristics of an item — these codes often con-tain redundancies and can become excessive in length — whereas a *non-significant* code value in no way describes the properties of the object of the coding.

6.2.1   Some Coding Schemes

1. *Serial codes* — objects are denoted by values in some range $M..N$, the actual values being meaningless other than as identification. These values are usually assigned in the order in which the objects come into existence. For example, the United Kingdom universities might be coded as

University	Code number
Oxford	01
Cambridge	02
Durham	03
...	
Ulster	47

If, when this coding scheme was first adopted, the code numbers had been allocated instead in alphabetic order, then of course it would not be possible to incorporate new universities in the list with-out changing many of the existing code numbers.

2. *Block codes* — objects are formed into blocks according to some classification attribute, with particular subranges being allo-cated to each category, e.g., the universities might be organized into four groups, corresponding to the four countries of the United King-dom.

Group	Range of codes
English	01 — 50
Scottish	51 — 70
Welsh	71 — 85
Irish	86 — 99

In this case the code value identifies the category — note that all the code numbers are the same length. New code numbers can be easily allocated provided that the block concerned does not already contain its maximum number of objects.

3. *Significant digit codes* — the particular digit positions have significant meanings, e.g., a clothing wholesaler might use an eight-digit coding scheme to identify his stock. The first two digits might identify the type of clothing, the next whether it is men's, women's or unisex clothing, the next two the size, and the last three digits the material, color and style, respectively.

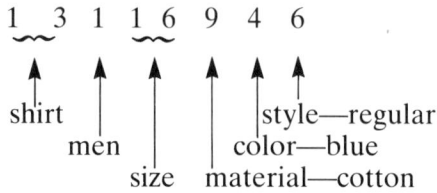

$$1 \quad 3 \quad 1 \quad 1 \; 6 \quad 9 \quad 4 \quad 6$$

shirt

men

size

style—regular

color—blue

material—cotton

4. *Mnemonic codes* — mnemonics are used in the code instead of digits — this makes the codes easier to handle from the human point of view, although this may not be the case from the computer aspect.

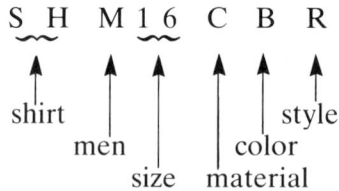

$$S \quad H \quad M \; 1 \; 6 \quad C \quad B \quad R$$

shirt

men

size

style

color

material

5. *Hierarchical codes* — the code value in this case describes not only the object but also where it fits into some overall system. The coding scheme divides objects into progressively more strictly defined groups, with each group adding a new level to the code number. For any given level the code numbers are allocated serially. For instance, taking our university example further, the faculties of a university and the departments within a faculty may be assigned codes within the particular university and faculty respectively, e.g., 24.2 might refer to the Arts Faculty of the University of Leeds and 24.2.7 might refer to the History department within that faculty. In this case the length of the code number depends upon the object's position within the hierarchy defined by the coding system.

6. *Self-checking codes* — errors in the transcription of code numbers from source documents to other documents and computer input media have been analyzed with the following results:

(a) single transcription errors (i.e., incorrect copying of a character) such as recording 578268 as 578368 account for about 85% of the errors made;

(b)   transposition errors (interchanging of two characters), e.g.,
      recording 578268 as 528768, account for a further 8% approxi-
      mately;
(c)   the remaining errors are made up mainly of insertion and omis-
      sion erors.

Self-checking code numbers have an extra character appended
to them in order to enable their correctness to be checked. The most
frequently used scheme is the *Modulus 11* system in which an extra,
redundant, digit in the range 0..10 (10 is usually represented by X) is
added to the code number so that the sum of the products of the digits
and their weights is divisible by 11. Normally the rightmost digit is the
check digit; usually the weights are assigned from 1 upwards starting
from the rightmost digit, i.e., the check digit necessary to make
578268 into a seven digit Modulus 11 number according to this
scheme would be 6.

number 5   7   8   2   6   8   6   ◄—check digit
weight 7   6   5   4   3   2   1

The Modulus 11 system is made use of in the *International Standard Book Number* (ISBN) coding scheme. An ISBN has ten digits of
which the last one is a Modulus 11 check digit. The first field (usually
one digit) of an ISBN refers to the area in which the book was published (e.g., 0 for U.S.A. and U.K.). The next field refers to the publisher, and the third field to the book itself. The scheme is hierarchical
in that the length of the publisher field is determined by the size
(number of books published) of the publisher — small publishers
have longer publisher fields and shorter book number fields than
large publishers. The first digit of the publisher field indicates its
length.

area	publisher	book-number	check digit
a	0p	bbbbbb	c
a	1p	bbbbbb	c
a	2pp	bbbbb	c
		...	
a	6pp	bbbbb	c
a	7ppp	bbbb	c
a	8pppp	bbb	c
a	9ppppp	bb	c

Examples:
   0 14 002087 X   Faulkner, *The Sound and the Fury* (Penguin).
   0 201 13795 X   Sommerville, *Software Engineering* (Addison-
                   Wesley).

0 87769 076 6   Pollack, *Compiler Techniques* (Auerbach).
3 437 40109 2   Welsh and Elder, *Einfuhrung in Pascal* (Gustav Fischer).

It can be shown that the Modulus 11 check digit scheme will detect over 99% of all possible errors — including all single transcription errors and transposition errors, and almost 91% of other random errors. The scheme can be used effectively for up to 10 digit numbers (including the check digit).

Analysis of Modulus N check digit system
The weights must lie in the range $1..N-1$ since, for a weight w,
$\quad w > N$ is equivalent to a weight $w \bmod N$
$\quad w = N$ is equivalent to a weight 0, which is ineffective
Given a code number $n1n2...nk$
and weights $\qquad w1w2...wk$
let S denote sum $(ni*wi)$ for all i in $1..k$
then $S \bmod N = 0$ is the condition that we require for the number to be valid.

Consider a single transcription error, i.e., ni transcribed as x
The change in S is $(ni-x)wi$
If this is divisible by N then the error will not be detectable
Assume that the digits ni are the digits $0..M$ (say), then
$$1 <= abs\,(ni-x) <= M$$
For the error to be detectable

1. N must not divide $(ni-x)$ $=> N > M$
2. N must not divide wi $=> 0 < wi < N$
3. N must not divide $(ni-x)wi => N$ must be prime

Hence N must be a prime greater than any weight and also greater than any digit occurring in the code number, and the weights must be positive values.

Consider the transposition of ni and nj
The change in S is $(ni-nj)wi + (nj-ni)\,wj = (ni-nj)(wi-wj)$
For the error to be detectable

1. N must not divide $(ni-nj)$ => $N > M$
2. N must not divide $(wi-wj)$ =>   weights all different and in the range $1..N-1$
3. N must not divide product => N prime

Hence all single transcription and transposition errors are detectable provided that N is a prime greater than any digit appearing in the code number, also greater than any of the weights, and the weights must all be positive and different (hence the length of the code number cannot be greater than the total number of weights available — M in this case).

6.3 DATA VALIDATION PROGRAMS

Good data capture methods and well-organized physical handling of the data can assist in the reduction of input data errors. However, these will not avoid some errors getting through and so the system must itself guard against the entry of erroneous data by performing an initial validation of the data. Hence all files of input source data should be subjected to examination by a data validation program which exhaustively inspects the file records looking for possible errors.

All files of input data should be labelled (e.g., magnetic tape files should always have labels, and source files in general should have batch header records) and every program using a file should check the label and batch header records of the file to ensure that it is indeed processing the required file.

Validation programs detect the following types of errors

- data fields containing illegal characters, e.g., numeric fields containing I instead of 1 as a result of a keying error, or other non-digits;
- radix errors, e.g., minutes $\geqslant 60$;
- out of range values, e.g., hours worked per week > 70 (say);
- inconsistent data, e.g., 29 Feb 1982;
- erroneous values, by the use of batch and control totals;
- illegal code numbers (by the use of check digit schemes);
- non-existent code numbers, by searching a table or file of legal numbers;
- data records in the wrong order, by the use of sequence numbers.

Sometimes values may have the correct format and legal contents, but appear to have unusual values, e.g., a customer may normally use a very large number of units of electricity but his latest meter card record may show a low reading for the last period. In such cases the data validation program might flag such records for further inspection.

6.4   CASE STUDY: TRANSACTIONS VALIDATION PROGRAM

We shall now design and implement a data validation program (*PROGRAM2* described in Chapter 1) which examines the files of transaction records input to the Model Savings Bank system. Transactions without errors are to be written to a magnetic tape file called TRANSACTIONS (which is to be sorted later in preparation for use in *PROGRAM4*, the sequential file update program) held on tape drive 1. Details of all erroneous transactions, and a summary of the total number of transactions examined, passed, and rejected are to be printed, together with a listing (for verification purposes) of the records written to TRANSACTIONS. The input transactions file is to be held on disk drive 1, while the printer output is to be directed to line printer 1. The file of transactions will have been produced previously by a key-to-disk operation which generates a disk file which is then loaded onto disk drive 1 prior to running this validation program.

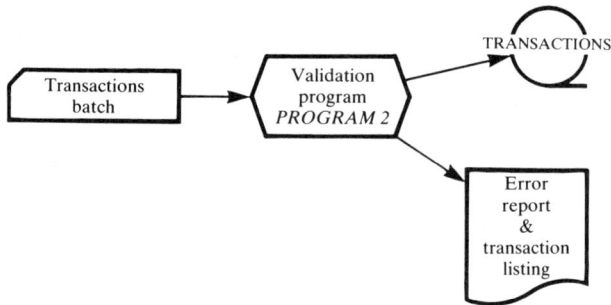

Figure 6.1   Transaction validation program

The validation checks to be performed are:

1.   that all fields contain legal characters;
2.   that the date is feasible;
3.   that the transactions are in non-descending date order;
4.   that all account numbers are valid Modulus 11 numbers;
5.   that the transaction kind is valid;
6.   that no debit exceeds the permitted maximum of $2000.

The input transactions file is simply an input text file, while the listing file is an output text file, i.e., they are instances of

class *inputtextfile* **in library**

and

class *outputtextfile* **in library**

respectively. The valid transactions file contains records of the type *transaction* already defined in the sequential file update program, i.e.,

```
type accountnumber = environment.string;
     transtype = (addition, deletion, credit, debit);
     money = environment.numeric;
     transaction = record
                    date : environment.string;
                    key : accountnumber;
                    kind : transtype;
                    amount : money;
                    clientidentity : environment.string;
                    other : environment.string
                  end;
class transfile = sequentialfile in library
                 (where type itemtype = transaction);
```

and the physical file, denoted by the identifier *VTF* (for Valid Transactions File), is declared as

```
instance VTF : transfile (environment.MT1,
                          'TRANSACTIONS', true,
                          environment.blocksize, 2)
```

The basic program structure is simply

```
begin { main program }
    validatebatch;
    listvalidtransactions
end.
```

The process of validating the transaction batch involves declaration of a double buffered *inputtextfile* instance, viz.,

```
instance disk : inputtextfile (environment.DA1, 2);
```

and an output processing instance of *VTF*

```
instance validtransactions : VTF.output (environment.simple, 100);
```

so that its action may be expressed as

```
begin
    {initialize data}
    reportheading;
```

```
disk.readline (thistransaction, endofinput);
while not endofinput do
begin
   checktransaction;
   disk.readline (thistransaction, endofinput)
end;
   reportfooting
end;
```

where *reportheading* and *reportfooting* are responsible for printing out the validation error report headings and final control totals using a file

instance *errorreport* : *outputtextfile* (*environment. LP1*, 2);

The checking of a transaction involves the use of a variable *transrecord* which is assigned the value of any successfully checked transaction prior to its output to the valid transactions file. The structure of the checking process is determined by the structure of a transaction record, viz.,

```
begin
   errorcount: = 0;
   checkdate;
   checkaccountnumber;
   checktranskind (ok);
   if ok then checkrestoftransaction;
   if errorcount > 0
   then reporterrors
   else validtransactions.write (transrecord)
end;
```

Note that the checking of the amount and client identity fields (by *checkrestoftransaction*) is dependent upon the kind of transaction having been successfully established.

The *checkdate* process must read the first six characters of a transaction and assign them as the date field of *transrecord*. This is achieved by a call of

getstring (*thistransaction*, 1, 6, *transrecord.date*)

In order to inspect the two-digit year, month, and day fields separately these subfield values are obtained by calls of

getinteger (*thistransaction*, 1, 2, *yearfield*, *ok*)
getinteger (*thistransaction*, 3, 2, *monthfield*, *ok*)
getinteger (*thistransaction*, 5, 2, *dayfield*, *ok*)

respectively. If any of these calls results in the parameter variable *ok* being assigned the value *false,* then it may be deduced that the field concerned contained non-digit characters. Having obtained these integer values the correctness of the date they represent is determined using a table *daysinmonth* which contains the number of days in each month of the year. The checking of the date sequencing of transaction records is implemented simply as a string comparison of the current and previous (valid) transaction dates.

The account number validation involves inspecting the eight account number characters in various different ways. First of all, the leading seven characters of the current input transaction must be checked to ensure that they are digits — this is achieved by using the *getnumeric* operator to obtain these seven characters as a numeric value and checking the value returned by the *ok* parameter. The check digit is read in as a character and inspected to ensure that it is a digit or X. To perform the Modulus 11 check the values of the individual digits in the account number can be obtained by calls of *getinteger* using a field length parameter value of 1.

The checking of the transaction kind also involves the transformation of the character value read to a value of the enumerated type *transtype* and its assignment to *transrecord.kind.*

Finally, the checking done by *checkrestoftransaction* depends upon the transaction kind. The client identity is checked in the case of a new account transaction to ensure that it is non-empty and, for credits and debits, the amount field is checked to ensure that it is numeric and also (for debits) not greater than the maximum debit permitted (denoted by the numeric value *maxdebit*).

The errors for each transaction are recorded by the procedure *recorderror* in a list *errorlist.* For any erroneous transaction the procedure *reporterrors* will print out the offending transaction together with its position in the overall batch and a list of the relevant error messages.

The listing of the valid transaction file is performed by the procedure *listvalidtransactions* which declares another printer file instance (again using line printer unit 1) together with an input processing instance of the file *VTF.*

```
instance listfile : outputtextfile (environment.LP1, 2);
instance validtransactions : VTF.input (environment.locked);
```

Listing 10 gives the full coding of *PROGRAM2.* Listing 11 illustrates the contents of a typical batch of unvalidated transactions, presented as input to a run of this program, and the validation report produced as output is given in Listing 12. The contents of the valid transactions tape file produced are listed in Listing 13.

LISTING 10 : PROGRAM2

```
program PROGRAM2 {data validation} ;

    class module environment in library ;

    const firstyear = 81 ;
          lastyear = 82 ;
          daysinFebruary = 28 ;
          maxwithdrawal = 2000 ;
          cardwidth = environment.cardwidth ;
          printerwidth = environment.printerwidth ;

    type accountnumber = environment.string ;
         transtype =(addition, deletion, credit, debit) ;
         money = environment.numeric ;
         transaction = record
                           date : environment.string ;
                           key : accountnumber ;
                           kind : transtype ;
                           amount : money ;
                           clientidentity : environment.string ;
                           other : environment.string
                       end ;

    class transfile = sequentialfile in library
                           (where type itemtype = transaction) ;

    instance VTF : transfile (environment.MT1, 'TRANSACTIONS', true,
                              environment.blocksize, 2) ;

    class inputtextfile in library ;

    class outputtextfile in library ;

    procedure validatebatch ;

        const errormax = 9 ;
              maxerrorspercard = 5 ;

        type errorrange = 1..errormax ;

        instance disk : inputtextfile (environment.DA1, 2) ;
        instance errorreport : outputtextfile (environment.LP1, 2) ;
        instance validtransactions : VTF.output (environment.simple, 100) ;

        var endofinput : boolean ;
            transcount, erroneoustransactions : integer ;
            transrecord : transaction ;
            thistransaction, lastdate, allspaces : environment.string ;
            maxdebit : environment.numeric ;
            daysinmonth : array [1..12] of 28..31 ;
            errorcount : 0..maxerrorspercard ;
            errorlist : array [1..maxerrorspercard] of errorrange ;
            errormessage : array [errorrange] of
                               packed array [1..35] of char ;

        procedure reportheading ;
            var outputline : environment.string ;
            begin
               with environment, errorreport do
               begin
                  newpage ;
                  setall (outputline, printerwidth, ' ') ;
                  puttext (outputline, 'VALIDATION REPORT', 31, 20) ;
                  writeline (outputline) ;
                  putall (outputline, '*', 1, 80) ;
                  writeline (outputline)
               end
            end {reportheading} ;
```

```
procedure reportfooting ;
   var outputline : environment.string ;
   begin
      with environment, errorreport do
      begin
         setall (outputline, printerwidth, ' ') ;
         putall (outputline, '*', 1, cardwidth) ;
         newlines (2) ; writeline (outputline) ; newlines (1) ;
         puttext (outputline, 'TOTAL TRANSACTIONS EXAMINED =',
                  1, cardwidth) ;
         putinteger (outputline, transcount, 30, 6) ;
         writeline (outputline) ;
         puttext (outputline,
                  'TOTAL TRANSACTIONS IN ERROR =', 1, 40) ;
         putinteger (outputline, erroneoustransactions, 30, 6) ;
         writeline (outputline) ;
         puttext (outputline,
                  'TOTAL CORRECT TRANSACTIONS  =', 1, 40) ;
         putinteger (outputline, transcount - erroneoustransactions,
                     30, 6) ;
         writeline (outputline) ;
         putall (outputline, '*', 1, cardwidth) ;
         newlines (1) ; writeline (outputline)
      end
   end {reportfooting} ;

procedure recorderror (errorindex : errorrange) ;
   begin
      if errorcount < maxerrorspercard
      then begin
              errorcount := errorcount + 1 ;
              errorlist [errorcount] := errorindex
           end
   end {recorderror} ;

procedure reporterrors ;
   var i : integer ;
       thiscard, outputline : environment.string ;
   begin
      with environment, errorreport do
      begin
         erroneoustransactions := erroneoustransactions + 1 ;
         newlines (1) ;
         setall (outputline, printerwidth, ' ') ;
         puttext (outputline,
                  'ERRORS FOUND IN TRANSACTION', 1, 29) ;
         putinteger (outputline, transcount, 30, 6) ;
         writeline (outputline) ;
         getstring (thistransaction, 1, cardwidth, thiscard) ;
         putstring (outputline, thiscard, 1, cardwidth) ;
         writeline (outputline) ;
         for i := 1 to errorcount do {output message}
         begin
            puttext (outputline, errormessage [errorlist[i]],
                     1, printerwidth) ;
            writeline (outputline)
         end
      end
   end {reporterrors} ;

procedure checktransaction ;

   var ok : boolean ;

   procedure checkdate ;
      var dateok, monthok, ok : boolean ;
          yearfield, monthfield, dayfield : integer ;

      procedure errorindate (i : errorrange) ;
         begin
            dateok := false ; recorderror (i)
         end {errorindate} ;
```

```
procedure sequencecheck ;
   begin
      if environment.lessthan (transrecord.date, lastdate)
      then recorderror (3)
      else lastdate := transrecord.date
   end {sequencecheck} ;

begin {checkdate}
   with environment do
   begin
      dateok := true ; monthok := true ;
      getstring (thistransaction, 1, 6, transrecord.date) ;
      getinteger (thistransaction, 1, 2, yearfield, ok) ;
      if not ok
      then errorindate (1)
      else if not (yearfield in [firstyear..lastyear])
           then errorindate (2) ;
      getinteger (thistransaction, 3, 2, monthfield, ok) ;
      if not ok
      then begin errorindate (1) ; monthok := false end
      else if not (monthfield in [1..12])
           then begin errorindate (2) ; monthok := false end ;
      getinteger (thistransaction, 5, 2, dayfield, ok) ;
      if not ok
      then errorindate (1)
      else if monthok
           then if dayfield > daysinmonth [monthfield]
                then errorindate (2) ;
      if dateok then sequencecheck
   end
end {checkdate} ;

procedure checkaccountnumber ;
   var checkdigit : char ;
       first7digits : environment.numeric ;
       sum, i, : integer ;
       digit : 0..9 ;
   begin
      with environment do
      begin
         getstring (thistransaction, 7, 8, transrecord.key) ;
         getnumeric (thistransaction, 7, 7, 0,
                     first7digits, ok) ;
         getchar (thistransaction, 14, checkdigit) ;
         if not (ok and (checkdigit in ['0'..'9', 'X']))
         then recorderror (4)
         else begin {modulus 11 check}
                 sum := 0 ;
                 for i := 1 to 7 do {weight digit}
                 begin
                    getinteger (thistransaction, i+6, 1,
                                digit, ok) ;
                    sum := sum + (9-i) * digit
                 end ;
                 if checkdigit = 'X'
                 then sum := sum + 10
                 else sum := sum + ord (checkdigit) - ord ('0') ;
                 if sum mod 11 <> 0 then recorderror (5)
              end
      end
   end {checkaccountnumber} ;

procedure checktranskind (var ok : boolean) ;
   var transkind : char ;
   begin
      with environment do
      begin
         getchar (thistransaction, 15, transkind) ;
         ok := true ;
         if transkind in ['C', 'D', 'N', 'X']
         then with transrecord do
         case transkind of
```

```
                    'C' : kind := credit ;
                    'D' : kind := debit ;
                    'N' : kind := addition ;
                    'X' : kind := deletion ;
                    end
              else begin ok := false ; recorderror (6) end
          end
      end {checktranskind} ;

    procedure checkrestoftransaction ;
        var ok : boolean ;
        begin
            with environment, transrecord do
            begin
                case kind of
                addition : begin
                              getstring (thistransaction, 22, 30,
                                           clientidentity) ;
                              if equal (clientidentity, allspaces)
                              then recorderror (8)
                           end ;
                deletion : ;
                credit,
                debit    : begin {check amount}
                              getnumeric (thistransaction, 16, 6, 2,
                                            amount, ok) ;
                              if not ok
                              then recorderror (7)
                              else if (kind = debit) and
                                      numgreaterthan (amount, maxdebit)
                                 then recorderror (9)
                           end
                end ;
                getstring (thistransaction, 52, 29, other)
            end
        end {checkrestoftransaction} ;

    begin
        errorcount := 0 ;
        checkdate ;
        checkaccountnumber ;
        checktranskind (ok) ;
        if ok then checkrestoftransaction ;
        if errorcount > 0
        then reporterrors
        else validtransactions.write (transrecord)
    end {checktransaction} ;

begin
    environment.construct (lastdate, '000000') ;
    environment.integertonumeric (maxwithdrawal, maxdebit) ;
    environment.setall (allspaces, 30, ' ') ;
    daysinmonth [1] := 31 ;
    daysinmonth [2] := daysinFebruary ;
    daysinmonth [3] := 31 ;
    daysinmonth [4] := 30 ;
    daysinmonth [5] := 31 ;
    daysinmonth [6] := 30 ;
    daysinmonth [7] := 31 ;
    daysinmonth [8] := 31 ;
    daysinmonth [9] := 30 ;
    daysinmonth [10] := 31 ;
    daysinmonth [11] := 30 ;
    daysinmonth [12] := 31 ;
    errormessage [1] := 'ILLEGAL CHARACTER IN DATE       ' ;
    errormessage [2] := 'INVALID DATE                    ' ;
    errormessage [3] := 'DATE OUT OF SEQUENCE            ' ;
    errormessage [4] := 'ILLEGAL CHARACTER IN A/C NUMBER ' ;
    errormessage [5] := 'INVALID ACCOUNT NUMBER          ' ;
    errormessage [6] := 'INVALID TRANSACTION KIND        ' ;
    errormessage [7] := 'AMOUNT IS NOT NUMERIC           ' ;
    errormessage [8] := 'IDENTITY FIELD IS MISSING       ' ;
```

```
            errormessage [9] := 'DEBIT AMOUNT EXCEEDS LIMIT
            transcount := 0 ;
            erroneoustransactions := 0 ;
            reportheading ;
            disk.readline (thistransaction, endofinput) ;
            while not endofinput do
            begin
                transcount := transcount + 1 ;
                checktransaction ;
                disk.readline (thistransaction, endofinput)
            end ;
            reportfooting
        end {validatebatch} ;

    procedure listvalidtransactions ;

        instance listfile : outputtextfile (environment.LP1, 2) ;
        instance validtransactions : VTF.input (environment.locked) ;

        var transrecord : transaction ;
            endoffile : boolean ;
            outputline : environment.string ;

        begin
            with environment, listfile, transrecord do
            begin
                newpage ;
                construct (outputline,
                         'LISTING OF VALID TRANSACTIONS FILE') ;
                writeline (outputline) ;
                validtransactions.read (transrecord, endoffile) ;
                while not endoffile do
                begin
                    setall (outputline, printerwidth, ' ') ;
                    putstring (outputline, date, 6, 6) ;
                    putstring (outputline, key, 15, 8) ;
                    case kind of
                        credit : begin
                                    putchar (outputline, 'C', 26) ;
                                    putnumeric (outputline, amount, 30, 6, 2)
                                 end ;
                        debit  : begin
                                    putchar (outputline, 'D', 26) ;
                                    putnumeric (outputline, amount, 30, 6, 2)
                                 end ;
                        addition : begin
                                      putchar (outputline, 'N', 26) ;
                                      putstring (outputline,
                                               clientidentity, 39, 30)
                                   end ;
                        deletion : putchar (outputline, 'X', 26)
                    end ;
                    putstring (outputline, other, 70, 30) ;
                    writeline (outputline) ;
                    validtransactions.read (transrecord, endoffile)
                end ;
                puttext (outputline, 'END OF FILE', 1, 100) ;
                writeline (outputline)
            end
        end {listvalidtransactions} ;

    begin {main program}
        validatebatch ;
        listvalidtransactions
    end.
```

LISTING 11 : THE INPUT TRANSACTIONS BATCH

```
        date   account amount        client
               number                identity
                         trans
                         kind



       82020110118632C005000
       82020160598409C012345
       82020150227327D105437
       82020130111110N        J.FRAZER
       82020140216640D 54376
       8202012028277XN         W.COEY
       82020110464182C300000
       82020110182047C 10000
       82020110223983D 20000
       82020110141103C005000
       82020160598409D001234
       82020130124123D 68025
       82020110272569C 10000
       82020110354603D 20000
       82020150111116N        D.FLYNN
       82020120575629D 10000
       82020150553755C 10000
       82020140495647C 10000
       82020150111116C050000
       82010110175229D005000
       82020130214122D 25877
       82020140111113N        H.WILSON         ·
       82020110464182C800000
       82020120564880D030000
       82020110422609C 10000
       82020130214122X
       82020120260156C 10000
       82020120174462D 10000
       82020130146542C 10000
       82020110192446C005000
       82020140111113C100000
       82020160424265C 10000
       8202014055872XD 10000
       82020130227623C 10000
       82020110182446D 10000

       82020130283175D 10000
       82020150118730C 10000
       82020160517743D 10000
       82020110I83272D005000
       82020230137624R005000
       82020260598409D000123
       82020230124123D100000
       82020230214122X
       82020210464182D300000
       82020210497323D 10000
       82020230342678C 10000
       82020220346387D 10000
       82020260587652C 10000
       82020220393342C 10000
       82020250154257C 10000
       82020230414164C 10000
       82020230214122D000500
```

```
82020220436831D 10000
82020260168145C 10000
82020210253866C 10000
82020220473648C 10000
82020230468515D 10000
82020250238825D 10000
82020230436168C005000
82020240158225N
82020260598409C 10000
82020240111113D010000
82020250111116D050000
82020240216640X
82020240216640X
82020210464182C400000
82020210543937C 10000
82020210326960D 10000
82020230534070C 10000
82020260236604D 10000
82020250324462C 10000
82020240113124D 10000
82020210464182C400000
82020210388354C 10000
82020210498613D100000
82020240167259C 10000
82020250347756D 10000
82020260326441C 10000
82020240443914D300000
82020360598409C   5000
82020350111116X
82020340216640N        T.PATTERSON
82020330528232X
82020320011690XD 10000
82020340246183D 10000
82020340216640C100000
82020310586563C 10000
82020350427091C 10000
820203502X8131C111111
82020340316432C 10000
8202031058725XD 10000
82020350111116C100000
82020360347198D 10000
82020340345815D 10000
82020350518305D 10000
82020320165919C 10000
82020340443914C 10000
82020320266170D 10000
82022910124268D005000
```

LISTING 12 : VALIDATION REPORT


```
                              VALIDATION REPORT
************************************************************************

ERRORS FOUND IN TRANSACTION      10
82020110141103C005000
ILLEGAL CHARACTER IN DATE
ILLEGAL CHARACTER IN DATE

ERRORS FOUND IN TRANSACTION      20
82010110175229D005000
DATE OUT OF SEQUENCE

ERRORS FOUND IN TRANSACTION      30
82020110192446C005000
INVALID ACCOUNT NUMBER

ERRORS FOUND IN TRANSACTION      40
82020110I83272D005000
ILLEGAL CHARACTER IN A/C NUMBER

ERRORS FOUND IN TRANSACTION      41
82020230137624R005000
INVALID TRANSACTION KIND

ERRORS FOUND IN TRANSACTION      60
82020230436168C005000
AMOUNT IS NOT NUMERIC

ERRORS FOUND IN TRANSACTION      61
82020240158225N
IDENTITY FIELD IS MISSING

ERRORS FOUND IN TRANSACTION      80
82020240443914D300000
DEBIT AMOUNT EXCEEDS LIMIT

ERRORS FOUND IN TRANSACTION      90
820203502X8131C111111
ILLEGAL CHARACTER IN A/C NUMBER

ERRORS FOUND IN TRANSACTION     100
82022910124268D005000
INVALID DATE


************************************************************************

TOTAL TRANSACTIONS EXAMINED =    100
TOTAL TRANSACTIONS IN ERROR =     10
TOTAL CORRECT TRANSACTIONS  =     90

************************************************************************
```

LISTING 13 : VALID TRANSACTIONS FILE CONTENTS

```
LISTING OF VALID TRANSACTIONS FILE
82020110118632C005000
82020160598409C012345
82020150227327D105437
82020130111110N       J.FRAZER
82020140216640D054376
8202012028277XN       W.COEY
82020110464182C300000
82020110182047C010000
82020110223983D020000
82020160598409D001234
82020130124123D068025
82020110272569C010000
82020110354603D020000
82020150111116N       D.FLYNN
82020120575629D010000
82020150553755C010000
82020140495647C010000
82020150111116C050000
82020130214122D025877
82020140111113N       H.WILSON
82020110464182C800000
82020120564880D030000
82020110422609C010000
82020130214122X
82020120260156C010000
82020120174462D010000
82020130146542C010000
82020140111113C100000
82020160424265C010000
8202014055872XD010000
82020130227623C010000
82020110182446D010000
82020160134666D010000
82020130283175D010000
82020150118730C010000
82020160517743D010000
82020260598409D000123
82020230124123D100000
82020230214122X
82020210464182D300000
82020210497323D010000
82020230342678C010000
82020220346387D010000
82020260587652C010000
82020220393342C010000
82020250154257C010000
82020230414164C010000
82020230214122D000500
82020220436831D010000
82020260168145C010000
82020210253866C010000
82020220473648C010000
82020230468515D010000
82020250238825D010000
82020260598409C010000
82020240111113D010000
```

```
82020250111116D050000
82020240216640X
82020240216640X
82020210464182C400000
82020210543937C010000
82020210326960D010000
82020230534070C010000
82020260236604D010000
82020250324462C010000
82020240113124D010000
82020210464182C400000
82020210388354C010000
82020210498613D100000
82020240167259C010000
82020250347756D010000
82020260326441C010000
82020360598409C005000
82020350111116X
82020340216640N        T.PATTERSON
82020330528232X
82020320116900XD010000
82020340246183D010000
82020340216640C100000
82020310586563C010000
82020350427091C010000
82020340316432C010000
8202031058725XD010000
82020350111116C100000
82020360347198D010000
82020340345815D010000
82020350518305D010000
82020320165919C010000
82020340443914C010000
82020320266170D010000
END OF FILE
```

The implementation of *PROGRAM2* in COBOL is described in Chapter 14.

EXERCISES

1. (a) Add an extra, final, digit to each of the following numbers to make them into valid Modulus 11 numbers:
   000000164   000027598   003062584
   (b) Which of the following are valid ISBNs?
   0220668647   0876266943   600001132X

2. Define a suitable form for a Modulus 7 check digit sytem.
   A transposition error is one in which one digit of a number is interchanged with another digit of the number, e.g., 12543 instead of 12345. Show whether the Modulus 7 check system can detect all single transposition errors.

3. A company's employees and customers and suppliers are identified by their names but many mistakes are made in the copying and punching of names.

(a) Show, in detail, how the names may be protected by check characters to ensure that all single errors of transcription will be detectable. Assume that names are shorter than 30 characters and are composed from the letters A to Z (capitals only), space, apostrophe, hyphen, and full stop.

(b) Why might a numeric coding scheme be preferred to the use of names?

(c) How can the scheme of part (a) be modified to handle names of up to 118 characters? Assume that each character is stored in six bits and that the complete character set contains a further 34 characters in addition to the 30 used in names.

4. (a) List, with brief explanations, six requirements one should consider when designing a coding scheme for identifying, say, manufactured products. To what extent does the International Standard Book Number (ISBN) coding scheme meet these requirements?

(b) A 'seesaw' error is defined to be an error in which one digit of a number is increased by some amount while another digit is decreased by the same amount. Is the Modulus 11 check digit system adequate to detect a seesaw error in an ISBN? Can it detect a pair of seesaw errors in an ISBN?

5. What manual and computational precautions should be taken to minimize the occurrence of erroneous input data and to maximize the detection of such data?

6. The transactions batch input to the data validation program developed in this chapter is to be preceded by a batch header record containing the following data:

in columns   1 – 6: the current date (in YYMMDD format)
in columns   7 – 12: the date of the first transaction appearing in the batch
in columns 13 – 17: the number of transactions in the batch
in columns 18 – 28: a batch total which has been computed as the sum of the
                     amount fields appearing in all credit and debit records

Amend the program given in Listing 10 so that the program

(a) prints out the current date in the validation report heading;

(b) checks that no transaction is dated prior to the given first transaction date;

(c) prints out the input transaction count and batch total given in the batch header;

(d) computes and prints out its own batch total for the amount fields of the transaction batch.

7 SORTING FILES

Sorting involves forming a sequence of records into a key-ordered sequence. Although many files are structured to facilitate searching, it is often the case that the records in a file need to be sorted into some significant order in order to perform efficiently certain processing of the records. For example, we have already seen that sorting is required when batches of transactions are used to update a sequential organization master file. After validation of the transactions they are written to a temporary file, following which the transaction records are sorted into the required key order.

Although sorting is such a common activity in data processing that most manufacturers provide standard sorting packages, and most commercial programming languages contain sorting facilities, an installation may have particular sorting requirements that make it necessary to build in-house sorting programs. In this chapter we shall examine some of the more popular sorting algorithms and also construct a general purpose procedure for sorting files. For fuller details of the algorithms described, and their implementation (in Pascal), the reader is referred to Wirth (1976).

We shall describe two types of sorting algorithm in this chapter: *external* sorting algorithms, which are used solely for sorting files of records, and *internal* sorting algorithms which are used to sort groups of records which are small enough for an entire group to be accommodated in main memory. We shall see that external sorting algorithms usually require the use of an internal sorting algorithm to increase the efficiency of their initial phase, and hence of the file sorting process as a whole.

7.1   EXTERNAL SORTING

Given a sequence of record keys a_1, a_2,...,a_n, an ascending ordered
subsequence (or ascending *run*) a_i,...,a_j is such that

$$a_{i-1} > a_i$$
$$a_k <= a_{k+1} \quad \text{for all } k = i,...,j-1$$
$$a_j > a_{j+1}$$

and similarly for a descending run. As we saw in Chapter 5, merging
is the combination of two or more runs into a single run.

Each operation that treats the entire sequence of records consti-
tutes a *pass*. A file sort is thus made up of a number of passes.

In general, the number of records in a file to be sorted is very
much greater than the available main memory, and so the records
cannot all be read into main memory and sorted there. Instead file
sorting methods usually involve first distributing the records to a
number of auxiliary files and then merging the records from these
files to produce runs; this process continues with longer runs being
formed until eventually a single run is formed. The more efficient
methods usually take account of any existing order among the records
of the file to be sorted.

7.1.1   Balanced *N*-way Merge Sorting

This sorting method normally employs $2N$ auxiliary files and builds an
ordered file by merging fixed-length runs. Figure 7.1 shows the steps
involved in such a sort for $N=2$.

In the first pass the unordered records are read (in groups of S
records) from the file F which is to be sorted into main memory and
each group sorted (using an array sorting algorithm). The resultant
runs are written to two other files A and B alternately. Hence this pass
distributes runs of S records and, if there are R records to be sorted,
then A and B will each contain $R/2S$ runs at the end of the distribution
pass. The size of S is determined by the amount of main memory
available to sort records. The sorting of groups of S records may be
performed using any of the normal array sorting algorithms, e.g.,
straight selection, insertion, quicksort. Some of these algorithms are
described in the next section of this chapter.

In the second pass a run is read from each file and merged to form
a single run of length $2S$, which is then written to a third auxiliary file
C. The second runs on A and B are merged and the resultant run sent
to the fourth auxiliary file D. Such a merge is known as a *2-way merge*
since runs are merged from two input files. It is a *balanced* merge

since there are equal numbers of input and output files used in each
merge. This merging process continues with runs written to C and D
in turn, until all the runs of A and B have been merged. There are now
$R/4S$ runs of length $2S$ on each of C and D.

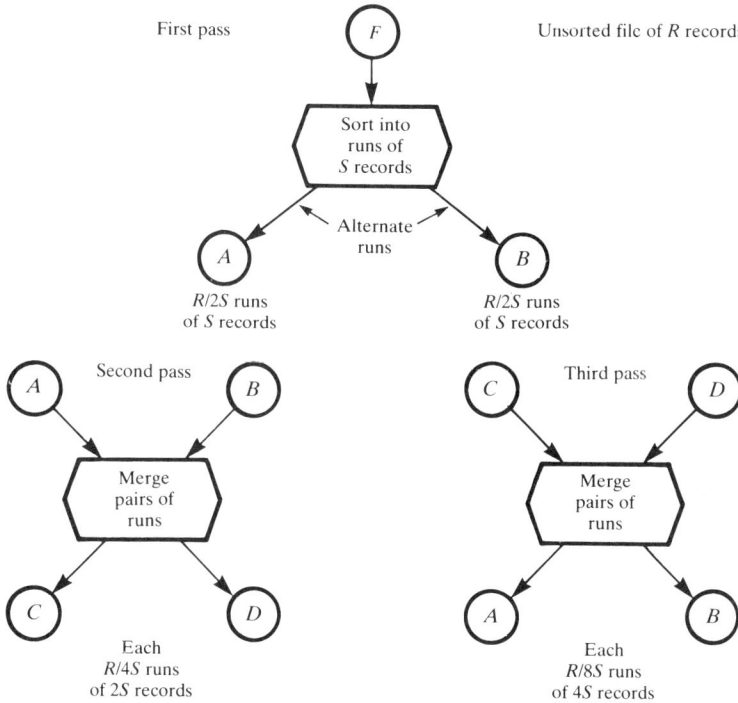

First pass F Unsorted file of R records

Sort into
runs of
S records

Alternate
runs

A B

$R/2S$ runs $R/2S$ runs
of S records   of S records

A Second pass B C Third pass D

Merge
pairs of
runs

Merge
pairs of
runs

C D A B

Each   Each
$R/4S$ runs $R/8S$ runs
of $2S$ records   of $4S$ records

Figure 7.1 Balanced 2-way merge sort

The third pass operates in exactly the same way as the second
pass except that runs are read and merged from C and D to be written
to A and B alternately. Subsequent passes continue to merge and distribute runs, with the length of the runs doubling in each pass, until a
merging pass produces a single run — which is the original file in
sorted order.

Since the runs double in length in each merging pass the total
number of merge passes required is $\log_2 R/S$ if R/S is an integer power
of 2, otherwise it is the first integer value greater than $\log_2 R/S$. In general, for an N-way merge, the number of merge passes is approximately $\log_N R/S$.

As an example, consider the sorting of a file containing records with the following keys

70   24   3   84   25   91   32   76   85   90   5   18   14   19   48   17

We assume for simplicity that it is not possible to sort groups of records in main memory during the distribution phase, i.e., $S=1$.

Pass 1: distribute runs of length 1 to A and B alternately
   A 70′ 3′ 25′ 32′ 85′ 5′ 14′ 48′
   B 24′ 84′ 91′ 76′ 90′ 18′ 19′ 17′
The primes mark the end of the runs generated

Pass 2: merge pairs of runs of length 1 and distribute to C and D
   C 24 70′ 25 91′ 85 90′ 14 19′
   D 3 84′ 32 76′ 5 18′ 17 48′

Pass 3: merge pairs of runs of length 2 and distribute to A and B
   A 3 24 70 84′ 5 18 85 90′
   B 25 32 76 91′ 14 17 19 48′

Pass 4: merge pairs of runs of length 4 and distribute to C and D
   C 3 24 25 32 70 76 84 91′
   D 5 14 17 18 19 48 85 90′

Pass 5: merge pairs of runs of length 8 → sorted sequence sent to A
   A 3 5 14 17 18 19 24 25 32 48 70 76 84 85 90 91′
   B empty

Note that the number of merge passes is four, i.e., $\log_2 16$, as expected. During the sorting process the original file F is not used (for security purposes, in case of a software or hardware malfunction so that the original file is still intact for a rerun of the sort program).

7.1.2   Von Neumann Merge Sort

The straight merge sort described above completely ignores any ordering which may initially exist among the records of the file to be sorted. In particular, notice what would have happened if the file records had in fact already been in sorted order. The initial pass would have distributed individual records to the two output files alternately, thus destroying the existing ordering, and the process of reconstruction of the initial sorted order would have required exactly the same effort as for a randomly ordered file.

The Von Neumann merge sort is an example of a *natural merge sort* which is similar in operation to the straight merge sort except that, instead of merging fixed-length runs, it takes advantage of any existing runs within the file to be sorted (which there almost certainly will be) by distributing runs from the initial unsorted file to the auxiliary files and then merging these runs. Again the process continues until only one run remains, which is in the desired order.

For example, consider the sorting of the 16 record file previously sorted using the 2-way merge sort. In the first pass the file *F* is distributed run-by-run to *A* and *B* alternately. There are in fact eight runs on *F* to begin with, viz.,

    F   70' 24' 3 84' 25 91' 32 76 85 90' 5 18' 14 19 48' 17'

and the initial distribution to *A* and *B* gives

    A   70' 3 84' 32 76 85 90' 14 19 48'
    B 24 25 91' 5 18' 17'

Note that, although the runs 24 and 25 91 were written to *B* as separate runs, they will form a single run when *B* is subsequently read. Hence they have been marked above as a single run.

Pass 2: merge runs from *A* and *B*; distribute to *C* and *D* alternately.
    C 24 25 70 91' 17 32 76 85 90'
    D   3 5 18 84' 14 19 48'
Here the final merge involves merging 14 19 48 from *C* with an empty run from *D*.

Pass 3: merge runs from *C* and *D*; distribute to *A* and *B* alternately.
    A   3 5 18 24 25 70 84 91'
    B 14 17 19 32 48 76 85 90'

Pass 4: final merge onto *C*.
    C 3 5 14 17 18 19 24 25 32 48 70 76 84 85 90 91'
    D empty

Here only three merges were required (since there were just seven runs resulting from the initial distribution). Compare the behavior of the two sorting methods considered so far when the file *F* is already sorted to begin with — whereas the Von Neumann method will detect this existing sequencing during the initial pass, the 2-way merge sort will break the file down into fixed-length runs and proceed to gradually re-build the sorted file. Indeed, a good test of any sorting algorithm is its efficiency when presented with an already sorted file.

7.1.3 Unbalanced Merge Sort

If an odd number $2N+1$ of auxiliary files is available, then it is not possible to use them all in a *balanced* merge sort (i.e., a sort with the same number of input files in each merge pass). In this case the auxiliary files are split into two groups — one containing $N+1$ files and the other N files. During the first pass runs are distributed to each of the files in the $N+1$ file group in turn. The first merge takes runs from these $N+1$ files and writes the resultant runs to each file of the N file group in turn. This process continues with alternate merge passes from the $N+1$ file group to the N file group, and vice versa. Figure 7.2 illustrates this for the case of five auxiliary files.

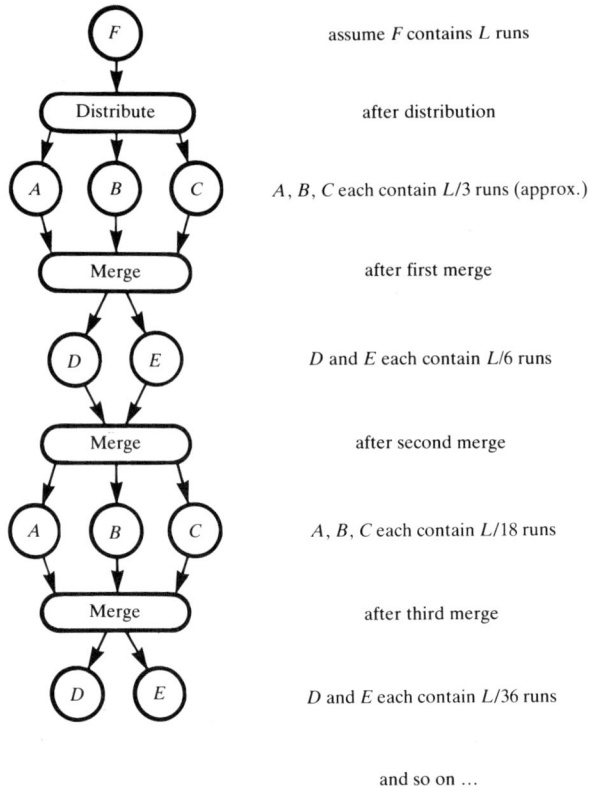

assume F contains L runs

after distribution

A, B, C each contain $L/3$ runs (approx.)

after first merge

D and E each contain $L/6$ runs

after second merge

A, B, C each contain $L/18$ runs

after third merge

D and E each contain $L/36$ runs

and so on ...

Figure 7.2   Unbalanced merge sort with five files

If the file F to be sorted contains L runs then, at the end of the distribution pass, there will be $L/3$ runs (approximately) on each of A, B, and C. The first merge from A, B, and C to D and E results in D and E each receiving $L/6$ runs. After the next merge A, B, and C will each contain $L/18$ runs. Consider again the sorting of the previous file, this time using five auxiliary files:

after the distribution pass:
```
A  70'  25   91'  14   19   48'
B  24   32   76   85   90'  17'
C   3   84'   5   18'
```
(note that two sucessive runs distributed to B form a single run on that file)

after the first merge:
```
D  3   24   32   70   76   84  85  90'  14  19  48'
E  5   17   18   25   91'
```

after the second merge
```
A  3   5   17   18  24  25  32  70  76  84  85  90  91'
B  14  19  48'
C  empty
```

and the sort is completed on the third merge.

7.1.4 Polyphase Merge Sort

The efficiency of the merge sorts examined so far depends upon the number of input files used in the merging. To obtain maximum efficiency, i.e., to maximize the length of the runs formed at each pass, it is necessary to maximize the number of input files used in each merge. If there are N auxiliary files, then the maximum number of input files that can be used is obviously $N-1$ since at least one file is required to receive the resulting runs. However, should all the input files become empty at the same time, no advantage is gained because it is then necessary to perform some redistribution of the records from the output file to the other files in preparation for the next merge. By arranging the number of runs on each input file to be different from each other, one input file will become exhausted at a time, and when it is exhausted it may then be used as the output file for the next merge. The previous output file then becomes an input file. This is the principle underlying the *polyphase* merge sort.

In Figure 7.3 there are four auxiliary files being used for merging purposes. The files $F1$, $F2$, and $F3$ are being merged and there are $n1$, $n2$, and $n3$ runs on each file respectively, where $n1>n2>n3$. A 3-way merge takes place to $F4$. After $n3$ merges have taken place there will be $n3$ runs on $F4$, $F3$ will be empty, and $F1$ and $F2$ will still have $n1-n3$ and $n2-n3$ runs awaiting merging.

At this stage the completely read file $F3$ changes roles with $F4$, i.e., $F4$ is then used in a 3-way merge with $F1$ and $F2$, the merged runs being written to $F3$. When one of $F1$, $F2$, or $F4$ becomes empty it changes roles with $F3$. Provided that $n1$, $n2$, and $n3$ are chosen

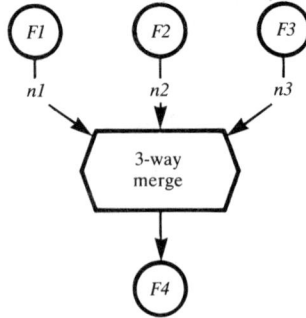

Figure 7.3   Polyphase merge sort (four files)

appropriately, each of the files becomes empty in turn and eventually the merges produce a single run, the sorted file.

In Figure 7.4 the progress of a polyphase sort using four work files is illustrated. Assume that initially the three input files $F1$, $F2$, and $F3$ contain 13, 11, and 7 runs, respectively. In the first merge pass 7 runs are merged from $F1$, $F2$, and $F3$ to $F4$ leaving 6 runs on $F1$, 4 on $F2$, 7 on $F4$, and $F3$ is empty (thus becoming the output file for the next merging pass); in the second merge 4 runs are merged from $F1$, $F2$, and $F4$ to $F3$, and so on. At the end of the complete series of merges $F4$ contains the sorted records.

	F1	F2	F3	F4
	13	11	7	0
first merge				
	6	4	0	7
second merge				
	2	0	4	3
third merge				
	0	2	2	1
fourth merge				
	1	1	1	0
fifth merge				
	0	0	0	1

Figure 7.4   Polyphase merge sort of 31 runs using four files

How do we determine a suitable initial distribution of the records among the $N-1$ files to be used in the first merge so that the merges function properly? By working backwards from the required final dis-

tribution (which is 1 run on one file and all the others empty) Figure
7.5 is obtained. On the right-hand side the numbers of runs on the
four files are given in descending order.

F1	F2	F3	F4	Total	Ordered			
1	0	0	0	1	1	0	0	0
0	1	1	1	3	1	1	1	0
1	0	2	2	5	2	2	1	0
3	2	0	4	9	4	3	2	0
7	6	4	0	17	7	6	4	0
0	13	11	7	31	13	11	7	0
13	0	24	20	57	24	20	13	0
		.		.				
		.		.				
		.		.				

Figure 7.5   Perfect distribution for four files

The numbers in the first column of the Ordered table

$$1,1,2,4,7,13,24,\ldots$$

are *Fibonacci numbers* of order 2 in which each number is the sum of
its three predecessors (except the first three numbers 1,1,2). Hence,
the numbers of runs initially on each of the three files *F1*, *F2*, *F3* must
be the sum of 3, 2, and 1 consecutive numbers of order 2 (e.g., 13 =
7+4+2, 11 = 7+4, 7 = 7, in the example of Figure 7.5). In general,
the ideal numbers of runs on each work file to achieve a perfect
polyphase sort with N work files are the sums of $N-1$, $N-2$,...,1 consecutive Fibonacci numbers of order $N-2$, all containing the same
Fibonacci number as their highest number.

But what if the number of runs on the file to be sorted is not the
sum of $N-1$ such Fibonacci sums (e.g., not 1, 3, 5, 9, 17, 31, or 57, etc.
in the example above)? The answer is to pad out the work files initially with sufficient 'dummy' or empty runs to achieve an ideal distribution. During merging the existence of these dummy runs must be
recognized so that any merge which involves such a dummy run
ignores that run, but any merge which involves dummy runs on all
input files produces a single dummy run on the output file. Wirth's
polyphase sort program demonstrates how the existence of these
dummy runs need only be hypothetical, i.e., it is not necessary to
explicitly write them to the output files during distribution and subsequent merging.

   To illustrate how the initial distribution might be performed,

consider the sorting into ascending sequence of a file with the following record keys

99 91 90 85 84 76 70 48 32 25 24 19 18 17 14 13 5

using four auxiliary files. For simplicity we have chosen the file to
contain exactly 17 records which are in descending key order (i.e.,
thus containing 17 runs).

The required sums of Fibonacci numbers of order 2 determining
the initial numbers of runs on each file are generated as the distribution progresses. An array named TARGET is used in Figure 7.6 to
hold the next distribution goal to be achieved at any stage. The initial
distribution goal is (1,1,1) — we ignore (1,0,0) — so TARGET is
initialized as in Figure 7.6(a), and the first three runs read from the
file to be sorted are sent to *F1*, *F2*, and *F3*, thus meeting the first
target. The next target is computed by adding the first element value
in the array to each of the other two elements, and rotating the three
elements one position leftwards (this method of determining the distribution follows from the Fibonacci properties of the sums we are
trying to generate), as in Figure 7.6(b). Thus the next two runs are
written to *F1* and *F2*, respectively.

(a)   TARGET | 1 | 1 | 1 | 99->*F1* ; 91->*F2* ; 90->*F3*

(b)   TARGET | 2 | 2 | 1 | 85->*F1* ; 84->*F2*

(c)   TARGET | 4 | 3 | 2 | 76->*F1* ; 70->*F2* ; 48->*F3* ; 32->*F1*

(d)   TARGET | 7 | 6 | 4 | 25->*F1* ; 24->*F2* ; 19->*F3* ; 18->*F1* ;
                                 17->*F2* ; 14->*F3* ; 13->*F1* ; 5->*F2*

Figure 7.6   Initial distribution of runs in four auxiliary file polyphase sort

The next target becomes (4,3,2) which requires two runs to be
added to *F1*, and one to each of *F2* and *F3* (runs are always distributed
to each of the files in turn until the target has been met) to produce the
situation shown in Figure 7.6(c). The next target is computed to be
(7,6,4); when it has been met the file to be sorted has been completely
distributed and the initial distribution is as shown below.

F1   99' 85' 76' 32' 25' 18' 13'
F2   91' 84' 70' 24' 17' 5'
F3   90' 48' 19' 14'
F4   empty

the first merge produces
F1   25' 18' 13'
F2   17' 5'
F3   empty
F4   90 91 99' 48 84 85' 19 70 76' 14 24 32'

and the second merge produces
F1   13'
F2   empty
F3   17 25 90 91 99' 5 18 48 84 85'
F4   19 70 76' 14 24 32'

the fourth merge leads to
F1   empty
F2   13 17 19 25 70 76 90 91 99'
F3   5 18 48 84 85'
F4   14 24 32'

and the sort is completed with the fifth merge
F1   5 13 14 17 18 19 24 25 32 48 70 76 84 85 90 91 99'
F2   empty
F3   empty
F4   empty

Although this polyphase sort requires five merges, which is the same as would have been required in a 2-way balanced merge sort of the same input file, the total number of records transferred between files (which is the true measure of efficiency of a sorting algorithm) is very much less for the polyphase sort. Since each record is transferred once in each pass of a balanced merge sort, the total number of records transferred in a sort of a 17 record file (i.e., requiring a distribution and five further merges) will be 17 times 6, i.e., 102 records. In the above polyphase sort only 65 transfers take place in the distribution and five merge passes.

One complication mentioned previously in the Von Neumann sort occurs again here — two runs written consecutively to an output file may produce a single run on that file and thereby cause the number of runs to vary from the required distribution. To avoid this possibility, the program performing the sort must check, during the initial distribution and each merge, for any occurrence of consecutive runs and adjust the number of runs distributed to the file concerned by the introduction of dummy runs. The resultant program is thus somewhat complex as may be observed from Program 2.16 in Wirth (1976).

7.2   INTERNAL SORTING

We shall describe just two array sorting methods that are commonly used — the simple straight selection sort which illustrates the characteristics of major sorting methods, and the famous Quicksort algorithm devised by C.A.R. Hoare which is generally the fastest array sorting method. We shall also introduce the Heapsort algorithm — a so-called *replacement* sorting technique which uses an array to generate longer strings for use in the initial distribution phase of a file sort. Once again the reader is referred to Wirth (1976) for a more complete review of array sorting methods.

7.2.1   Straight Selection Sort

Given an array A of n elements the straight selection algorithm may be expressed as

```
for i := 1 to n−1 do
begin
  find the least value of A[i],...,A[n] ;
  exchange A[i] and the least element value
end ;
```

For example, the sorting of an array of six integer elements by this straight selection method proceeds as shown in Figure 7.7.

$i = 1$	47	56	18	33	64	23
$i = 2$	18	56	47	33	64	23
$i = 3$	18	23	47	33	64	56
$i = 4$	18	23	33	47	64	56
$i = 5$	18	23	33	47	64	56

Figure 7.7   Straight selection sort

The complete form of a library sort operator using straight selection is given below. This operator is characterized by the type of the array elements to be sorted and the type of the values used to index the array elements (this must be an ordered type). It takes as parameters the array to be sorted (declared as a conformant array, thus allowing arrays of any length to be passed to the operator), and a function defining the ordering between values of the elements of the array being sorted.

```
procedure sortbystraightselection
            (var items : array [m..n : indextype] of elementtype ;
            function inorder (e1, e2 : elementtype) : boolean) ;
  { assumes type elementtype = type of array elements, with := defined }
  {                          and <= defined by function inorder   }
  {           type indextype = ordinal array index type,          }
  var firstunsorted, least, next : indextype ;
      leastvalue : elementtype ;
  begin
    for firstunsorted := m to pred (n) do
    begin
      least := firstunsorted ;
      for next := succ (firstunsorted) to n do
        if not inorder (items[least], items[next])
        then least := next ;
      leastvalue := items[least] ;
      items[least] := items[firstunsorted] ;
      items[firstunsorted] := leastvalue
    end
  end {sortbystraightselection} ;
```

Since *indextype* must be an ordered type, the standard Pascal functions *succ* and *pred* are applicable to its values.
This procedure might be used to sort an array

A : **array** [1..10] **of** *real*

thus

```
procedure sort = sortbystraightselection in library
                    (where type indextype = 1..10 ; {or just integer}
                                      elementtype = real) ;
function realsinorder (r1, r2 : real) : boolean ;
  begin realsinorder := (r1 <= r2) end ;
begin
    ...
    sort (A, realsinorder)
    ...
end
```

7.2.2 Quicksort

The straight selection method illustrates that the cost of sorting an array increases nonlinearly with the array length. The cost of sorting can be reduced by a recursive *divide-and-conquer* strategy such as

```
procedure sort {an array A} ;
   begin
      if sorting is needed
      then begin
               split A into segments S1, S2 ;
               sort (S1) ;
               sort (S2)
            end
   end ;
```

For this procedure to be correct the segments S1 and S2 must be such that sorting each completes the sorting of A, i.e., all elements in S1 must already be sorted with respect to all elements in S2, or

$$inorder \ (S1[i], \ S2[j]) \ for \ all \ valid \ i \ and \ j$$

In a practical sorting algorithm we wish to avoid the use of additional storage and to minimize the movement of items, so the segments S1 and S2 must be held within A. Hence our solution is reformulated as :

```
procedure sort (first, last : indextype) ;
   begin
      if first < last
      then begin
               partition A [first..last] into two segments ;
               sort (first, lastoffirstsegment) ;
               sort (firstoflastsegment, last)
            end
   end ;
```

How is the partitioning operation performed? Suppose we define the goal to be an initial segment of elements not greater than some partition value x, and a final segment of elements whose value is not less than x. We can define the partitioning process as one which begins with both segments initially empty and repeatedly extends each segment until they meet. Extension is trivial when the next element already fits that segment. When this is not so the stopper values can be interchanged and the process continued :

```
x := some suitable value ;
i := first ; j := last ;
repeat
   while inorder (A[i], x) do i := i+1 ;
   while inorder (x, A[j]) do j := j-1 ;
   if i <= j
   then begin
            interchange A[i] and A[j] ;
            i := i+1 ; j:= j-1
```

```
      end
   until i > j
```

How is *x* chosen? Ideally it should be the median value of those to be sorted so as to give two partitions of the same length. In practice we might settle for some arbitrary value chosen from those to be sorted, e.g.,

$$x := A \left[(first + last) \ \textbf{div} \ 2 \right]$$

However, this arbitrary choice means that the partition value *x* may be either the 'least' or 'greatest' of those to be partitioned, in which case one or other of the while loops above will increase *i* beyond *last* or decrease *j* below *first*. To avoid this the while loops can be rewritten to stop on an element value 'equal' to the partition value *x* and (unnecessarily) have it swapped into the other segment. In terms of the *inorder* function this is achieved by re-expressing the while loops as:

```
      while not inorder (x, A[i]) do i := i+1 ;
      while not inorder (A[j], x) do j := j−1 ;
```

In practice the unnecessary element changes caused by this modification are significant only if the array being sorted contains large numbers of 'equal' items.

It should be noted that when the partition loop terminates the values of *i* and *j* are not necessarily adjacent, but if they are not, the element values *A*[*j*+1], *A*[*j*+2],..., *A*[*i*−1] are all equal to the chosen partition value *x* and require no further consideration in the sort process. Thus, for the purpose of the following recursive *quicksort* procedure applied to an array *items* of values of some *elementtype* and index type *indextype*, it is sufficient to take *i* as *firstoflastsegment* and *j* as *lastoffirstsegment* so that the procedure becomes:

```
procedure quicksort (first, last : indextype) ;
   var i, j : indextype ;
       x, y : elementtype ;
   begin
    if first < last
    then begin
          x := items [(first + last) div 2] ;
          i := first ; j := last ;
          repeat
            while not inorder (x, items[i]) do i := i+1 ;
            while not inorder (items[j], x) do j := j−1 ;
            if i <= j
            then begin
                  y := items[i] ; items[i] := items[j] ;
```

$$items[j] := y \; ;$$
$$i := i+1 \; ; j := j-1$$
end
until $i > j$;
quicksort (*first*, *j*) ;
quicksort (*i*, *last*)
end
end {*quicksort*} ;

The overall sort process then contains *quicksort* as a local procedure and consists of an initial call of *quicksort* to sort the array passed as parameter, viz.,

procedure *sortbyquicksort*
                (**var** *items* : **array** [*m..n* : *indextype*] **of** *elementype* ;
                function *inorder* (*e1*, *e2* : *elementtype*) : *boolean*)
{ *assumes type elementtype = type of array elements,*   }
{   *with := defined and <= defined by*   }
{   *function inorder*   }
{   *type indextype   = ordinal array index type*   }
procedure *quicksort* (*first, last* : *indextype*) ; ... {*as above*} ... ;
begin
    quicksort (*m, n*)
end {*sortbyquicksort*} ;

This procedure might be used to sort the array

A : **array** [1..10] **of** *real*

thus

procedure *sort* = *sortbyquicksort* **in library**
                (**where type** *indextype* = 1..10 ; *elementtype* = *real*) ;
function *realsinorder* (*r1, r2* : *real*) : *boolean* ;
    begin *realsinorder* := (*r1* <= *r2*) **end** ;
begin
    ...
    sort (*A*, *realsinorder*)
    ...
end

i.e., exactly as before except that the quicksort procedure is now retrieved from the library instead of the straight selection sort operator.

7.2.3 Heapsort

The straight selection and quicksort algorithms are such that, if S records can be accommodated in main memory, then these can be sorted to produce runs of length S for distribution in the initial phase of an external sorting procedure. An alternative technique for use in the distribution phase that enables runs longer than S records to be generated involves the use of one of a number of so-called *replacement* algorithms, the best known of which is the *heapsort* algorithm.

Given a group of S records in main memory, the record with the least key (m, say) is selected, written away to an output file, and replaced by another record from an input file; the record with the smallest key greater than or equal to m is then selected, written away, and replaced; and so on, until all the records in the group have key values less than that of the last record written away. This will, in general, result in the generation of a run of length $2S$, assuming that the input file record keys are randomly distributed. This technique may be implemented using a *heap* which may be represented diagrammatically as in Figure 7.8.

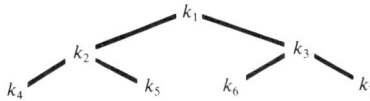

Figure 7.8   Structure of a heap

The record with key k_i sits 'above' the records with keys k_{2i} and k_{2i+1}; the records are arranged in the heap so that $k_i <= k_{2i}$ and $k_i <= k_{2i+1}$. Thus k_1 is the smallest key; when it is selected it is replaced at the top of the heap by the next input file record that has a key value greater than k_1 (records with keys less than k_1 are used to construct another heap which will be used to generate the next run). The new record is then 'sifted' down through the heap until it finds its correct place. If it is at position i then it is compared with the keys at positions $2i$ and $2i+1$; if it is not greater than either then it has found its correct position, otherwise it changes place with the record with the lesser key, and the sifting process continues at the next level in the heap. When the other heap (of records with keys too small for this heap) has been filled, i.e., the first heap has been emptied, a complete run has been generated. The other, full, heap is then used to generate the next run with the first heap used to hold records with smaller keys.

Figure 7.9 illustrates the sifting of a record value through a heap large enough to hold seven records. The state of the heap immediately before the topmost item in the heap is written away is shown in Figure 7.9(a) and the heap resulting from the acceptance and sifting of the next input file record is shown in Figure 7.9(b).

The program to implement the generation of runs using such a heap must first construct an initial heap, then pass input records through the heap and thence to an output file, and when the input file is exhausted finally 'flush' the residual records from the heap.

(a) before removal

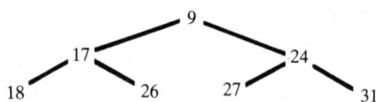

```
                         9
              17               24
        18        26     27        31
```

```
25  16 . . .
```
input file

(b) after removal

```
                        17
              18               24
        25        26     27        31
```

```
16 . . .
```
input file

Figure 7.9   Sifting through a heap

Note that, because of the simple relationships among the positions in the heap (which is effectively a binary tree) no explicit links need to be stored. Instead the two heaps involved may co-habit in a single array, and the size of one heap increases at the expense of the other.

In the heapsort algorithm given below three sequential files must be supplied as parameters — an input file and two output files to which alternate runs generated by the heapsort will be written. The array *heap* is used to hold the two heaps identified above with the value of the variable *endoflowerheap* denoting the boundary between the two heaps. Initially (step 1) the lower half of the *heap* array is filled with records from the input file and then (step 2) the rest of the heap is filled with input records each of which is sifted into its correct position, thus completing the construction of an initial heap (the second heap is empty at this stage). As new input values are read in those input values which can be accepted into the lower heap are sifted to their appropriate position (step 3). Those which do not belong to the current lower heap are put into the upper heap, the size of the lower heap is reduced by one, and (if necessary) the new input value is sifted through the upper heap (step 4). When the lower heap becomes empty the upper heap is then occupying the entire array and hence it becomes the lower heap and is used to generate the next output run (step 5). When the input file is exhausted the lower heap is flushed to complete the current run (step 6) and, at the same time, the upper heap moves down the array in preparation for it to be flushed to generate the next and final run (step 7).

```
procedure heapsort (instance F1, F2, F3 : seqfile) ;
  { assumes const heapsize (of type integer)              }
  {          class seqfile = sequentialfile (of items of)  }
  {          type itemtype with := defined, as well as      }
  {          function inorder (i1, i2 : itemtype) : boolean }
  instance infile : F1.input (environment.simple) ;
  instance outfile1: F2.output (environment.simple, 100) ;
  instance outfile2: F3.output (environment.simple, 100) ;
  type heapindex = 0..heapsize ;
  var nextrecord : itemtype ;
      out1current : boolean ;
      heap : array [1..heapsize] of itemtype ;
      endoflowerheap, midheap, lastelement, i : heapindex ;
  procedure writeouttopofheap ;
    begin
      if out1current
      then outfile1.write (heap[1])
      else outfile2.write (heap[1])
    end ;
  procedure switchoutputfile ;
    begin out1current := not out1current end ;
  procedure sift (first, last : heapindex) ;
    label 1 ;
    var i, j : indextype ;
        siftelement : itemtype ;
    begin
      i := first ; j := 2*first ; siftelement := heap[first] ;
      while j <= last do
      begin
        if j < last
        then if not inorder (heap[j], heap[j+1]) then j := j+1 ;
        if inorder (siftelement, heap[j]) then goto 1 ;
        heap[i] := heap[j] ; i := j ; j := 2*i
      end ;
      1 : heap[i] := siftelement
    end {sift} ;
  begin
    midheap := heapsize div 2 ;
    infile.read (nextrecord, eof) ;
    out1current := true ;
    { step 1 }
    for i := midheap + 1 to heapsize do
    begin heap[i] := nextrecord ; infile.read (nextrecord, eof) end ;
    { step 2 }
    for i := midheap downto 1 do
```

```
            begin
                heap[i] := nextrecord ; sift (i, heapsize) ;
                infile.read (nextrecord, eof)
            end ;
            endoflowerheap := heapsize ;
            while not eof do
            begin
                writeouttopofheap ;
                if inorder (heap[1], nextrecord)
                then begin { step 3 }
                        heap[1] :=nextrecord ; sift (1, endoflowerheap)
                     end
                else begin { step 4 }
                        heap[1] := heap[endoflowerheap] ;
                        sift (1, endoflowerheap – 1) ;
                        heap[endoflowerheap] := nextrecord ;
                        if endoflowerheap <= midheap
                        then sift (endoflowerheap, heapsize) ;
                        { step 5 }
                        endoflowerheap := endflowerheap – 1 ;
                        if endoflowerheap = 0
                        then begin
                                endoflowerheap := heapsize ;
                                switchout putfile
                             end
                     end ;
                infile.read (nextrecord, eof) ;
            end ;
            { step 6 }
            lastelement := heapsize ;
            for i := endoflowerheap downto 1 do
            begin
                writeouttopofheap ;
                heap[1] := heap[i] ; sift (1, i–1) ;
                heap[i] := heap[lastelement] ;
                lastelement := lastelement – 1 ;
                if i <= midheap then sift (i, lastelement)
            end ;
            { step 7 }
            switchoutputfile ;
            for i := lastelement downto 1 do
            begin
                writeouttopofheap ;
                heap[1] := heap[i] ; sift (1, i)
            end
        end {heapsort} ;
```

7.3   AN EXTERNAL SORTING ABSTRACTION

In this section we concentrate upon the design of a library procedure suitable for sorting a file of any sequential file class based upon our *sequentialfile* abstraction. This sorting procedure will perform a Von Neumann merge sort using four auxiliary sequential disk files, i.e., its distribution phase will be required to generate runs of records for subsequent 2-way balanced merging.

This library procedure, which we name *Generalfilesort*, will take as parameters two instances of a sequential file class *seqfile* which are the file to be sorted and the file which is to receive the sorted records, respectively, as well as an ordering function for the type *recordtype* of the file records. Hence *Generalfilesort* will have the following heading:

```
procedure Generalfilesort
        (instance unsortedfile, sortedfile : seqfile ;
            function inorder (r1, r2 : recordtype) : boolean)
    {  assumes class seqfile (= sequentialfile of)            }
    {           type recordtype, with := defined, and <=      }
    {                       defined by a function inorder      }
```

and its retrieval from the library will require the specification of the file record type and the sequential file class concerned, i.e., its use in an actual program would take the form

```
type somerecordtype = ... ;
class somefileclass = sequentialfile in library
                    (where type itemtype = somerecordtype) ;
instance F1 : somefileclass (...) ;
instance F2 : somefileclass (...) ;
function ordering (r1, r2 : somerecordtype) : boolean ; ... ;
procedure Generalfilesort in library
            (where type recordtype = somerecordtype ;
                class seqfile = somefileclass) ;
begin
    ...
    Generalfilesort (F1, F2, ordering) ;
    ...
end
```

The sort will use four auxiliary files of class *seqfile* (Figure 7.10). Identifying these files by integers in the range 1..4 they may be declared as an array of instances, viz.,

```
instance auxfile : array [filerange] of seqfile
                    (environment.DA1, 'aux1',
                    true, environment.blocksize, 2)
```

$(environment.DA2, 'aux2',$
  $true, environment.blocksize, 2)$
$(environment.DA3, 'aux3',$
  $true, environment.blocksize, 2)$
$(environment.DA4, 'aux4',$
  $true, environment.blocksize, 2)$;

where each file is assigned to a different disk drive, uses standard blocks, and is double buffered.

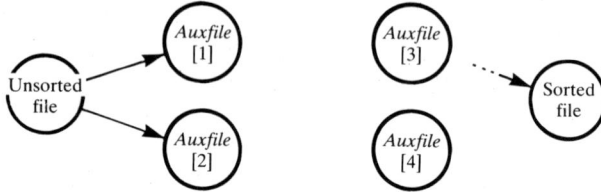

Figure 7.10   Files involved in sort

The basic program structure is thus

> **begin**
>   *distribute records from unsorted file*
>   *to auxfile*[1] *and auxfile*[2] ;
>   *perform merges* ;
>   *copy sorted records to sorted file*
> **end**

The action of *performmerges* will be to perform a series of merges of runs from *auxfile*[1] and *auxfile*[2] to *auxfile*[3] and *auxfile*[4], and vice versa, so that each auxiliary file is used as an input file and output file by alternate merge passes.

For the distribution phase we shall employ the heapsort procedure developed in the previous section using a heap of size 30, say.

> **procedure** *distribute* = *heapsort* **in library**
>   (**where const** *heapsize* = 30 ;
>   **type** *itemtype* = *recordtype*) ;

In this case it is not necessary to provide specifications for *seqfile* and *inorder* since there is no re-naming required. This procedure is called as

> *distribute (unsortedfile, auxfile*[1], *auxfile*[2])

The procedure *performmerges* will carry out the merging operations and assign to its variable formal parameter *sortedrecordson* the

Index of the auxiliary file containing the final sorted run. It operates by repeatedly calling a procedure *pass* to perform each individual merge until *pass* reports that a merge is not possible due to one of its input files being empty. *pass* is supplied with a pair of indexes indicating the first of the two input files and the first of the two output files to be used in the particular merge, e.g., the call

$$pass\ (1, 3, sortcomplete)$$

would cause *pass* to attempt a merge from *auxfile*[1] and *auxfile*[2] to *auxfile*[3] and *auxfile*[4] — if either of *auxfile*[1] or *auxfile*[2] is empty the call of *pass* will assign *true* to the variable parameter *sortcomplete*. Hence *performmerges* take the form

```
begin
    in := 1 ; out := 3 ;
    repeat
        pass (in, out, sortcomplete) ;
        if not sortcomplete
        then begin x := in ; in := out ; out := x end
    until sortcomplete ;
    sortedrecordson := in
end {performmerges} ;
```

Each activation of

procedure *pass* (*in1*, *out1* : *filerange* ; **var** *sortcomplete* : *boolean*) ;

declares four file processing instances — an input processing instance is defined for each auxiliary file to be used as an input file in the pass, and an output processing instance for each auxiliary file to be used as an output file, thus

```
instance infile1 : auxfile [in1].input (environment.simple) ;
instance infile2 : auxfile [in1+1].input (environment.simple) ;
instance outfile1 : auxfile [out1].output (environment.simple, 100) ;
instance outfile2 : auxfile [out1+1].output (environment.simple, 100) ;
```

pass begins by checking if either input file is empty and, if not, merges runs from the two input files until the end of one file is reached. The tail of the other file must then be copied run by run. Merged runs must be sent to each of the two output files in turn – the variable *out1iscurrent* is used to determine which is the current output file. Hence *pass* takes the form

```
begin
    out1iscurrent := true ;
    infile1.read (record1, endof1) ; infile2.read (record2, endof2) ;
    sortcomplete := endof1 or endof2 ;
```

```
        if not sortcomplete
        then begin
                repeat
                    mergeapairofruns ;
                    out1iscurrent := not out1iscurrent ;
                until endof1 or endof2 ;
                while not endof1 do
                begin copyrun1 ; out1iscurrent := not out1iscurrent end ;
                while not endof2 do
                begin copyrun2 ; out1iscurrent := not out1iscurrent end
            end
    end {pass} ;
```

The procedure *copyrun1* makes use of a procedure *copy1* to transfer a record from the input file *infile1* to the current output file and determine when the end of a run on *infile1* has been reached. We thus introduce a boolean variable local to *pass* whose value indicates whether or not the end of a run has been reached. This will be set by *copy1*.

```
procedure copyrun1 ;
    begin {copy one run from infile1 to current output file}
        repeat copy1 until endofrun
    end {copyrun1} ;
```

copy1 is simply expressed in terms of file operations on *infile1* and the current output file. To determine the end of a run, the last record transferred from *infile1* must be retained for comparison with its successor (if there is one), using the formal function parameter *inorder* of *Generalfilesort*.

```
procedure copy1 ;
    var temprecord : recordtype;
    begin
        if out1iscurrent
        then outfile1.write (record1)
        else  outfile2.write (record1) ;
        temprecord := record1 ;
        infile1.read (record1, endof1) ;
        if endof1
        then endofrun := true
        else  endofrun := inorder (record1, temprecord)
    end {copy1} ;
```

Similar procedures *copyrun2* and *copy2* are provided for *infile2* — unfortunately these must be separate procedures since the two input files *infile1* and *infile2* are of different classes and hence cannot be passed as parameters to more general *copyrun* and *copy* procedures.

mergeapairofruns produces a merged run on the current output
file formed from a run of each of *infile1* and *infile2*. It operates by
comparing the records in corresponding runs on *infile1* and *infile2*,
again using the *inorder* parameter function. *copy1* and *copy2* are then
used to transfer the selected records to the output file. This process
terminates when the end of one of the two input runs is reached, at
which point the tail of the other run is copied to the output file.

```
begin
  repeat
    if inorder (record1, record2)
    then begin copy1 ; if endofrun then copyrun2 end
    else  begin copy2 ; if endofrun then copyrun1 end
  until endofrun
end {mergeapairofruns} ;
```

Thus the development of our *Generalfilesort* abstraction is completed
and is given in full in Listing 14. Its use in an actual program is illustrated by the transaction sorting case study program in Section 7.4.

```
         LISTING 14 : GENERAL FILE SORT PROCEDURE

procedure Generalfilesort
            (instance unsortedfile, sortedfile : seqfile ;
             function inorder (r1, r2 : recordtype) : boolean) ;

  { assumes class seqfile (= sequentialfile of)            }
  {          type recordtype, with := defined, and <=      }
  {                       defined by the function inorder } 

  type filerange = 1..4 ;

  instance auxfile : array [filerange] of seqfile
                        (environment.DA1, 'aux1',
                         true, environment.blocksize, 2)
                        (environment.DA2, 'aux2',
                         true, environment.blocksize, 2)
                        (environment.DA3, 'aux3',
                         true, environment.blocksize, 2)
                        (environment.DA4, 'aux4',
                         true, environment.blocksize, 2)

  var filecontainingsortedrecords : filerange ;

  procedure distribute = heapsort in library
                        (where const heapsize = 30 ;
                             type itemtype = recordtype) ;

  procedure performmerges (var sortedrecordson : filerange) ;

    var in, out, x : filerange ;
        sortcomplete : boolean ;

    procedure pass (inl, outl : filerange ; var sortcomplete : boolean) ;

      instance infile1 : auxfile [inl].input (environment.simple) ;
      instance infile2 : auxfile [inl+1].input (environment.simple) ;
      instance outfile1 : auxfile [outl].output
                                  (environment.simple, 100) ;
```

```
      instance outfile2 : auxfile [out1+1].output
                                    (environment.simple, 100) ;

   var endof1, endof2, outliscurrent : boolean ;
      record1, record2 : recordtype ;
      endofrun : boolean ;
   procedure copy1 ;
      var temprecord : recordtype ;
      begin
         if outliscurrent
         then outfile1.write (record1)
         else outfile2.write (record1) ;
         temprecord := record1 ;
         infile1.read (record1, endof1) ;
         if endof1
         then endofrun := true
         else endofrun := inorder (record1, temprecord)
      end {copy1} ;

   procedure copy2 ;
      var temprecord : recordtype ;
      begin
         if outliscurrent
         then outfile1.write (record2)
         else outfile2.write (record2) ;
         temprecord := record1 ;
         infile2.read (record1, endof2) ;
         if endof2
         then endofrun := true
         else endofrun := inorder (record2, temprecord)
      end {copy1} ;

   procedure copyrun1 ;
      begin {copy one run from infile1 to current output file}
         repeat copy1 until endofrun
      end {copyrun1} ;

   procedure copyrun2 ;
      begin {copy one run from infile2 to current output file}
         repeat copy2 until endofrun
      end {copyrun2} ;

   procedure mergeapairofruns ;
      begin
         repeat
            if inorder (record1, record2)
            then begin copy1 ; if endofrun then copyrun2 end
            else begin copy2 ; if endofrun then copyrun1 end
         until endofrun
      end {mergeapairofruns} ;

   begin {pass}
      outliscurrent := true ;
      infile1.read (record1, endof1) ;
      infile2.read (record2, endof2) ;
      sortcomplete := endof1 or endof2 ;
      if not sortcomplete
      then begin
              repeat
                 mergeapairofruns ;
                 outliscurrent := not outliscurrent ;
              until endof1 or endof2 ;
              while not endof1 do
              begin
                 copyrun1 ; outliscurrent := not outliscurrent
              end ;
              while not endof2 do
              begin
                 copyrun2 ; outliscurrent := not outliscurrent
              end
           end
   end {pass} ;
```

```
begin
   in := 1 ; out := 3 ;
   repeat
      pass (in, out, sortcomplete) ;
      if not sortcomplete
      then begin x := in ; in := out ; out := x end
   until sortcomplete ;
   sortedrecordson := in
end {performmerges} ;

procedure copy (filecontainingsortedrecords : filerange) ;
   instance infile : auxfile [filecontainingsortedrecords].input
                                            (environment.locked) ;
   instance outfile : sortedfile.output (environment.simple, 100) ;
   var nextrecord : recordtype ;   endoffile : boolean ;
   begin
      infile.read (nextrecord, endoffile) ;
      while not endoffile do
      begin
         outfile.write (nextrecord) ;
         infile.read (nextrecord, endoffile)
      end
   end {copy} ;

begin {Generalfilesort}
   distribute (unsortedfile, auxfile[1], auxfile[2]) ;
   performmmerges (filecontainingsortedrecords) ;
   copy (filecontainingsortedrecords)
end  {Generalfilesort}
```

In the case of a disk sort such as above the number of disk drives critically affects the efficiency of the sort. For example, when copying a file *A* to a file *B* it is desirable that both files should be on different disk drives — otherwise every block which is read and written will require two seeks. The first seek will locate the block on file *A* and read it into a main memory buffer, after which a seek will be used to seek the destination cylinder of file *B* to write out the block. There will then be a seek back to the first file, and so on.

The ideal situation is therefore to have one auxiliary file associated with each i/o channel. Hence our auxiliary sort files have been assigned to four different disk drives.

7.4 CASE STUDY: SORTING THE VALID TRANSACTIONS FILE

The validated transactions stored on the magnetic tape file TRANS-ACTIONS by the validation program of the previous chapter have to be sorted into date within account number order in preparation for their input to the sequential master file update program of Chapter 5. Figure 7.11 shows the sort program (*PROGRAM3*) and its associated files.

The sorted records are to be written to a tape file labelled SORTED-TRANS and a listing of the sorted records is to be produced on line printer unit 1 for verification purposes. The input file is held on magnetic tape unit 1, the sorted file on magnetic tape unit 2.

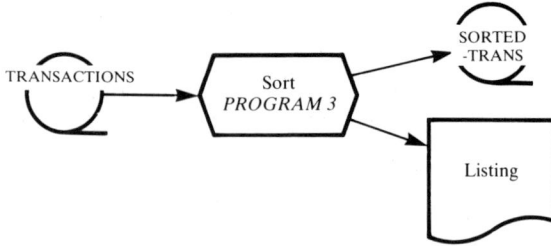

Figure 7.11   Sort program

      TRANSACTIONS and SORTED-TRANS will be denoted by the program identifiers *VTF* and *STF* (Sorted Transactions File) respectively. These files contain records of the type *transaction* defined previously and hence we have

> **class** *transfile = sequentialfile* **in library**
>   (**where type** *itemtype = transaction*) ;
> **instance** *VTF* : *transfile* (*environment.MT1*,
>   *'TRANSACTIONS'*, *false*,
>   *environment.blocksize*, 2) ;
> **instance** *STF* : *transfile* (*environment.MT2*,
>   *'SORTED-TRANS'*, *true*,
>   *environment.blocksize*, 2) ;

where both files are again double buffered for sequential processing.
      The library procedure *Generalfilesort* will be used to perform the sorting and is retrieved as

> **procedure** *Generalfilesort* **in library**
>   (**where type** *recordtype = transaction* ;
>   **class** *seqfile = transfile*)

The program structure is

> **begin**
>   *Generalfilesort* (*VTF*, *STF*, *transinorder*) ;
>   *listSTF*
> **end**

where the function *transinorder* will define the ordering between records of type *transaction* and the procedure *listSTF* will list the records of *STF* on a printer file (this procedure is almost identical to the transaction listing procedure in the previous chapter).

> **function** *transinorder* (*t1*, *t2* : *transaction*) : *boolean* ;
>   **begin**

$$transinorder := environment.lessthan\ (t1.key, t2.key)\ \textbf{or}$$
$$environment.equals\ (t1.key, t2.key)\ \textbf{and}$$
$$\textbf{not}\ environment.lessthan\ (t2.date, t1.date)$$
end

where transactions with the same account number key are to be ordered by date. The complete program expressed in our extended version of Pascal is thus as given in Listing 15. Listing 13 (Chapter 6) shows the input file of validated transactions used in a run of the program, and the sorted transactions output file so produced is that given in Chapter 5 as Listing 5 (the transactions file input to the sequential file update program *PROGRAM4*).

```
                    LISTING 15 : PROGRAM3

program PROGRAM3 {sorting of transactions} ;

    class module environment in library ;

    const printerwidth = environment.printerwidth ;

    type accountnumber = environment.string ;
         transtype =(addition, deletion, credit, debit) ;
         money = environment.numeric ;
         transaction = record
                          date : environment.string ;
                          key : accountnumber ;
                          kind : transtype ;
                          amount : money ;
                          clientidentity : environment.string ;
                          other : environment.string
                       end ;

    class transfile = sequentialfile in library
                          (where type itemtype = transaction) ;

    instance VTF : transfile (environment.MT1, 'TRANSACTIONS', false,
                              environment.blocksize, 2) ;
    instance STF : transfile (environment.MT2, 'SORTED-TRANS', true,
                              environment.blocksize, 2) ;

    procedure Generalfilesort in library
                (where type recordtype = transaction ;
                       class seqfile = transfile) ;

    function transinorder (t1, t2 : transaction) : boolean ;
        begin
            transinorder := environment.lessthan (t1.key, t2.key) or
                            environment.equals (t1.key, t2.key) and
                            not environment.lessthan (t2.date, t1.date)
        end ;

    procedure listSTF ;

        class outputtextfile in library ;

        instance listfile : outputtextfile (environment.LP1, 2) ;
        instance sortedfile : VTF.input (environment.locked) ;

        var transrecord : transaction ;
            endoffile : boolean ;
            outputline : environment.string ;

        begin
            with environment, listfile, transrecord do
```

```
begin
    construct (outputline,
                'LISTING OF SORTED TRANSACTIONS FILE') ;
    writeline (outputline) ;
    sortedfile.read (transrecord, endoffile) ;
    while not endoffile do
    begin
        putall (outputline, 1, printerwidth, ' ') ;
        putstring (outputline, date, 6, 6) ;
        putstring (outputline, key, 15, 8) ;
        case kind of
        credit : begin
                    putchar (outputline, 'C', 26) ;
                    putnumeric (outputline, amount, 30, 6, 2)
                 end ;
        debit  : begin
                    putchar (outputline, 'D', 26) ;
                    putnumeric (outputline, amount, 30, 6, 2)
                 end ;
        addition : begin
                    putchar (outputline, 'N', 26) ;
                    putstring (outputline, clientidentity,
                                39, 30)
                   end ;
        deletion : putchar (outputline, 'X', 26) ;
        end ;
        putstring (outputline, other, 70, 30) ;
        writeline (outputline) ;
        sortedfile.read (transrecord, endoffile)
    end ;
    puttext (outputline, 'END OF FILE', 1, printerwidth) ;
    writeline (outputline)
end
end {listSTF} ;

begin
    Generalfilesort (VTF, STF, transinorder) ;
    listSTF
end.
```

EXERCISES

1. A file contains records with the following keys:
    ```
    1   19  37   7  67  47  17  54  61  29
    3    6  41  11  92  53  19  20  22  31
    5   24  43  13  44  59  23  36   4   8
    ```
    The file is to be sorted into ascending order of this key field value. For each of the following sorting methods show how the sort progresses, indicating the contents of each file at the end of each pass:

    (a) merge sort using six files;
    (b) Von Neumann sort using six files;
    (c) polyphase sort using three files.

2. An array of eight elements is available for use in a heapsort (based upon the procedure given in this chapter) to generate initial runs from the file shown above. What runs result from this heapsort?
    Trace the Von Neumann sort using six files to sort the file above if the initial runs are distributed using such a heapsort.

3. (a) Why is the Von Neumann merge sort better than the balanced N-way merge sort?

(b) Why is the polyphase merge sort better than the balanced N-way merge sort?
(c) How does the use of the replacement selection technique improve the initial distribution phase of any merge sort?

4. A computer installation has four magnetic tape decks which are to be used to sort a tape file on ascending key. It is not known in advance how many records are to be sorted.
   (a) For:
      (i) a balanced 2-way merge sort,
      (ii) a Von Neumann sort,
      show diagrammatically how each sort progresses, making it clear which records are on which tapes at each stage, and which tapes are rewound and when. Use as your example a file containing records with the following keys:
      47 23   1   2 82 43 48 84
      92 93 97   8 10   4 14 34
      Assume that the records are so large that no sorting may be done in main store, other than simple merging of records from different tapes.
   (b) If a fifth tape deck were available how might these sorts take advantage of it?

5. Replace the *distribute* procedure in the *Generalfilesort* procedure of Section 7.3 by one of the internal sorting procedures developed in Section 7.2 and which uses an array of 200 elements.

6. Rewrite the *Generalfilesort* procedure of Section 7.3 so that it performs a polyphase merge sort, again using four auxiliary files.

7. A library class providing an abstraction of a sequential organization file is specified as

```
class sequentialfile (identity : packed array [m..n : integer] of char ;
                      newfile : boolean) ;
{assumes type itemtype with := defined}
type*processing modes = ( *input, *output ) ;
procedure *open (mode : processingmodes) ; ... ;
procedure *close ; ... ;
procedure *read (var i : itemtype ; var eof : boolean) ; ... ;
procedure *write (i :itemtype) ; ... ;
begin
   {attach file} ; *** ; {release file}
end
```

and a general file sorting procedure with the heading

```
procedure filesort (instance unsortedfile,
                    sortedfile : seqfile ;
            function inorder (r1, r2 : recordtype) : boolean) ;
   { assumes class seqfile derived from class sequentialfile of }
   {           type recordtype                                  }
```

is also held in the library.

A sequence of four digit numbers is to be generated in which all the numbers, other than the first two, are obtained by taking the sum modulus 10 000 of the previous two numbers in the sequence. Write a progam, using the above abstractions, which reads in the first two numbers of the sequence, generates the next fifty numbers of the sequence, and outputs the sorted sequence to the operator's console, followed by the message '*sort complete*'. The use of the console is specified by the following library class

class *console* ;
  procedure **read* (**var** *i : integer*) ; ... ;
  procedure **write* (*i : integer*) ; ... ;
  procedure **message* (*m* : **packed array** [*u..v : integer*] **of** *char*) ; ... ;
begin ∗∗∗ **end**

8 PROCESSING INDEXED SEQUENTIAL FILES

8.1 INTRODUCTION

So far we have organized the master account file for the Model Savings Bank system as a sequential file. However, the use of such a file imposes severe constraints on the usability of the system. For instance, the delays caused by the batching of the transactions means that the system only contains up-to-date information on the customers' accounts immediately following an update run (and even then it may be out-of-date). For a customer actually at a teller's position in a branch the status of his account cannot be obtained immediately for two reasons – firstly, the organization of the master file records makes such access to his account record impractical, and, secondly, if such an access were performed there would not be any guarantee that the data contained therein was up-to-date.

Immediate access to account records has two obvious advantages from the point of view of the bank. Attempts to overdraw accounts would be detectable by a teller instead of remaining undetected until the file update run. Performing an immediate update for any account changes would also require transactions to be validated as they were being made by a customer and the need to sort transaction batches into account number order would be avoided.

We concentrate first upon the problem of organizing the master file records so that it is possible to obtain immediate access to its records. This requires the storage of the file on a direct-access device such as a disk drive. Since many of the other applications in the banking system will still require sequential processing of the account records the most suitable form of file organization is as an indexed sequential file (since such files can be accessed both sequentially and

randomly). Storing the master file on disk also means that the generation of multiple versions of the master file is avoided — although
there is then the problem of maintaining the security of the master
file.

Hence we redesign the system around an indexed sequential
master file. For the moment we shall continue to update this file using
a file of transactions — however, the transaction batch will not be
required to be in sorted order, although we assume that the transactions have already passed through a data validation phase (the inte-
gration of the validation and update phases is trivial and is set as an
exercise for the reader).

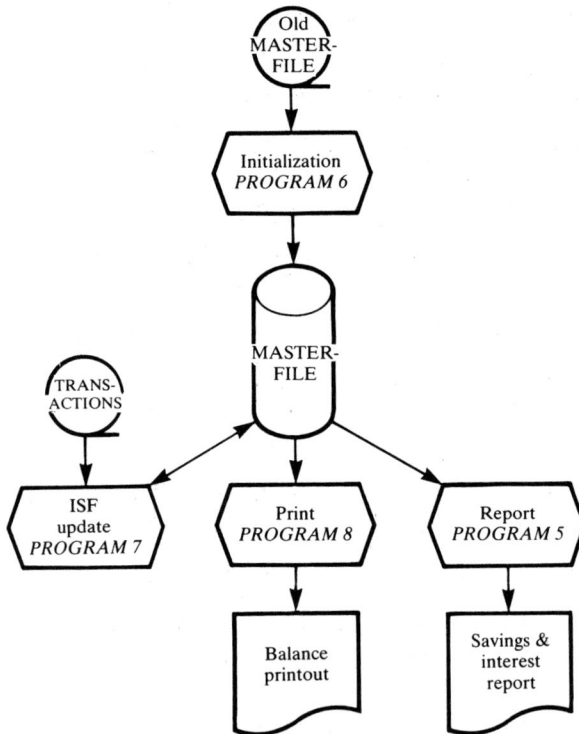

Figure 8.1   System based on indexed sequential master file

In Figure 8.1 the file initialization program *PROGRAM6* is used
to create an indexed sequential master file from the latest version of
the sequential master file. *PROGRAM7* performs the updating of
this file using the unsorted valid transactions file TRANSACTIONS

and employing random access to the file records — in practice these transactions might arrive and be processed in real time. However, conceptually they may just be considered as a file of transactions which has been generated by some validation phase.

PROGRAM8 prints out the master file records in account number order to produce a report on the status of each customer's account — this is basically the same program as was used to print out the sequential file contents. Instead of writing it as a separate program we shall incorporate it in *PROGRAM6*. *PROGRAM5* is the overall savings report and interest payment program described in Chapter 1 — the development of this program is performed in Chapter 10.

As we saw in Chapter 3, indexed sequential files may be stored only on direct-access media such as magnetic disk. Logically an indexed sequential file consists of a sequence of records in ascending key order value, together with an index which enables the position of any record in the file to be determined, given its key value. This logical structure is illustrated in Figure 8.2, where $k1..kn$ are the keys of the records, and $k1 < k2 < ... < kn$. In practice the physical organization of an index may actually be as a multi-level, tree-structured, index.

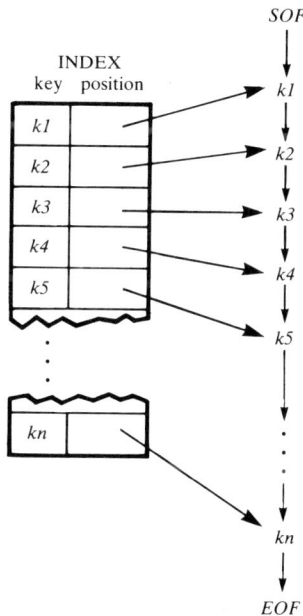

Figure 8.2   Logical structure of an indexed sequential file

There are two basic methods of access to records in an indexed sequential file — *sequential* and *indexed* access. Sequential access is such that the next record accessed by a read operation will be the successor in the key ordered sequence of the previous record read. For indexed access any record may be accessed by using its key value in a search of the index to determine its position within the sequence. Indexed sequential files may be processed using sequential access only or indexed access only, depending upon the nature of the application. They may also be processed using a mixture of both access methods, i.e., a particular record may be read using indexed access (via the index) and records subsequently accessed using sequential read operations, i.e., these records will be the successors of the initially read record. Files accessed in this way are said to to be accessed *dynamically*.

Indexed sequential files are generally used in applications where the file being processed has a very low hit ratio (e.g., less than 5%), in which case the use of indexed access is necessary for efficient processing. In such processing, if the references to the file records are not made in key order, there will be considerable arm movement and hence (see Section 3.4.3) it is desirable (if possible) to presort the updating data into key order sequence also — the disk arms will thus move smoothly across the cylinders in a single sweep, i.e., with minimum arm movement, and the cylinder indexes need only be read from the disk once per cylinder instead of once per record.

The other category of application for which an indexed sequential organization is well-suited is any in which the file records may be processed randomly by some programs and in key order sequence by other programs. In such cases the availability of both indexed and sequential access to the records in the file makes both types of processing convenient (and acceptably efficient).

8.2   SPECIFICATION OF AN INDEXED SEQUENTIAL FILE ABSTRACTION

We now, as in the case of sequential files, develop an abstract data type specification for indexed sequential files. Such an abstraction is characterized by the type of the records in the file, which we will denote by the type identifier *elementtype*, and also the type of the primary search key for the records, say type *keytype*. This abstraction will also require the definition of an operator (*getkey*) which defines how the key value of a record is extracted from the record itself, and two comparison operators *samekey* and *keyorder* which determine whether two keytype values are equal, and in key order, respectively. An instance of this data type, which we name *indexedsequentialfile*, will require the same set of physical parameters as was supplied for sequential file instances (with the added restriction that the file must be held on a direct-access device). Thus the heading of the indexed sequential file abstraction is

```
class indexedsequentialfile
      (device : environment.directdevices ;
      identity : packed array [m..n : integer] of char ;
      newfile : boolean ;
      bucketsize : environment.blockrange;
      numberofbuffers : environment.bufferrange) ;
    { assumes type elementtype with := defined                     }
    {          type keytype      with := defined                    }
    {          procedure getkey (v : elementtype ; var k : keytype) }
    {          function samekey (k1, k2 : keytype) : boolean        }
    {          function keyorder (k1, k2 : keytype) : boolean       }
begin
    { attach file to program }
    ***
    { release file from program }
end {indexedsequentialfile}
```

Hence, assuming that we wish to use an indexed file of records of the following type

```
type datatype =  record
                    number : integer ;
                    restofdata : sometype
                 end ;
```

where the field *number* is the key field uniquely identifying the records in such a file, we must define operators

```
procedure getnumber (d : datatype ; var i : integer) ;
   begin i := d.number end ;
function samenumber (i1, i2 : integer) : boolean ;
   begin samenumber := (i1 = i2) end ;
function numbersinorder (i1, i2 : integer) : boolean ;
   begin numbersinorder := (i1 < i2) end ;
```

and then specify the required file type as

```
class ISfile =  indexedsequentialfile in library
                (where type elementtype = datatype ;
                       keytype = integer ;
                 procedure getkey = getnumber ;
                 function samekey = samenumber ;
```

        function *keyorder = numbersinorder*) ;

An instance of this type might be declared as

    instance *codefile* : *ISfile* (*environment.DA1*, *'1983-codes'*, *false*, 1024, 1)

    Three sets of operations will be provided by the *indexedsequen-tialfile* data type, corresponding to the three modes of file access identified above. Hence, within the *indexedsequentialfile* type, we define instances of three local abstract data types providing the required access abstractions, viz.,

    class *indexedsequentialfile* (...) ;
      class module *sequential ; ... ;
      class module *indexed ; ... ;
      class module *dynamic ; ... ;
      begin
        ***
      end {*indexedsequentialfile*}

    Each of these access abstractions will then, in turn, provide a set of abstractions corresponding to the processing modes and associated operations available to a file being accessed in the mode concerned, e.g.,

    class module *sequential ;
      class *input (...) ; ... *specification of input operations* ... ;
      class *output (...) ; ... *specification of output operations* ... ;
      class *inputoutput (...) ; ... *specification of inputoutput operations* ... ;
      begin
        ***
      end {*sequential*}

    Hence, to perform processing of the above file *codefile* as a sequentially accessed input file, we would declare an instance

      instance *L* : *codefile.sequential.input* (...) ;

As for sequential files, the initialization of any such instance will open the file concerned ready for the required mode of processing, and the finalization will close the file in the closing mode defined by a parameter, viz.,

    instance *L* : *codefile.sequential.input* (*environment.locked*) ;

We shall now develop each of the access mode abstractions in turn.

8.2.1 Sequential Access

For sequentially accessed indexed sequential files the open, close, and file access operations provided are as for sequential files. The effect of these operations is precisely as described in Chapter 5 with two minor, but important, exceptions. The *write* operator checks that the key of the record being written to the file preserves the key ordering; e.g., in Figure 8.3 the operation *write (R)* is legal, given the current file window position, provided the key value extracted from *R* is 'greater' than *k2* and 'less' than *k3*. The *getkey* operator defines the record key value given the record value *R*, and the ordering relations are defined by the *keyorder* operator.

Figure 8.3   Sequential insertion

The *replace* operator must check that the key value of the new record value being written to the file is the same as that of the record being replaced, i.e., given the state of the file in Figure 8.3, the operation *replace (R)* is legal only if the key value of the record *R* has the same value as *k3* (the *samekey* operator defines this equality test).

Hence, following upon our *sequentialfile* abstraction in Chapter 5, we have

```
class module *sequential ;
   class *input (closingmode : environment.closingmodes) ;
      procedure *read (var v : elementtype ; var eof : boolean) ;
      begin
         {open file as an input file}
         ***
         {close file}
      end ; {input}
   class *output ( closingmode : environment.closingmodes ;
                   bucketoccupancy : environment.percentage) ;
      procedure *write (v : elementtype ; var error : boolean) ;
      begin
         {open file as an output file}
         ***
         {close file}
      end ; {output}
   class *inputoutput (closingmode : environment.closingmodes) ;
      procedure *read (var v : elementtype ; var eof : boolean) ;
      procedure *write (v : elementtype ; var error : boolean) ;
      procedure *replace (v : elementtype ; var error : boolean) ;
      procedure *delete ;
      begin
```

{*open file as an inputoutput file*}

***

{*close file*}

end ; {*inputoutput*}

begin

***

end {*sequential*}

Note that the *replace* and *write* operators have boolean variable parameters *error* which are used by the operators to indicate the success of the attempted operations — a *write* operation will fail if it does not maintain the key ordering, likewise a *replace* operation will fail if it attempts to alter the key of the record being replaced.

The *bucketoccupancy* parameter of the *output* class indicates to what degree the file buckets are to be filled when the file is initially written.

8.2.2   Indexed Access

For indexed access the effect of the open operation is to leave the initial position of the file window undefined.

The *read* operator

procedure *read (*k* : *keytype* ; **var** *v* : *elementtype* ;
          var *successful* : *boolean*) ;

accesses the record in the file with key value *k* and assigns the value of this record to the variable *v*. The file window is set to contain the record thus read. However, if there is no record in the file with key value *k*, then the *keyread* operation is unsuccessful, no value is assigned to *v*, and the file window position becomes undefined. This operator (in common with the other indexed access operators below) assigns a boolean value to the parameter *successful* to indicate the success or otherwise of the attempted operation.

The *deletion* operator

procedure *delete (*k* : *keytype* ; **var** *successful* : *boolean*) ;

deletes the record with key value *k* from the file. If no such record exists, then the operation is unsuccessful. The file window position always becomes undefined.

The *replacement* operator

procedure *replace (*v* : *elementtype* ; **var** *successful* : *boolean*) ;

replaces the record of the file with the same key value as *v* by the record value *v*. However, the operation will succeed only if there is currently a record in the file with the same key value as *v*. Again this operator leaves the file window position undefined.

The *write* operator

procedure **write* (*v* : *elementtype* ; **var** *successful* : *boolean*) ;

adds the record value *v* to the file in such a position that the key ordering of the records is maintained. The file window position becomes undefined. The write operation will be unsuccessful if a record with the same key value as *v* is already in the file.

Figure 8.4 shows the operations which may be applied to indexed sequential files opened in each of the three possible processing modes for indexed access. The full specification of the indexed abstraction is given below.

	Processing mode		
	Input	Output	Input–output
read	X		X
delete			X
replace			X
write		X	X

Figure 8.4   Permitted indexed access operations

```
class module *indexed ;
  class *input (closingmode : environment.closingmodes) ;
    procedure *read (k : keytype ; var v : elementtype ;
                         var successful : boolean) ;
  begin
    {open file as an input file}
    ***
    {close file}
  end ; {input}
  class *output (closingmode : environment.closingmodes) ;
    procedure *write (v : elementtype ; var successful : boolean) ;
    begin
    {open file as an output file}
    ***
    {close file}
  end ; {output}
  class *inputoutput (closingmode : environment.closingmodes) ;
    procedure *read (k : keytype ; var v : elementtype ;
                         var successful : boolean) ;
    procedure *delete (k : keytype ; var successful : boolean) ;
    procedure *replace (v : elementtype ; var successful : boolean) ;
```

```
procedure *write (v : elementtype ; var successful : boolean) ;
begin
    {open file as an inputoutput file}
    ***
    {close file}
    end ; {inputoutput}
begin
    ***
end {indexed}
```

8.2.3 Dynamic Access

When a file is first opened it may be processed using either sequential or indexed access operations. If sequential access is chosen, then a subsequent switch to indexed access is achieved simply by performing any indexed access operation. A switch from indexed access to sequential access occurs as the result of using any sequential access operation — processing then begins at the current file window position (provided it was defined by an immediately preceding indexed access *read* operation — this is the only indexed access operation which defines the file window position). Hence groups of successive records in an indexed sequential file may be accessed by reading the first record with an indexed access *read* operation and then reading each of the succeeding records by a sequential *read* operation, prior to performing other sequential access operations on those records — this is sometimes referred to as *selective–sequential processing*.

In practice dynamic access involves only input or input–output processing since the read operations which define the window position are not available for output processing. Therefore the dynamic access abstraction consists of two local data types each containing an appropriate combination of sequential access and indexed access operators.

```
class module *dynamic ;
    class *input (closingmode : environment.closingmodes) ;
        procedure *seqread (var v : elementtype ; var eof : boolean) ;
        procedure *keyread (k : keytype ; var v : elementtype ;
                            var successful : boolean) ;
        begin
            {open file as an input file}
            ***
            {close file}
            end ; {input}
    class *inputoutput (closingmode : environment.closingmodes) ;
        procedure *seqread (var v : elementtype ; var eof : boolean) ;
```

```
procedure *seqwrite (v : elementtype ; var error . boolean) ;
procedure *seqreplace (v : elementtype ; var error : boolean) ;
procedure *seqdelete ;
procedure *keyread (k : keytype ; var v : elementtype ;
                            var successful : boolean) ;
procedure *keydelete (k : keytype ; var successful : boolean) ;
procedure *keyreplace (v : elementtype ; var successful : boolean) ;
procedure *keywrite (v : elementtype ; var successful : boolean) ;
begin
   {open file as an inputoutput file}
   ***
   {close file}
end ; {inputoutput}
begin
   ***
end {dynamic}
```

Given

```
instance F : codefile.dynamic.input (environment.simple) ;
var R : datatype ;
    t : integer ;
    ok, eof : boolean ;
```

the following sequence of operations will read and process a sequence of records beginning with the record containing the key value *t* :

```
begin
   F.keyread (t, R, ok) ;
   if not ok
   then error ('record not in file')
   else repeat
           process (R) ;
           F.seqread (R, eof) ;
       until eof
end
```

8.3   CASE STUDY: INDEXED SEQUENTIAL MASTER FILE INITIALIZATION

The indexed sequential master file to be used in the Model Savings Bank system must initially be created by copying the records of the sequential master file held on magnetic tape to the disk file, as shown in Figure 8.5.

To illustrate sequential access to an indexed sequential file more fully, we shall also incorporate in the master file initialization a process which prints out the contents of the file (identified as *PRO-GRAM8* in the first section of this chapter). The magnetic tape master file will be held on tape unit 1, the disk file on disk drive 1, and the listing will be printed on line printer unit 1. The disk file will consist of buckets of the standard sector size, i.e., *environment.sectorsize*.

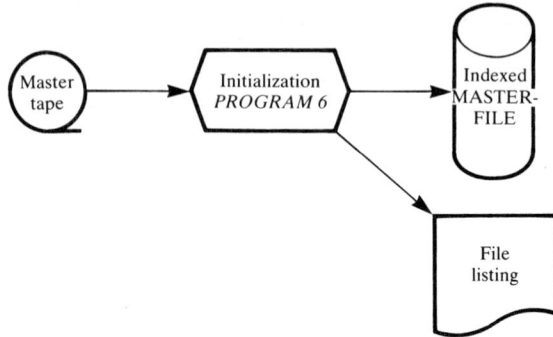

Figure 8.5 Initialization of indexed sequential master file

The master file records are of the type *masterrecord* defined previously and the sequential master file is declared as

class *seqmasterfile* = *sequentialfile* **in library**
(**where type** *itemtype* = *masterrecord*) ;
instance *MTfile* : *seqmasterfile* (*environment.MT1*,
'*MASTER-FILE*', *false*,
environment.blocksize, 2) ;

The indexed sequential master disk file is declared as

class *ISmasterfile* = *indexedsequentialfile* **in library**
(**where type** *elementtype* = *masterrecord* ;
keytype = *accountnumber* ;
procedure *getkey* = *getacnumber* ;
function *samekey* = *sameacnumber* ;
function *keyorder* =
acnumbersinorder) ;
instance *ISfile* : *ISmasterfile* (*environment.DA1*,
'*MASTER-FILE*', *true*,
environment.sectorsize, 2) ;

where the operators *getacnumber*, *sameacnumber*, and *acnumbersinorder* must be declared in the initialization program. They take the form

```
procedure getacnumber (m : masterrecord ; var k : accountnumber) ,
   begin k := m.key end ;
function sameacnumber (k1, k2 : accountnumber) : boolean ;
   begin sameacnumber := environment.equals (k1, k2) end ;
function acnumbersinorder (k1, k2 : accountnumber) : boolean ;
   begin
      acnumbersinorder := environment.lessthan (k1, k2)
   end ;
```

The main program then calls procedures *createISfile* and *listISfile*. The master disk file will be accessed sequentially by both procedures (hence it uses two buffers), and is processed as an output file by *createISfile* and as an input file by *listISfile*. Hence *createISfile* declares a local instance

> **instance** *newmaster* : *ISfile.sequential.output* (*environment.simple*, 60) ;

(The second parameter value indicates that, when the file is being written, the buckets of the file are to be filled to 60% of their maximum record capacity, thus leaving space for later insertions into the file.) *listISfile* declares a local instance

> **instance** *newmaster* : *ISfile.sequential.input* (*environment.locked*) ;

createISfile reads the tape file records and writes each one to the indexed sequential file by means of calls of

> *newmaster.write* (*nextrecord, invalidkey*)

The parameter *invalidkey* is set to *true* by *newmaster.write* if and only if the key value of *nextrecord* is not greater than the key of the previous record written to the file. This invalid key condition should not arise in this program since the tape file records are themselves organized in ascending key sequence.

listISfile uses the sequential input operator *newmaster.read* to obtain, in key sequence, the records whose details are to be listed on the printer file.

Listing 16 gives the complete implementation of the file initialization program. The output listing produced will be the same as that produced in Chapter 5 by *PROGRAM1* (the sequential file initialization program) and contained in Listing 3.

```
                    LISTING 16 : PROGRAM6

program PROGRAM6 {initialize indexed sequential master file} ;

   class module environment in library ;

   type accountnumber = environment.string ;
```

```
          money = environment.numeric ;
          masterrecord = record
                          key : accountnumber ;
                          clientidentity : environment.string ;
                          currentbalance, minimumbalance : money
                        end ;

   class seqmasterfile = sequentialfile in library
                          (where type itemtype = masterrecord) ;

   procedure getacnumber (m : masterrecord ; var k : accountnumber) ;
      begin k := m.key end ;

   function sameacnumber (k1, k2 : acccountnumber) : boolean ;
      begin sameacnumber := environment.equals (k1, k2) end ;

   function acnumbersinorder (k1, k2 : accountnumber) : boolean ;
      begin acnumbersinorder := environment.lessthan (k1, k2) end ;

   class ISmasterfile = indexedsequentialfile in library
                          (where type elementtype = masterrecord ;
                                      keytype = accountnumber ;
                              procedure getkey = getacnumber ;
                              function samekey = sameacnumber ;
                              function keyorder = acnumbersinorder) ;

   class outputtextfile in library ;

   instance MTfile  : seqmasterfile (environment.MT1, 'MASTER-FILE',
                                      false, environment.blocksize, 2) ;

   instance ISfile : ISmasterfile (environment.DA1, 'MASTER-FILE', true,
                                    environment.sectorsize, 2) ;

   procedure createISfile ;

      instance oldmaster : MTfile.input (environment.locked) ;
      instance newmaster  : ISfile.sequential.output
                                            (environment.simple, 60) ;

      var nextrecord : masterrecord ;
         eof, invalidkey : boolean ;

      procedure error (message : packed array [m..n : integer] of char) ;
         begin
            { print out some diagnostic information }
         end ;

      begin
         oldmaster.read (nextrecord, eof) ;
         while not eof do
         begin
            newmaster.write (nextrecord, invalidkey) ;
            if invalidkey then error ('key sequence error') ;
            oldmaster.read (nextrecord, eof)
         end
      end {createISfile} ;

   procedure listISfile ;

      instance printfile : outputtextfile (environment.LP1, 2) ;
      instance newmaster : ISfile.sequential.input (environment.locked) ;

      var newrecord : masterrecord ;
         endofnewmaster : boolean ;
         outputline : environment.string ;

      begin
         with environment do
         begin
            setall (outputline, environment.printerwidth, ' ') ;
```

```
newmaster.read (newrecord, endofnewmaster) ;
while not endofnewmaster do
   with newrecord do
   begin
      putstring (outputline, key, 6, 8) ;
      putstring (outputline, clientidentity, 19, 30) ;
      putnumeric (outputline, currentbalance, 54, 8, 2) ;
      putnumeric (outputline, minimumbalance, 67, 8, 2) ;
      printfile.writeline (outputline) ;
      newmaster.read (newrecord, endofnewmaster)
   end
end
end {listISfile} ;

begin
   createISfile ;
   listISfile
end.
```

8.4 CASE STUDY: INDEXED SEQUENTIAL MASTER FILE UPDATE

The indexed sequential master file update program *PROGRAM7* uses the file TRANSACTIONS of validated but unsorted transactions to update the file MASTER-FILE initialized by the previous case study program. Any errors detected in the update process will be reported on a line printer (Figure 8.6).

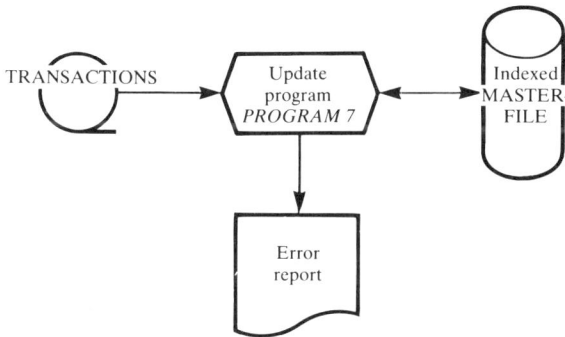

Figure 8.6   Indexed sequential master file update

The design of this file update program is based upon the direct-access file update algorithm developed in Section 4.3, except that we now use the indexed sequential file abstraction. It is assumed that the master file is held on disk drive 1, the unsorted transactions file on tape unit 1, and the error report on line printer 1.

The transactions file has the same form as in the previous case study programs, viz.,

> **class** *transfile* = *sequentialfile* **in library**
> (**where type** *itemtype* = *transaction*) ;
> **instance** *TF* : *transfile* (*environment.MT1*, *'TRANSACTIONS'*,
> *false*, *environment.blocksize*, 2) ;

The indexed sequential file *ISfile* is declared exactly as in the initialization program except that for indexed access we use only a single buffer. It uses the same *getacnumber*, *sameacnumber*, and *acnumbersinorder* operators as *PROGRAM6* (these are now assumed to have been made available in the library since they will be required by all programs accessing the indexed sequential version of the master file).

The file update procedure then follows closely the form of the program in Figure 4.3. Since the disk file is to be accessed randomly an input–output processing instance of the master file is declared local to the update procedure, viz.,

> **instance** *master* : *ISfile.indexed.inputoutput* (*environment.locked*) ;

getinitialstatus calls

> *master.read* (*currentacnumber*, *newrecord*, *originallyinfile*)

to determine whether a given account number has an associated record in the file. If it has, then the record is assigned to *newrecord* and *originallyinfile* is assigned *true*, otherwise *false* is assigned to *originallyinfile*. *recordfinalstatus* attempts to delete, replace, and write records using the appropriate indexed access operators of *master*. These should always function correctly in this program and so it does not bother to inspect the values assigned to the variable parameter *ok*. As the updating routine *applytransactiontomasterrecord* is exactly as for the sequential file update program, we assume that it is available also in the library. Listing 17 gives the complete update program.

LISTING 17 : PROGRAM7

```
program PROGRAM7 {indexed sequential master file update} ;

    class module environment in library ;

    const maxsavings = 20000 ;

    type   accountnumber = environment.string ;
           transtype = (addition, deletion, credit, debit) ;
           money = environment.numeric ;
           transaction = record
```

```
                             date : environment.string ;
                             key : accountnumber ;
                             kind : transtype ;
                             amount : money ;
                             clientidentity : environment.string ;
                             other : environment.string
                          end ;
      masterrecord = record
                          key : accountnumber ;
                          clientidentity : environment.string ;
                          currentbalance, minimumbalance : money
                       end ;

procedure getacnumber in library ;

function sameacnumber in library ;

function acnumbersinorder in library ;

class ISmasterfile = indexedsequentialfile in library
                        (where type elementtype = masterrecord ;
                               keytype = accountnumber ;
                               procedure getkey = getacnumber ;
                               function samekey = sameacnumber ;
                               function keyorder = acnumbersinorder) ;

class transfile = sequentialfile in library
                     (where type itemtype = transaction) ;

class outputtextfile in library ;

instance ISfile : ISmasterfile (environment.DA1, 'MASTER-FILE', false,
                                environment.sectorsize, 1) ;

instance TF : transfile (environment.MT1, 'TRANSACTIONS', false,
                         environment.blocksize, 2) ;

instance errorreport : outputtextfile (environment.LP1, 2)


procedure update ;

   instance master : ISfile.indexed.inputoutput (environment.locked) ;
   instance transfile : TF.input (environment.locked) ;

   var sentinelacnumber, transacnumber,
         currentacnumber : accountnumber ;
      transrecord : transaction ;
      newrecord : masterrecord ;
      originallyinfile, infile : boolean ;
      savingslimit : money ;

   procedure getnexttransaction (var acnumber : accountnumber) ;
      var endoftransactions : boolean ;
      begin
         transfile.read (transrecord, endoftransactions) ;
         if endoftransactions
         then acnumber := sentinelacnumber
         else acnumber := transrecord.key
      end ;

   procedure choosenextkeytoprocess (var acnumber : accountnumber) ;
      begin
         acnumber := transacnumber
      end ;

   procedure getinitialstatus ;
      begin
         master.read (currentacnumber, newrecord, originallyinfile) ;
         infile := originallyinfile
      end ;
```

```
procedure applytransactiontomasterrecord in library ;

procedure recordfinalstatus ;
    var ok : boolean ;
    begin
        if infile
        then if originallyinfile
                then master.replace (newrecord, ok)
                else master.write (newrecord, ok)
            else if originallyinfile
                then master.delete (currentacnumber, ok)
    end ;

begin { update }
    with environment do
    begin
        construct (sentinelacnumber, 'XXXXXXXX') ;
        zeroize (savingslimit, 7, 2) ;
        integertonumeric (maxsavings, savingslimit) ;
        getnexttransaction (transacnumber) ;
        choosenextkeytoprocess (currentacnumber) ;
        while not equals (currentacnumber, sentinelacnumber) do
        begin {process one item number}
            getinitialstatus ;
            while equals (currentacnumber, transacnumber) do
            begin {process one transaction}
                applytransactiontomasterrecord ;
                getnexttransaction (transacnumber)
            end ;
            recordfinalstatus ;
            choosenextkeytoprocess (currentacnumber)
        end
    end
end ; { update }

begin
    update ;
end.
```

Given the unsorted transactions file validated previously (see Listing 13, Chapter 6) and assuming that the indexed sequential file was in the same initial state as the old sequential master file of Listing 3, the error report produced by an execution of this update program will contain the same error diagnostics as the sequential update error report of Listing 7, except that the invalid transactions will be listed not in account number order but rather in the order in which they appeared in the original transactions batch. The state of the records of the updated indexed sequential master file will be the same as that of the new master sequential file shown in Listing 6.

8.5   PHYSICAL FILE STRUCTURE

Figure 8.7 shows how the storage used by an indexed sequential file which occupies N cylinders of a disk pack might be organized. The storage area is divided into *index areas*, *prime data areas*, and *overflow data areas*.

Track	Cylinder 1	2	3			N−1	N
1	Master index cylinder index	Cylinder index	Cylinder index				
2 3 4 5 6 7 8 9	Prime data area	Prime data area	Prime data area			Global overflow area	Global overflow area
10	Overflow area	Overflow area	Overflow area				

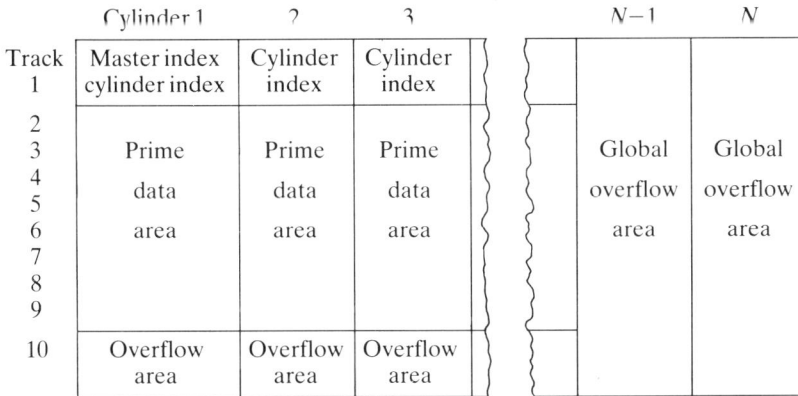

Figure 8.7 Physical organization of an indexed sequential file

At the start of the first cylinder there is a master index (see Section 3.4.3) which, for each cylinder containing prime data areas, gives the highest record key on the cylinder together with the address of the index for that cylinder. Each cylinder index will contain entries giving the highest record key in each prime data track together, possibly, with the address of the associated track index.

The prime data areas contain the file records organized in ascending key sequence — this sequencing may be determined by the order in which the records are physically stored, or by the addresses held in the entries within the indexes. Space is left in each bucket of these areas to allow new records to be added as the file is updated. An existing record is deleted by either setting a special indicator bit in the record, or by omitting the record from the bucket and closing the resulting gap. As new records are added to the file they are inserted into the appropriate bucket so as to maintain the key ordering of the records.

In spite of any deletions which have occurred it may happen that a bucket becomes full and there is no room for an insertion. Two different strategies are employed in such cases and involve the use of overflow areas. *ISAM* (*indexed sequential access method*) involves reorganizing the file structure and *VSAM* (*virtual storage access method*) involves reorganizing the indexes.

With ISAM any record which cannot be located in its proper (home) bucket is written to an overflow bucket and a pointer to this bucket is placed in the home bucket (Figure 8.8 illustrates the storage of a record with key 164 when its home bucket is full).

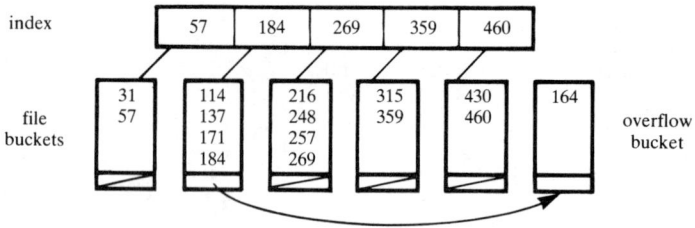

Figure 8.8   ISAM overflow handling

Any other buckets which overflow also place records in this same overflow bucket. When this overflow bucket itself becomes full a second overflow bucket is used and chained to the previous one. Provision for overflow buckets is usually made at the end of each cylinder — overflowed records can thus be retrieved without further disk head movement. These cylinder overflow areas might themselves fill up and so some global overflow areas are provided in the last few cylinders of the file. However, access to records in these areas will involve additional head movement. Once lengthy overflow chains have been created retrieval will slow down and hence, from time to time, it may be necessary to run a file reorganization program which empties the overflow areas by redistributing the records among the prime data areas and rewrites all the indexes.

The ISAM method does not involve changing the indexes of the file when an overflow occurs. VSAM operates by splitting the records of an overflowed bucket into two halves, placing the half which does not contain the new record key into a new bucket, and creating a new index entry for that new bucket. Figure 8.9 shows the result of adding the record with key 164 to the same file as was updated by ISAM in Figure 8.8.

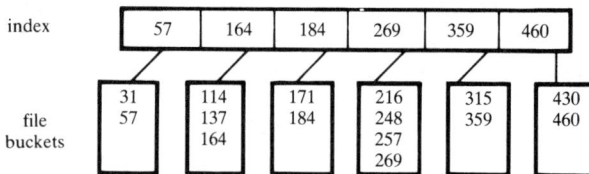

Figure 8.9   VSAM overflow handling

For multi-level indexes this creation of a new index entry may cause the bucket containing the index concerned to overflow, in which case the same splitting operation is applied to the index bucket and hence a new index entry is created at the next higher level of indexing. The VSAM method leads to more efficient record retrieval since all buckets are in prime data areas and hence directly locatable via an index — this method is therefore to be preferred for large files.

8.6 AN IMPLEMENTATION OF INDEXED SEQUENTIAL FILES

As in the chapter on sequential files we again present a high-level description of a possible implementation of the indexed sequential file abstraction. We restrict our description to that of files in which the index is held in the first bucket and is a single-level index containing the key of the highest record in each of the succeeding buckets of the file (Figure 8.10). We shall ignore the problems of bucket overflow. The extension to more sophisticated index structures and overflow handling is not difficult, but is left as an exercise.

Figure 8.10   Indexed file structure

8.6.1 The Block Control Abstraction

The file block control abstraction developed in Chapter 5 is used again here but is augmented with two operators to manipulate the file index:

    function **number* (*key* : *indexkeytype*) : *integer*

which returns the number of the bucket which should contain the record with the given key value, and

    procedure **writeindexentry* (*blocknumber* : *integer* ; *maxkey* : *indextype*)

which creates an index entry designating *maxkey* as the greatest key value in bucket *blocknumber*.

This block control abstraction, which we name *isfblockcontrol*, will require the type of the record keys (*indextype*) and a key ordering operator (*indexkeyorder*, for searching the index) to be supplied as well as the type *recordtype* of the file records. Its full specification is

```
class isfblockcontrol (device : environment.directdevices ;
                       id : packed array [m..n : integer] of char ;
                       newfile : boolean ;
                       bucketsize : environment.blockrange ;
                       numberofbuffers : environment.bufferrange) ;
{ assumes type recordtype with := defined                              }
{          type indextype with := defined                              }
{          function indexkeyorder (k1, k2 : indextype) : boolean       }
instance interface : environment.fileinterface
                     (device, id, newfile,
                      bucketsize, numberofbuffers) ;
var *length : integer ;
procedure *get ( var blocknumber : integer ; sequential : boolean ;
                 var found : boolean) ;
procedure *put (blocknumber : integer) ;
procedure *getrecord (j : integer ; var v : recordtype) ;
procedure *replacerecord (j : integer ; v : recordtype) ;
procedure *deleterecord (j : integer) ;
procedure *putrecord (j : integer ; v : recordtype) ;
procedure *clear ;
function *number (key : indextype) : integer ;
procedure *writeindexentry (blocknumber : integer ;
                            maxkey : indextype) ;
begin
***
end {isfblockcontrol} ;
```

8.6.2 Implementation Details

The *indexedsequentialfile* class will make use of an instance, *block*, of the *isfblockcontrol* class to provide access to the file blocks required during file processing using both sequential and indexed access — when retrieved from the library *isfblockcontrol* must be supplied with the file record and key types as well as the key ordering operator, viz.,

```
class isfblockcontrol in library
    (where type recordtype = elementtype ;
               indextype = keytype ;
           function indexkeyorder = keyorder) ;
instance block : isfblockcontrol (device, identity, newfile,
                                  bucketsize, numberofbuffers) ;
```

Again local operators are provided to handle logical file opening and closing, and error reporting. The *indexedsequentialfile* class initialization checks that the file is a disk file and determines the blocking factor for the file records.

We will not describe the sequential access operations since they are almost identical with those for sequential organization files except that the first records of the file are located in bucket 2 and the *write* operator for a newly created file being processed as an output file must fill buckets to the required occupancy and also create index entries. Likewise the dynamic access operators are just a combination of the various sequential and indexed access operators.

For indexed access the input, output, and input–output classes each provides a subset of the *read*, *write*, *replace*, and *delete* operations. These operators use a local procedure *obtain* which, given a bucket number, ensures that the block control instance obtains the required bucket from the file. If this bucket is different from the previous bucket accessed and that previous bucket was changed in any way, then that bucket is first written back to the file. Those operators which are given a record value as parameter extract the key value from the record by means of the *getkey* procedure. Another local procedure *findrecord* performs a binary search of the records in the current bucket to locate the record with a given key — this procedure uses the *samekey* and *keyorder* operators to perform key comparisons. Individual records in a bucket are processed using the *getrecord*, *putrecord*, *deleterecord*, and *replacerecord* operators of the block control instance. The *write* operator rejects any attempts to insert a record into an already full bucket. Listing 18 gives the implementation of the indexed access operations for an indexed sequential file.

```
         LISTING 18  :   INDEXED SEQUENTIAL FILE IMPLEMENTATION


class indexedsequentialfile
        (device : environment.directdevices ;
         identity : packed array [m..n : integer] of char ;
         newfile : boolean ;
         bucketsize : environment.blockrange ;
         numberofbuffers : environment.bufferrange) ;

   { assumes type elementtype with := defined                     }
   {          type keytype      with := defined                     }
   {          procedure getkey (v : elementtype ; var k : keytype)  }
   {          function samekey (k1, k2 : keytype) : boolean          }
   {          function keyorder (k1, k2 : keytype) : boolean         }

   class isfblockcontrol in library
      (where type recordtype = elementtype ;
             indextype = keytype ;
             function indexkeyorder = keyorder) ;

   instance block : isfblockcontrol (device, identity, newfile,
                            bucketsize, numberofbuffers) ;
```

```
type filestatus = (opened, closed, locked) ;

var status : filestatus ;
    blockingfactor : integer ;

procedure error (message : packed array [m..n : integer] of char) ;
   begin
      writeln (identity, ' - ', message) ;
      halt
   end { error } ;

procedure openfile ;
   begin
      case status of
      opened : error ('file already in use') ;
      closed : status := opened ;
      locked : error ('file closed in lock mode')
      end
   end {openfile} ;

procedure closefile (closingmode : environment.closingmodes) ;
   begin
      case closingmode of
      environment.simple   : status := closed ;
      environment.locked   : status := locked ;
      environment.norewind : status := closed
      end
   end {closefile} ;

class module *sequential ; ... ;
class module *dynamic ; ... ;

class module *indexed ;

   var currentblock : integer ;
       blockchanged : boolean ;

   procedure open ;
      begin
         openfile ;
         block.clear ; blockchanged := false ; currentblock := 0
      end {open} ;

   procedure close (closingmode : environment.closingmodes) ;
      begin
         if blockchanged then block.put (currentblock) ;
         closefile (closingmode)
      end {close} ;

   procedure obtain (blocknumber : integer ; var exists : boolean) ;
      begin
         if currentblock <> blocknumber
         then begin
                 if blockchanged then block.put (currentblock) ;
                 block.get (blocknumber, false, exists) ;
                 blockchanged := false ;
                 if exists
                 then currentblock := blocknumber
                 else currentblock := 0
              end
         else exists := true
      end ; {obtain}

   procedure findrecord (key : keytype ; var found : boolean ;
                         var position : integer) ;
      var first, last, mid : integer ;
          k : keytype ;
          v : elementtype ;
      begin
         first := 1 ; last := block.length ; found := false ;
```

```
                while not found and (first <= last) do
                begin
                  mid := (first + last) div 2 ;
                  block.getrecord (mid, v) ;
                  getkey (v, k) ;
                  if samekey (k, key)
                  then found := true
                  else if keyorder (key, k)
                       then last := mid - 1
                       else first := mid + 1
              end ;
              if found then position := mid else position := first
          end ; {findrecord}

      procedure readelement (k : keytype ; var v : elementtype ;
                             var successful : boolean) ;
         var position : integer ;
         begin
            obtain (block.number (k), successful) ;
            if successful
            then begin
                    findrecord (k, successful, position) ;
                    if successful then block.getrecord (position, v)
                 end
         end ; {readelement}

      procedure writeelement (v : elementtype ;
                              var successful : boolean) ;
         var k : keytype ; found, full : boolean ; position : integer ;
         begin
            getkey (v, k) ; obtain (block.number (k), successful) ;
            if successful
            then begin
                    findrecord (k, found, position) ;
                    full := (block.length = blockingfactor) ;
                    if found
                    then successful := false
                    else if full
                         then error ('bucket overflow') ;
                         else begin
                                 block.putrecord (position, v) ;
                                 successful := true ;
                                 blockchanged := true
                              end
                 end
         end ; {writeelement}

      procedure deleteelement (k : keytype ; var successful : boolean) ;
         var position : integer ;
         begin
            obtain (block.number (k), successful) ;
            if successful
            then begin
                    findrecord (k, successful, position) ;
                    if successful
                    then begin
                            block.deleterecord (position, v) ;
                            blockchanged := true
                         end
                 end
         end ; {deleteelement}

      procedure replaceelement (v : elementtype ;
                                var successful : boolean) ;
         var k : keytype ; position : integer ;
         begin
            getkey (v, k) ;
            obtain (block.number (k), successful) ;
            if successful
            then begin
                    findrecord (k, successful, position) ;
```

```
                    if successful
                    then begin
                            block.replacerecord (position, v) ;
                            blockchanged := true
                         end
             end
    end ; {replaceelement}

  class *input (closingmode : environment.closingmodes) ;
     procedure *read = readelement ;
     begin
        open ;
        *** ;
        close (closingmode)
     end ; {input}

  class *output (closingmode : environment.closingmodes) ;
     procedure *write = writeelement ;
     begin
        open ;
        *** ;
        close (closingmode)
     end ; {output}

  class *inputoutput (closingmode : environment.closingmodes) ;
     procedure *read = readelement ;
     procedure *delete = deleteelement ;
     procedure *replace = replaceelement ;
     procedure *write = writeelement ;
     begin
        open ;
        *** ;
        close (closingmode)
     end ; {inputoutput}


  begin
     ***
  end ; {indexed}
begin
  if not (device in environment.directaccessdevices)
  then error ('not a disc file')
  else begin
          status := closed ;
          blockingfactor := (blocksize-1) div size (elementtype)
          ***
       end
end {indexedsequentialfile}
```

To avoid the overhead of calling the *readelement*, *writeelement*, *deleteelement*, and *replaceelement* procedures from within the various *read*, *write*, *delete*, and *replace* operators of the processing classes we have used the same procedure renaming convention, e.g.,

procedure *read = readelement* ;

as is used for procedure renaming within library retrieval specifications.

It was mentioned previously that the sequential access output class is responsible for writing the index entries and initially filling buckets. This class takes the form

```
class *output (closingmode ; environment closingmodes ;
              bucketoccupancy : environment.percentage) ;
   var currentblock, loadingfactor : integer ;
       lastkey : keytype ;
   procedure recordlastkey (var v : elementtype) ;
      begin getkey (v, lastkey) end ;
   procedure *write (v : elementtype ; var error : boolean) ;
      begin
         with block do
         begin
            if length = loadingfactor
            then begin
                    writeindexentry (currentblock, lastkey) ;
                    put (currentblock) ;
                    currentblock := currentblock + 1 ;
                    clear
                 end ;
            putrecord (length + 1, v) ; recordlastkey (v)
         end
      end {write} ;
   begin
      openfile;
      block.clear ; currentblock := 2 ;
      loadingfactor := round (blockingfactor * bucketoccupancy / 100) ;
      *** ;
      with block do
      if length > 0
      then begin
              writeindexentry (currentblock, lastkey) ;
              put (currentblock)
           end ;
      closefile (closingmode)
   end {output};
```

The implementation of the block control abstraction must be extended to handle the file index and its associated operators. The approach to obtaining the index from the first bucket and writing it back is the same as that employed for mapping records onto blocks (Section 5.6). The first memory unit of bucket 1 contains the number

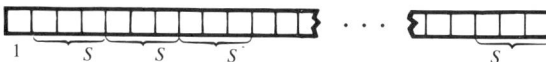

$S = size\ (indextype)$

Figure 8.11   Structure of index bucket

of entries in the index, and the remainder of the first bucket is organized as groups of *S* memory units, where S is the storage size required for a key value (Figure 8.11).

Declaring

```
const maxdatabuckets = ... ;
var   index : array [2..maxdatabuckets] of indextype ;
      indexlength, keylength : integer ;
```

the initialization of the *isfblockcontrol* class involves reading the index from bucket 1, and the finalization writes back the index. The mapping between groups of memory units and index values again involves the use of a Pascal variant record structure as used in Chapter 5, i.e., by declaring

```
type twotypes = (aninteger, akey) ;
var keydummy = record
                 case twotypes of
                 aninteger : (word : array [1..size(indextype)]
                                     of integer) ;
                 akey       : (keyvalue : indextype)
               end
```

The enhancements which have to be made to the *blockcontrol* implementation of Section 5.6 to support the required additional indexed sequential file blockcontrol facilities are given below.

```
class isfblockcontrol (...) ;
   { assumes type recordtype with := defined                         }
   {          type indextype with := defined                         }
   {          function indexkeyorder (k1, k2 : indextype) : boolean  }
   { operators *length, *get, *put, *getrecord, *replacerecord       }
   {          *deleterecord, *putrecord, *clear as before            }
   const maxdatabuckets = ... ;
   var index : array [2..maxdatabuckets] of indextype ;
       indexlength, keylength : integer ;
   type twotypes = (aninteger, akey) ;
   var keydummy = record
                    case twotypes of
                    aninteger : (word : array [1..size(indextype)]
                                        of integer) ;
                    akey       : (keyvalue : indextype)
                  end ;
   procedure readindex ;
      var i, j, next : integer ;
          found : boolean ;
      begin
          interface.getblock (1, block, found) ;
          if found then indexlength := block [1] else indexlength := 0 ;
```

```
      next := 1 ;
      for ı := 1 to indexlength do
      begin {obtain next entry}
        for j := 1 to keylength do keydummy.word [j] := block [next+j] ;
        index [i+1] := keydummy.keyvalue ;
        next := next + keylength
      end
    end {readindex} ;
  procedure writeindex ;
    var i, j, next : integer ;
    begin
      block [1] := indexlength ;
      next := 1 ;
      for i := 1 to indexlength do
      begin {add next entry]
        keydummy.keyvalue := index [i+1] ;
        for j := 1 to keylength do
          block [next+j] := keydummy.word [j] ;
        next := next + keylength
      end ;
      interface.putblock (1, block)
    end {writeindex} ;
  function *number (key : indextype) : integer ;
    var first, last, mid : integer ;
    begin
      first := 2 ; last := indexlength ;
      while first <= last do
      begin
        mid := (first + last) div 2 ;
        if indexkeyorder (index[mid], key)
        then first := mid + 1
        else last := mid - 1
      end ;
      number := first
    end {number} ;
  procedure *writeindexentry (blocknumber : integer ;
                              maxkey : indextype) ;
    begin index [blocknumber] := maxkey end ;
  begin
    recordlength := size (recordtype) ;
    keylength := size (indextype) ;
    if not newfile then readindex ;
    *** ;
    writeindex
  end {isfblockcontrol} ;
```

EXERCISES

1. For what types of application would an indexed sequential file be used?

2. Amend the design of the update program so that it takes the unvalidated trans-
    actions file and applies only valid transactions to the indexed sequential master
    file. This should make use of the validation routines constructed for the data vali-
    dation program *PROGRAM2* in Chapter 6. The transactions file is to be held on
    disk drive 4, the master file on disk drive 1. Details of invalid transactions and the
    summary report should be output to line printer 1.

3. Implement the sequential access operations for the *indexedsequentialfile* class.

4. Extend the implementation of the random access operators of *indexedsequen-
    tialfile*, and the operations provided by the *isfblockcontrol* class, to
    (i) provide a two-level index structure;
    (ii) handle overflow from buckets using either the ISAM or VSAM approach.

9 PROCESSING RANDOM ORGANIZATION FILES

9.1 INTRODUCTION

We now return to the problem discussed in the introduction to Chapter 8 of obtaining rapid access to the records in a file so that, for instance, a teller in a branch of our savings bank, or a customer at an automatic teller terminal, may have an account record made available to him almost instantaneously. Figure 9.1 illustrates a possible on-line system to support such a facility. Details of transactions are input at a number of video/keyboard terminals which are connected to a central machine (possibly through a concentrator device). The master file is a direct-access file and the file update program is required to validate each incoming transaction before using it in a file enquiry or file update operation (or the transactions may be validated locally at any VDU if it is an intelligent terminal). Indeed the transactions may be generated interactively by means of a conversation

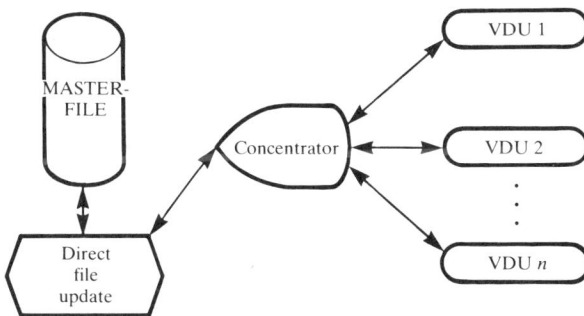

Figure 9.1   On-line system

between the update program and the terminal operator. In such an on-line system the file update program might have to be capable of handling communication with a number of users simultaneously, and the file access speed would have to be sufficiently fast to avoid terminal users having to wait long periods (i.e., more than a few seconds) for a response.

Although organizing the master file records as an indexed sequential file provides direct access to a file record given its key value, even faster record access may be achieved by organizing the file records as a random organization file where the records are positioned in the file using some addressing algorithm. Provided a simple yet effective algorithm is chosen (for a discussion of effectiveness see the next section) record access will generally be faster than for indexed access since the latter may involve a number of searches through a multi-level index before a record position can be located.

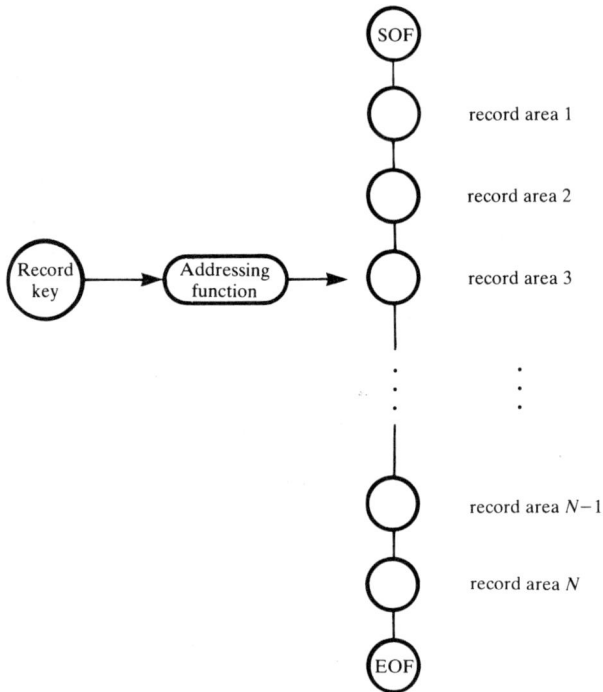

Figure 9.2   Random organization file structure

Random organization files were introduced in Chapter 3. Such files are always stored on a direct-access medium. Since the layout and retrieval of records are based upon the use of an addressing algorithm which calculates the position of a record in a file from its key field value, random files are used in real-time applications where access speed is of crucial importance.

The logical structure of a random organization file is an ordered sequence of record areas, each of which is capable of holding one record. Each record area in the sequence is identified by a *relative record number*, on the basis of which records are stored and retrieved. If there are N record areas in the file then each record area is distinguished by a unique integer in the range $1..N$, as illustrated in Figure 9.2.

9.2 ADDRESSING ALGORITHMS

The choice of addressing algorithm used to organize records in a random organization file depends upon the nature of the key field values. The addressing algorithm is a function which maps a value of the record key type onto a relative record number, i.e., if there are N record areas in the file then we have

$$addressing function : keytype \rightarrow 1..N$$

Once the relative record number has been established for a given key value the physical address of the record area concerned can be calculated quite simply, provided the record areas form a contiguous storage area on the physical file.

Many different functions are employed in practice — we now give a few examples:

(a) *self-addressing* or *self-indexing* — the key value itself defines the relative record number, e.g., in our savings bank system the first seven digits of each account number are unique (since the final digit is merely an additional check digit) and so a file of 10 million record areas could be used to hold the account records. The record for account number 2028277X would then be stored in record area 2028277 of the file. This is an ideal method for a very dense set of key values but also means that there may be many unused record areas in the file due to unallocated account numbers. Files organized in this way are often known as *self-indexed files*.

The advantage of this particular addressing function is its simplicity and efficiency when appropriately applied. The major drawback is that, unless the vast majority of possible key values are

actually assigned, large numbers of record areas will remain unoccupied. It relies upon a key range which is in unbroken sequence. Provided that our savings bank has close to 10 000 customers in each
branch, 100 branches in each area, and ten areas in all, then self-indexing is an ideal method of organizing the records. However, the bank
does not have that many branches in each area and so large ranges of
possible account numbers will not be used in practice.

In the case where the actual key values form a sparse set of the
possible key values, i.e., only a small proportion of the key type
values (the total number of possible values of a type is known as its
cardinality) is assigned as record keys, then the addressing function
chosen must map the key values onto some dense set with values
$1..N$, where the total number of record areas N in the file will be very
much less than the cardinality of the key type but greater than the
number of key values actually allocated.

In the following examples we assume a seven digit key value and
a file of 1000 record areas.

(b) *prime division* — the key value is divided by the nearest
prime number below the number of record areas in the file and the
remainder after this division plus 1 gives the relative record number,
e.g., for the above file

$$2028277 \rightarrow 2028277 \textbf{ mod } 997 + 1 \rightarrow 380$$

(c) *mid-square method* — the key value is squared and the
middle digits (which will be the most random) are used to obtain the
relative record number, e.g.,

$$2028277 \rightarrow 4113907588729 \rightarrow 075 + 1 \rightarrow 76$$

(d) *folding algorithm* — the key value is split into a number of
parts which are added together and the result mod 1000 (plus 1) is
taken as the relative record number, e.g., adding the first three,
middle three, and last three digits gives

$$2028277 \rightarrow (202 + 282 + 277) \textbf{ mod } 1000 + 1 \rightarrow 762$$

(e) *radix transformation* — the key value is considered to be
expressed in a radix greater than 10 (such as 11) and then converted
to radix 10, e.g.,

$$2028277 \rightarrow 3583378 \rightarrow \text{relative record number } 379$$

Of course, non-numeric key values must first be transformed to
corresponding numeric values before these algorithms may be
applied but such transformation is simple to perform on a computer.

Thus, if an algorithm other than self-indexing is used, one important consequence is that it is no longer possible to access the file records in key value sequence. In order to print out the customer balances in account number order in our savings system it will first be necessary to sort the master file records to produce a sequential version of that file. Hence the Model Savings Bank system of Figure 8.1 would have to be modified as shown in Figure 9.3 if a random organization master file was used.

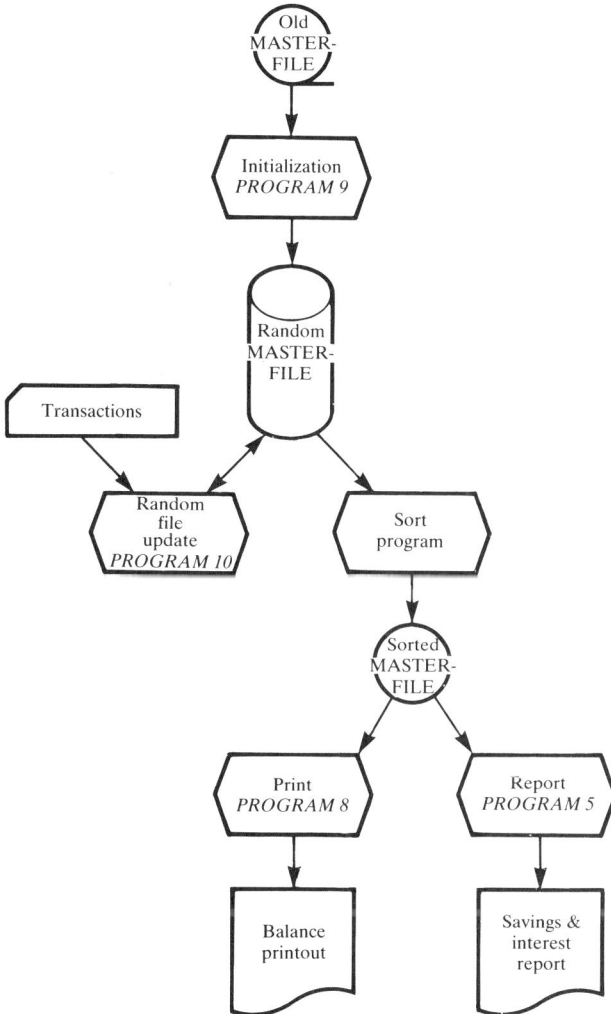

Figure 9.3   System based on random organization master file

The problem with the last four functions given above is that, because there are fewer record areas than possible key values, they produce synonyms or *collisions*, i.e., they map different key values on to the same relative record number. For instance, the prime division function used above maps keys with values 0, 997, 1994, 2991 all onto relative record area 1. This means that it may not be possible to store a record (or subsequently find it) at the preferred position generated by the addressing function. Where is the record stored in the event of its preferred position already being occupied?

Two possible strategies were outlined in Chapter 3. The first was to introduce a *re-hashing function* which enables possible alternative positions to be determined. Hence, when adding a record to a random file, it is placed either in the position specified by the application of the hashing function to its key value (its preferred position) or, if this position is occupied, at the first of the unoccupied alternative positions determined by applying the re-hashing function to its key. The simplest re-hashing function just involves placing the record in the first unoccupied position after its preferred position, where the file is considered to be cyclic in structure, i.e., the last record is followed by the first record — this is known as *linear re-hashing*. Other possible re-hashing methods are referenced in the Bibliography.

Another approach to overcoming the collision problem is to increase the size of each record area. In this case the record area is usually chosen to be equal in size to a file bucket. The addressing algorithm then generates a logical bucket number from a record key, and the bucket thus identified is the preferred bucket for the storage of the record (see Figure 3.17). Locating a record then involves the determination of its *logical bucket number* followed by a search of the records in the bucket concerned. Special overflow buckets are normally reserved for the storage of new records whose preferred buckets are full at the time of insertion into the file.

Addressing algorithms should be designed to minimize the amount of computation involved and also to minimize the number of collisions or bucket overflows that occur (as these result in longer access paths to the records concerned) — an effective algorithm is one which, by distributing the actual record keys evenly over the file locations, produces a low number of collisions or bucket overflows and can also be evaluated quickly. Thus the design of the addressing function for a random organization file is a critical factor in obtaining fast access to its records and requires careful study of the nature of the actual key values in order to produce an algorithm which gives the most even spread of preferred record positions. After designing an algorithm it is worthwhile carrying out a simulation of the behavior of the function and modifying it until satisfactory results are achieved.

9.3 SPECIFICATION OF A RANDOM FILE ABSTRACTION

We now, as in the case of sequential and indexed sequential files, develop an abstract data type specification for random organization files. We consider a random file to be a sequence of N buckets, each containing records of some type *elementtype* (the maximum number of records that can be accommodated in a bucket will depend upon the relative sizes of the buckets and the records) and identified by a logical bucket number in the range $1..N$. The preferred bucket for storage of a record will be determined by application of an addressing function to the record key value. Problems of bucket overflow will be handled automatically and remain transparent to the user.

Such an abstraction is characterized by the number of buckets in the file, the type *elementtype* of the records in the file, the type of the primary key for the records, say *keytype*, and an addressing function *bucketnumber* which transforms a record key value into a logical bucket number. This abstraction will also require the definition of an operator (*getkey*) which defines how the key of a record is extracted from the record itself, and a comparison operator (*samekey*) which determines whether two *keytype* values are equal.

An instance of this data type, which we name *randomfile*, will require the same set of physical parameters as was supplied for sequential and indexed sequential file instances (with the restriction that the file must be held on a direct-access device). Thus the heading of the random file abstraction is

```
class randomfile (device : environment.directdevices ;
                  identity : packed array [m..n : integer] of char ;
                  newfile : boolean ;
                  bucketsize : environment.blockrange ;
                  numberofbuffers : environment.bufferrange) ;
   { assumes const numberofbuckets (of type integer)        }
   {          type elementtype with := defined              }
   {          type keytype                                  }
   {          function bucketnumber (k : keytype) : integer }
   {          procedure getkey (v : elementtype ; var k : keytype) }
   {          function samekey (k1, k2 : keytype) : boolean }
begin
   { attach file to program }
   ***
   { release file from program }
end {randomfile}
```

Hence, assuming that we wish to use a random file, of say 47 buckets, containing records of the following type

```
type datatype = record
                number : integer ;
                restofdata : sometype
         end
```

where the field *number* is the key field uniquely identifying the records in a file, we must define operators

```
procedure getnumber (d : datatype ; var i : integer) ;
   begin i := d.number end ;
function samenumber (i1, i2 : integer) : boolean ;
   begin samenumber := (i1 = i2) end ;
```

and an addressing function which maps a record key of type *integer* onto a value in the logical bucket number range 1..47, e.g.,

```
function address (i : integer) : integer ;
   begin {use prime division by 47}
      address := i mod 47 + 1
   end {address} ;
```

in order to specify the required file type as

```
class randomfile in library
      (where const numberofbuckets = 47 ;
             type elementtype = datatype ;
                  keytype = integer ;
             function bucketnumber = address ;
             procedure getkey = getnumber ;
             function samekey = samenumber) ;
```

An instance of this type might be declared as

```
instance codefile : randomfile (environment.DA1, '1983-codes',
                    false, 1024, 1)
```

For new files (i.e., files whose actual *newfile* parameter values are *true*) the *randomfile* data type will automatically initialize such files to consist of as many home buckets as specified (by the value of *numberofbuckets*) each of the size specified by the *bucketsize* parameter.

Three sets of operations will be provided by the *randomfile* data type, corresponding to the three possible modes of file access. Hence, within the *randomfile* type, we again provide single instances of three local abstract data types providing the required access abstractions, viz.,

```
class randomfile (...) ;
   class module *sequential ; ... ;
```

```
class module *direct ; ... ;
class module *dynamic ; ... ;
begin
    ***
end {randomfile}
```

Each of these access abstractions provides a set of abstractions corresponding to the three possible processing modes and specifying associated operations available to a file being accessed in the mode concerned, e.g.,

```
class module *sequential ;
    class *input (...) ; ... specification of input operations ... ;
    class *output (...) ; ... specification of output operations ... ;
    class *inputoutput (...) ; ... specification of input–output operations ... ;
    begin
        ***
    end {sequential}
```

Hence, to perform processing of the above file *codefile* as a directly accessed input file, we would declare an instance

instance *L* : *codefile.direct.input* (...)

As for sequential and indexed files, the initialization of any such instance will open the file concerned ready for the required mode of processing, and the finalization will close the file in the closing mode defined by a parameter, viz.,

instance *L* : *codefile.direct.input* (*environment.locked*)

9.3.1 Sequential Access

Since a random organization file may be viewed as a sequence of consecutively numbered buckets, its sequential access operations are the same as for sequential files as described in Chapter 5 with two minor exceptions. These are that the *write* operator checks that the transformed bucket number of the key of a record being written to a file is appropriate for the bucket into which an attempt is being made to write the record, and the *replace* operator must check that the bucket number defined by the key value of the new record value being written to the file is the same as that of the record being replaced. The *samekey* operator defines this equality test.

The *read* operator accesses the successor record of the previous record read from the sequence forming the file and advances the conceptual file window exactly as for a sequential file. Hence we have

```
class module *sequential ;
  class *input (closingmode : environment.closingmodes) ;
    procedure *read (var v : elementtype ; var eof : boolean) ;
    begin
      {open file as an input file}
      * * *
      {close file}
    end ; {input}
  class *output (closingmode : environment.closingmodes) ;
    procedure *write (v : elementtype ; var error : boolean) ;
    begin
      {open file as an output file}
      * * *
      {close file}
    end ; {output}
  class *inputoutput (closingmode : environment.closingmodes) ;
    procedure *read (var v : elementtype ; var eof : boolean) ;
    procedure *write (v : elementtype ; var error : boolean) ;
    procedure *replace (v : elementtype ; var error : boolean) ;
    procedure *delete ;
    begin
      {open file as an inputoutput file}
      * * *
      {close file}
    end ; {inputoutput}
  begin
    * * *
  end {sequential}
```

In this case the *output* class does not require a *bucketoccupancy* parameter. Note that the *replace* and *write* operators have boolean variable parameters *error* which are used by the operators to indicate the success of the attempted operations — both operations will fail if the record key is inappropriate to the bucket currently containing the file window.

9.3.2 Direct Access

For direct access the operators specified are exactly as for indexed access to indexed sequential files — only the implementation of these operators will reflect the fact that access is via the file's addressing function rather than by use of indexes.

The full specification of the direct access abstraction is thus :

```
class module *direct ;
  class *input (closingmode : environment.closingmodes) ;
```

```
procedure *read (k . keytype , var v : elementtype ;
                      var successful : boolean) ;
begin
   {open file as an input file}
   ***
   {close file}
end ; {input}
class *output (closingmode : environment.closingmodes) ;
   procedure *write (v : elementtype ;
                      var successful : boolean) ;
   begin
      {open file as an output file}
      ***
      {close file}
   end ; {output}
class *inputoutput(closingmode : environment.closingmodes) ;
   procedure *read (k : keytype ; var v : elementtype ;
                      var successful : boolean) ;
   procedure *delete (k : keytype ; var successful : boolean) ;
   procedure *replace (v : elementtype ; var successful : boolean) ;
   procedure *write (v : elementtype ; var successful : boolean) ;
   begin
      {open file as an input–output file}
      ***
      {close file}
   end ; {input–output}
begin
   ***
end (direct)
```

9.3.3 Dynamic Access

Again dynamic access operations are defined exactly as for indexed files and also have the same effect from the user's viewpoint. Thus the dynamic access abstraction takes the same form as for indexed sequential files, consisting of two local data types each providing an appropriate combination of sequential access and direct access operators.

```
class module *dynamic ;
   class *input (closingmode : environment.closingmodes) ;
      procedure *seqread (var v : elementtype ;
                         var eof : boolean) ;
      procedure *keyread (k : keytype ; var v : elementtype ;
                         var successful : boolean) ;
```

```
begin
    {open file as an input file}
    ***
    {close file}
end ; {input}
class *inputoutput (closingmode : environment.closingmodes) ;
    procedure *seqread (var v : elementtype ;
                        var eof : boolean) ;
    procedure *seqwrite (v : elementtype ; var error : boolean) ;
    procedure *seqreplace (v : elementtype ;
                           var error : boolean) ;
    procedure *seqdelete ;
    procedure *keyread (k : keytype ; var v : elementtype ;
                        var successful : boolean) ;
    procedure *keydelete (k : keytype ;
                          var successful : boolean) ;
    procedure *keyreplace (v : elementtype ; var successful : boolean) ;
    procedure *keywrite (v : elementtype ;
                         var successful : boolean) ;
    begin
        {open file as an input–output file}
        ***
        {close file}
    end ; {input–output}
begin
    ***
end ; {dynamic}
```

9.4 CASE STUDY: RANDOM ORGANIZATION MASTER FILE INITIALIZATION

We shall organize the random organization master file to be used in the Model Savings Bank system so that it uses 1024 character buckets (i.e., the buckets are two sectors long, which should enable 12 to 15 of our account records to be stored in each bucket, depending on how

Figure 9.4 Initialization of random organization master file

the environment string and numeric types are implemented) and there will be 997 home buckets in the file — the logical bucket number of any account record will be determined by taking the remainder plus 1 after division of the first seven digits of the account number by the prime number 997. This version of the master file is initially created by copying the records of the sequential master file held on magnetic tape to the disk file, as shown in Figure 9.4.

The master file records are of the type *masterrecord* defined in earlier programs and the sequential master file is declared as

```
class seqmasterfile = sequentialfile in library
                    (where type itemtype = masterrecord) ;
instance MTfile : seqmasterfile (environment.MT1,
                                 'MASTER-FILE', false,
                                 environment.blocksize, 2) ;
```

The random organization master disk file is declared as

```
class randomfile in library
                    (where const numberofbuckets = 997 ;
                           type elementtype = masterrecord ;
                                keytype = accountnumber ;
                           function bucketnumber = address ;
                           procedure getkey = getacnumber ;
                           function samekey = sameacnumber) ;
instance randommaster : randomfile (environment. DA1,
                                    'MASTER-FILE', true,
                                    2*environment.sectorsize,
                                    1) ;
```

where the file will be initialized automatically to consist of 997 home buckets since it is a new file ; single buffering is used since we shall be employing direct access to the file records ; and the operators *getacnumber*, *sameacnumber*, and *address* must be declared in the initialization program. *getacnumber* and *sameacnumber* are exactly as for the processing of the indexed sequential master file, viz.,

```
procedure getacnumber (m : masterrecord ; var k : accountnumber) ;
    begin k := m.key end ;
function sameacnumber (k1, k2 : accountnumber) : boolean ;
    begin sameacnumber := environment.equals (k1, k2) end ;
```

and the address operator takes the form of a function

```
function address (key : accountnumber) : integer ;
    const prime = 997 ;
    var value : environment.numeric ;
        n : integer ;
        ok : boolean ;
```

```
begin
    {this assumes the implementation supports 7 digit integer values}
    with environment do
    begin
        getnumeric (key, 1, 7, 0, value, ok) ;
        numerictointeger (value, n) ;
        address := n mod prime + 1
    end
end {address} ;
```

We will assume that this function is also held in the library since it will be required by all other programs which use direct access to this master file.

The main program then calls a procedure *createrandomfile* which directly accesses the record locations of the master disk file and processes it as an output file. Hence *createrandomfile* declares a local instance

instance *newmaster* : *randommaster.direct.output* (*environment.simple*) ;

createrandomfile reads the tape file records and writes each one to the random organization file by means of calls of

newmaster.write (*nextrecord, invalidkey*)

The parameter *invalidkey* is set to true by a call of *newmaster.write* if and only if the bucket in which the record is to be stored does not exist, which should not happen if our *address* function is programmed correctly. The complete text of *PROGRAM9* is thus as shown in Listing 19.

```
                        LISTING 19 : PROGRAM9


program PROGRAM9 {initialize random master file} ;

    class module environment in library ;

    type accountnumber = environment.string ;
         money = environment.numeric ;
         masterrecord = record
                            key : accountnumber ;
                            clientidentity : environment.string ;
                            currentbalance, minimumbalance : money
                        end ;

    class seqmasterfile = sequentialfile in library
                            (where type itemtype = masterrecord) ;

    procedure getacnumber in library ;

    function sameacnumber in library ;

    function address in library ;
```

```
class randomfile in library
                  (where const numberofbuckets = 997 ;
                         type elementtype = masterrecord ;
                              keytype = accountnumber ;
                         procedure bucketnumber = address ;
                         procedure getkey = getacnumber ;
                         function samekey = sameacnumber) ;

instance MTfile  : seqmasterfile (environment.MT1, 'MASTER-FILE',
                                  false, environment.blocksize, 2) ;

instance randommaster : randomfile (environment.DA1, 'MASTER-FILE',
                                    true, 2*environment.sectorsize,
                                    1) ;

procedure createrandomfile ;

    instance oldmaster : MTfile.input (environment.locked) ;
    instance newmaster : randommaster.direct.output
                                          (environment.locked) ;

    var nextrecord : masterrecord ;
        eof, invalidkey : boolean ;

    procedure error (message : packed array [m..n : integer] of char) ;
       begin
          { some suitable diagnostic message }
          halt
       end {error} ;

    begin
       oldmaster.read (nextrecord, eof) ;
       while not eof do
       begin
          newmaster.write (nextrecord, invalidkey) ;
          if invalidkey then error ('invalid bucket number') ;
          oldmaster.read (nextrecord, eof)
       end
    end {createrandomfile} ;

begin
   createrandomfile
end.
```

9.5 CASE STUDY: RANDOM ORGANIZATION MASTER FILE UPDATE

At the start of this chapter we introduced an on-line version of the master file update program in which a random organization file was updated by transactions arriving in real time from user terminals. Conceptually we may still view the incoming transactions as a sequential file and construct the update program to process the transactions as such. Assuming, for simplicity, that the transactions have already been validated (the incorporation of validation routines into the update program is a simple matter) we may construct the random organization master file update program *PROGRAM10* to use the file TRANSACTIONS of validated but unsorted transactions, produced by the validation program of Chapter 6, in the update of the file

MASTER-FILE initialized by the previous case study program. Any errors detected in the update process will be reported on a line printer (Figure 9.5).

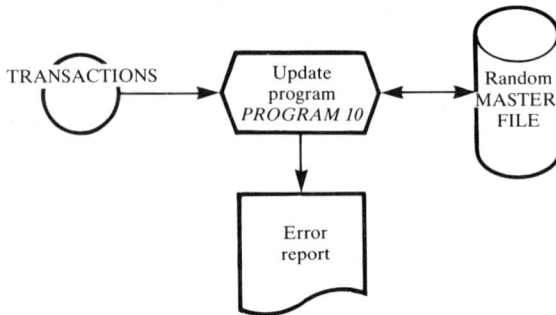

Figure 9.5   Random organization master file update

The design of this file update program is again based upon the direct-access file update algorithm developed in Section 4.3, except that we now use the random organization file abstraction. It is assumed that the master file is held on disk drive 1, the transactions file on tape unit 1, and the error report on line printer 1.

The unsorted transactions file has the same form as in the previous case study programs, viz.,

> **class** *transfile* = *sequentialfile* **in library**
> **(where type** *itemtype* = *transaction*) ;
> **instance** *TF* : *transfile* (*environment.MT1*, *'TRANSACTIONS'*,
> *false*, *environment.blocksize*, 2) ;

The random organization file *randommaster* is declared exactly as in the initialization program *PROGRAM9* and obviously uses the same *getacnumber*, *sameacnumber*, and *address* operators.

The file update procedure again follows closely the form of the program in Figure 4.3. Since the disk file records are to be accessed directly an input–output processing instance of the master file is declared local to the update procedure, viz.,

> **instance** *master* : *randommaster.direct.inputoutput* (*environment.locked*) ;

Otherwise the update procedure is exactly as in the indexed sequential master file update program except that it deals with one transaction at a time rather than one key value. Listing 20 gives the complete update program.

LISTING 20 : PROGRAM10

```
program PROGRAM10 { random master file update } ;

    class module environment in library ;

    const maxsavings = 20000 ;

    type  accountnumber = environment.string ;
          transtype = (addition, deletion, credit, debit) ;
          money = environment.numeric ;
          transaction = record
                            date : environment.string ;
                            key : accountnumber ;
                            kind : transtype ;
                            amount : money ;
                            clientidentity : environment.string ;
                            other : environment.string
                        end ;
          masterrecord = record
                            key : accountnumber ;
                            clientidentity : environment.string ;
                            currentbalance, minimumbalance : money
                        end ;

    procedure getacnumber in library ;

    function sameacnumber in library ;

    function address in library ;

    class randomfile in library
                    (where const numberofbuckets = 997 ;
                           type elementtype = masterrecord ;
                                keytype = accountnumber ;
                           function bucketnumber = address ;
                           procedure getkey = getacnumber ;
                           function samekey = sameacnumber) ;

    class transfile = sequentialfile in library
                    (where type itemtype = transaction) ;

    class outputtextfile in library ;

    instance randommaster : randomfile (environment.DA1, 'MASTER-FILE',
                                        false, 2*environment.sectorsize,
                                        1) ;

    instance TF : transfile (environment.MT1, 'TRANSACTIONS', false,
                             environment.blocksize, 2) ;

    instance errorreport : outputtextfile (environment.LP1, 2)


    procedure update ;

        instance master : randommaster.direct.inputoutput
                                        (environment.locked) ;
        instance transfile : TF.input (environment.locked) ;

        var sentinelacnumber, transacnumber,
               currentacnumber : accountnumber ;
            transrecord : transaction ;
            newrecord : masterrecord ;
            originallyinfile, infile : boolean ;
            savingslimit : money ;

        procedure getnexttransaction (var acnumber : accountnumber) ;
          var endoftransactions : boolean ;
          begin
```

```
          transfile.read (transrecord, endoftransactions) ;
          if endoftransactions
          then acnumber := sentinelacnumber
          else acnumber := transrecord.key
      end ;

procedure choosenextkeytoprocess (var acnumber : accountnumber) ;
      begin
          acnumber := transacnumber
      end ;

procedure getinitialstatus ;
      begin
          master.read (currentacnumber, newrecord, originallyinfile) ;
          infile := originallyinfile
      end ;

procedure applytransactiontomasterrecord in library ;

procedure recordfinalstatus ;
      var ok : boolean ;
      begin
          if infile
          then if originallyinfile
              then master.replace (newrecord, ok)
              else master.write (newrecord, ok)
          else if originallyinfile
              then master.delete (currentacnumber, ok)
      end ;

begin { update }
      with environment do
      begin
          construct (sentinelacnumber, 'XXXXXXXX') ;
          zeroize (savingslimit, 7, 2) ;
          integertonumeric (maxsavings, savingslimit) ;
          getnexttransaction (transacnumber) ;
          choosenextkeytoprocess (currentacnumber) ;
          while not equals (currentacnumber, sentinelacnumber) do
          begin {process one transaction}
              getinitialstatus ;
              applytransactiontomasterrecord ;
              recordfinalstatus ;
              getnexttransaction (transacnumber) ;
              choosenextkeytoprocess (currentacnumber)
          end
      end
  end ; { update }

begin
   update ;
end.
```

The error report produced by an execution of this update program on the file of unsorted transactions produced as output by the validation program *PROGRAM2* will be exactly the same as for an execution of *PROGRAM7*, the indexed sequential file update program (Listing17).

9.6   IMPLEMENTATION OF RANDOM FILES

Since the physical structure of a random organisation file is simply a sequence of numbered disk blocks, the *randomfile* class will make use of an instance, *block*, of the same *blockcontrol* class as was used in the implementation of the *sequentialfile* data type (Chapter 5). This will provide access to the file blocks required during file processing using both sequential and direct access — when retrieved from the library *blockcontrol* must be supplied with the appropriate file record type, viz.,

> **class** *blockcontrol* **in library** (**where type** *recordtype* = *elementtype*) ;
> **instance** *block* : *blockcontrol* (*device*, *identity*, *newfile*,
>   *bucketsize*, *numberofbuffers*) ;

Again local operators are provided to handle logical file opening and closing, and error reporting. The *randomfile* class initialization checks that the file is a disk file and determines the blocking factor for the file records as well as initializing a new file to contain the appropriate number of empty home buckets.

We will not describe the sequential access operations since they are almost identical with those for sequential organization files. Likewise the dynamic access operators are just a combination of the various sequential and direct access operators.

For direct access each of the *input*, *output*, and *inputoutput* classes provides a subset of the *read*, *write*, *replace*, and *delete* operations. These operators use a local procedure *obtain* which, given a logical bucket number determined by applying the *bucketnumber* function to the key of the record concerned, ensures that the block control instance obtains the required bucket from the file. If this bucket number is different from that of the previous bucket accessed and the previous bucket was changed in any way, then that bucket is first written back to the file. Those operators which are given a record value as parameter extract the key value from the record by means of the *getkey* procedure. Another local procedure *findrecord* performs a linear search of the records in the current bucket to attempt to locate the record — this procedure uses the *samekey* operator to perform key comparisons. Individual records in a bucket are processed using the *getrecord*, *putrecord*, *deleterecord*, and *replacerecord* operators of the block control instance.

In the implementation given in Listing 21 the problems of bucket overflow are ignored, thus the *write* operator rejects any attempts to insert a record into an already full bucket. The extension of the implementation to handle bucket overflow is left as an exercise.

```
            LISTING 21 : RANDOM FILE IMPLEMENTATION

class randomfile (device : environment.directdevices ;
                  identity : packed array [m..n : integer] of char ;
                  newfile : boolean ;
                  bucketsize : environment.blockrange ;
```

```
                        numberofbuffers : environment.bufferrange) ;

{ assumes const numberofbuckets (of type integer)               }
{          type elementtype with := defined                     }
{          type keytype                                         }
{          function bucketnumber (key : keytype) : integer      }
{          procedure getkey (v : elementtype ; var k : keytype) }
{          function samekey (k1, k2 : keytype) : boolean        }

class blockcontrol in library (where type recordtype = elementtype) ;

instance block : blockcontrol (device, identity, newfile,
                               bucketsize, numberofbuffers) ;

type filestatus = (opened, closed, locked) ;

var status : filestatus ;
    blockingfactor : integer ;

procedure error (message : packed array [m..n : integer] of char) ;
   begin
      { output some suitable error diagnostic message }
      halt
   end { error } ;

procedure openfile ;
   begin
      case status of
      opened : error ('file already in use') ;
      closed : status := opened ;
      locked : error ('file closed in lock mode')
      end
   end {openfile} ;

procedure closefile (closingmode : environment.closingmodes) ;
   begin
      case closingmode of
      environment.simple   : status := closed ;
      environment.locked   : status := locked ;
      environment.norewind : status := closed
      end
   end {closefile} ;


class module *sequential ; ... ;
class module *dynamic ; ... ;

class module *direct ;

   var currentblock : integer ;
       blockchanged : boolean ;

   procedure initializefile ;
      var i : integer ;
      begin
         block.clear ;
         for i := 1 to numberofbuckets do block.put (i)
      end {initializefile} ;

   procedure open ;
      begin
         openfile ;
         block.clear ; blockchanged := false ; currentblock := 0
      end {open} ;

   procedure close (closingmode : environment.closingmodes) ;
      begin
         if blockchanged then block.put (currentblock) ;
         closefile (closingmode)
      end {close} ;
```

```
procedure obtain (blocknumber : integer ; var exists : boolean) ;
   begin
      if (blocknumber < 1) or (blocknumber > numberofblocks)
      then error ('bucket number out of range')
      else if currentblock <> blocknumber
           then begin
                   if blockchanged then block.put (currentblock) ;
                   block.get (blocknumber, false, exists) ;
                   blockchanged := false ;
                   if exists
                   then currentblock := blocknumber
                   else currentblock := 0
                end
           else exists := true
   end ; {obtain}

procedure findrecord (key : keytype ; var found : boolean ;
                      var position : integer) ;
   var i : integer ; k : keytype ; v : elementtype ;
   begin
      found := false ; i := 0 ;
      while not found and (i < block.length) do
      begin
         i := i+1 ; block.getrecord (i, v) ; getkey (v, k) ;
         found := samekey (key, k)
      end ;
      if found then position := i
   end ; {findrecord}

procedure readelement (k : keytype ; var v : elementtype ;
                       var successful : boolean) ;
   var position : integer ;
   begin
      obtain (bucketnumber (k), successful) ;
      if successful
      then begin
              findrecord (k, successful, position) ;
              if successful then block.getrecord (position, v)
           end
   end ; {readelement}

procedure writeelement (v : elementtype ;
                        var successful : boolean) ;
   var k : keytype ; found, full : boolean ; position : integer ;
   begin
      getkey (v, k) ; obtain (bucketnumber (k), successful) ;
      if successful
      then begin
              findrecord (k, found, position) ;
              full := (block.length = blockingfactor) ;
              if found
              then successful := false
              else if full
                   then error ('bucket overflow') ;
                   else begin
                           block.putrecord (block.length + 1, v) ;
                           successful := true ;
                           blockchanged := true
                        end
           end
   end ; {writeelement}

procedure deleteelement (k : keytype ; var successful : boolean) ;
   var position : integer ;
   begin
      obtain (bucketnumber (k), successful) ;
      if successful
      then begin
              findrecord (k, successful, position) ;
              if successful
              then begin
```

```
                                 block.deleterecord (position, v) ;
                                 blockchanged := true
                             end
                     end
             end ; {deleteelement}

         procedure replaceelement (v : elementtype ;
                                   var successful : boolean) ;
             var k : keytype ; position : integer ;
             begin
                 getkey (v, k) ; obtain (bucketnumber (k), successful) ;
                 if successful
                 then begin
                         findrecord (k, successful, position) ;
                         if successful
                         then begin
                                 block.replacerecord (position, v) ;
                                 blockchanged := true
                             end
                     end
             end ; {replaceelement}

         class *input (closingmode : environment.closingmodes) ;
             procedure *read = readelement ;
             begin
                 open ;
                 *** ;
                 close (closingmode)
             end ; {input}

         class *output (closingmode : environment.closingmodes) ;
             procedure *write = writeelement ;
             begin
                 open ;
                 *** ;
                 close (closingmode)
             end ; {output}

         class *inputoutput (closingmode : environment.closingmodes) ;
             procedure *read = readelement ;
             procedure *delete = deleteelement ;
             procedure *replace = replaceelement ;
             procedure *write = writeelement ;
             begin
                 open ;
                 *** ;
                 close (closingmode)
             end ; {inputoutput}


         begin
             ***
         end ; {direct}

 begin
     if not (device in environment.directaccessdevices)
     then error ('not a disc file')
     else begin
             if newfile then initializefile ;
             status := closed ;
             blockingfactor := (blocksize-1) div size (elementtype) ;
             ***
         end
 end {randomfile}
```

EXERCISES

1. A disk file of 10 000 records is stored on a disk pack beginning at cylinder 8. Each cylinder contains 100 records and each track contains 10 records. Calculate the address of a record with key 87654321 if the file is organized as a random file and the following address-generation algorithms are used :

    (a) self-addressing using the last four digits;
    (b) prime division;
    (c) the mid-square method;
    (d) a folding algorithm which halves the key into two four-digit numbers;
    (e) radix transformation from base 11.

2. Extend the random file update program *PROGRAM10* so that it also validates incoming transactions.

3. Implement the sequential-access operations for random files.

4. Extend the implementation of the *randomfile* class so that it handles bucket overflow. Assume that it allocates reserved overflow buckets such that there is one overflow bucket per ten home buckets.

5. The following is a specification of a library class which provides an abstraction of a random organization file

    class *randomfile* (*identity* : **packed array** [*m..n* : *integer*] **of** *char*) ;
      { *assumes type elementtype with* := *defined*   }
      {   *type keytype*   }
      {   *function address* (*k* : *keytype*) : *integer*   }
      {   *procedure getkey* (*v* : *elementtype* ; **var** *k* : *keytype*)   }
      {   *function samekey* (*k1*, *k2* : *keytype*) : *boolean*   }
      var *operationok : *boolean* ;
      procedure *read (*k* : *keytype* ; **var** *v* : *elementtype*) ; ... ;
      procedure *delete (*k* : *keytype*) ; ...;
      procedure *replace (*v* : *elementtype*) ; ... ;
      procedure *write (*v* : *elementtype*) ; ...;
      begin
        { *open file for input–output processing* }
        *** ;
        { *close file* }
      end

    A random organization master file maintains credit ratings on a company's customers, where each customer has a unique six-digit account number. The customer records are defined as

    type *masterrecord* = **record**
                      key : *accountnumber* ;
                      rating : *integer*
              end

    The master file identity is *RATINGS*. Using a suitable addressing algorithm, write a program which enables access to, insertion of, and updating of, credit ratings in this file.

10 REPORT PRODUCTION

10.1 INTRODUCTION

One of the major activities in commercial data processing is the production of reports from the contents of files, e.g., in our model banking system the master accounts file may be used to produce reports giving information such as the current balance of each customer's account, or the total savings in each of the branches and areas, or simply to produce a mailing list. In other systems customer account files might be used to generate statements to be sent to customers; stock files could be used to produce reports detailing products which need to be re-ordered or manufactured; payroll files could be used to print summaries of wages paid, e.g., for tax returns.

Such applications generally have a standard form — the file involved usually consists of records sorted in some significant order, and the report generation program processes the file sequentially one record at a time, printing details extracted from the records and possibly accumulating required aggregate totals.

Listing 22 illustrates a report produced as output by the program *PROGRAM5* described in Chapter 1. The sequential and indexed sequential versions of the master file for the Model Savings Bank both consist of a sequence of customer account records in ascending account number. At the end of each month the bank management is required to pay monthly interest to all of its customers (at a rate of 0.75% of their minimum balance in the previous month if it is less than $5000 — for larger balances the excess of the minimum balance over $5000 earns interest at 1%). As part of the same process the bank management also requires details of the total savings currently invested, and interest paid for the previous month in the bank as a

254

whole, as well as in each of the regional areas and branches. The current state of each customer's account is also required. Since the first digit of each customer's account number is the area number of his branch, and the next two digits are the branch number, the master file is already ordered by area number, and by branch number within area number. Hence the file is suitably structured for generation of such a report.

The report illustrated in Listing 22 is printed using the first 66 lines of each page. It begins with a *report heading* 'SAVINGS SUMMARY BY AREA AND BRANCH' on a single page, and ends with a *report footing* 'END OF REPORT' also on a single page. The intervening pages contain the details of the current balance (after interest has been awarded) of each customer, and the total savings at, and interest paid for the previous month by, each branch, each area, and the entire bank. Each page begins with a *page heading* (just a page number in this case) and ends with a *page footing* (the page number again). The lines which give the details of each customer are known as *detail lines*. The details of the customers in each branch are preceded by a single line heading (known as a *control heading*) giving the branch number, and are followed by a two line footing (known as a *control footing*) giving the branch number as well as the total amount invested in the branch and aggregate interest paid for the last month at the branch.

Likewise, the details of all the branches in an area are preceded by a control heading giving the area number and are followed by a control footing giving the area number, total savings invested, and total monthly interest paid in that area. The branch control headings and footings are known as *minor control headings* and *minor control footings* since they correspond to values of the minor key field on which the master file is sorted, whereas the area headings and footings are *major control headings* and *footings* since they correspond to values of the major sorting key of the master file. In turn the details of all the areas are preceded and followed by a *final control heading* 'BANK REPORT' and *final control footing* (giving the total savings and interest paid by the bank), respectively.

The page numbers are printed on lines 2 and 62 of each page, with the control headings, footings, and details appearing between lines 4 and 56.

If the detail lines (i.e, the customers' balances) are omitted from the report it is then known as a *summary report*. Listing 23 shows part of a summary report produced from the same input file as above. In this example not only the actual customer details have been omitted but also the branch minor control headings.

LISTING 22 : SAVINGS AND INTEREST REPORT

SAVINGS   SUMMARY   BY   AREA   AND   BRANCH ←report heading

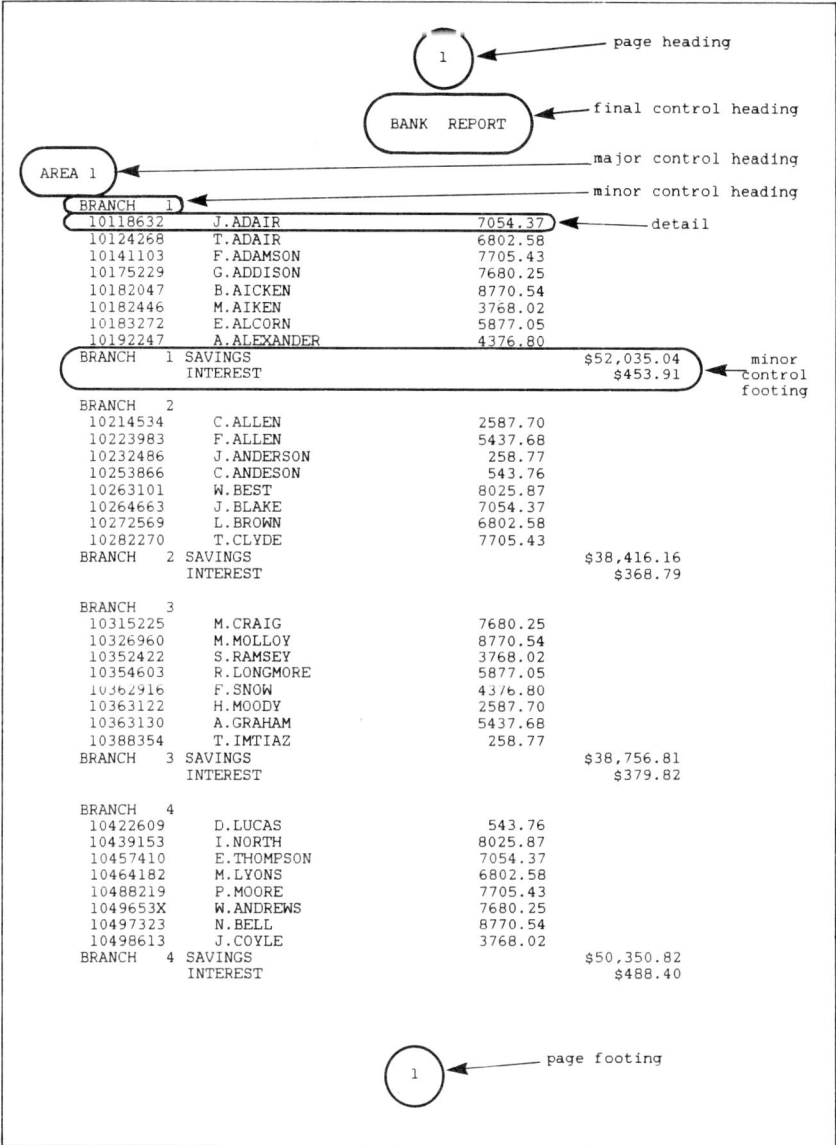

```
                                    ( 1 )  ◄────────── page heading

                              ┌──────────────┐
                              │ BANK   REPORT │ ◄──── final control heading
                              └──────────────┘
  ┌─────────┐                                    ◄── major control heading
  │ AREA 1  │ ◄─────────────────────────────────
  └─────────┘
  ┌──────────────────┐                           ◄── minor control heading
  │ BRANCH    1      │
  │ 10118632     J.ADAIR              7054.37  ◄──────── detail
  └──────────────────────────────────────────
    10124268     T.ADAIR              6802.58
    10141103     F.ADAMSON            7705.43
    10175229     G.ADDISON            7680.25
    10182047     B.AICKEN             8770.54
    10182446     M.AIKEN              3768.02
    10183272     E.ALCORN             5877.05
    10192247     A.ALEXANDER          4376.80
  ┌───────────────────────────────────────────────┐
  │ BRANCH    1 SAVINGS              $52,035.04     │            minor
  │             INTEREST                $453.91     │ ◄────────  control
  └───────────────────────────────────────────────┘            footing

    BRANCH    2
    10214534     C.ALLEN              2587.70
    10223983     F.ALLEN              5437.68
    10232486     J.ANDERSON            258.77
    10253866     C.ANDESON             543.76
    10263101     W.BEST               8025.87
    10264663     J.BLAKE              7054.37
    10272569     L.BROWN              6802.58
    10282270     T.CLYDE              7705.43
    BRANCH    2 SAVINGS              $38,416.16
                INTEREST                $368.79

    BRANCH    3
    10315225     M.CRAIG              7680.25
    10326960     M.MOLLOY             8770.54
    10352422     S.RAMSEY             3768.02
    10354603     R.LONGMORE           5877.05
    10362916     F.SNOW               4376.80
    10363122     H.MOODY              2587.70
    10363130     A.GRAHAM             5437.68
    10388354     T.IMTIAZ              258.77
    BRANCH    3 SAVINGS              $38,756.81
                INTEREST                $379.82

    BRANCH    4
    10422609     D.LUCAS               543.76
    10439153     I.NORTH              8025.87
    10457410     E.THOMPSON           7054.37
    10464182     M.LYONS              6802.58
    10488219     P.MOORE              7705.43
    1049653X     W.ANDREWS            7680.25
    10497323     N.BELL               8770.54
    10498613     J.COYLE              3768.02
    BRANCH    4 SAVINGS              $50,350.82
                INTEREST                $488.40




                                    ( 1 )  ◄────────── page footing
```

```
                                    2


        BRANCH   5
          10516670        E.DICKSON             5877.05
          10517588        F.ELMORE              4376.80
          10528121        J.GILBERT             2587.70
          10543937        W.HARBINSON           5437.68
          10572708        W.REDMOND              258.77
          10586563        J.MCALISTER            543.76
          1058725X        W.THOMPSON            8025.87
          10596534        W.MORGAN              7054.37
        BRANCH   5 SAVINGS                              $34,162.00
                   INTEREST                                $314.29

   AREA 1 SAVINGS                                                  $213,720.83
          INTEREST                                                   $2,004.49

                                                      major control
   AREA 2                                             footing

        BRANCH   1
          2011690X        G.ARMSTRONG           6802.58
          20125267        R.BITTLES             7705.43
          20159110        I.BOAL                7680.25
          20165277        W.BROWN               8770.54
          20165919        E.COE                 3768.02
          20174462        S.CRYMBLE             5877.05
          20176597        B.MCATEER             4376.80
          20183143        T.BOYLE               2587.70
        BRANCH   1 SAVINGS                              $47,568.37
                   INTEREST                                $428.12

        BRANCH   2
          20231997        J.SPRATT              5437.68
          20242441        J.MCBRIDE              258.77
          20260156        S.MORT                 543.76
          20266170        W.GRAHAM              8025.87
          20266200        A.IRWIN               7054.37
          20274386        J.REID                6802.58
          2028277X        P.MCCALLION           7705.43
          20283229        G.HANLON              7680.25
        BRANCH   2 SAVINGS                              $43,508.71
                   INTEREST                                $387.23

                                      .
                                      .
                                      .
```

```
                    .
                    .
                    .

    60422246      F.GORMAN              3768.02
    60424265      D.LEITCH              5877.05
    60434333      H.MCVEIGH             4376.80
    60436581      L.SHIVERS             2587.70
    60444053      S.LIDSTER             5437.68
    60453389      R.TAYLOR               258.77
 BRANCH    4 SAVINGS                              $38,756.81
             INTEREST                                 $377.24

 BRANCH    5
    60517743      U.BAYER                543.76
    60524545      F.BREEN              8025.87
    6055438X      M.CALDWELL           7054.37
    60581840      R.CARLISLE           6802.58
    60584033      R.COURTNEY           7705.43
    60587652      B.HANNA              7680.25
    60588381      B.LIVINGSTONE        8770.54
    60598409      L.MAGEE              3768.02
 BRANCH    5 SAVINGS                              $50,350.82
             INTEREST                                 $492.76

 AREA 6 SAVINGS                                  $210,434.48
        INTEREST                                   $1,994.63

 BANK   TOTAL   SAVINGS                         $1,281,779.95
               INTEREST                            $11,697.78
```

◄── final control footing

8

```
                              ╭──────────────────────╮
                              │                      │ ◄────── report footing
                              │   END  OF   REPORT   │
                              ╰──────────────────────╯
```

LISTING 13 : SUMMARY REPORT EXTRACT

```
                                  1

                           BANK   REPORT

AREA 1

     BRANCH   1 SAVINGS                       $52,035.04
              INTEREST                           $453.91

     BRANCH   2 SAVINGS                       $38,416.16
              INTEREST                           $368.79

     BRANCH   3 SAVINGS                       $38,756.81
              INTEREST                           $379.82

     BRANCH   4 SAVINGS                       $50,350.82
              INTEREST                           $488.40

     BRANCH   5 SAVINGS                       $34,162.00
              INTEREST                           $314.29

AREA 1 SAVINGS                                              $213,720.83
       INTEREST                                               $2,004.49


AREA 2

     BRANCH   1 SAVINGS                       $47,568.37
              INTEREST                           $423.36

     BRANCH   2 SAVINGS                       $43,508.71
              INTEREST                           $382.88

     BRANCH   3 SAVINGS                       $31,620.32
              INTEREST                           $265.62

     BRANCH   4 SAVINGS                       $55,684.11
              INTEREST                           $501.16

     BRANCH   5 SAVINGS                       $35,087.53
              INTEREST                           $301.75

AREA 2 SAVINGS                                              $213,469.04
       INTEREST                                               $1,874.77


AREA 3

     BRANCH   1 SAVINGS                       $46,203.47
              INTEREST                           $401.47

     BRANCH   2 SAVINGS                       $46,841.57




                                  1
```

10.2   DESIGNING A REPORT GENERATION PROGRAM

We now return to consideration of the problem of generating printed reports, such as those illustrated in Listings 22 and 23, from the sequential versions of the master file in the Model Savings Bank system. For the random organization master file the records would first have to be sorted into ascending account number order before production of such a report could be achieved since, as we shall see, the production of such reports depends upon the file records being accessible in order of their key field values.

The required program is to perform two tasks — the addition of interest to each account, and the production of the printed report detailing balances and interest paid. This program would be run at the end of each month and award interest according to the formula given at the start of this chapter, i.e., 0.75% on the first $5000 minimum balance, and 1% for any additional minimum balance.

10.2.1   The Input File Structure

The records in the sequential and indexed sequential versions of the master accounts file are ordered by customer number within branch number within area number. Hence the area field (the first digit in each account number) is said to be the *major control key* for the file and the branch field (the second and third digits) is known as the *minor control key*. All records with the same area digit in their account numbers form a *major control group*. Within each major control group all records with the same branch value in their account numbers form a *minor control group*. Thus, as the records are ordered by area number and by branch number within area number (since they are in account number order), the file has a hierarchical structure, consisting of a number of major control groups, each of which is made up of several minor control groups containing account records. These records are known as *detail* records. The overall file of records is known as the *final control group*. Figure 10.1 lists parts of the master file and illustrates the structure of the record control groups within the file.

When a record in a file is followed by a record with a different branch number value, a *minor control break* is said to occur between the two records. Hence all the minor control groups are separated by minor control breaks. When a record is followed by one with a different area digit a *major control break* occurs (and also therefore a minor control break since a change in area number implies a change in branch number also). All the major control groups are separated

account number	client-identity	current balance	minimum balance	
major control key	*minor control key*			
10118632	J.ADAIR	7054.37	0.00 ←	*detail record*
10124268	T.ADAIR	6802.58	5802.58	
10141103	F.ADAMSON	7705.43	5705.43	
10175229	G.ADDISON	7680.25	4680.25	
10182047	B.AICKEN	8770.54	4770.54	
10182446	M.AIKEN	3768.02	568.02	
10183272	E.ALCORN	5877.05	777.05	
10192247	A.ALEXANDER	4376.80	66.80	*minor control*
10214534	C.ALLEN	2587.70	77.70	*break*
10223983	F.ALLEN	5437.68	37.68	
10232486	J.ANDERSON	258.77	258.77	
10253866	C.ANDESON	543.76	443.76	
10263101	W.BEST	8025.87	6025.87	
10264663	J.BLAKE	7054.37	4054.37	
10272569	L.BROWN	6802.58	2802.58	
10282270	T.CLYDE	7705.43	2705.43	
10315225	M.CRAIG	7680.25	1680.25	
10326960	M.MOLLOY	8770.54	1770.54	
10352422	S.RAMSEY	3768.02	268.02	
10354603	R.LONGMORE	5877.05	477.05	
10362916	F.SNOW	4376.80	46.80	
10363122	H.MOODY	2587.70	2587.60	
10363130	A.GRAHAM	5437.68	5435.68	
10388354	T.IMTIAZ	258.77	138.77	
10422609	D.LUCAS	543.76	323.76	
10439153	I.NORTH	8025.87	5004.87	
10457410	E.THOMPSON	7054.37	4024.37	
10464182	M.LYONS	6802.58	6702.58	
10488219	P.MOORE	7705.43	7505.43	
1049653X	W.ANDREWS	7680.25	7380.25	
10497323	N.BELL	8770.54	8370.54	
10498613	J.COYLE	3768.02	3268.02	
10516670	E.DICKSON	5877.05	5277.05	
10517588	F.ELMORE	4376.80	4046.80	
10528121	J.GILBERT	2587.70	2067.70	
10543937	W.HARBINSON	5437.68	0.00	
10572708	W.REDMOND	258.77	234.56	
10586563	J.MCALISTER	543.76	345.89	
1058725X	W.THOMPSON	8025.87	7632.67	
10596534	W.MORGAN	7054.37	500.00	*major* and *minor*
2011690X	G.ARMSTRONG	6802.58	4687.23	*control breaks*
		·		
		·		
20594984	R.MCCOMB	6802.58	5435.68	*major* and *minor*
30114985	K.JAMES	7705.43	2000.00	*control breaks*
30124123	T.JOHNSON	7680.25	2000.00	
30137624	J.RAWE	8770.54	3500.00	
30146542	R.ROSE	3768.02	2587.70	
30156904	J.MCCOOK	5877.05	0.00	

minor control group

major control group

account number	client-identity	current balance	minimum balance

major *minor*
control *control*
    key *key*

30168945	B.NEESON	4376.80	0.00
3017614X	S.STEVENSON	2587.70	2587.70
30184983	N.ATALLI	5437.68	3368.02
30214122	W.BEATTIE	258.77	0.00
30227623	M.BOYCE	543.76	100.00
30236541	J.BRIGGS	8025.87	3265.70
30246903	G.BUNN	7054.37	5435.68
3026894X	R.CAMERSON	6802.58	2000.00
30276144	M.CONNOLLY	7705.43	4550.00
30283175	A.HAWTHORNE	7680.25	3500.00
30298830	W.MCCOURT	8770.54	7000.00
30318610	M.OWENS	3768.02	2000.00
30328233	S.ROBERTS	5877.05	3000.00
30337321	A.MCCROSSAN	4376.80	3500.00
30342678	F.MAGUIRE	2587.70	2587.70
30356199	M.SINNAMON	5437.68	3368.02
30365716	J.CASSIDY	258.77	50.00
30373344	G.CLAKE	543.76	0.00
30374413	E.CRAWFORD	8025.87	3265.70
30414164	J.CURRY	7054.37	5435.68
3042433X	P.DONAGHY	6802.58	2000.00
30436168	C.FENTON	7705.43	4550.00
30448611	W.FULTON	7680.25	3368.02
30452376	J.HOLOHAN	8770.54	7770.54
30468515	P.MCDALD	3768.02	3500.00
30478561	W.GREEN	5877.05	2000.00
30484936	S.ROBINSON	4376.80	2587.70
30515467	G.MALONE	2587.70	0.00
30527473	H.MCDOWELL	5437.68	3265.70
30528232	L.PATIENCE	258.77	50.00
30534070	F.TURNER	543.76	100.00
30546524	W.AYTON	8025.87	3368.02
30552346	S.BEGGS	7054.37	2000.00
30566053	M.BOYD	6802.58	5435.68
30572525	D.BRITTON	7705.43	4550.00
40113124	D.BURNS	7680.25	3500.00

major and *minor*
control breaks

60336927	J.DUNLEA	8025.87	5435.68
60343249	W.FOYE	7054.37	3265.70
60347198	C.HILL	6802.58	5500.00
60356855	G.LATIMER	7705.43	4550.00
60414359	M.NIXON	7680.25	3500.00
60415223	M.QUIGG	8770.54	2587.70
60422246	F.GORMAN	3768.02	3000.00
60424265	D.LEITCH	5877.05	3000.00
60434333	H.MCVEIGH	4376.80	3500.00
60436581	L.SHIVERS	2587.70	2587.70
60444053	S.LIDSTER	5437.68	2587.70
60453389	R.TAYLOR	258.77	50.00

account number	client-identity	current balance	minimum balance

major control key   *minor control key*

60517743	U.BAYER	543.76	100.00
60524545	F.BREEN	8025.87	5435.68
6055438X	M.CALDWELL	7054.37	3265.70
60581840	R.CARLISLE	6802.58	5500.00
60584033	R.COURTNEY	7705.43	4550.00
60587652	B.HANNA	7680.25	6000.00
60588381	B.LIVINGSTONE	8770.54	5435.68
60598409	L.MAGEE	3768.02	3265.70

final, major and minor control breaks

Figure 10.1   Input file structure

by major and minor control breaks — a control break at one level always implies control breaks at all lower levels in the hierarchical structure of the file records. The final record in the file is assumed to be followed by a *final control break* — thus causing major and minor control breaks also.

10.2.2   The Report Program Structure

From the input file structure it can be seen that the basic structure of the program to generate the required report will take the form

```
begin
    print heading for the bank ;
    for each area do
    begin
        print heading identifying the area ;
        for each branch do
        begin
            print heading identifying the branch ;
            for each account do
            begin
                award interest ;
                print balance
            end ;
            print total savings and interest paid for branch
        end ;
```

> *print total savings and interest paid for area*
> **end** ;
> *print total savings and interest paid for bank*
> **end**

The *logical* structure of the report thus consists of a final control group containing a number of major control groups (one per area) each in turn containing a number of minor control groups (one per branch). Each minor control group contains a sequence of detail records (one for each customer in the branch concerned). In general therefore a report consists of a final control group containing a heading, a sequence of items, and a footing; each item may itself be a similarly structured control group at the next lower level, or a detail record.

The report thus makes explicit the hierarchical structure of the record control groups which is implicit in the input file, by printing a control heading immediately before, and a control footing immediately after, the constituents of each control group. The control heading usually includes the value of the control key associated with that control group (e.g., in our report the area and branch numbers are printed out in the control headings) and the control footings (if included) often consist of the control key value and other information pertaining to the detail records included in the control group concerned. In our example the total savings and interest paid in branches and areas are included in the control footings. Final control headings and footings are also included — in our example the control heading is the string 'BANK REPORT' and the control footing gives the entire savings held in, and interest paid for the previous month by, the bank. Control headings, control footings, and detail lines are known collectively as *logical report groups*. As we have already noted, a report in which the detail lines are omitted is known as a *summary report*.

However, this is not actually the report that is required, for it is not formatted into pages with headings and footings, and does not have a report heading or a report footing. The report is to be printed on pages containing a certain number of lines, i.e., the report also has a *physical* structure of which the report generation program must take account. The report must begin with a report heading and conclude with a report footing and each intermediate page must have both a page heading and a page footing. The end of one page and the start of the next is termed a *page break*. Each logical report group (control heading, footing, or detail) must be printed entirely on one page. Hence a *report group length* must be associated with each logical report group — in our example the various control headings and footings are always preceded by a certain number of blank lines, control headings and details themselves occupy one line, and control footings occupy two lines in the report.

We may view the generation of the report as consisting of the two processes identified above — one generating the sequence of logical report groups, and the other forming this sequence into a paged report with page and report headings and footings. These two processes may be considered as executing concurrently and communicating via a buffering data structure (Figure 10.2). As the first process *generatelogicalreportgroups* produces logical report groups these will be appended to the buffer — each time that the process *printpagedreport* requires another logical report group it will obtain it from the buffer. *generatelogicalreportgroups* will indicate that the entire logical report group sequence has been generated by appending a special terminator report group to the buffer.

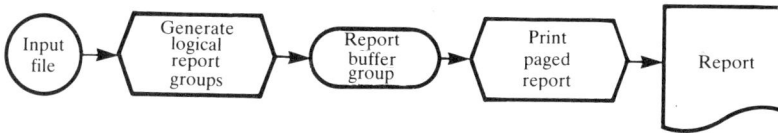

Figure 10.2   Producing the report using concurrent processes

In this example a logical report group consists of up to two lines (each of which is a string) preceded by a number of blank lines. Each report group also contains a field whose value indicates whether or not this is the special final group marking the end of the sequence. Hence a logical report group takes the form

```
type line = environment.string ;
    logicalreportgroup =
        record
            case endofreportgroupsequence : boolean of
            true : ( ) ;
            false : (linestoskip : 0..maxint ;
                    numberoflines : 0..maxlines ;
                    contents : array [1..maxlines] of line)
        end ;
```

The variant corresponding to *endofreportsequence* being true is used only in the construction of the end of sequence group.

For the buffer itself we assume that the buffer monitor constructed in Chapter 2 has been made available in the library, thus

monitor module *buffer* **in library**
  (**where type** *infotype* = *logicalreportgroup* ;
     const $N = 20$)

Hence a report group R is appended to the buffer by means of a call

$$buffer.add\ (R)$$

and the report group value which has been in the buffer for the longest time is assigned to a variable L by a call of

$$buffer.obtain\ (L)$$

The structure of the process *generatelogicalreportgroups* is based, as we have already seen, upon the structure of the accounts file. A procedure

procedure *readmasterfile* (**var** *thisrecord* : *masterrecord* ;
                  var *controlbreakstatus* : *break*)

where

type *break* = (*none, minor, major, final*)

obtains the next record from the accounts file and, if the reading of this record causes a control break to occur, then the level of that control break is assigned to *controlbreakstatus*, otherwise it is assigned the value *none*.

    With this procedure available it is straightforward to derive the basic structure of the logical report group generation process. At the start of each control group a control heading is constructed and added to the buffer — counter variables associated with that group are also initialized. At the end of each control group various counter values associated with that control level are added to counter values at the next higher level, e.g., branch totals are added to area totals. This incrementing action is known as *rolling forward* the counter values. The processing of detail records involves calculation of the interest, addition of the interest and resultant current balance to the branch totals (known as *sub-totalling*), resetting the minimum balance for an account to the new current balance, and returning the updated account record to the master file. As each logical report group is thus constructed it is appended to the buffer.

process *generatelogicalreportgroups* ;
  begin
    send final control heading to buffer ;
    set bank totals to zero ;
    readmasterfile (*thisrecord, controlbreakstatus*) ;
    while *controlbreakstatus* < *final* **do**

```
begin {process next major control group}
    send major control heading to buffer ;
    set area totals to zero ;
    while controlbreakstatus < major do
    begin {process next minor control group}
        send minor control heading to buffer ;
        set branch totals to zero ;
        while controlbreakstatus < minor do
        begin {process next detail record}
            calculate interest from minimum balance in this record ;
            add interest to current balance in this record ;
            reset minimum balance for this record ;
            increment branch totals ;
            send detail record to buffer ;
            master.rewrite (this record, ok) ;
            readmasterfile (this record, controlbreakstatus)
        end ;
        increment area totals by branch totals ;
        send minor control footing to buffer
    end ;
    increment bank totals by area totals ;
    send major control footing to buffer
end ;
send final control footing to buffer ;
send end of report sequence signal to buffer
end {generatelogicalreportgroups} ;
```

The *printpagedreport* process defines the significant lines of the page for printing purposes, viz.,

```
const pageheadingline = ...;
      pagefootingline = ... ;
      reportheadingline = ... ;
      reportfootingline = ... ;
      firstdetailline = ... ;
      lastdetailline = ... ;
```

Its action is basically to print a report heading, construct pages containing a page heading, logical report groups, and a page footing, followed by a report footing. Hence its structure may be summarized as

```
process printpagedreport ;
    begin
        print report heading ;
        pagecount := 0 ;
        get first logical report group from buffer ;
        repeat
            increment pagecount ;
```

> *print page heading on page heading line of new page* ;
> *prepare to print from first detail line* ;
> *linecount* := *firstdetailline* − 1 ;
> **with** *next logical report group* **do**
> **repeat**
>   *skip required number of lines* ;
>   *print contents on required number of lines* ;
>   *increment linecount* ;
>   *get next logical report group from buffer* ;
>   *length* := *linestoskip* + *numberoflines*
> **until** *endofreportgroupsequence*
>   **or** (*linecount* + *length* > *lastdetailline*) ;
> *print page footing on pagefootingline*
> **until** *end of logical report groups has been reached* ;
> *print report footing*
> **end** {*printpagedreport*} ;

In the complete text of *PROGRAM5* given below in Listing 24
generatelogicalreportgroups uses the indexed sequential master file
(see Chapter 8) and *printpagedreport* uses an output text file sent to
a line printer. *generatelogicalreportgroups* constructs the lines of
report groups using the string and numeric operations provided by
the *environment* module, and the various arithmetic quantities are
declared to be of type *environment.numeric*.

```
                    LISTING 24 : PROGRAM5

program PROGRAM5 {generate report using concurrent processes} ;

    class module environment in library ;

    const maxlines = 2 ;

    type line = environment.string ;

        logicalreportgroup =
                    record
                        case endofreportgroupsequence : boolean of
                        true  : ( ) ;
                        false : (linestoskip : 0..maxint ;
                                 numberoflines : 0..maxlines ;
                                 contents : array [1..maxlines] of line)
                    end ;

    monitor module buffer in library
        (where const N = 20 ;
                type infotype = logicalreportgroup) ;

    process generatelogicalreportgroups ;

        type accountnumber = environment.string ;
             money = environment.numeric ;
             masterrecord = record
                        key : accountnumber ;
                        clientidentity : environment.string ;
                        currentbalance, minimumbalance : money
                    end ;
```

```
procedure getacnumber in library ;

function sameacnumber in library ;

function acnumbersinorder in library ;

class indexedsequentialfile in library
      (where type elementtype = masterrecord ;
                  keytype = accountnumber ;
             procedure getkey = getacnumber ;
             function samekey = sameacnumber ;
             function keyorder = acnumbersinorder ) ;

instance ISfile : indexedsequentialfile
                      (environment.DA1, 'MASTER-FILE',
                       true, environment.sectorsize, 2) ;

instance master : ISfile.sequential.inputoutput
                                  (environment.locked) ;

type reportgrouptypes = (finalheading, areaheading, branchheading,
                          detail,
                          branchfooting, areafooting, finalfooting) ;
     break = (none, minor, major, final) ;


var thisarea, areanumber, thisbranch, branchnumber : 1..maxint ;
    banktotal, bankinterest, areatotal, areainterest,
    branchtotal, branchinterest, interest : money ;
    thisrecord : masterrecord ;
    controlbreakstatus : break ;

procedure readmasterfile (var thisrecord : masterrecord ;
                          var controlbreakstatus : break) ;
    var eof, ok : boolean ;
    begin
        master.read (thisrecord, eof) ;
        if eof
        then controlbreakstatus := final
        else with environment, thisrecord do
             begin
                getinteger (key, 1, 1, thisarea, ok) ;
                getinteger (key, 2, 2, thisbranch, ok) ;
                if thisarea <> areanumber
                then controlbreakstatus := major
                else if thisbranch <> branchnumber
                      then controlbreakstatus := minor
                      else controlbreakstatus := none
             end
    end {readmasterfile} ;

procedure sendtobuffer (grouptype : reportgrouptypes) ;
    var nextgroup : logicalreportgroup ;
    begin
        with environment, nextgroup do
        begin
           endofreportgroupsequence := false ;
           setall (contents[1], printerwidth, ' ') ;
           setall (contents[2], printerwidth, ' ') ;
           case grouptype of
           finalheading :
              begin
                 linestoskip := 3 ; numberoflines := 1 ;
                 puttext (contents[1], 'BANK  REPORT', 37, 12)
              end ;
           finalfooting :
              begin
                 linestoskip := 3 ; numberoflines := 2 ;
                 puttext (contents[1],
                          'BANK  TOTAL  SAVINGS', 1, 20) ;
                 putnumeric (contents[1], banktotal, 66, 14, 2) ;
```

```
                    puttext (contents[2], 'INTEREST', 13, 8) ;
                    putnumeric (contents[2], bankinterest, 66, 14, 2)
                end ;
            areaheading :
                begin
                    linestoskip := 2 ; numberoflines := 1 ;
                    puttext (contents[1], 'AREA', 1, 4) ;
                    putinteger (contents[1], areanumber, 6, 1)
                end ;
            areafooting :
                begin
                    linestoskip := 1 ; numberoflines := 2 ;
                    puttext (contents[1], 'AREA', 1, 4) ;
                    putinteger (contents[1], areanumber, 6, 1) ;
                    puttext (contents[1], 'SAVINGS', 8, 7) ;
                    putnumeric (contents[1], areatotal, 66, 14, 2) ;
                    puttext (contents[2],'INTEREST', 8, 8) ;
                    putnumeric (contents[2], areainterest, 66, 14, 2)
                end ;
            branchheading :
                begin
                    linestoskip := 1 ; numberoflines := 1 ;
                    puttext (contents[1], 'BRANCH', 5, 6) ;
                    putinteger (contents[1], branchnumber, 13, 2)
                end ;
            branchfooting :
                begin
                    linestoskip := 0 ; numberoflines := 2 ;
                    puttext (contents[1], 'BRANCH', 5, 6) ;
                    putinteger (contents[1], branchnumber, 13, 2)
                    puttext (contents[1], 'SAVINGS', 16, 7) ;
                    putnumeric (contents[1], branchtotal, 53, 14, 2) ;
                    puttext (contents[2],'INTEREST', 16, 8) ;
                    putnumeric (contents[2], branchinterest, 53, 14, 2)
                end ;
            detail :
                with thisrecord do
                begin
                    linestoskip := 0 ; numberoflines := 1 ;
                    putstring (contents[1], key, 6, 8) ;
                    putstring (contents[1], clientidentity, 19, 21) ;
                    putnumeric (contents[1], currentbalance, 41, 8, 2)
                end
            end
        end ;
        buffer.add (nextgroup)
    end {sendtobuffer} ;

procedure calculateinterest (balance : money ;
                             var interest : money) ;
    const threshold = 5000 ; lowerrate = 0.0075 ; upperrate = 0.1 ;
    var amount, r : real ;
    begin
        with environment do
        begin
            numerictoreal (balance, amount) ;
            if amount > threshold
            then r := threshold * lowerrate
                    + (amount - threshold) * upperrate
            else r := amount * lowerrate ;
            realtonumeric (r, interest)
        end
    end {calculateinterest} ;

procedure signalendoflogicalreportgroups ;
    var nextgroup : logicalreportgroup ;
    begin
        nextgroup.endofreportgroupsequence := true ;
        buffer.add (nextgroup)
    end {signalendoflogicalreportgroups} ;
```

```
        begin
          with environment do
          begin
             sendtobuffer (finalheading)   ;
             zeroize (banktotal, 10, 2) ; zeroize (bankinterest, 8, 2) ;
             areanumber := 1 ; branchnumber := 1 ;
             readmasterfile (thisrecord, controlbreakstatus) ;
             while controlbreakstatus < final do
             begin {process next major control group}
                areanumber := thisarea ;
                sendtobuffer (areaheading) ;
                zeroize (areatotal, 10, 2) ;
                zeroize (areainterest, 8, 2) ;
                while controlbreakstatus < major do
                begin {process next minor control group}
                   branchnumber := thisbranch ;
                   sendtobuffer (branchheading)   ;
                   zeroize (branchtotal, 8, 2) ;
                   zeroize (branchinterest, 8, 2) ;
                   while controlbreakstatus < minor do
                   with thisrecord do
                   begin {process next detail record}
                      zeroize (interest, 8, 2) ;
                      calculateinterest (minimumbalance, interest) ;
                      addnumeric (currentbalance, interest) ;
                      addnumeric (branchtotal, currentbalance) ;
                      addnumeric (branchinterest, interest) ;
                      minimumbalance := currentbalance ;
                      sendtobuffer (detail) ;
                      master.rewrite (thisrecord, ok) ;
                      readmasterfile (thisrecord, controlbreakstatus)
                   end ;
                   addnumeric (areatotal, branchtotal) ;
                   addnumeric (areainterest, branchinterest) ;
                   sendtobuffer (branchfooting)
                end ;
                addnumeric (banktotal, areatotal) ;
                addnumeric (bankinterest, areainterest) ;
                sendtobuffer (areafooting)
             end ;
             sendtobuffer (finalfooting)   ;
             signalendoflogicalreportgroups
          end
     end {generate logical report groups } ;


process printpagedreport ;

     const reportheadingline = 20 ;
           reportfootingline = 20 ;
           pageheadingline   =  2 ;
           pagefootingline   = 62 ;
           firstdetailline   =  4 ;
           lastdetailline    = 56 ;

     type reportgrouptypes = (reportheading, reportfooting, pageheading,
                              pagefooting) ;

     class outputttextfile in library ;

     instance savingsprintout : outputtextfile (environment.LP1, 2) ;

     var pagecount, linecount : 0..maxint ;
         nextgroup : logicalreportgroup ;
         i : 1..maxlines ;

     procedure print (grouptype : reportgrouptypes) ;
        var line : environment.string ;
        begin
           with environment, savingsprintout do
```

```
        begin
            setall (line, printerwidth, ' ') ;
            case grouptype of
            reportheading :
                begin
                    { new page has been taken automatically }
                    {  in the initialisation of the file      }
                    newlines (reportheadingline - 1) ;
                    puttext (line,
                                    'SAVINGS   SUMMARY  BY  AREA  AND  BRANCH',
                                    20, 39) ;
                    writeline (line)
                end ;
            reportfooting :
                begin
                    newpage ;
                    newlines (reportfootingline - 1) ;
                    puttext (line, 'END  OF  REPORT', 29, 15) ;
                    writeline (line)
                end ;
            pageheading :
                begin
                    newpage ;
                    newlines (pageheadingline - 1) ;
                    putinteger (line, pagecount, 39, 3) ;
                    writeline (line) ;
                    newlines (firstdetailline - pageheadingline - 1)
                end ;
            pagefooting :
                begin
                    newlines (pagefootingline - linecount - 1) ;
                    putinteger (line, pagecount, 39, 3) ;
                    writeline (line) ;
                end
            end
        end
    end {print};

begin
    with nextgroup, savingsprintout do
    begin
        print (reportheading) ;
        pagecount := 0 ;
        buffer.obtain (nextgroup) ;
        repeat
            pagecount := pagecount + 1 ;
            print (pageheading) ;
            linecount := firstdetailline - 1 ;
            repeat
                newlines (linestoskip) ;
                for i := 1 to numberoflines do writeline (contents[i]) ;
                linecount := linecount + linestoskip + numberoflines ;
                buffer.obtain (nextgroup)
            until endofreportgroupsequence or
                    (linecount + linestoskip + numberoflines >
                                                lastdetailline) ;
            print (pagefooting)
        until endofreportgroupsequence ;
        print (reportfooting)
    end
end {printpagedreport} ;



begin {main program}
    ***
end.
```

If a summary report is required, i.e., as in Listing 23 with branch headings and details omitted, then it is necessary to remove only the procedure statements

sendtobuffer (branchheading)

and

sendtobuffer (detail)

from the process *generatelogicalreportgroups*.

10.3   RESOLVING THE STRUCTURAL CLASH

How can we implement this program in a language which does not provide concurrent processes, e.g., in a sequential programming language such as Pascal or COBOL? The process *generatelogicalreportgroups* which generates the logical structure of the report consists of a nested set of loops reflecting the hierarchy of control groups which make up the report. The process *printpagedreport* that imposes the physical structure upon the report also consists of a pair of nested loops reflecting the line and page structure of the printed report. However, the two sets of nested loops do not nest with respect to one another, but overlap in an arbitrary way. Hence we cannot produce a sequential program merely by nesting one process within the other and are faced with a structural clash which must be reconciled in order to produce a sequential report generation program. How can this structural clash be resolved?

(a) By implementing the processes as two *sequential programs*. The processes are written as sequential programs and the two programs are run in sequence. First *generatelogicalreportgroups* generates and leaves its logical report groups in an intermediate file of logical report groups and then *printpagedreport* reads this file and constructs the paged report (Figure 10.3). Each call of *buffer.add* in *generatelogicalreportgroups* becomes an output statement which sends the report group concerned to the sequential intermediate file, and each call of *buffer.obtain* in *printpagedreport* becomes an input statement which reads the next logical report group from the file. The communication buffer between the two programs is thus a file and so the overall report generation takes longer as compared with the use of concurrent processes due to the amount of input–output activity involved.

Input file → Generate logical report groups → Report group file

Report group file → Print paged report → Report

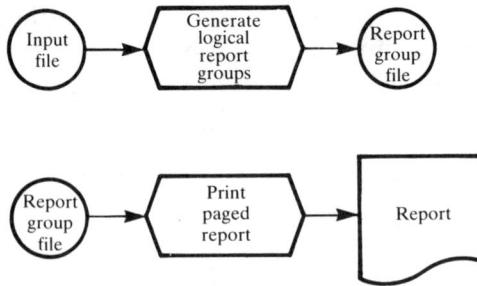

Figure 10.3   Producing the report in two passes

(b) By implementing the processes as *coroutines* — in a programming language such as Simula the processes *generatelogicalreportgroups* and *printpagedreport* might be implemented as coroutines (cooperating routines). Each time that *generatelogicalreportgroups* produces a logical report group it assigns the details of the report group to a global variable acting as a buffer, and then transfers control to *printpagedreport* via a coroutine *resume* statement. This suspends *generatelogicalreportgroups* and recommences execution of *printpagedreport* at the point at which *printpagedreport* previously relinquished control to *generatelogicalreportgroups*. *printpagedreport* then adds this logical report group to the printed report and transfers control back to *generatelogicalreportgroups* (again via a *resume* statement) which continues at the point from which it transferred control to *printpagedreport* previously. Hence each call of *buffer.add* in *generatelogicalreportgroups* is replaced by an assignment to the global communication variable followed by a *resume*, and each call of *buffer.obtain* in *printpagedreport* is replaced by a *resume* followed by an inspection of the value of the global communication variable. Thus the necessary interleaving of the actions of the two processes is obtained.

(c) By using the *Program Inversion* technique — if the implementation language provides neither parallel programming facilities nor coroutines, but only a subroutine facility, then one of the two processes *generatelogicalreportgroups* and *printpagedreport* (usually *generatelogicalreportgroups*) is inverted with respect to the other (i.e., *generatelogicalreportgroups* becomes a subroutine of *printpagedreport*). Thus, whenever *printpagedreport* wants some input it calls *generatelogicalreportgroups*, but each such call of *generatelogicalreportgroups* should only execute part of its overall action, viz., from the point of output of the previous logical report group to the point of output of the next — thus *generatelogicalreportgroups* must remember where its next invocation is to begin by assigning some suitable value to a global variable (the *switch variable*) immediately prior to relinquishing control, and transfer control to the point indicated when it is next invoked. Hence each call of *buffer. obtain* in *printpagedreport* is replaced by a call of *generatelogicalreportgroups*, and each call of *buffer.add* in *generatelogicalreportgroups* is replaced by an assignment to the switch variable followed by a subroutine exit. Each entry to *generatelogicalreportgroups* must first execute a statement which switches control to the appropriate re-entry point according to the switch value. Depending upon the language used, the calls of *generatelogicalreportgroups* may involve that procedure in assigning the next logical report group value to a variable parameter or else to a global buffer variable. This technique, which was developed by Michael Jackson as part of his Jackson Structured Programming (JSP) methodology, is illustrated by the COBOL version of the report generation program presented in Chapter 18.

(d) The three techniques described above are general methods for resolving structural clashes. The Report Writer facility of COBOL, as well as similar facilities in some special-purpose languages, provides special features for report-writing. The production of reports is so commonplace that, rather than include special report-writing facilities in an existing language, as in COBOL, non-procedural languages have been developed which use the report generation process as the basic run-time execution pattern and allow the user to supply various parameters (input file descriptions, calculations, report formats) from which a program is generated that will produce the required report from the given input files. RPG II is the best known of these non-procedural languages. The COBOL Report Writer is discussed in Chapter 18.

EXERCISES

1. Implement the report generation program in Pascal as two programs run in sequence and using an intermediate sequential file of logical report groups.

2. Implement the report generation program using coroutines.

3. You are designing a data processing language which is to provide a feature for automatic generation of reports from the contents of input files. What facilities would you provide for the specification of
   (a) the logical structure of the input file;
   (b) the physical layout of the report?

Part 2

FILE PROCESSING
IN
COBOL

11 AN INTRODUCTION TO COBOL

In May 1959 a committee (known as CODASYL — Conference on Data Systems Languages) sponsored by the US Department of Defense (the world's largest computer user, then and now) produced a definition of a programming language intended for business data processing applications. In 1960 this definition was published as COBOL (COmmon Business Oriented Language).

Since 1960 COBOL has become the most widely implemented programming language and is certainly the language most widely used by professional programmers. Compilers for COBOL are available on almost all mainframe machines as well as most minicomputers and many microcomputers. One of the features of COBOL has been its evolution, by means of a regular series of revisions to its definition, since 1960. COBOL-61, COBOL-Edition 65, and COBOL-68 all defined extensions to the original language. In 1974 ANSI approved a new definition, COBOL-74, as a 540 page document. The language is now very considerably larger than in 1960 and, as CODASYL currently have committees working on data base, mass storage, and asynchronous language facilities, the expansion seems far from over.

11.1 AN OVERVIEW OF COBOL

The basic data structure of the language is the record. Data within a record is structured in a hierarchical manner, and names may be associated with any of the substructures of a record. Arrays are also provided (known in COBOL as *tables*), and tables of records, or records containing tables, may be declared. Elementary data items must be fully declared as to type and size — the PICTURE facility enables the construction of an unbounded set of possible type definitions. The basic elementary data types are numbers and character strings.

The primitive operators of COBOL include simple arithmetic, logical and relational operators as well as character string operators. Assignment is provided with automatic type conversion because of the potentially large number of types that a programmer may construct. The dependence of business data processing on file-handling necessitates the provision of a wide range of powerful facilities for file-handling, including primitives for manipulating sequential, indexed-sequential, and random organization files; primitives for sorting and merging data files; and an automatic facility for generating printed reports from the contents of data files.

Structured statements include an alternation (IF) statement, a multibranch GO TO statement for multi-way selection in limited circumstances, and a PERFORM statement which acts as both a loop constructor and a (parameterless) procedure call statement. The language is based upon a single module program structure allowing only global data. There is no means by which a programmer can define his own functions. An exception-handling facility is provided for use when input–output errors, etc., occur.

Of all the commonly used programming languages none has a more readable syntax than COBOL. Even simple arithmetic operations may be written as statements which involve the use of English verbs rather than mathematical symbols — the language also provides a wide range of 'noise' words which may be included in a program to enhance its readability.

11.2   STRUCTURE OF COBOL PROGRAMS

11.2.1   The Four Divisions

A COBOL program must be organized according to a standard predetermined hierarchical structure. The order of structures in the hierarchy is division, section, paragraph, sentence, statement, clause.

To a person picking up a COBOL program for the first time, its outstanding feature is the organization of the program into four divisions — the IDENTIFICATION, ENVIRONMENT, DATA and PROCEDURE divisions, in that order (see Listing 25 for an example of a COBOL program).

(a) The purpose of the IDENTIFICATION DIVISION is purely documentary — to identify the source program, its author, and origins. The PROGRAM-ID paragraph is mandatory, while the AUTHOR, INSTALLATION, DATE-WRITTEN and DATE-COMPILED paragraphs are optional. The entries in each of the last four paragraphs are known as comment-entries and serve solely as documentation. Thus the program text itself contains the basic identifying documentation. Such documentation is obviously necessary in a situation where a data processing department will have (probably) hundreds of COBOL programs amounting to many millions of lines of program text.

```
IDENTIFICATION DIVISION.
PROGRAM-ID.  program-name.
[AUTHOR.   [comment-entry] ]
[INSTALLATION.    [comment-entry] ]
[DATE-WRITTEN.    [comment-entry] ]
[DATE-COMPILED.   [comment-entry] ]
```

A *comment-entry* is any sequence of characters.

```
{character} ...
```

(b) The ENVIRONMENT DIVISION defines system-specific information about the compiling and object computers, as well as the peripheral devices used. This division has two sections: CONFIGURATION and INPUT-OUTPUT.

```
ENVIRONMENT DIVISION.
CONFIGURATION SECTION.
SOURCE-COMPUTER.    computer-name.
OBJECT-COMPUTER.    computer-name.
[SPECIAL-NAMES.     special-names-entry ]
[INPUT-OUTPUT SECTION.
 FILE-CONTROL.      {file-control-entry} ...
 [I-O-CONTROL.      input-output-control-entry ] ]
```

The first section, the CONFIGURATION SECTION, has two mandatory paragraphs: SOURCE-COMPUTER, to specify the compiling computer, and OBJECT-COMPUTER, to specify the executing computer, which may be different from the compiling computer if the compiler is a cross-compiler. The optional paragraph is the SPECIAL-NAMES paragraph, which allows the programmer to associate his own names with those objects (e.g., peripheral devices) which are given names by the particular COBOL implementation, and hence facilitates transfer of programs between different systems. The second section, INPUT-OUTPUT, has two major paragraphs — FILE-CONTROL which names the files used by a program and defines the external media on which they reside, as well as organizational and access information; and I-O-CONTROL, which specifies special input–output control techniques to be used in the object program.

Since a COBOL program may be compiled and executed on many different computer systems, and in many data processing installations with different peripheral devices, the ENVIRONMENT DIVISION serves a useful purpose in isolating the environment-dependence of the rest of the program. Transporting a program to a different environment will then require the rewriting of the ENVIRONMENT DIVISION and, hopefully, a minimum of changes to the remainder of the program.

(c) All the declarations of data used in a COBOL program appear in the DATA DIVISION, which consists of several sections according to the usage of the particular data items. For our purposes we shall consider only three of the five possible sections:

1. the FILE SECTION describes the format of all data held on external files and transmitted into or out of main memory, as well as the format of data held on internal sort files;
2. the WORKING-STORAGE SECTION describes all temporary data items generated during the execution of the program;
3. the REPORT SECTION is used to declare the data and report formats by which the Report Writer Control System can construct a report.

```
DATA DIVISION.
FILE SECTION.
   [ file-description-entry ] ...
WORKING-STORAGE SECTION.
   [ data-item-description ] ...
REPORT SECTION.
   [ formatted-report-description ] ...
```

(d) the PROCEDURE DIVISION contains the executable statements. In its simplest form it consists of a sequence of procedures. A procedure is a *paragraph* or *section*, where a section is a named group of paragraphs. If one paragraph is in a named section, then all paragraphs must be in sections. Hence there are two formats possible for the PROCEDURE DIVISION. Either

```
PROCEDURE DIVISION.
{section-name SECTION.
[paragraph-name.   [sentence] ...] ...} ...
```

or

```
PROCEDURE DIVISION.
{paragraph-name.   [sentence] ...} ...
```

Section names must be unique and paragraph names must be unique within a section. Each sentence in the PROCEDURE DIVISION consists of one or more statements, separated by semicolons or spaces. Execution of a program begins at the first statement of the PROCEDURE DIVISION.

11.2.2 Notation for Defining COBOL Syntax Rules

Throughout this second part of the book we shall give various syntax rules which define the formats in which the words and other elements of the COBOL language may be arranged to form valid COBOL constructs such as divisions, sections, paragraphs, and sentences. The possible structures of the four divisions of a COBOL program have already been described in the previous section by such rules.

All words printed in upper case appearing within part of a syntax rule are key words which must appear if that part is used (e.g., IDENTIFICATION, DIVISION, etc.). Words printed in lower case are the names of other COBOL structures whose possible forms are described by means of other syntax rules defined elsewhere.

Any portion of a syntax rule that is enclosed in square brackets, [ ], may be included or omitted as the programmer wishes. Thus, in the IDENTIFICATION DIVISION, not only are the AUTHOR, INSTALLATION, DATE-WRITTEN, and DATE-COMPILED paragraphs optional, but so also are the comment-entries within those paragraphs. The term *comment-entry* is used in this syntax rule and is then defined immediately afterwards.

Braces, { }, enclosing a portion of a rule indicate that one of the options contained within the braces must be selected. The choices are usually presented in a vertical column.

The ellipsis mark (...) appearing in a rule indicates the position at which the programmer may repeat some preceding portion, which is determined as follows: Given ... in a syntax rule, begin scanning right to left, determine the first] or } to the left of the ... ; continue scanning right to left and determine the logically matching [or { ; the ... then applies to the words between the pair of delimiters so determined. When braces enclose a portion of a rule, but only one possibility is shown, the function of the braces is to delimit that portion of the rule to which a following ellipsis applies. From the ENVIRONMENT DIVISION format defined earlier, we can see that the FILE-CONTROL paragraph may consist of one or more *file-control-entries*. In the DATA DIVISION the FILE SECTION consists of zero or more *file-description-entries*. If it contains sections then the PROCEDURE DIVISION structure is such that it consists of one or more sections, each with a section heading (*section-name* SECTION) followed by zero or more paragraphs, each containing zero or more sentences. Structures such as *file-control-entry* and *file-description-entry* will be defined at a later and more appropriate stage.

The punctuation characters comma and semicolon appear in many syntax rules. They may be included or omitted by the programmer, and are also interchangeable.

11.2.3 Presentation of COBOL Programs

COBOL programs make use of 'words' and 'literals' (constants). A word is composed of up to 30 letters, digits, and hyphens — it must neither begin nor end with a hyphen. When a programmer is required to declare a word (e.g., as the name of a data item or paragraph) there are a number of reserved words (about 350!) that must be avoided — only a few of these contain digits or hyphens. Such a user-defined word introduced as the name of a data item should begin with a letter, although this restriction does not apply to section and paragraph names. A numeric literal consists of up to 18 decimal digits and may contain a decimal point but must not finish with one; it may be immediately preceded by a plus or minus sign. A non-numeric literal (i.e., a string) consists of up to 120 characters and is enclosed in quote characters ("), e.g.,

```
"THIS IS AN EXAMPLE OF A STRING"
```

A single quote character within a non-numeric literal is denoted by writing the quote character twice, e.g.,

```
"THE WORD HE SPOKE WAS ""MAGIC""!"
```

The normal mode of presentation of COBOL programs to a compiler is as lines of text as reflected by the layout of a COBOL program sheet (Figure 11.1). Columns 1 to 6 of each line may be used to hold line sequence numbers — numbers should originally be multiples of 10 or 100 to allow subsequent insertions. The actual COBOL program text in most lines of the program begins in column 12 (the B margin) but certain lines (i.e., division, section, and paragraph headings) begin in column 8 (the A margin).

Programs may also contain *comment-lines* — such lines contain an asterisk character ('*') in column 7 and the contents of the line are taken by the compiler to be intended as documentation. Any line containing a slash character ('/') in column 7 is also a comment-line but the printing of that line during compilation will cause a page throw in the listing produced by the COBOL compiler.

Column 7 is used not only to indicate comment-lines but also to indicate the overflow of one line into the next (this is useful for continuing strings which are too long to fit on a single line — in which case the continuation of the string on the next line is indicated by a hyphen in column 7 and there must be a quotation mark to the right of the B margin preceding the continuation of the string — see the example in Figure 11.1 on the lines numbered 220 and 230).

All sections begin with a section heading starting in the A margin, viz.

section-name SECTION.

followed by a series of paragraphs. Paragraph names are written starting in the A margin and followed by a full stop; the body of the paragraph follows on subsequent lines. The end of one paragraph or section is indicated by the beginning of the next or the end of the program. The body of a paragraph consists of a sequence of sentences, each of which starts in the B margin (or later) and is terminated by a full stop.

11.3   AN EXAMPLE COBOL PROGRAM

A COBOL program and a description of its contents and operation are now presented in order to illustrate the structure of COBOL programs and to give a brief introduction to, and illustration of, some of the more frequently used language features.

```
Sequence no.
1   6 7 8  11 12  15    20    25    30    35    40    45    50    55    60    65  70 72 73  75    80
          A   B

010*       THIS LINE IS A COMMENT
020/       THIS COMMENT WILL APPEAR AT THE TOP OF A NEW PAGE IN THE
030*          LISTING PRODUCED BY THE COMPILER

210        77 MY-NAME PIC X(10) VALUE "JOHN ELDER".
220        77 MY-ADDRESS PIC X(55) VALUE "22A, ROBINSON ROAD, BANGOR, NORTHERN I
230-                                      "RELAND, BT19 2NJ.".

710 PROCEDURE DIVISION.
720 THE-FIRST SECTION.
730 PARAGRAPH-1.
740        DISPLAY MY-NAME, MY-ADDRESS
750 PARAGRAPH-2.
```

Figure 11.1 Layout of COBOL text

The purpose of presenting an example program at this stage is primarily to give the reader a flavor of what COBOL programs look like, and the sort of features that the language provides for the programmer. Chapter 12 gives a more thorough introduction to the basic data and algorithm structuring features of COBOL than is provided in this chapter. Details of various specialized data processing facilities provided in COBOL are presented in most of the succeeding chapters. However, this text concentrates only on giving a general description of the features concerned and illustrating their application rather than attempting to give exhaustive coverage of the detailed language rules. These are best learned by actually writing COBOL programs and having them compiled and executed on a computer — at that stage the use of the reference manuals for your particular COBOL implementation will prove invaluable.

Program specification: A file of 80 character records contains details of the current state of members' accounts in a savings bank. The format of each record is shown below

1	8	9	38	39	45	46	52	53	80
account number		member identity		current balance		minimum balance		other details	

The fields of each record contain, from left to right, an eight-character account number, a thirty-character member identification, a seven-digit value denoting the amount currently in the account, another seven-digit value giving the minimum balance held in the account since annual interest was last paid, and the final 28 characters contain other information in which we are not interested. The current balance and the minimum balance held in an account are recorded as a number of cents (e.g., 0205476 represents $2054.76). A printed report is to be produced detailing the annual interest due to each member, calculated as follows: the first $5000 of the minimum balance held in a member's savings account during the present interest period earns interest at a current lower rate of 9.5%; if the minimum balance exceeds $5000 then the excess above $5000 attracts interest at a current higher rate of 10.75%. The program is to print out the total number of members and aggregate interest paid to those members.

In the description which follows, reference is made to the line numbers of Listing 25, the program *PROGRAM0*.

LISTING 25 : *PROGRAM0*

```
010 IDENTIFICATION DIVISION.
020 PROGRAM-ID.        PROGRAM0.
030 INSTALLATION.      QUB.
040 AUTHOR.            JOHN ELDER.
050 DATE-WRITTEN.      JANUARY 1983.
060 DATE-COMPILED.     01/10/8.
070
080* A PROGRAM TO READ ACCOUNT RECORDS FROM A PUNCHED CARD FILE,
090* COUNT THE TOTAL NUMBER OF CUSTOMERS,
100* AND CALCULATE THE TOTAL INTEREST TO BE PAID.
110* INTEREST PER ACCOUNT CALCULATED AS FOLLOWS :
120*    FIRST $5000 OF MINIMUM BALANCE AT LOWER-RATE
130*    EXCESS AT HIGHER-RATE  (SEE WORKING-STORAGE SECTION)
140
150 ENVIRONMENT DIVISION.
160
170 CONFIGURATION SECTION.
180 SOURCE-COMPUTER.   SUPER-2000.
190 OBJECT-COMPUTER.   SUPER-2000.
200
210 INPUT-OUTPUT SECTION.
220 FILE-CONTROL.
230     SELECT CLIENT-DATA ASSIGN TO CARD-READER 1.
240     SELECT INTEREST-REPORT ASSIGN TO PRINTER 1.
250
260
270 DATA DIVISION.
280
290 FILE SECTION.
300 FD CLIENT-DATA LABEL RECORDS OMITTED.
310 01 CLIENT-RECORD.
320     02 ACCOUNT-NUMBER    PIC XXXXXXXX.
330     02 CLIENT-IDENTITY   PIC X(30).
340     02 CURRENT-BALANCE   PIC 9(5)V99.
350     02 MINIMUM-BALANCE   PIC 9(5)V99.
360     02 FILLER            PIC X(28).
370 FD INTEREST-REPORT LABEL RECORDS OMITTED.
380 01 OUTPUT-LINE          PIC X(120).
390
400 WORKING-STORAGE SECTION.
410 77 THRESHOLD           PIC 9(4) VALUE 5000.
420 77 OVER-THRESHOLD      PIC 9(5)V99.
430 77 REGULAR-INTEREST    PIC 9(4)V99 USAGE COMP.
440 77 EXTRA-INTEREST      PIC 9(5)V99 USAGE COMP.
450 77 TOTAL-INTEREST      PIC 9(5)V99 USAGE COMP.
460 77 AGGREGATE-INTEREST  PIC 9(7)V99 USAGE COMP VALUE ZERO.
47ᴜ 77 CLIENT-COUNT        PIC 9999     USAGE COMP VALUE ZERO.
480 77 EOF                 PIC 9 VALUE ZERO.
490    88 END-OF-DATA      VALUE 1.
500 01 CLIENT-LINE.
510     02 ACCOUNT-NUMBER    PIC X(8).
520     02 CLIENT-IDENTITY   PIC X(30).
530     02 FILLER            PIC X(12) VALUE " INTEREST = ".
540     02 INTEREST          PIC $$$,$$9.99.
550 01 SUMMARY-LINE.
560     02 FILLER            PIC X(19) VALUE "NUMBER OF CLIENTS =".
570     02 CLIENT-TOTAL      PIC ZZZ9.
580     02 FILLER            PIC X(24) VALUE "     EARNED INTEREST =".
590     02 INTEREST-TOTAL    PIC $$,$$$,$$9.99.
600 77 LOWER-RATE     PIC V9999 VALUE 0.0950.
610 77 HIGHER-RATE    PIC V9999 VALUE 0.1075.
620
630
640 PROCEDURE DIVISION.
650 MAIN-PARAGRAPH.
660     OPEN INPUT CLIENT-DATA , OUTPUT INTEREST-REPORT.
670     PERFORM READ-A-CARD.
```

```
680      PERFORM PROCESS-CLIENT UNTIL END-OF-DATA.
690      PERFORM CLOSE-DOWN.
700      STOP RUN.
710 READ-A-CARD.
720      READ CLIENT-DATA AT END MOVE 1 TO EOF.
730 PROCESS-CLIENT.
740      PERFORM CALCULATE-INTEREST.
750      ADD 1 TO CLIENT-COUNT.
760      ADD TOTAL-INTEREST TO AGGREGATE-INTEREST.
770      MOVE CORRESPONDING CLIENT-RECORD TO CLIENT-LINE.
780      MOVE TOTAL-INTEREST TO INTEREST.
790      WRITE OUTPUT-LINE FROM CLIENT-LINE AFTER ADVANCING 1 LINE.
800      PERFORM READ-A-CARD.
810 CALCULATE-INTEREST.
820      IF MINIMUM-BALANCE IS GREATER THAN THRESHOLD PERFORM FORMULA-2
830          ELSE MULTIPLY MINIMUM-BALANCE BY LOWER-RATE
840                  GIVING TOTAL-INTEREST.
850 FORMULA-2.
860      MULTIPLY THRESHOLD BY LOWER-RATE GIVING REGULAR-INTEREST.
870      SUBTRACT THRESHOLD FROM MINIMUM-BALANCE GIVING OVER-THRESHOLD.
880      MULTIPLY OVER-THRESHOLD BY HIGHER-RATE GIVING EXTRA-INTEREST.
890      ADD REGULAR-INTEREST, EXTRA-INTEREST GIVING TOTAL-INTEREST.
900 CLOSE-DOWN.
910      MOVE CLIENT-COUNT TO CLIENT-TOTAL.
920      MOVE AGGREGATE-INTEREST TO INTEREST-TOTAL.
930      WRITE OUTPUT-LINE FROM SUMMARY-LINE AFTER ADVANCING 2 LINES.
940      CLOSE CLIENT-DATA , INTEREST-REPORT.
```

```
IDENTIFICATION DIVISION.
PROGRAM-ID.             PROGRAMO.
INSTALLATION.           QUB.
AUTHOR.                 JOHN ELDER.
DATE-WRITTEN.           JANUARY 1983.
DATE-COMPILED.
```

Lines 010–060 form the IDENTIFICATION DIVISION of the program, and serve purely as documentation. The division header on line 010 is required, as is the PROGRAM-ID paragraph, but all other paragraphs are optional. When the program is written the DATE-COMPILED paragraph is often left empty. During compilation of the program the compiler will insert the current date as the comment-entry for the DATE-COMPILED paragraph (or replace any existing comment-entry with the current date), which will then be printed in the compilation listing, as shown in Listing 25. Our COBOL compiler presents the date of compilation in the form month/day/year, where each component of the date is represented by two digits.

Lines 080–140 are comment-lines giving the reader some information about the purpose of the program.

Lines 150–240 form the ENVIRONMENT DIVISION with the division header on line 150 required.

Lines 270–610 form the DATA DIVISION as indicated by the compusory header on line 270. All data used in the program is declared here.

Lines 640–940 are the PROCEDURE DIVISION which begins with the mandatory header and is broken up into named paragraphs which may be referenced by subroutine calls (PERFORM statements) and GO TO statements. Program execution begins at line 650, the first statement of the first paragraph (MAIN-PARA-GRAPH). In this example the PROCEDURE DIVISION is not written in sections. Hence the structure of the PROCEDURE DIVISION corresponds to the second format given in Section 11.2.1.

```
CONFIGURATION SECTION.
SOURCE-COMPUTER.    SUPER-2000.
OBJECT-COMPUTER.    SUPER-2000.
```

These lines form the CONFIGURATION SECTION — the computer on which the program is to be compiled is specified in the SOURCE-COMPUTER paragraph, and the OBJECT-COMPUTER paragraph specifies the name of the computer on which the object program will be executed (see description of line 240 for full details of the name).

```
INPUT-OUTPUT SECTION.
FILE-CONTROL.
    SELECT CLIENT-DATA
       ASSIGN TO CARD-READER 1.
    SELECT INTEREST-REPORT
       ASSIGN TO PRINTER 1.
```

The INPUT-OUTPUT SECTION consists, in this case, of only a FILE-CONTROL paragraph associating data files declared in the program with actual files on physical hardware devices. The file named CLIENT-DATA in the program is actually a punched card file held on CARD-READER 1 (a standard device name defined by the COBOL implementation to denote the card reader which will hold the card file when the program is executed). The printed output from the program is formed in a file INTEREST-REPORT which is actually a line printer file (PRINTER 1 is the system-name for the line printer designated as number 1 in the configuration).

Each implementation of COBOL defines a set of so-called *system-names*, local standard names for the devices forming the physical hardware configuration available to COBOL programs during execution. These names are required for, e.g., the computer itself (to identify it in the ENVIRONMENT DIVISION) and all the card readers, line printers, magnetic tape, and disk drives on which files used in a COBOL program may reside. In our implementation the computer itself has the name SUPER-2000 (as used in both the SOURCE-COMPUTER and OBJECT-COMPUTER paragraphs) and its card readers (of which there are two), card punch (one only), line printers (two in all), magnetic tape, and magnetic disk drives (four of each) are denoted by the system-names CARD-READER, CARD-PUNCH, PRINTER, TAPE, and DISK, respectively, followed by an integer specifying the particular device of that class.

Lines 290–380 form the FILE SECTION in which all files introduced in the FILE-CONTROL paragraph are defined in terms of their characteristics and record formats.

```
FD CLIENT-DATA LABEL RECORDS OMITTED.
```

The file description (FD) for the input file CLIENT-DATA. Since this file is held on a card reader little information is required. The LABEL RECORDS OMITTED clause indicates that the file is not preceded by a special label card containing identification information relating to the file. This FD description, together with the FILE-CONTROL entry, gives sufficient information to the compiler to enable the file to be accessed at run-time.

```
01 CLIENT-RECORD.
   02 ACCOUNT-NUMBER    PIC XXXXXXXX.
   02 CLIENT-IDENTITY   PIC X(30).
   02 CURRENT-BALANCE   PIC 9(5)V99.
   02 MINIMUM-BALANCE   PIC 9(5)V99.
   02 FILLER            PIC X(28).
```

These lines define the format of records in the file CLIENT-DATA. This declaration causes storage to be allocated in main memory for a record of the specified format, and each time a record is read from the CLIENT-DATA file it will be stored in the data item named CLIENT-RECORD.

Line 310: the entire input record structure is named CLIENT-RECORD — the level number 01 (level numbers indicate the hierarchical structure of the record) denotes that this is an entire structure.

Lines 320–360: CLIENT-RECORD is made up of five fields; the first four fields are as described in the program specification and the

fifth field, which has no particular significance in this particular application, is given the standard COBOL name FILLER, which may be
used in place of a data-name for a field if that field is never referred to
explicitly by any operation within the program.

Line 320: the type of the field ACCOUNT-NUMBER is given
using a PIC (picture) clause XXXXXXXX specifying an eight-character string — each X indicates an alphanumeric character.

Line 330: CLIENT-IDENTITY is a string of 30 alphanumeric
characters — X(30) is shorthand for a picture of thirty Xs.

Lines 340 and 350: CURRENT-BALANCE and MINIMUM-
BALANCE are both seven-digit character strings (9 in a picture represents a digit position) with the V indicating that there is an implied
decimal point between the fifth and sixth digits, i.e., no decimal point
actually occurs on the punched card record, but any operation using
these values will treat them as if a decimal point is present at the indicated position.

Line 360: in this program the last 28 characters of a punched card
record do not require a unique name.

```
FD INTEREST-REPORT LABEL RECORDS OMITTED.
01   OUTPUT-LINE           PIC X(120).
```

The file INTEREST-REPORT is a printer file, hence LABEL
RECORDS OMITTED (printer files do not have any form of file-
labelling associated with them in most implementations). Since we
wish to output two types of records with different formats to this file
the record structure OUTPUT-LINE is defined simply as a 120 character string, the length of a line on the printer used. The actual lines to
be output will be built up elsewhere and moved to OUTPUT-LINE
immediately prior to output.

Lines 400–600 form the WORKING-STORAGE SECTION
which contains declarations of working data items, i.e., those not
directly associated with any file, but which are used by the program in
performing calculations and generating output records.

```
77 THRESHOLD             PIC 9(4) VALUE   5000.
```

An unstructured data item (denoted by level number 77) named
THRESHOLD is a four-digit number with initial value 5000.

```
77 OVER-THRESHOLD        PIC 9(5)V99.
```

An uninitialized seven-digit data item with two implied places of deci-
mals.

```
77 REGULAR-INTEREST        PIC 9(4)V99 USAGE COMP.
```

USAGE COMP specifies that REGULAR-INTEREST is to be used primarily in arithmetic calculations and should therefore be stored in a form (often binary unless the computer provides decimal arithmetic facilities) appropriate for efficient hardware arithmetic.

```
77 EXTRA-INTEREST          PIC 9(5)V99 USAGE COMP.
77 TOTAL-INTEREST          PIC 9(5)V99 USAGE COMP.
77 AGGREGATE-INTEREST      PIC 9(7)V99
                           USAGE COMP VALUE ZERO.
77 CLIENT-COUNT            PIC 9999
                           USAGE COMP VALUE ZERO.
```

Lines 440–470 declare similar data items. However, AGGREGATE-INTEREST and CLIENT-COUNT are both given initial values of zero. ZERO is a COBOL *figurative constant*, i.e., a predefined data name which identifies a constant value, in this case the integer 0.

```
77 EOF                 PIC 9 VALUE ZERO.
   88 END-OF-DATA VALUE 1.
```

A single-digit numeric data item EOF is initialized here to zero. The level 88 data item END-OF-DATA is associated with the preceding declaration of EOF and is effectively a boolean variable whose value is *true* if and only if the current value of EOF is 1.

```
01 CLIENT-LINE.
   02 ACCOUNT-NUMBER    PIC X(8).
   02 CLIENT-IDENTITY   PIC X(30).
   02 FILLER            PIC X(12)
            VALUE " INTEREST = ".
   02 INTEREST          PIC $$$,$$9.99.
```

A record structure CLIENT-LINE (all records have level number 01) is used to hold the details of a member's account and interest due, prior to printing. The anonymous field at line 530 contains a constant string value " INTEREST = " which forms part of every CLIENT-LINE value generated by the program. The INTEREST field contains the value of the interest due to a member. The picture clause specifies special editing actions to be performed whenever a value is moved to the field during program execution — these editing actions are intended to produce a suitable printed form of the value. $$$,$$9.99 indicates that the value will be less than 100 000 with two digits after the decimal point (all but the leading $ is effectively a 9). A decimal point will be inserted between the fifth and sixth digits, any leading zeroes beyond the unit's digit will be suppressed and replaced by blanks, a comma will be inserted if necessary, and a single $ will be placed immediately to the left of the leading digit. Hence INTEREST is a ten-character field. If the value 4321.23 were moved to this field by the program its resultant value would be equal to the string " $4,321.23".

```
01 SUMMARY-LINE.
   02 FILLER              PIC X(19)
      VALUE "NUMBER OF CLIENTS  =".
   02 CLIENT-TOTAL        PIC ZZZ9.
   02 FILLER              PIC X(24)
      VALUE "       EARNED INTEREST  =".
   02 INTEREST-TOTAL PIC $$,$$$,$$9.99.
```

These lines define a similar record type used for constructing the final line of the report giving the total of members and interest due.

```
77 LOWER-RATE    PIC V9999 VALUE 0.0950.
77 HIGHER-RATE   PIC V9999 VALUE 0.1075.
```

LOWER-RATE and HIGHER-RATE are two constant-valued data items — if the rates of interest paid to members are changed, then the only modification required to the program is to change the initial values given to both these data items.

The PROCEDURE DIVISION begins with the division header on line 640. The first statement of the program to be executed will be the first statement of the first paragraph.

```
MAIN-PARAGRAPH.
   OPEN INPUT CLIENT-DATA, OUTPUT INTEREST-REPORT.
```

The files CLIENT-DATA and INTEREST-REPORT are opened ready for input and output, respectively. All files used in a COBOL program must be opened before processing of their contents may commence.

```
   PERFORM READ-A-CARD.
```

The single statement (line 720) of the body of the paragraph READ-A-CARD (line 710) is executed as a procedure, after which control returns to line 680.

```
   PERFORM PROCESS-CLIENT UNTIL END-OF-DATA.
```

While the value of the data item END-OF-DATA is not true (i.e., the value of EOF equals zero) the statements of the paragraph PROCESS-CLIENT are repeatedly executed — the PERFORM ... UNTIL ... statement of COBOL is equivalent to the while-statement of Pascal.

```
PERFORM CLOSE-DOWN.
```

causes execution of the paragraph named CLOSE-DOWN (at line 890).

```
STOP RUN.
```

This statement, when executed, causes the program to terminate.

```
READ-A-CARD.
        READ CLIENT-DATA AT END MOVE 1 TO EOF.
```

Line 710 is the heading of the paragraph READ-A-CARD. At line 720 the next record of the punched card file CLIENT-DATA is read and its characters are stored in the record item named CLIENT-RECORD. If, however, the end of the file has been reached and no such next record exists to be read, then 1 is assigned to EOF (and the value of END-OF-DATA thus becomes equal to *true*).

```
PERFORM CALCULATE-INTEREST.
```

Execution of this statement in turn causes execution of the paragraph CALCULATE-INTEREST (which calculates the total interest due to the member whose account was last read into ACCOUNT-RECORD, and leaves its value in the data item TOTAL-INTEREST).

```
ADD 1 TO CLIENT-COUNT.
```

increments the value of the numeric data item CLIENT-COUNT by 1.

```
ADD TOTAL-INTEREST TO AGGREGATE-INTEREST.
```

increments the value of the data item AGGREGATE-INTEREST by that of the data item TOTAL-INTEREST.

```
MOVE CORRESPONDING CLIENT-RECORD TO CLIENT-LINE.
```

The values of the fields of the record item CLIENT-RECORD which have the same names as fields of the record item CLIENT-LINE (i.e.,

ACCOUNT-NUMBER and CLIENT-IDENTITY) are moved to
these corresponding fields of CLIENT-LINE.

```
MOVE TOTAL-INTEREST TO INTEREST.
```

The total interest payable to the member is moved to the
INTEREST field of CLIENT-LINE (where the editing described
previously takes place).

```
WRITE OUTPUT-LINE FROM CLIENT-LINE
    AFTER ADVANCING 1 LINE.
```

The contents of CLIENT-LINE (this record data item is effectively
a 60 character string) are moved into the first 60 characters of the
record OUTPUT-LINE, the remaining 60 characters space-filled,
and the value of OUTPUT-LINE is then output to the printer file
INTEREST-REPORT on its next printing line. The AFTER
ADVANCING clause specifies how far the carriage control of the
printer is to move before printing this output line.

```
PERFORM READ-A-CARD.
```

reads in the next card by calling the paragraph READ-A-CARD.

```
CALCULATE-INTEREST.
    IF MINIMUM-BALANCE IS GREATER THAN
        THRESHOLD PERFORM FORMULA-2
    ELSE MULTIPLY MINIMUM-BALANCE
        BY LOWER-RATE
        GIVING TOTAL-INTEREST.
```

The paragraph called as a subroutine from line 740 calculates the
interest to be paid on the account currently being processed. An IF
statement determines which interest calculation is required by testing the value of the account's MINIMUM-BALANCE field.

```
FORMULA-2.
    MULTIPLY THRESHOLD BY LOWER-RATE
        GIVING REGULAR-INTEREST.
    SUBTRACT THRESHOLD FROM MINIMUM-BALANCE
        GIVING OVER-THRESHOLD.
    MULTIPLY OVER-THRESHOLD BY HIGHER-RATE
        GIVING EXTRA-INTEREST.
    ADD REGULAR-INTEREST, EXTRA-INTEREST
        GIVING TOTAL-INTEREST.
```

The paragraph FORMULA-2 is executed for minimum balances
greater than the threshold value. Depending on the processor

involved numeric data items declared with USAGE COMP may
have to be converted from string form to binary form before arithmetic operations are carried out on their values. Note the forms of
the ADD, SUBTRACT, and MULTIPLY verbs which include an
implicit assignment operation.

```
CLOSE-DOWN.
        MOVE CLIENT-COUNT TO CLIENT-TOTAL.
        MOVE AGGREGATE-INTEREST TO INTEREST-TOTAL.
        WRITE OUTPUT-LINE FROM SUMMARY-LINE
            AFTER ADVANCING 2 LINES.
        CLOSE CLIENT-DATA, INTEREST-REPORT.
```

The final paragraph CLOSE-DOWN is executed (by a call from line
690) when the CLIENT-DATA file has been completely processed.
The final summary line giving details of the total number of members and aggregate interest paid to them is constructed (with editing
carried out similar to that described at line 540) and printed (with a
preceding blank line). Both of the files are then closed.

    If the card file whose contents are shown in Listing 2 (see Chap-
ter 5) is input to *PROGRAM0*, then the output produced by the
execution of *PROGRAM0* on this file is shown in Listing 26. In
order to save space only the first and last parts of this print-out have
been shown.

```
            LISTING 26  :   INTEREST LISTING


10118632J.ADAIR                     INTEREST =         $0.00
10124268T.ADAIR                     INTEREST =       $561.27
10141103F.ADAMSON                   INTEREST =       $550.83
10175229G.ADDISON                   INTEREST =       $444.62
10182047B.AICKEN                    INTEREST =       $453.20
10182446M.AIKEN                     INTEREST =        $53.96
10183272E.ALCORN                    INTEREST =        $73.81
10192247A.ALEXANDER                 INTEREST =         $6.34
10214534C.ALLEN                     INTEREST =         $7.38
10223983F.ALLEN                     INTEREST =         $3.57
10232486J.ANDERSON                  INTEREST =        $24.58
10253866C.ANDESON                   INTEREST =        $42.15
10263101W.BEST                      INTEREST =       $585.28
10264663J.BLAKE                     INTEREST =       $385.16
10272569L.BROWN                     INTEREST =       $266.24
10282270T.CLYDE                     INTEREST =       $257.01
10315225M.CRAIG                     INTEREST =       $159.62
10326960M.MOLLOY                    INTEREST =       $168.20
10352422S.RAMSEY                    INTEREST =        $25.46
10354603R.LONGMORE                  INTEREST =        $45.31
10362916F.SNOW                      INTEREST =         $4.44
10363122H.MOODY                     INTEREST =       $245.82
10363130A.GRAHAM                    INTEREST =       $521.83
10388354T.IMTIAZ                    INTEREST =        $13.18
10422609D.LUCAS                     INTEREST =        $30.75
```

.
.
.

```
60254181P.KYLE                      INTEREST =      $332.50
6026439XN.SHERMAN                   INTEREST =      $245.83
60316527W.MCQUEEN                   INTEREST =      $190.00
60326441R.CARSWELL                  INTEREST =       $14.25
60332271L.CHURMS                    INTEREST =       $14.25
60336544V.CONEY                     INTEREST =        $4.75
60336927J.DUNLEA                    INTEREST =      $521.83
60343249W.FOYE                      INTEREST =      $310.24
60347198C.HILL                      INTEREST =      $528.75
60356855G.LATIMER                   INTEREST =      $432.25
60414359M.NIXON                     INTEREST =      $332.50
60415223M.QUIGG                     INTEREST =      $245.83
60422246F.GORMAN                    INTEREST =      $285.00
60424265D.LEITCH                    INTEREST =      $285.00
60434333H.MCVEIGH                   INTEREST =      $332.50
60436581L.SHIVERS                   INTEREST =      $245.83
60444053S.LIDSTER                   INTEREST =      $245.83
60453389R.TAYLOR                    INTEREST =        $4.75
60517743U.BAYER                     INTEREST =        $9.50
60524545F.BREEN                     INTEREST =      $521.83
6055438XM.CALDWELL                  INTEREST =      $310.24
60581840R.CARLISLE                  INTEREST =      $528.75
60584033R.COURTNEY                  INTEREST =      $432.25
60587652B.HANNA                     INTEREST =      $582.50
60588381B.LIVINGSTONE               INTEREST =      $521.83
60598409L.MAGEE                     INTEREST =      $310.24

NUMBER OF CLIENTS = 240     EARNED INTEREST =    $70,285.28
```

EXERCISE

1. (Programming exercise) In a particular implementation of COBOL columns 1–6 and 73–80 of each line of a program are reserved for use for sequence numbering and program identification, respectively. However, many programmers do not make use of these facilities or else their sequence numbering sometimes needs reorganization.

Write a COBOL program which will read in the source text of any COBOL program, preceded by a line containing
in columns   1–6   999999
in columns 73–80   the program identification
and produce as output a new version of the input COBOL program with the program identification appearing in columns 73–80 of every card, and sequence numbers (with increments of 10) in columns 1–6.

This simple utility may then be used to create fresh editions of any COBOL program.

Use this program (preceded by a suitable first line) as its own data. Assign the input file and output file to suitable device names, as defined by your own COBOL implementation.

12 BASIC COBOL DATA AND PROGRAM STRUCTURES

In this chapter we give an introduction to the basic data structuring and program structuring facilities of standard COBOL. The properties of the simple numeric and alphanumeric data types, and structured types in the form of records and arrays, are described together with the arithmetic operators, composition, selection, procedurization, and repetition control structures. The special primitive operators for table handling and string manipulation are also introduced. The intention is not to give an exhaustive description of the COBOL features concerned but rather to give the reader sufficient knowledge of the language to enable him to fully understand the case study Model Savings Bank programs appearing in later chapters. The reader, after studying the material contained in this chapter, should be capable of constructing COBOL programs of a similar nature. For some of the COBOL features introduced here, the full range of options associated with them is not covered, but rather some suitable subset has been chosen which should prove adequate in most circumstances. In subsequent chapters additional COBOL features concerned with the various aspects of file handling will be presented as appropriate.

12.1 DATA IN COBOL

12.1.1 Basic Data Types

The basic data types provided by COBOL are numbers and alphanumeric strings. The source program representation of constants of these types has already been described in Chapter 11.

Each working variable is declared in the Working-Storage Section by giving it a level number of 77 and a unique data-name followed by a *picture* describing the data type of the variable; the declaration ends with a period. Level 77 data items are known as *non-contiguous* data items since they are not subordinate to any other data item and are not themselves composed of any subitems. A picture is analogous to a Pascal type definition in that it denotes what values a variable may take. Every elementary data item must have a picture specified for it — an *elementary* data item is one that does not contain any subordinate data items.

If a data-name refers to a non-negative five-digit numeric value, then its picture is

$$99999 \quad \text{or} \quad 9(5)$$

i.e., each 9 represents a digit position in the data value. The position of any decimal point is indicated by a V in the picture; thus, if the value can range from 0.00 to 99.99 its picture is

$$99V99 \quad \text{or} \quad 9(2)V9(2)$$

The decimal point is not actually stored but its position is taken into account whenever the data item is used. At program execution time data items with the above pictures would occupy 5 and 4 characters of storage, respectively. Some examples of numeric data declarations:

```
77 HOURS          PICTURE 99V9.
77 HOURLY-RATE    PICTURE 9V99.
77 DAILY-RATE     PICTURE 99V99.
```

Note that PICTURE may be abbreviated to PIC.

Numeric data items are described by pictures containing only the symbols 9, P, S, and V, and the number of digit positions indicated must not be greater than 18.

For data values which may be negative, the character S in a picture represents an implied sign (otherwise the item is treated as positive), e.g., a picture of S9 indicates that the numeric value is a single digit value with its sign represented in some way (often by the use of a bit that is normally unused in the decimal representation of the leading digit). An S must always be the leftmost symbol in a picture.

The character P in a picture indicates that the value stored for the data item is to be scaled to obtain the true value, e.g.,

$$99PP$$

indicates that an integer is stored as a value 100 times less than its true value. Hence the stored value 23 represents the actual value 2300 if the associated picture is 99PP.

Some examples of pictures and their meanings are shown in Figure 12.1 (a digit with a bar above it in the column of stored values indicates that a minus sign is represented within the stored representation of that digit).

Picture	Size (characters)	Stored value	Actual value
999	3	432	+432
S999	3	432	+432
S999	3	$\overline{4}$32	−432
9V9	2	67	+6.7
99V	2	84	+84
V99	2	49	+0.49
PP99	2	36	+0.0036
99P	2	28	+280
SVP99	2	$\overline{1}$7	−0.017
SVP99	2	17	+0.017

Figure 12.1

Data items with non-numeric values have pictures such as

XXXXXXX

or

X(7)

where each X represents an alphanumeric character. At program execution time a data item with the above picture would occupy 7 characters of storage. Hence the following data item

```
77 EMPLOYEE-NAME PICTURE X(15).
```

is an alphanumeric data item whose value will be a string of 15 characters.

12.1.2 Usage

The value of a numeric data item may be represented in either binary or decimal form depending upon the computer concerned. Decimal forms are usually expressed in binary-coded decimal (BCD), and the use of such a representation normally permits the direct transfer of numeric data between main memory and external text files. The format in which a data item is stored is known as its *usage*. Decimal and character representations are known in COBOL as DISPLAY usage.

However, on machines which do not provide decimal arithmetic facilities, it is necessary to convert a numeric value used in an arithmetic operation and stored in decimal (DISPLAY) form to (probably) binary representation, perform the operation, and convert back again to decimal form. This inefficiency can be avoided by declaring a data item to have USAGE COMPUTATIONAL (or COMP) which causes the item to be stored in the appropriate hardware numeric representation. This representation may, but does not necessarily, use the minimum number of bits required. Thus execution speed can be increased but at the cost of machine independence of data item length. The standard DISPLAY representation is the default, as in the examples of Section 12.1.1.

Examples:
```
77   V-1   PIC 9.
77   V-2   PIC 9 USAGE COMPUTATIONAL.
77   V-3   PIC 9(4) USAGE COMP.
77   V-4   PIC S9(5) USAGE COMP.
```

On a machine using binary numeric representation the storage requirement for V-1 is 1 character while for V-2, V-3, and V-4 it is at least 4, 14, and 18 bits respectively (including one bit for the sign in the case of V-4).

Thus, with regard to object program speed, it pays to hold data in its dominant usage. In passing it should be noted that various manufacturers provide additional non-standard COMPUTATIONAL usages to reflect the facilities of their particular machines such as floating-point and double-precision arithmetic.

12.1.3 Synchronization

Most computer memories are organized in such a way that there are natural addressing boundaries in the memory (e.g., word, byte, and character boundaries). The manner in which storage for data items is allocated is determined by the compiler, and COBOL compilers usually do not respect these natural boundaries, i.e., a single data item may lie across a natural boundary, or two or more data items may be stored between a pair of adjacent boundaries. This costs a price in program execution speed when accessing the items, since parts of them may share storage units lying between natural addressing boundaries with other data items and will then have to be unpacked. COBOL provides a means of data alignment whereby data items may be forced to begin or end on a natural boundary, and no data items share storage between two adjacent boundaries — this is achieved by means of the SYNCHRONIZED (or SYNC) clause following the picture of the item.

```
77  STRING-EXAMPLE  PIC X(15)  SYNC LEFT.
```

specifies that this data item is to be stored beginning at the leftmost character position following a natural boundary, and any unused positions up to the next rightmost boundary delimiting the data item are to remain unused. So, on a 4 character per word machine, the storage layout associated with the data item STRING-EXAMPLE might be as shown in Figure 12.2.

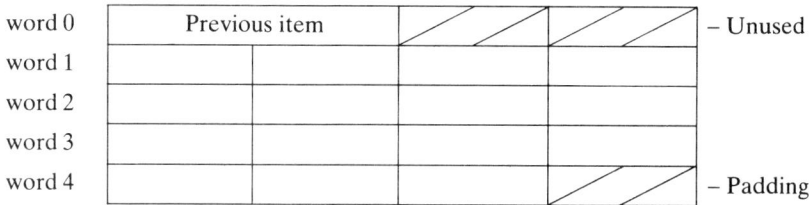

Figure 12.2   Storage allocation for a left-synchronized data item

The item might have been declared as SYNC RIGHT, in which case word 1 would have an unused leftmost character position and the end of the item would have been aligned with the end of word 4 (Figure 12.3).

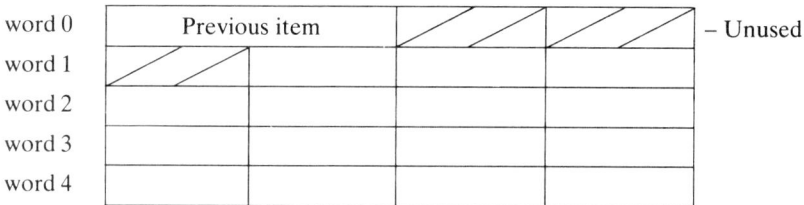

Figure 12.3   Storage allocation for a right-synchronized data item

Synchronization of numeric items may be to the left or right also, thereby causing appropriate word alignment and the introduction of unused padding storage. Numeric items are normally aligned to the right of a word. On a 4 character per word machine the storage allocation caused by the declarations

```
77  V-1  PIC 99 SYNC RIGHT.
77  V-2  PIC 9 USAGE COMP SYNC RIGHT.
```

```
77  V-3  PIC 9(4) USAGE COMP.
77  V-4  PIC 9(4) USAGE COMP SYNC RIGHT.
```

might be as shown in Figure 12.4.

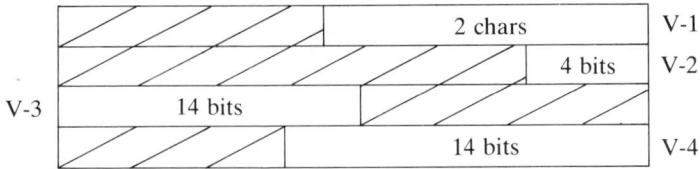

Figure 12.4   Storage layout for right-synchronized data items

Thus COMP SYNC RIGHT is the usual declaration for data items that are used frequently in arithmetic operations, i.e., a data item declared as an integer (or integer subrange) or real variable in Pascal is normally declared in COBOL as a COMP SYNC RIGHT data item.

12.1.4 Justification

In Pascal the assignment of string values requires that the variable concerned and the string value being assigned are of the same type, i.e., have the same lower and upper bounds. However, when a new value is assigned to a COBOL alphanumeric data item and the data item and assigned character string involved are of different lengths, the following actions will occur: if the assigned string is too long then its excess characters are truncated at the right; if it is shorter than the receiving item then it is aligned to the left with space-fill to the right. This is known as *left justification*.

In order to reverse these rules, i.e., align to the right or truncate at the left, the receiving data item must be described as JUSTIFIED RIGHT in its declaration, e.g.,

```
77  STRING-EXAMPLE  PIC X(15)  JUSTIFIED RIGHT.
```

Example:

```
77  STRING-1  PIC X(15).
77  STRING-2  PIC X(15) JUSTIFIED RIGHT.
MOVE "SHORT STRING" TO STRING-1, STRING-2.
```

STRING-1 | SHORT STRING |
STRING-2 | SHORT STRING |

```
MOVE "A VERY LONG STRING...." TO STRING-1,STRING-2.
```

STRING-1 | A VERY LONG STR |
STRING-2 | LONG STRING. ... |

The JUSTIFIED clause must not be applied to any numeric data item.

If a new value is assigned to a DISPLAY usage numeric data item, the assigned data value is always aligned by its decimal point and moved to the receiving data item with zero fill or truncation at either end, as required. For example, given four numeric DISPLAY data items

```
77   N-1   PIC 99V99.
77   N-2   PIC 9V9.
77   N-3   PIC 9.
77   N-4   PIC V9.
```

the effect of moving the value 1.3 to each is as follows

```
MOVE  1.3 TO N-1     N-1     | 0 | 1 | 3 | 0 |
MOVE  1.3 TO N-2     N-2     | 1 | 3 |
MOVE  1.3 TO N-3     N-3     | 1 |
MOVE  1.3 TO N-4     N-4     | 3 |
```

The stricter type rules of Pascal would not permit a real to integer assignment such as that to N-3.

12.1.5 Initialization

The only means of assigning an initial value to a Pascal variable is by the execution of an assignment statement or input statement, whereas in the Working-Storage Section of the DATA DIVISION of a COBOL program (and also in the Report Section) initial values may be assigned to data items by means of the VALUE clause following the picture clause, e.g., the declaration

```
77   STRING-1   PIC X (15)   JUSTIFIED RIGHT
                             VALUE "TEST-VALUE".
```

produces the following storage initialization for STRING-1

| T E S T - V A L U E |

Numeric data items in the Working-Storage Section may also be initialized, e.g.,

```
77   ITEM-COUNTER   PIC 999   COMP SYNC RIGHT
                              VALUE IS 0.
77   SIGNED-VALUE   PIC S9   VALUE -1.
```

At this stage we introduce a few reserved words of COBOL (known as *figurative constants*) which are provided to represent standard values. These include

ZERO/ZEROS/ZEROES	standing for as many zeroes as required
SPACE/SPACES	standing for as many spaces as required
ALL *character-string*	standing for as many
ALL *figurative-constant*	instances of the character-string or figurative constant as required
LOW-VALUE/LOW-VALUES	standing for as many instances of the character with the lowest value in the computer's collating sequence as required
HIGH-VALUE/HIGH-VALUES	character with the highest value in the collating sequence

These constants may be used anywhere in a program and can be particularly useful when long strings of identical characters have to be constructed, e.g.,

```
77  ITEM-NUMBER    PIC 9 VALUE ZERO.
77  STRING-1       PIC X(15) VALUE SPACES.
77  STRING-2       PIC X(48) VALUE ALL "ABC".
```

ITEM-NUMBER will be given an initial value of 0; STRING-1 will be assigned a string of fifteen spaces; and the value of STRING-2 will initially consist of sixteen consecutive sequences of the string "ABC".

12.1.6 Records

It is often desirable to be able to treat a number of elementary items as a whole data item (known as a *group item*) for some purpose, i.e., to treat them as a record. COBOL records consist of data items organized in a hierarchical manner by means of data-names and level numbers. The record itself is given a level number 01 and each hierarchical sublevel is given an increasingly higher level number of up to 49. Elementary items of a record are given full data descriptions while groups of elementary items (group items) may be given properties (e.g., usage, synchronization) which then apply to all

subordinate items of that group Thus the details of an employee
and his hours worked may be described as

```
01  TIME-CARD.
   02  EMPLOYEE-DATA.
      03  NAME       PIC X(30).
      03  EMP-NO     PIC 9(5).
   02  HOURS-WORKED.
      03  BASIC      PIC 99.
      03  OVERTIME   PIC 99.
```

where the record TIME-CARD is made up of two fields
EMPLOYEE-DATA and HOURS-WORKED, each of which is
itself composed of two sub-fields. All group items, irrespective of
the type of any subordinate data items, are themselves
alphanumeric. Hence EMPLOYEE-DATA is equivalent to an
X(35) item, and HOURS-WORKED is an X(4) item.

This record item could be declared in Pascal as

var *timecard* : **record**
           employeedata : **record**
                  name : **packed array** [1..30]
                        of *char* ;
                  empno : 0..99999
                end ;
           hoursworked : **record**
                  basic, overtime : 0..99
                end
      end ;

Elementary items or group items at the same level may have
similar names as long as each is uniquely qualified in that some
higher level has a different name. Qualification is by means of OF or
IN, e.g., if both level 02 fields above had contained a further level
03 field called, say, EXTRA-FIELD, then reference to these fields
would require qualification to resolve the ambiguity, i.e.,

```
EXTRA-FIELD IN EMPLOYEE-DATA
```
{Pascal — *timecard.employeedata.extrafield*}
```
EXTRA-FIELD IN HOURS-WORKED
```
{Pascal — *timecard.hoursworked.extrafield*}

If there is no ambiguity, then fields may be named directly, e.g.,
NAME, BASIC. (In Pascal this is not possible and a field must
always be fully qualified, e.g., *timecard.employeedata.name*, unless
the field is referenced within a with statement).

The record structure is the basic means by which the formats of
all files and working-storage structures can be defined. The above

record TIME-CARD is thus a character string with the sublevel data names identifying substrings, i.e., TIME-CARD is an X(39) data item structured as shown below.

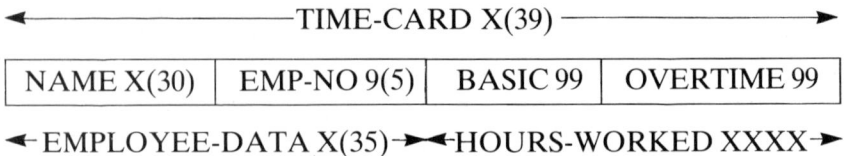

◄───────────────TIME-CARD X(39)───────────────►

NAME X(30)	EMP-NO 9(5)	BASIC 99	OVERTIME 99

◄─EMPLOYEE-DATA X(35)─►◄─HOURS-WORKED XXXX─►

12.1.7   Redefinition of Data Structures

It is often the case that we wish to give alternative definitions for a data structure. For example, we may wish to extend the time-card description to cover both daily paid and hourly paid employees, which have different attributes associated with them. In Pascal this is denoted by a variant record description in which a tag field is introduced to distinguish among the alternative forms, e.g.,

```
var timecard :   record
                 name : packed array [1..30] of char ;
                 empno : 0..99999 ;
                 case category : (hourly,daily) of
                     hourly : (basic, overtime : 0..99) ;
                     daily : (days : 0..7)
             end ;
```

To describe this structure in COBOL a further field CATEGORY might be added to the record to distinguish the employee's category (e.g., this field might contain H for hourly paid workers and D for daily paid workers). The record TIME-CARD now has two different formats but the CATEGORY, NAME, and EMP-NO fields are common to both; we therefore declare these as before. The HOURS-WORKED group is then also defined as before but must now be redefined as, say, DAYS-WORKED in the alternative structure, to cater for the description of daily paid workers.

```
01   TIME-CARD.
   02   NAME          PIC  X(30).
   02   EMP-NO        PIC  9(5).
   02   CATEGORY      PIC  X.
   02   HOURS-WORKED.
      03   BASIC       PIC  99.
      03   OVERTIME    PIC  99.
   02   DAYS-WORKED  REDEFINES  HOURS-WORKED.
      03   DAYS        PIC  9.
      03   FILLER      PIC  999.
```

The level numbers of both redefined and redefining data must be the same. Notice that the group field HOURS-WORKED consists of four characters, whereas the number of DAYS worked in a week can be expressed as a single digit value; however, when the field being redefined is not at level 01, the redefining structure must be the same size as that which it redefines and so, in this case, it must be padded out with a three-digit FILLER (remember FILLER is the standard COBOL name given to fields to which we will not refer explicitly in a program). Hence care must be taken when redefining to ensure that the storage sizes of the two descriptions match where necessary — this is troublesome when the descriptions contain synchronized or computational items whose length is dependent upon the architecture of the computer concerned, especially if the program is transferred to a machine with a different word structure, in which case the new storage sizes will almost certainly not match.

Redefining data may not be initialized but redefined data may be (obviously to initialize both would not make sense).

12.1.8 Tables

Pascal provides arrays with any number of dimensions and the index types may be any ordinal types. COBOL provides arrays of up to three dimensions, known as *tables*, in which each dimension has a lower default bound of 1 and some program-specified upper bound. They are denoted by the OCCURS clause in the description of a data item (which must not be a level 01 or 77 item), e.g., suppose it is wished to construct a table of the number of hours worked by each hourly paid employee and that the number of such employees lies between 1 and 200, viz.,

```
02 HRS   PIC 99   OCCURS 200 TIMES.
```

This defines a table of 200 two-digit numeric values. The elements of the table may be referenced as HRS (1), HRS (2), etc., or HRS (I) where I (known as the *subscript*) is a data item with value in the range 1..200. Subscripts must be either positive integer constants or non-subscripted numeric data items. A space must be left after the commas separating the subscripts of a two- or three-dimensional array.

To refer to the table as a whole rather than to particular individual elements requires it to be given a data name at a higher level, e.g.,

```
01  HOURS-TABLE.
   02  HRS  PIC 99  OCCURS 200 TIMES.
```

HOURS-TABLE is thus the entire table of 200 integer values, i.e., it is effectively a PIC X(400) data item.

Tables may have up to three dimensions. Suppose that each employee's time-card record is also to contain the number of hours worked on each day of the week. BASIC and OVERTIME then become one-dimensional tables of seven elements each, thus

```
01  TIME-CARD.
    02  NAME        PIC X(30).
    02  EMP-NO      PIC 9(5).
    02  BASIC       PIC 99 OCCURS 7 TIMES.
    02  OVERTIME    PIC 99 OCCURS 7 TIMES.
```

From such records we might wish to construct a table showing, for each employee, the number of hours worked each day of the week and the total number of hours worked each week. Again assuming that there are no more than 200 employees the definition of HOURS-TABLE could be expanded to:

```
01  HOURS-TABLE.
    02  EMPLOYEE-RECORD OCCURS 200 TIMES.
        03  HRS       PIC 99 OCCURS 7 TIMES.
        03  TOTAL     PIC 99.
```

In Pascal this structure could be realized as

```
var hourstable :   array [1..200] of
                   record
                   hrs : array [1..7] of  0..99 ;
                   total : 0..99
                   end ;
```

The number of hours worked by employee E on day D is then given by the value of HRS (E, D) and the total number of hours worked by him in the week by the value of TOTAL (E).

This method of identifying a table element may seem strange to the reader familiar with Pascal-like array notations, but it is (unfortunately) the way chosen in COBOL. In Pascal the above values would be denoted as

$$hourstable[E].hrs[D]$$

and

$$hourstable[E].total$$

assuming the declaration of hourstable above.

An example of a three-dimensional array in COBOL is

```
01  THREE-DIMENSIONAL-ARRAY.
    02  PLANE OCCURS 20 TIMES.
```

```
03  ROW OCCURS 30 TIMES.
   04  ELEMENT OCCURS 10 TIMES PIC 9.
```

which is declared in Pascal as

var *plane* :   **array** [1..20] **of**
                array [1..30] **of**
                    array [1..10] **of** 0..9;

This is a 20 by 30 by 10 table of digit values and parts of the table may be denoted as, e.g.,

```
ELEMENT (1, 2, 3)  ROW (4, 5)  PLANE (6)
```

{Pascal—   *plane* [1,2,3]   *plane* [4,5]   *plane* [6] }

ELEMENT (1, 2, 3) is a PIC 9 data item; ROW (4, 5) is effectively a table of ten PIC 9 items (i.e., a PIC X(10) item); and PLANE (6) is effectively a 30 by 10 item table (i.e., a PIC X(300) item).

Tables may not be initialized using the VALUE clause. However, this restriction may be overcome by the use of redefinition. A table of names of US states may be initialized as shown below:

```
01  US-STATES.
   02  STATE-SPELLINGS.
      03  FILLER  PIC X(20)  VALUE "ALABAMA".
      03  FILLER  PIC X(20)  VALUE "ARKANSAS".
                        .
                        .
                        .
      03  FILLER  PIC X(20)  VALUE "WASHINGTON".
   02  STATE-NAMES REDEFINES STATE-SPELLINGS.
   03  STATE  PIC X(20) OCCURS 50 TIMES.
```

Hence STATE (1) has the value "ALABAMA   ".
    Variable-length tables may also be declared, e.g.,

```
01  VARIABLE-LENGTH-EXAMPLE.
   02  VARIABLE-TABLE  PIC 9 OCCURS 1 TO 10
                        TIMES DEPENDING ON I.
```

indicates that the number of values held in the table at any time is given by the value of another data-item I (which must not be a field of VARIABLE-TABLE) where the value of I will always be between 1 and 10. This permits the saving of space when such a table is written out to a backing-store file and thus enables variable-length records to be created on tape and disk files (see Chapter 3). Pascal provides no equivalent feature for declaring variable-length arrays.

12.2   ARITHMETIC FACILITIES

The arithmetic operations required in business programming are usually simple and can be provided by a small range of operators — addition, subtraction, multiplication, division, and assignment. The use of mathematical functions such as square root, logarithm, etc., is rarely necessary.

12.2.1   Assignment

The basic COBOL verb for assigning values is the MOVE verb

> MOVE *operand* TO *identifier-list*

where *operand* is an identifier or literal, and *identifier-list* is a sequence of one or more identifiers separated by commas. An identifier is defined to be a unique data-name (i.e., a data-name which may have been subscripted or qualified in order to make it unique within the program). The value of the operand is assigned as the new value of each data item so identified according to their data descriptions, working from left to right through the identifier-list. Only numeric values should be assigned to numeric data items; only strings should be assigned to alphanumeric data items (although the actual COBOL assignment rules are somewhat less strict).

```
            COBOL
MOVE 6.5 TO X
MOVE ZERO TO A, B
MOVE C TO D
MOVE 3 TO I, A (I)
MOVE SPACES TO Y
MOVE A (I) TO I, B (I)
```

$$Pascal$$
$$X := 6.5$$
$$A := 0 \; ; \; B := 0$$
$$D := C$$
$$I := 3 \; ; \; A[I] := 3$$
$$Y := ' \qquad '$$
$$TEMP := A[I] \; ; \; I := TEMP \; ; \; B[I] := TEMP$$

where, in the last example, *TEMP* is some intermediate variable. If the data type of a numeric data item in the identifier-list differs from that of an operand, then an automatic type conversion is applied to the operand, which may involve truncation — for example, moving 1.5 to a PIC 9 field causes the receiving field to take the value 1. In the case of assignment to an alphanumeric data item the value is stored in the receiving data item after any necessary storage justification.

If both the operand and receiving data item are elementary, then the move is elementary; otherwise the MOVE is treated as though it were an elementary alphanumeric to alphanumeric MOVE, e.g.,

```
MOVE "4311" TO HOURS-WORKED
```

would be a legal assignment to the HOURS-WORKED field of the TIME-CARD record declared in Section 12.1.6.

The use of the same name to identify fields in different records is taken advantage of in the MOVE CORRESPONDING form. This gives the capability to access, in the same statement, various fields which have the same name in different records, e.g.,

```
MOVE CORRESPONDING X TO Y
```

will move the values of all the fields in the record data item X whose names correspond to those of fields in the record data item Y, to the appropriate fields of Y. In effect it is equivalent to a series of simple MOVE statements. For the names of pairs of fields to correspond they are not required to occupy identical positions within the record structures but must obey the rules that each pair have the same name qualification, and that at least one member of each pair must be elementary. Redefined items and tables are ignored for the purpose of establishing correspondence.

```
01  A.                        01  B.
    02  P PIC 9.                  02  P PIC 9.
    02  Q.                        02  U.
        03  V PIC 9.                  03  V PIC 9.
    02  R.                        02  R.
        03  S PIC 9.                  03  T PIC X.
        03  T PIC 9.                  03  S PIC 9.
```

In the above records the fields P, T, and S correspond. The V fields do not correspond since the first is V OF Q, the other V OF U.

Thus MOVE CORRESPONDING B TO A is equivalent to

```
MOVE P OF B TO P OF A.
MOVE T OF B TO T OF A.
MOVE S OF B TO S OF A.
```

12.2.2 Arithmetic

The arithmetic operators are provided in COBOL by the verbs ADD, SUBTRACT, MULTIPLY, and DIVIDE, all of which incorporate an assignment operation.

> ADD *operand, operand-list* GIVING *identifier*
> SUBTRACT *operand-list* FROM *operand* GIVING *identifier*
> MULTIPLY *operand* BY *operand* GIVING *identifier*
> DIVIDE *operand* INTO *operand* GIVING *identifier*
> $\qquad\qquad\qquad\qquad\qquad$ [REMAINDER *identifier*]

where the COBOL statements

```
ADD A, B, 7 GIVING C
SUBTRACT 1 FROM J GIVING K
MULTIPLY 2 BY A GIVING X
DIVIDE 2 INTO X GIVING Y
DIVIDE 2 INTO X GIVING Y REMAINDER T
```

correspond to the Pascal statements

$C := A+B+7$
$K := J-1$
$X := 2*A$
$Y := X/2$
$Y := X$ **div 2** ; $T := X$ **mod 2**
(assuming integer X and Y)

All identifiers and literals used in arithmetic operations must be numeric in type.

There are also abbreviated forms of these verbs for use when the result identifier is also one of the operands:

> ADD *operand-list* TO *identifier*
> SUBTRACT *operand-list* FROM *identifier*
> MULTIPLY *operand* BY *identifier*
> DIVIDE *operand* INTO *identifier*

where the COBOL statements

```
ADD A, B TO C
SUBTRACT 1, A FROM J
MULTIPLY 3 BY R
DIVIDE X INTO Y
ADD A, B TO B, C (B)
```

correspond to the Pascal statements

$C := C+A+B$
$J := J-(1+A)$
$R := 3*R$
$Y := Y/X$
$TEMP := A+B$; $B := B+TEMP$; $C[B] := C[B]+TEMP$

An entry in the table named HOURS-TABLE declared in Section 12.1.8 to hold the hours worked by each employee, can be constructed by a statement such as

```
ADD BASIC (DAY-NO), OVERTIME (DAY-NO)
    GIVING HRS (EMP-NO, DAY-NO)
```

Where necessary truncation takes place automatically, but the programmer may request rounding instead, e.g.,

```
                ADD A, B TO C ROUNDED
```

If C is a PIC 9 field and the result of the addition is, say, 1.6, then rounding gives the value of 2 to C, whereas if the ROUNDED option had not been used, the value 1 would have been assigned to C. Note that rounding is performed on the absolute value, i.e., -3.56 rounds to -4.

The equivalent of the Pascal assignment statement

$$PAY := HOURLYRATE * (BASIC + 1.5 * OVERTIME)$$

could be expressed in three COBOL statements.

```
MULTIPLY 1.5 BY OVERTIME GIVING HOURS
ADD BASIC TO HOURS
MULTIPLY HOURLYRATE BY HOURS GIVING PAY ROUNDED
```

This unnecessary verbosity may be avoided by use of the COMPUTE statement

COMPUTE *identifier-list* [ROUNDED] = *arithmetic-expression*

which allows a series of operators and operands to be combined into a single expression. The expression is evaluated from left to right using the following operator precedence (in decreasing order)

( )
   –   unary minus
  **   exponentiation
  * /
  + –

Arithmetic operators must be written with a preceding and following space, since they are effectively COBOL key words. Thus,

```
COMPUTE PAY ROUNDED
    = HOURLYRATE * (BASIC + 1.5 * OVERTIME)
```

All of the above arithmetic verbs allow the specification of action to be taken when the result value is too large for the receiving field, using the SIZE ERROR option, e.g., for the ADD verb

> ADD *operand-list* TO *identifier* [ROUNDED]
> [ON SIZE ERROR *imperative-statement*]

If such overflow occurs then the receiving item is not assigned the result value but instead the *imperative-statement* is obeyed. Thus,

```
MULTIPLY A BY B ON SIZE ERROR GO TO OVERFLOW-ROUTINE
```

causes control to be transferred to the paragraph or section named OVERFLOW-ROUTINE in the event of the product of A and B being larger than the maximum value permitted by the picture for B, and the value of B remains as before the attempted multiplication. If overflow occurs and no SIZE ERROR phrase is specified, then the value of the receiving item is undefined (as is the case in Pascal). Note that assignment using the MOVE verb cannot cause overflow — any necessary truncation takes place automatically (which is not the case in Pascal when an assigned value lies outside the range of values declared for the assigned variable), as indicated in Sections 12.1.4 and 12.2.1.

The CORRESPONDING form may be used for the ADD and SUBTRACT verbs subject to the extra correspondence condition that a pair of like-named data items correspond only if they are both elementary and numeric. Thus, in the example given earlier,

```
SUBTRACT CORRESPONDING A FROM B
```

the effect is equivalent to

```
SUBTRACT P OF A FROM P OF B
SUBTRACT S OF A FROM S OF B
```

i.e., T OF A and T OF B do not correspond, since T OF B is alphanumeric.

12.3   PROGRAM SEQUENCE CONTROL IN COBOL

Execution of a COBOL program always begins at the first statement of the PROCEDURE DIVISION and continues statement by statement unless a switch of control occurs.

12.3.1   Composition

A group of COBOL statements may be formed into a *sentence* by joining them using semicolons, commas, or simply spaces as statement separators, and terminating the sentence with a period.

There are two types of sentence which concern us at this stage — *imperative* and *conditional* sentences (there is a third type — *declarative* sentences — but we shall introduce them later).

An imperative sentence is an *imperative-statement-sequence*, i.e., a sequence of imperative statements separated by semicolons, commas, or spaces. In the COBOL subset which we are considering here the imperative statements include the following verbs:

```
ACCEPT              GO                  RELEASE
ADD (1)             INITIATE            REWRITE (2)
CLOSE               INSPECT             SET
COMPUTE (2)         MOVE                SORT
DELETE (2)          MULTIPLY (1)        STOP
DISPLAY             OPEN                SUBTRACT (1)
DIVIDE (1)          PERFORM             TERMINATE
EXIT                READ (2)            WRITE (2)
GENERATE
```

(1) without an ON SIZE ERROR phrase
(2) without an INVALID KEY phrase.

Most of these verbs have not yet been described but are introduced and listed here for ease of reference.

The following is thus an imperative sentence:

```
ADD A TO B ; SUBTRACT 4 FROM C ; GO TO PARAGRAPH-1.
```

A conditional sentence is a conditional statement, optionally preceded by an *imperative-statement-sequence*. The conditional statements which we shall be considering are the following

- IF, SEARCH, and RETURN statements
- READ statements with an AT END or INVALID KEY phrase
- REWRITE, WRITE or DELETE statements with an INVALID KEY phrase
- ADD, COMPUTE, MULTIPLY, DIVIDE, or SUBTRACT statements with an ON SIZE ERROR phrase

The following are both valid conditional sentences:

```
SUBTRACT 4 FROM C
    ON SIZE ERROR GO TO PARAGRAPH-2.
ADD A TO B ; IF B > ZERO GO TO PARAGRAPH-3.
```

If it is required to compose a group of sentences into a single compound statement, then they must be grouped into a named paragraph or section. This paragraph or section may then be executed in-line as the execution of the program proceeds through the text of the PROCEDURE DIVISION, or else out-of-line by means of a PERFORM statement (see Section 12.3.6).

12.3.2 Program Termination

A Pascal program terminates when the program execution reaches the end of the main program statements. The STOP verb is used to terminate a COBOL program, either temporarily or permanently. Its use is compulsory in COBOL whereas, in Pascal, a program terminates upon reaching the end of the main program statement-part. There are two formats for the STOP verb

$$\boxed{\text{STOP} \quad \left\{ \begin{array}{l} \text{RUN} \\ \textit{literal} \end{array} \right\}}$$

The first form (STOP RUN) is used for permanent halting. The second form (STOP *literal*) causes a temporary halt — the literal value is communicated to the system operator, and the program may subsequently be restarted by the operator at the statement following the STOP. Examples:

```
STOP RUN.
STOP "LOAD TAPE #17" ; OPEN INPUT-TAPE-FILE.
```

12.3.3 Unconditional Branching

$$\boxed{\text{GO TO } \textit{procedure-name}}$$

where *procedure-name* is the name of a paragraph or section, causes control to switch to the named paragraph or section, e.g.,

```
...
    GO TO PARA-1.
...
PARA-1.
...
...
```

We shall avoid the use of GO TO statements as far as possible since they tend to produce unstructured and unreadable programs unless great care is taken. However, we shall find that some of the structures provided in COBOL are such that we are forced to use the GO TO verb in certain circumstances.

12.3.4 Alternation

The Pascal if-statement is expressed in COBOL as

$$\boxed{\text{IF } \textit{condition} \left\{ \begin{array}{l} \textit{statement-1} \\ \text{NEXT SENTENCE} \end{array} \right\} \text{ ELSE } \left[\begin{array}{l} \textit{statement-2} \\ \text{NEXT SENTENCE} \end{array} \right]}$$

As in Pascal, the ELSE alternative may be omitted. *statement-1* and *statement-2* must be either *imperative-statement-sequences* or an *imperative-statement-sequence* followed by a conditional statement.

Example:
```
          IF CATEGORY IS EQUAL TO "H"
               MULTIPLY 1.5 BY OVERTIME GIVING HOURS ;
               ADD BASIC TO HOURS ;
               MULTIPLY HOURLY-RATE BY HOURS
                    GIVING TOTAL-PAY
          ELSE MULTIPLY DAILY-RATE BY DAYS
                    GIVING TOTAL-PAY.
```

There are several ways of constructing conditions using arithmetic expressions, relational and boolean operators (NOT, AND, OR), e.g.,

```
A = 1 OR B = 2 OR C = 3
A < B AND C > D
A < B AND A > C   (may also be written as A < B AND > C)
A = 1 OR 4 OR 7 OR 9
```

The relational operators may be represented lexically as

$$
\text{IS [NOT]} \left\{ \begin{array}{l} \text{GREATER THAN} \\ \text{EQUAL TO} \\ \text{LESS THAN} \end{array} \right\}
$$

```
e.g.,   X IS LESS THAN 6
        Y IS EQUAL TO "MAN-IN-THE-MOON"
```

All operators must be written with preceding and following spaces.

In the evaluation of conditions arithmetic expressions are evaluated first, then relational operators are applied, then negated conditions (i.e., involving NOT) are evaluated, and finally the AND and OR operators are applied. This is somewhat different from the Pascal precedence rules. Beware of the ambiguity that may arise in the use of the NOT operator, viz.,

```
A > B AND NOT > C OR D   is equivalent to
((A > B) AND (A NOT > C)) OR (A NOT > D)
```

i.e., the NOT operator is effectively a part of any immediately following relational operator.

If the operands of a relational operator are numeric then the comparison is algebraic, otherwise the characters forming the values of the operands are compared using the character collating sequence of the object computer. Hence, the literal "COBOL-68" is greater in value than "COBOL-61" in all character sets (since the character 1 will always precede the character 8 in collating sequences on any

machine) and "M'LEAN" is less than "MCLEAN" provided ' precedes C in the relevant character set, since the characters of the two
operands are compared one-by-one from left to right until two different characters are compared. "WILLIAMS" is less than
"WILLIAMSON" if the space character precedes O but "SMITH"
is always equal to "SMITH " as shorter values are padded out with
trailing spaces before comparison with longer values.

From the syntax of an IF statement given at the start of this section it follows that an IF statement can appear only at the end of a
statement sequence and so nesting of IF statements may become difficult to achieve. If a statement sequence is at all complicated it is
better written as a separate paragraph and executed as a procedure
using the PERFORM verb (see Section 12.3.6).

The contents of a DISPLAY usage data item may be checked to
ensure that they contain only numeric or alphabetic information by
means of the IS NUMERIC and IS ALPHABETIC class conditions, i.e.,

$$\text{identifier IS [NOT] } \begin{Bmatrix} \text{NUMERIC} \\ \text{ALPHABETIC} \end{Bmatrix}$$

e.g.,

```
IF ITEM-NUMBER IS NOT NUMERIC
   ADD 1 TO ERROR-COUNT
```

For the purposes of these tests an item is considered to be numeric
if it consists of nothing but digit characters, with or without an oper-
ational sign (denoted by an S in its picture). In particular, if it contains any spaces it is not numeric. Leading spaces in a numeric data
item may replaced by zeroes using the INSPECT verb (see Section
12.5). An item is considered to be alphabetic if it consists of letters
and spaces only, and this test obviously cannot be applied to an item
with a numeric data description.

The sign of numeric data or of an arithmetic expression may be
checked using the POSITIVE, NEGATIVE, and ZERO relations,
i.e.,

$$\begin{Bmatrix} \text{identifier} \\ \text{arithmetic-expression} \end{Bmatrix} \text{ IS [NOT]} \begin{Bmatrix} \text{POSITIVE} \\ \text{ZERO} \\ \text{NEGATIVE} \end{Bmatrix}$$

e.g.

```
IF A > 5 AND A - B IS NEGATIVE
   ADD 1 TO ERROR-COUNT
```

In the DATA DIVISION *condition-names* may be associated
with the values of elementary data items, e.g.,

```
77  ITEM PIC 9.
   88  ITEM-VALID VALUE IS 3,5 THRU 8.
   88  ITEM-ERROR VALUE IS 0,1,2,4,9.
```

In this case ITEM is known as a *conditional* data item, and the *condition-names* that follow (denoted by level numbers of 88) represent either a single value, a set, or a range of values of that item. At program execution time ITEM-VALID is true if and only if the current value of ITEM is 3, 5, 6, 7, or 8. Otherwise it is false. Likewise ITEM-ERROR is true only when the current value of ITEM is 0, 1, 2, 4 or 9. (Sets of values associated with different condition names need not be disjoint.) Compound conditions such as

```
IF ITEM IS NOT NUMERIC OR ITEM-ERROR
   PERFORM ERROR-ROUTINE
```

may then be constructed. The use of condition-names avoids the construction of long conditional expressions. The final format for a condition is thus

> [NOT] *condition-name*

12.3.5 Selection

An equivalent effect to that of the Pascal case statement can be achieved in COBOL by the use of the GO TO ... DEPENDING ON ... statement, viz.,

> GO TO *procedure-name* [, *procedure-name* ...]
> DEPENDING ON *identifier*

The identifier must be that of a numeric data item with an integer value. If its value is less than 1 or greater than the number of *procedure-names* listed then the statement execution has no effect; otherwise, if its value is I, control is transferred to the Ith *procedure-name* in the list.

Example: ```GO TO P-1, P-2, P-3, P-4
           DEPENDING ON ITEM-NUMBER```

If the value of ITEM-NUMBER is not in the range 1..4, then control passes to the next statement of the program. If its value is, say, 3 then control passes to the first statement of the paragraph or section named P–3.

In contrast to the Pascal case statement the GO TO ... DEPENDING ON ... statement is extremely restrictive in that the selector value must be an integer and the selected values effectively form an integer subrange with lower bound 1.

12.3.6   Procedurization

It has already been noted that one of the ways of constructing a compound statement in COBOL is to form the statements concerned into a paragraph or section and to execute it out-of-line as a procedure. In Pascal a procedure is invoked by writing the procedure name as a statement, in COBOL a procedure is invoked via the PERFORM verb naming the paragraph or section concerned. There is no means in COBOL of passing parameters.

> PERFORM *procedure-name*

e.g.,

```
PERFORM ERROR-REPORT
```

Execution of this PERFORM statement causes control to transfer to the section or paragraph ERROR-REPORT and, after its execution, control will normally return to the statement immediately following the PERFORM statement.

In the example program presented in Chapter 11 the main paragraph consisted of a statement to open the files required, then three PERFORM statements, and finally a STOP RUN statement. Most of our example programs will be structured in this way, i.e., the first paragraph will consist of a sequence of calls to other paragraphs.

The PERFORM statement is also useful for by-passing some of the problems associated with nested IF statements in COBOL. For instance, given a complex program structure expressible in Pascal as, say,

```
if C1
then begin
        S1 ;
        if C2 then S2 ;
        S3
     end
else if C3
     then S4
     else S5
```

this is not directly translatable into COBOL (especially if *S1*, *S2*, *S3*, *S4*, and *S5* are structured statements such as if statements) due to the restricted rules concerning the nesting of conditional statements (in particular, the if statement

```
if C2 then S2
```

forming part of the statement sequence

S1 ;
if *C2* **then** *S2* ;
S3

causes a problem since a conditional statement can only follow a
sequence of imperative statements in COBOL). A good general rule
for dealing with nested sequences of statements within IF statements
is, if they contain non-imperative statements, to express each of
them as a paragraph and PERFORM it, e.g., the above structure
might be expressed in COBOL as

```
IF C1 PERFORM PARA-1 ELSE PERFORM PARA-2.
  ...
PARA-1.
  PERFORM S1.
  IF C2 PERFORM S2.
  PERFORM S3.
PARA-2.
  IF C3 PERFORM S4 ELSE PERFORM S5.
  ...
```
definitions of paragraphs S1 , ... , S5

If any of the statements S1,...,S5 are (sequences of) imperative
statements, then it is not necessary to form them into a separate
paragraph but instead they may be executed in-line within the paragraphs PARA-1 and PARA-2.

If a PERFORMed procedure contains another PERFORM
statement, then the text of the second procedure must either be
totally included in, or totally excluded from, the text of the first.

The EXIT verb is used to provide a common end-point for a
section of paragraphs. It must be the only sentence of the last paragraph of such a section, e.g.,

```
P SECTION.
P-1.
  ...
  IF N < 0 GO TO P-3.
...
P-2.
  ...
P-3.
  EXIT.
```

Some examples of legal and illegal code sequences involving PER-
FORM statements:

PERFORM A.   PERFORM B.   PERFORM A-1.

```
A SECTION.
A-1.
    ...
    PERFORM A-3.
    ...
    IF X < 0 GO TO A-4.
    ...                        always          X>=0      X<0
A-2.                                            OK      program
    ...                        legal                     action
    PERFORM A-1.                                        undefined
    ...
A-3.
    ...
A-4.
    EXIT.
B SECTION.
B-1.
    ...
    IF P < Q GO TO B-2
      ELSE GO TO B-3.
    ...                        always
B-2.
    PERFORM A.                 legal
B-3.
    EXIT
```

No recursion is allowed in COBOL and a good general rule is to avoid PERFORMing procedures which attempt to jump outside their boundaries.

12.3.7 Repetition

The main repetitive construct of Pascal is the while statement. In COBOL the body of the loop is written as a separate paragraph or section and the effect of the while construct achieved by performing the execution of the paragraph or section repeatedly using various forms of the PERFORM verb.

> PERFORM *procedure-name* UNTIL *condition*

Note that the condition is evaluated before the first iteration (i.e., it is not equivalent to the Pascal repeat statement despite the textual resemblance between the two statements).

The equivalent effect to a for statement is obtained using the

> PERFORM *procedure-name* $\begin{Bmatrix} identifier \\ integer \end{Bmatrix}$ TIMES

form where the identifier must be a numeric integer data item. The named procedure is executed the number of times specified by the value of the integer or identifier indicated, except if this value is non-positive, in which case the PERFORM statement has no effect.

Alternatively, if the use of a loop counting variable is required

> PERFORM *procedure-name*
>
>   VARYING *identifier* FROM $\begin{Bmatrix} identifier \\ integer \end{Bmatrix}$ BY $\begin{Bmatrix} identifier \\ integer \end{Bmatrix}$
>
>   UNTIL *condition*

such loops may be nested to a maximum depth of 3:

> PERFORM ...
> VARYING ...
> [AFTER VARYING ...]
> [AFTER VARYING ...]

Examples:

```
(a)  PERFORM P-1 UNTIL X = 3.
(b)  PERFORM P-1 7 TIMES.
(c)  PERFORM CARD-ISSUE NUMBER-OF-COPIES TIMES.
(d)  PERFORM RATE-FORMULA VARYING AMOUNT
          FROM 50 BY 5 UNTIL AMOUNT > 200.
(e)  PERFORM ANALYSE-ELEMENT
          VARYING K FROM 1 BY 1 UNTIL K > 10
          AFTER VARYING J FROM 1 BY 1 UNTIL J > 30
          AFTER VARYING I FROM 1 BY 1 UNTIL I > 20.
```

These are equivalent to the Pascal statements:

(a)   **while** $x<>3$ **do** *p1*
(b)   **for** $i := 1$ **to** 7 **do** *p1*
(c)   **for** $i := 1$ **to** *numberofcopies* **do** *cardissue*
(d)   *amount* $:= 50$;
      while *amount* $<= 200$ **do** **begin**
                              rateformula ;
                              amount $:= amount + 5$
                         end
(e)   **for** $i := 1$ **to** 20 **do**
        for $j := 1$ **to** 30 **do**
          for $k := 1$ **to** 10 **do** *analyseelement*

12.4 LOW VOLUME INPUT AND OUTPUT

It is often necessary to transfer small amounts of information to or from peripherals such as the operator console, e.g., to input batch totals during validation of a batch of input records, or output diagnostic messages whenever error situations arise.

The COBOL verbs ACCEPT and DISPLAY are used for the
transfer of low-volume input and output involving low-speed
peripheral devices.

ACCEPT *identifier* [FROM *mnemonic-name*]
DISPLAY *operand* [, *operand*] ... [UPON *mnemonic-name*]

mnemonic-name is a programmer-defined name denoting a
hardware device (e.g., card or tape reader or operator console for
ACCEPT, printer or punch or console for DISPLAY), and must
have been specified in the SPECIAL-NAMES paragraph of the
CONFIGURATION SECTION in the ENVIRONMENT
DIVISION. If no *mnemonic-name* is specified, then the peripheral
device associated with the ACCEPT or DISPLAY is defined by
each COBOL implementation (often it is the operator console, or
its equivalent).

Examples:
```
ACCEPT CONTROL-TOTAL.
ACCEPT BATCH-TOTAL FROM CARDS.
DISPLAY CONTROL-TOTAL, BATCH-TOTAL.
DISPLAY "ERROR FOUND ON CARD",
        CARD-NUMBER UPON LP.
```

The mnemonics CARDS and LP must have been previously
defined in the SPECIAL-NAMES paragraph, e.g.,

```
ENVIRONMENT DIVISION.
CONFIGURATION SECTION.
   ...
SPECIAL-NAMES.
   PRINTER 1 IS LP.
   CARD-READER 1 IS CARDS.
   ...
```

PRINTER 1 and CARD-READER 1 are our system-defined names
for the printer and card-reader peripherals.

In on-line systems these verbs can also be useful for sending
messages (via DISPLAY) to a program user at a terminal in order
to instruct him as to what data to input, and then accepting (via
ACCEPT) the reply, e.g.,

```
DISPLAY "TYPE IN YOUR NAME NOW".
ACCEPT USER-NAME.
```

The ACCEPT statement can also be used to obtain calendar
and time of day information from the system for printing in reports
generated by a COBOL program.

$$\boxed{\text{ACCEPT } identifier \text{ FROM } \begin{Bmatrix} \text{DATE} \\ \text{DAY} \\ \text{TIME} \end{Bmatrix}}$$

DATE is the reserved COBOL name for a predeclared conceptual data item which behaves as if it were a PIC 9(6) item in which the current data is stored in year, month, day form (each component being represented as two digits); DAY (the year of the century and day of the year) is equivalent to a PIC 9(5) item; TIME (the elapsed time after midnight to one-hundredth of a second) is effectively a PIC 9(8) item. Given the data declarations shown below

```
77   DATE-TODAY   PIC 9(6).
77   DAY-TODAY    PIC 9(5).
77   TIME-NOW     PIC 9(8).
```

the effect of the following PROCEDURE DIVISION statements executed at exactly 1.31 p.m. on 3 January 1983

```
ACCEPT DATE-TODAY FROM DATE.
ACCEPT DAY-TODAY FROM DAY.
ACCEPT TIME-NOW FROM TIME.
```

would be assign the values 830103, 83003, and 13310000 to DATE-TODAY, DAY-TODAY, and TIME-NOW, respectively.

Other SPECIAL-NAMES facilities include:

1. DECIMAL-POINT IS COMMA — for exchanging the role of commas and periods in the definition of numeric values and picture clauses.
2. CURRENCY SIGN IS *literal* — for changing the currency symbol defined by the COBOL implementation to some other currency symbol (this might be useful for transporting a program written in the USA to, say, the UK).
3. Our COBOL system defines a system-name CHANNEL-1 to represent the printer carriage control hardware facility which moves the paper in the printer to the top of the next form ready for printing. In the SPECIAL-NAMES paragraph we could introduce our own name for this facility, e.g.,

```
        CHANNEL-1 IS NEWPAGE
```

NEWPAGE is then a mnemonic-name and may be used anywhere that a mnemonic-name is appropriate, e.g., in the ADVANCING clause of a WRITE statement, e.g.,

```
    WRITE OUTPUT-LINE AFTER NEWPAGE.
```

This mapping of system-names on to mnemonic-names is again of use in transporting programs, e.g., if a program is moved to a system where the system-name for this particular hardware facility is TOP-OF-FORM, say, then the only change required in the program is to change the SPECIAL-NAMES entry to

```
TOP-OF-FORM IS NEWPAGE
```

and the remainder of the program remains unaffected.

12.5   STRING HANDLING

Given a data item whose value is a string of characters, there are a number of different types of manipulation that we might envisage performing on such a string, such as

1. counting the number of occurrences of certain characters within the string, or one of its substrings;
2. replacing particular characters within the string, or a substring, by other characters or strings of characters;
3. breaking the string up into a number of separate substrings. Additionally, given a number of such strings, we might wish to
4. join these strings, or substrings within them, to form a single string.

COBOL provides three verbs to perform these four classes of string manipulation — the INSPECT, STRING, and UNSTRING verbs.

The STRING verb provides the ability to concatenate two or more strings, or substrings of these strings, into a single data item. It is particularly useful for applications such as the printing of names and addresses on correspondence, or setting up headings to be displayed as part of reports. The UNSTRING verb is used for splitting a string into smaller strings and is useful, for example, for isolating particular substrings within a larger string of text, or for overcoming the problems caused by having to specify rigid, fixed-length, fields in records of an input data file in COBOL.

It is possible to do most kinds of string processing without using these verbs but instead employing the data REDEFINES feature and the PERFORM verb, although these special string-handling verbs provide a simple, convenient, and flexible set of text processing facilities which add greatly to the power of the COBOL language. We shall not consider the STRING and UNSTRING verbs further but shall instead concentrate upon the INSPECT verb and the special data editing facilities provided in COBOL.

12.5.1   The INSPECT Verb

This verb provides the ability to carry out the first two categories of string processing activity identified above — the counting and/or replacement of occurrences of single characters or groups of characters (substrings) within any data item declared to have DISPLAY usage. It has three different formats.

The first format is that used for counting occurrences of characters and substrings.

INSPECT *identifier-1* TALLYING

$$\left\{ \textit{identifier-2} \quad \text{FOR} \quad \left\{ \begin{array}{c} \left\{ \begin{array}{c} \text{ALL} \\ \text{LEADING} \end{array} \right\} \qquad \left\{ \begin{array}{c} \textit{identifier-3} \\ \textit{literal-1} \end{array} \right\} \\ \text{CHARACTERS} \\ \left[\left\{ \begin{array}{c} \text{BEFORE} \\ \text{AFTER} \end{array} \right\} \quad \text{INITIAL} \quad \left\{ \begin{array}{c} \textit{identifier-4} \\ \textit{literal-2} \end{array} \right\} \right] \end{array} \right\} \right\}$$

...   ...

As an example, suppose we wish to count the total number of asterisk characters appearing within a piece of text held in an alphanumeric data item TEXT-ITEM. The statements required to count the blanks would be:

```
MOVE ZERO TO STAR-COUNT.
INSPECT TEXT-ITEM
    TALLYING STAR-COUNT FOR ALL "*".
```

Hence, if the value of TEXT-ITEM consisted of the 50 characters

```
*****THE*DOG*ATE*THE*CAT.**IT*DID*NOT*FEEL*WELL.**
```

then the value of STAR-COUNT after execution of the above statements would be 17.

Perhaps we might wish also to count the number of leading asterisks and (in case there are no leading asterisks) the number of characters preceding the first asterisk in the string. The code would be expanded to:

```
MOVE ZEROES TO STAR-COUNT,
    LEADING-STARS, BEFORE-FIRST-STAR.
INSPECT TEXT-ITEM
    TALLYING STAR-COUNT FOR ALL "*",
            LEADING-STARS FOR LEADING "*",
            BEFORE-FIRST-STAR FOR
                CHARACTERS BEFORE INITIAL "*".
```

For the above value of TEXT-ITEM the execution of these statements would assign the values 17, 5, 0 to STAR-COUNT, LEADING-STARS, and BEFORE-FIRST-STAR, respectively.

In the above syntax rule for INSPECT *identifier-1* is the string which is to be inspected. *identifier-2* names the data item (which must be a numeric DISPLAY item) to which the result of the counting (TALLYING) operation will be assigned. It must always be initialized prior to an INSPECTion. The phrases following TALLYING indicate the characters being counted — ALL implies that all substrings which match the value of *identifier-3* or *literal-1* will be counted, LEADING implies that only leftmost occurrences will be counted, while CHARACTERS implies that all characters in a leading or trailing substring of identifier-1 will be counted. CHARACTERS is normally used in conjunction with the BEFORE or AFTER phrases. These are used to delimit the part of the string to be inspected for counting purposes, i.e., they define either an initial or final substring. For example, in the above example we might wish to determine the length of the initial substring of TEXT-ITEM consisting wholly of non-asterisks, specified as

```
CHARACTERS BEFORE INITIAL "*"
```

i.e., the substring we require is delimited by the first asterisk (INITIAL "*") in TEXT-ITEM and the CHARACTERS option will cause the number of characters in this substring to be counted.

The second format for INSPECT provides a replacement facility — it operates in almost exactly the same way except that, instead of counting characters or substrings, it will replace them by other characters or strings. Additionally, it provides a facility for replacement of the first occurrence of a character or substring within a string.

INSPECT *identifier-1* REPLACING

$$
\left\{
\begin{array}{l}
\text{CHARACTERS BY} \begin{Bmatrix} \textit{identifier-6} \\ \textit{literal-4} \end{Bmatrix} \left[\begin{Bmatrix} \text{BEFORE} \\ \text{AFTER} \end{Bmatrix} \text{INITIAL} \begin{Bmatrix} \textit{identifier-7} \\ \textit{literal-5} \end{Bmatrix} \right] \\[4ex]
\begin{Bmatrix} \text{ALL} \\ \text{, LEADING} \\ \text{FIRST} \end{Bmatrix} \begin{Bmatrix} \textit{identifier-5} \\ \textit{literal-3} \end{Bmatrix} \quad \text{BY} \quad \begin{Bmatrix} \textit{identifier-6} \\ \textit{literal-4} \end{Bmatrix} \\[4ex]
\left[\begin{Bmatrix} \text{BEFORE} \\ \text{AFTER} \end{Bmatrix} \text{INITIAL} \begin{Bmatrix} \textit{identifier-7} \\ \textit{literal-5} \end{Bmatrix} \right] \Bigg\}_{...}
\end{array}
\right\}
$$

If we wished to replace all asterisk characters in TEXT-ITEM by slashes ("/"):

```
INSPECT TEXT-ITEM
    REPLACING ALL "*" BY "/".
```

This would have the effect of changing the value of TEXT-ITEM from

*****THE*DOG*ATE*THE*CAT.**IT*DID*NOT*FEEL*WELL.**

to

/////////THE/DOG/ATE/THE/CAT.//IT/DID/NOT/FEEL/WELL.//

There is also a combined form of the INSPECT verb which provides both tallying and replacement options. We shall not give a full definition of its syntax but some of the examples below illustrate its use.

Examples:

```
(a)  INSPECT A-1
         TALLYING COUNT-ITEM
           FOR CHARACTERS BEFORE INITIAL "B".
(b)  INSPECT A-1
         TALLYING COUNT-ITEM
            FOR LEADING "L" BEFORE INITIAL "A".
(c)  INSPECT A-1
         REPLACING FIRST "A" BY "Z".
(d)  INSPECT A-1
         REPLACING CHARACTERS BY
            "Z" BEFORE INITIAL "A".
(e)  INSPECT A-1
         REPLACING LEADING SPACES BY ZEROES.
(f)  INSPECT A-1
         REPLACING ALL "A" BY "X", "G" BY "Z"
            AFTER INITIAL "A".
(g)  INSPECT A-1
         TALLYING COUNT-ITEM FOR ALL "?"
         REPLACING ALL "?" BY "Z".
```

Figure 12.5 shows the values of data items A–1 and COUNT-ITEM after execution of each of the above seven INSPECT statements, given initial values of these items.

	A-1		COUNT-ITEM	
	Before	After	Before	After
(a)	?????ABC	?????ABC	0	6
(b)	LEADING.	LEADING.	0	1
(c)	?????ABC	?????ZBC	0	0
(d)	?????ABC	ZZZZZABC	0	0
(e)	@@@@1234	00001234	0	0
(f)	BANDAGES	BANDXZES	0	0
(g)	??A?B?C?	ZZAZBZCZ	0	5

Figure 12.5   Effect of INSPECT operations

12.5.2 Edited Data Items

As we have seen in our example programs the output produced by a data processing program is usually an updated magnetic tape or disk file, or else some form of report sent to a printer or video display unit. In the cases of printed and displayed reports the readability of the reports (which are often examined by non-computing personnel) depends greatly upon the format and presentation of the information contained in the reports. In Listing 22 of Chapter 10 various headings were interspersed with the details and report lines, numeric values were printed out with leading zeroes replaced by spaces, and symbols such as currency signs, commas, and decimal points were inserted to make the values meaningful to the reader.

COBOL provides a wide range of data-editing facilities, mainly through its PICTURE type definition facility. By giving suitable pictures for data items (which must have DISPLAY usage) that are to be printed, the values moved to these items may be modified (*edited*, in COBOL parlance) to include certain special characters (e.g., $, +, /, ., CR) or replace certain characters (such as leading spaces) or move characters into significant positions (e.g., numeric signs, currency symbols, asterisks for protecting sums printed on checks).

Below are listed some of the symbols concerned and their meanings when used in PICTURE definitions.

SYMBOL	EXAMPLE PICTURE	MEANING
.	9.9	insert a decimal point into value
,	99,999,999	insert commas into value
B	99B999B999	insert spaces into value

/	99/99/99	insert slash characters
0	9990	append a zero to value
$	$999	insert a currency symbol
+	+999	insert − if value moved is negative otherwise insert +
−	−999	insert − if value moved is negative otherwise insert a space
DB	9999DB	insert DB if value moved is negative otherwise insert two spaces
CR	9999CR	insert CR if value moved is negative otherwise insert two spaces
multiple Z	ZZZ9	replace leading zeroes in value moved by spaces
multiple $	$$$9	replace leading zeroes in value moved by spaces, except rightmost leading zero which is replaced by the currency symbol $ (known as *floating* the currency symbol)
multiple +	+++9	replace leading zeroes in value moved by spaces, except rightmost leading zero which is replaced by + or −, depending upon sign of value
multiple −	−−−9	as above except rightmost leading zero is replaced by space or −
multiple *	***9	replace leading zeroes by * (this is used for check protection)

Z, $, +, −, and * are effectively 9s (i.e., they denote digit positions) but have an additional editing meaning attributed to them. $ is used here as the currency symbol — however it is possible to use other characters as the curency symbol. An alternative character may be defined by particular COBOL implementations (e.g., £ in UK installations) or by specifying a different character in the CURRENCY SIGN clause of the SPECIAL-NAMES paragraph (see Section 12.4). This alternative character may then be used in place of the $ symbol in any of the editing examples given below, with exactly the same effect as if $ had been used.

A data item containing any of these special picture symbols is known as an *edited data item* and any value moved to such a field will be edited according to the picture of the receiving item. The full rules for the construction of edited pictures are quite complex and we shall restrict ourselves here to giving a range of typical examples.

For edited pictures containing a decimal point the position at which alignment of the assigned value is to take place is that occupied by the decimal point, e.g., moving 12.45 to a data item with the following picture

PIC +99.99

results in the item being assigned the value "+12.45".

An edited picture may contain an insertion symbol which is preceded in the picture by a symbol which causes replacement of a leading zero, e.g., in the picture

PIC $,$$9.99

the insertion symbol is preceded by $ which is a replacement symbol used for replacing leading zeroes by spaces (except for the rightmost leading zero, which will be replaced by the currency character). Should a value be moved to this item such that a replacement takes place in the character position preceding the comma insertion symbol, then the insertion symbol is itself replaced by the replacement symbol, e.g., moving 12.45 to the above item produces the edited string " $12.45" as its value.

Figure 12.6 gives various examples illustrating the effect of MOVE operations involving edited destination data items.

MOVE SOURCE-ITEM TO RECEIVING-FIELD			
SOURCE-ITEM		RECEIVING-FIELD	
Picture	Value	Picture	Edited result
999	245	ZZZ	245
999	045	ZZZ	%45
999	005	ZZZ	%%5
999	000	ZZZ	%%%
999	123	$$$$	$123
999	023	$$$$	%$12
999	003	$$$$	%%$3
999	000	$$$$	%%%%
999	000	$$$9	%%$0
999	123	999.9	123.0
999	123	+999	+123
S999	-123	+999	-123
999	123	++++	+123
999	012	++++	%+12
999	012	****.**	**12.00
999	000	****.**	******
9999V99	123456	ZZ,ZZ9.99	%1,234.56
999	212	ZZ,ZZ9.99	%%%212.00
S999	123	999CR	123
S999	-123	999CR	123CR
S999	123	999DB	123%%
S999	-123	999DB	123DB
99999	12345	ZZBZZZ	12 345
99999	00017	ZZBZZZ	%%%%17

999999	321321	$ZZZ,ZZZ.ZZ	$321,321.00
9(5)V9	UU1234	$$$$,$$$.99	%%%%$123.4U
S9(6)	-000123	ZZZZZZ-	%%%123-
S9(4)V99	-001234	$$,$$$.99CR	%%%$12.34CR
9(6)	123456	9BBB9(5)	1 23456
9(4)V99	000067	$***,***.99	$*******.67

{ % represents a leading space }

Figure 12.6   Effects of edited pictures

If the DECIMAL POINT IS COMMA clause has appeared in the SPECIAL-NAMES paragraph of a program (see Section 12.4) then the functions of the period and comma editing symbols are interchanged, i.e., the rules given above for the use of periods and commas (and their effects) are interchanged.

If a numeric display item is described as BLANK WHEN ZERO in its data declaration, then moving of the value zero to that item will cause the item to be assigned all spaces and the editing actions defined by its picture will be overridden, e.g.,

```
77 ITEM-1 PIC $$$.99 BLANK WHEN ZERO.
```

will result in ITEM-1 being assigned the value "$12.45" when the value 12.45 is moved to it, but its value will be "   " when zero is moved.

12.6   TABLE HANDLING

The construction of tables of data and the use of subscripting have already been described. Instead of subscripting a table with an integer data item, a special data item known as an *index* may be associated with a table and used only to address an element of that table. The value of an index item corresponds to the occurrence number of an element of its associated table. However, it differs from a subscript in that the method of representation and the value of the index (usually a memory address) is specified by the implementation and may only be used in special table-handling operations provided by certain COBOL verbs.

An index may be associated with a table in the data declaration of the table, e.g.,

```
01  TABLE-OF-DATA.
  02  TABLE-ITEM OCCURS 200 TIMES INDEXED BY I,J.
    03  FIELD-1 PIC 999.
    03  FIELD-2 PIC X(20).
```

I and J are thus declared as index-names associated with TABLE-OF-DATA and need not be declared elsewhere.

Index data-items may also be declared as working-storage variables with INDEX usage and then used as general table-indexing items, e.g.,

```
77   INDEX-1   USAGE INDEX.
77   INDEX-2   INDEX.
```

Note the difference between index-names (which are declared in conjunction with a table) and index data items (which are general-purpose indexes declared independently of any table).

Elements of a table such as TABLE-OF-DATA may then be referenced using I, J (its associated index-names), INDEX-1, or INDEX-2 (general index items). However, indexing and subscripting may not be mixed when identifying a particular multi-dimensional table element. Relational conditions may be constructed using indexes, e.g.,

I > J	– compares occurrence numbers
INDEX-1 > INDEX-2	– likewise
J = 7	– the occurrence number corresponding to the value of J is used
I < AA (numeric)	– likewise

Often tables will be constructed in which the elements are sorted according to a key field value in each element. Special operations, involving the use of index items, may be performed on such tables, e.g., linear and binary searching based upon the key field values, provided that the table has been suitably declared.

```
01   TABLE-OF-SORTED-DATA.
  02   SORTED-DATA OCCURS 500 TIMES
                   ASCENDING KEY IS SORT-KEY
                   INDEXED BY INDEX-A.
    03   SORT-KEY   PIC 9999
    03   DATE-FIELD PIC X(25).
```

The above table contains 500 elements with the element values in ascending order of the field SORT-KEY in each. It is the responsibility of the programmer to ensure that the values in the table remain in sorted order. INDEX-A is an index-name associated with the table. Tables may be declared to be in ascending or descending order of up to three key fields.

We now look at some of the special verbs used in conjunction with index data items. The only statements which can assign values to index data items are the SET and SEARCH verbs.

SET	$\begin{cases} \textit{index-name} \\ \textit{identifier} \end{cases}$	$\begin{cases} [\,\textit{index-name}\,]\,... \\ [\,\textit{identifier}\,\quad]\,... \end{cases}$	TO	$\begin{cases} \textit{index-name} \\ \textit{identifier} \\ \textit{integer} \end{cases}$
SET	*index-name*	$[\,\textit{index-name}\,]\,...$	$\begin{cases} \text{UP BY} \\ \text{DOWN BY} \end{cases}$	$\begin{cases} \textit{identifier} \\ \textit{integer} \end{cases}$

An index-name may be given an initial value by means of the first form of the SET verb, e.g.,

```
SET I TO 3
```

where the operand is an occurrence number (i.e., positive integer), arithmetic expression, or another index value. Care should be taken when assigning the value of an index to another index to ensure that both indexes currently refer to the same table.

Index data items may only be assigned the values of other indexes, i.e., they cannot be assigned integer values. Hence

```
SET INDEX-A TO I
```

is legal, but

```
SET INDEX-A TO 3
```

is not.

The values of index-names only may be incremented or decremented using the second form of this verb, e.g.,

```
SET I UP BY 2.
SET I DOWN BY 1.
```

The SEARCH verb is used to scan tables ordered on some key field value in order to find the first element which satisfies some specified condition:

SEARCH *data-name* [VARYING   *index-name*]
[AT END *imperative-statement*]
WHEN *condition* $\begin{cases} \text{NEXT SENTENCE} \\ \textit{imperative-statement} \end{cases}$
$\left[\text{WHEN } \textit{condition} \begin{cases} \text{NEXT SENTENCE} \\ \textit{imperative-statement} \end{cases} \right]...$

Example:
```
         SET I TO 1.
         SEARCH SORTED-DATA
           AT END PERFORM NOT-IN-TABLE
           WHEN SORT-KEY (I) IS EQUAL TO 1234
             NEXT SENTENCE.
```

The first index associated with SORTED-DATA (i.e., I) is initially set to indicate the first element of the table (the VARYING clause is for use when some other index is required). The search commences at the element of the table corresponding to the current value of the index associated with SORTED-DATA (i.e., element 1) and continues with I being incremented by one as each element is examined. If an element with key field value 1234 is found, then the search terminates and control passes to the next sentence of the program with I having the occurrence number value of the element concerned — otherwise, if no element with key value 1234 exists, then the procedure NOT-IN-TABLE is performed. When more than one index-name is associated with a table (e.g., SORTED-DATA has two associated index-names, I and J) the SEARCH statement will always use the first named, unless another index-name is cited in a VARYING phrase.

If the table has been declared as an ordered table (as has TABLE-OF-SORTED-DATA) then a binary search of the complete table may be effected using the SEARCH ALL form of this verb, e.g.,

```
SEARCH ALL SORTED-DATA
    AT END PERFORM NOT-IN-TABLE
    WHEN SORT-KEY (I) IS EQUAL TO 1234
    NEXT SENTENCE.
```

No VARYING clause is permitted in this form and only one WHEN clause. If the search condition is independent of the key field, then the search will again be linear. If the table is ordered on more than one key field value, then if the condition refers to a minor key field it must also refer to the major key fields.

In Pascal such array searches have to be implemented as procedures performing linear or binary searches, such as in Section 3.3.3.

12.7   THE COBOL LIBRARY

The library facility in COBOL is intended to reduce the work involved in writing a COBOL program, particularly where the program is one of a number making up a system, and to reduce the length of the text of the programs. The library contains pieces of COBOL source text which are available for inclusion in a program at compile-time. Typically these source text fragments are common file descriptions, record definitions, PROCEDURE DIVISION paragraphs and sections which may be used by more than one program (for instance, in the Model Savings Bank system the master file descriptions, transaction processing routines, and random file addressing algorithms will all be held in the library since they are each used by several of the case study programs).

The library is held on backing store; how it is set up, modified, and new entries added, is defined by the particular COBOL implementation concerned. It consists of a number of named pieces of text, each identified by a unique *text-name*. Any piece of text held in the library may be incorporated into a source program by means of the COPY verb, which may be used anywhere in a COBOL program that a character-string or separator may occur (except within another COPY statement). The COPY statement is then replaced in the source program by the named library text. Textual replacement during the copying operation is also provided.

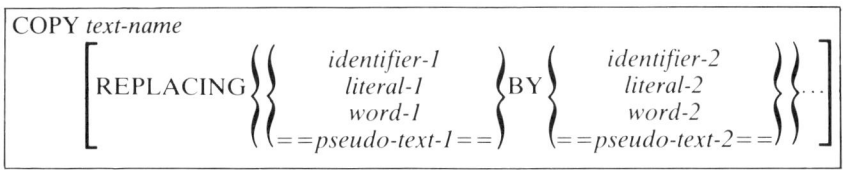

```
COPY text-name
    ⎡                ⎧⎧   identifier-1   ⎫    ⎧   identifier-2   ⎫⎫  ⎤
    ⎢ REPLACING ⎨⎨     literal-1      ⎬ BY ⎨     literal-2      ⎬⎬ ...
    ⎢                ⎨⎨     word-1         ⎬    ⎨     word-2         ⎬⎬
    ⎣                ⎩⎩ ==pseudo-text-1== ⎭    ⎩ ==pseudo-text-2== ⎭⎭  ⎦
```

pseudo-text-1 and *pseudo-text-2* consist of any sequence of characters (only *pseudo-text-2* may be an empty sequence).

Suppose that the library contains the following three pieces of text named IS-MASTER, MASTER-FD, and ADDRESS-ROUTINE:

```
IS-MASTER       SELECT MASTER-FILE
                    ASSIGN TO DISK
                    ORGANIZATION INDEXED ACCESS RANDOM
                    RECORD KEY R-K.
MASTER-FD      FD MASTER-FILE
                    BLOCK CONTAINS 512 CHARACTERS
                    LABEL RECORDS STANDARD
                    VALUE OF ID "XXX".
                01  MASTER-RECORD.
                    02  ACCOUNT-NUMBER  PIC X(8).
                    02  CLIENT-IDENTITY PIC X(30).
                    02  CURRENT-BALANCE PIC 9(5)V99
                                        COMP SYNC RIGHT.
                    02  MINIMUM-BALANCE PIC 9(5)V99
                                        COMP SYNC RIGHT.
ADDRESS-ROUTINE   DIVIDE F-1 INTO F-2
                      GIVING F-3 REMAINDER F-4.
                  ADD 1 TO F-4.
```

then the above entries could be incorporated into programs which require them, with suitable textual replacement of data-names, as shown below.

```
(a)  FILE-CONTROL.
         COPY IS-MASTER
             REPLACING R-K BY TRANSACTION-KEY
                            ==DISK==BY ==DISK 1==.
(b)  FILE SECTION.
         COPY MASTER-FD
             REPLACING "XXX" BY "MASTER-FILE".
(c)  GENERATE-BLOCK-NUMBER
         COPY ADDRESS-ROUTINE
             REPLACING
                 F-1 BY PRIME-DIVISOR
                 F-2 BY KEY-DIGITS
                 F-3 BY X-1
                 F-4 BY RECORD-NUMBER.
```

The resultant pieces of text which would be processed by the compiler are thus

```
(a)  FILE-CONTROL.
         SELECT MASTER-FILE
             ASSIGN TO DISK 1
             ORGANIZATION INDEXED ACCESS RANDOM
             RECORD KEY TRANSACTION-KEY.
(b)  FILE SECTION.
         FD MASTER-FILE
             BLOCK CONTAINS 512 CHARACTERS
             LABEL RECORDS STANDARD
             VALUE OF ID "MASTER-FILE".
         01  MASTER-RECORD.
             02  ACCOUNT-NUMBER    PIC X(8).
             02  CLIENT-IDENTITY   PIC X(30).
             02  CURRENT-BALANCE   PIC 9(5)V99
                                   COMP SYNC RIGHT.
             02  MINIMUM-BALANCE   PIC 9(5)V99
                                   COMP SYNC RIGHT.
(c)  GENERATE-BLOCK-NUMBER.
         DIVIDE PRIME-DIVISOR INTO KEY-DIGITS
             GIVING X-1 REMAINDER RECORD-NUMBER.
         ADD 1 TO F-4.
```

EXERCISES

In these exercises assume the computer for which the data declarations are being compiled is a four-byte per word machine, with the compiler allocating one byte to hold each character in a DISPLAY usage data item, and allocating the minimum number of bits to a COMPUTATIONAL usage item.

1. How much memory would be allocated to each of the following data items in an object program produced by this compiler?

```
77 DATA-ITEM-1   PICTURE 9.
77 DATA-ITEM-2   PICTURE S9.
77 DATA-ITEM-3   PICTURE S9 USAGE COMP.
77 DATA-ITEM-4   PICTURE S9(5) USAGE COMP.
77 DATA-ITEM-5   PICTURE 9(5)V9(4).
```

2. Twelve data items are defined by means of data descriptions of the form

```
77 A-n PIC S9(n) USAGE COMP.
```
    where n takes values from 1 to 12. Calculate the storage requirements of each of the twelve data items.
    What would be the effect on the storage requirements if the data items were also described as SYNC RIGHT?

3. (a)   A data item WORK-STORE consists of eight characters. In a calcula-tion PERFORM-1, comparisons will be made using the first four charac-ters and the last four characters separately. In a calculation PERFORM-2 comparisons will be made using the middle four characters. Write the data description for WORK-STORE so that the first four, middle four, and last four characters may each be referred to by single data-names.
   (b)   Write a data description for AMOUNT, a six-digit field including two decimal places, as an elementary item. It should also be possible to ex-amine the integer and fractional parts as separate items.

4. Write INSPECT statements to carry out the following operations on the characters of a data item named SAMPLE-ITEM:
   (a)   change all spaces into hyphens;
   (b)   count the number of leading zeroes;
   (c)   count the number of leading spaces and also replace them by periods;
   (d)   change all the characters up to the first X into Xs.

5. What are the contents of SAMPLE and COUNT-ITEM after the execution of each of the following INSPECT statements with the initial values of the eleven character data item SAMPLE as shown? Assume the value of COUNT is always zero prior to execution of each of the INSPECT statements.

   (a) `INSPECT SAMPLE`
`        TALLYING COUNT-ITEM FOR ALL CHARACTERS`
`                      BEFORE INITIAL ",".`
   (b) `INSPECT SAMPLE REPLACING ALL "*" BY "?".`
   (c) `INSPECT SAMPLE`
`        TALLYING COUNT-ITEM FOR ALL "-"`
`        REPLACING ALL "-" BY SPACE.`

```
(d)  INSPECT SAMPLE REPLACING FIRST "." BY "X".
(e)  INSPECT SAMPLE
        TALLYING COUNT-ITEM FOR ALL SPACES.
(f)  INSPECT SAMPLE
        TALLYING COUNT-ITEM FOR LEADING SPACES.
```

```
                      SAMPLE
         (a)  │$128,064.32│
         (b)  │$*****12.69│
         (c)  │535-22-1583│
         (d)  │9A6.77X.,XX│
         (e)  │ JOHN SMITH│
         (f)  │      1.23 │
```

6. The text of a piece of English prose consisting of letters, spaces, commas, and periods is stored in a string data item

```
77 TEXT-FRAGMENT  PIC X(1000).
```

All words are followed by a space, comma, or period. A comma is always followed by two spaces, a period by three spaces. Write COBOL statements to count the total number of words in the text held in TEXT-FRAGMENT.

7. How do the three different types of USAGE (viz., DISPLAY, COMPUTATIONAL and INDEX) differ? When should each be used?

8. Write the PROCEDURE DIVISION of a program to print cards 'two-up', i.e., two cards are to be printed side-by-side on each line. Only the first sixty characters of each card are to be printed. The file descriptions are

```
FD  CARD-FILE ...
   01  CARD-RECORD.
      02  CARD-DETAILS  PIC X(60).
      02  FILLER        PIC X(20).
FD  PRINT-FILE ...
   01  PRINT-RECORD.
      02  CARD-PLACES OCCURS 2 TIMES.
         03  FILLER     PIC X(60).
```

9. How much memory is allocated for each of the following eight COBOL data items?

```
77 X-1  PIC 99.
77 X-2  PIC S99.
77 X-3  PIC 99 USAGE COMP.
77 X-4  PIC S99 USAGE COMP.
```

```
77 X 5   PIC ZZZ.
77 X-6   PIC ***.
77 X-7   PIC 99V9.
77 X-8   PIC ++++.
```

What data will be stored as a result of each of the thirty-two statements

```
MOVE  12 TO X-n
MOVE -12 TO X-n
ADD 1 TO 1.9 GIVING X-n
ADD 1 TO 1.9 GIVING X-n ROUNDED
```

for n = 1,2,...,8?

10. What pictures may be legally constructed from the following five symbols:

$$9 \quad , \quad \$ \quad * \quad .$$

using each symbol at least once in every picture, and using no other symbol? What is the meaning of each picture?

11. What twenty-four values are stored as a result of moving each of the following four constants:

$$0 \quad 3.4 \quad 0.07 \quad -7.24$$

to each of six data items with the following pictures?

$$Z9 \quad +9 \quad -9 \quad S9 \quad +++ \quad \$*.**$$

12. Fill in the edited result column below.

SOURCE ITEM		RECEIVING ITEM	
PICTURE	Contents	PICTURE	Edited result
9(6)	000197	ZZZ999	
9(6)	290866	999B99B99	
9(6)	019113	Z(6)00	
9999V99	148143	ZZZ,ZZZ.Z	
S9(6)	543210	−999,999	
S9(6)	543210	+999,999	
99V999	03456	ZZV999	
X(6)	ABCDEF	X(7)	
X(6)	ABCDEF	XBXXXBBXX	
S9(6)	000312	ZZZ,ZZ9CR	

13. How much memory would each of the following data items occupy and what would be stored as a result of moving the value −123.456 to each (assuming standard COBOL is being used)?

```
77 A   PICTURE $9(6).99 .
77 B   PICTURE $(6)9.99 .
77 C   PICTURE $Z(6).99 .
77 D   PICTURE $***,***99DB .
77 E   PICTURE 999 USAGE IS COMPUTATIONAL .
77 F   PICTURE S99 .
77 G   PICTURE S99V99 .
77 H   PICTURE SVP9 .
```

13 SEQUENTIAL FILES

13.1 FILE DESCRIPTIONS IN COBOL

One of the features of COBOL that sets it apart from programming languages such as Pascal is its extensive range of facilities for input–output programming. COBOL supports sequential, indexed sequential and random file organizations with sequential, indexed, direct, and dynamic access, as appropriate.

The peripheral device on which a file is held is defined in the ENVIRONMENT DIVISION, together with declarations of the required organization and access methods. Properties of the file such as the block size, label contents, and record descriptions then appear in the DATA DIVISION.

13.1.1 File Descriptions in the ENVIRONMENT DIVISION

In the ENVIRONMENT DIVISION the programmer defines each of his files in terms of its implementation-dependent properties, i.e., the external device on which the file resides, the organization of the records in the file, the required mode of access to the records, and the degree of buffering to be used for the file. These specifications appear in the FILE-CONTROL paragraph of the INPUT-OUTPUT SECTION.

The general form of the FILE-CONTROL paragraph is as follows:

```
FILE-CONTROL.
   {  SELECT    file-name
      ASSIGN    TO  device-name   integer
      [RESERVE   integer   AREAS ]
                              (  INDEXED    )
      [ORGANIZATION  IS    {  RELATIVE   }  ]
                              ( SEQUENTIAL )
                          (  RANDOM    )
      [ACCESS  IS      {  DYNAMIC   }   ]      }  ...
                          ( SEQUENTIAL )
```

The SELECT clause names the file and the ASSIGN clause identifies its associated peripheral device. *device-name* is one of the system names defined by the COBOL implementation to denote the particular peripheral device concerned. The RESERVE clause specifies the degree of buffering required (the default in most COBOL implementations, including our case-study system, is single buffering).

The ORGANIZATION and ACCESS clauses specify the file organization method and file access method, respectively. The default for both of these clauses is SEQUENTIAL. RELATIVE organization is a COBOL form of random file organization. Both indexed and direct access are referred to as RANDOM access in COBOL.

Some examples of SELECT entries:

(a) SELECT MEMBER-DATA
        ASSIGN TO CARD-READER 1.
(b) SELECT STUDENT-FILE
        ASSIGN TO TAPE 2
        ORGANIZATION SEQUENTIAL
        RESERVE 2 AREAS.
(c) SELECT AN-INDEXED-FILE
        ASSIGN TO DISK 1
        ORGANIZATION IS INDEXED
        ACCESS IS RANDOM.

MEMBER-DATA is the name of a single-buffered, sequential access file held on the peripheral unit CARD-READER 1. STUDENT-FILE is a magnetic tape file (held on the tape drive designated as tape unit 2 by the implementation) which is double-buffered and, being a tape file, uses sequential organization and access. AN-INDEXED-FILE is a single-buffered disk file of records organized as an indexed sequential file which will be accessed randomly (i.e., via the file index).

13.1.2   File Descriptions in the DATA DIVISION

In the FILE SECTION a file description entry (i.e., beginning with the level indicator FD) is supplied for each of the files introduced in the FILE-CONTROL paragraph, giving details such as the presence or absence of labels (and their contents, if present), the size of the blocks or buckets in the file, followed by a sequence of descriptions of the various record types to be found in the file (in the form of *record-description-entries*).

When more than one record description is given the record data items so described all share the same storage area (known as the *file record area* and equal in size to the largest of the record items described), i.e., the file record area is implicitly redefined by each record description.

```
DATA DIVISION.
FILE SECTION.
[ FD    file-name
[ BLOCK CONTAINS    integer      {CHARACTERS}  ]
                                 { RECORDS   }
LABEL RECORDS {STANDARD  VALUE OF ID IS literal}.
              {OMITTED                         }
    record-description-entry
[ record-description-entry ] ...
] ...
```

Immediately after each FD entry (and there must be one for each file) there must be at least one record description defining the format of the file records. The BLOCK CONTAINS clause specifies the size of the blocks in a file in terms of either the number of records per block (the blocking factor) or number of characters per block. If it is omitted the file blocks will, by default, be assumed to contain just one record. For devices such as card readers and line printers which have only one physical record size, the BLOCK CONTAINS clause should not be specified. It is usual for tape and disk files to specify the block size in terms of characters rather than records and, indeed, most commercial installations use a standard block size for all their files. For instance, in the Model Savings Bank system, all tape and disk files employ a standard block size of 512 characters. To calculate the total size of a record in a tape or disk file, the length of the record count field (in our case we shall assume it to be four characters long) is added to the logical record size (i.e., the size of the largest record declared by the programmer) — see Section 3.2.3.

The mandatory LABEL RECORDS clause specifies whether the file contains labels. If it does then they must conform to the implementation standard. In the SUPER-2000 implementation of COBOL the VALUE OF ID clause occurring after LABEL RECORDS STANDARD will specify a string (of up to twenty characters), which is the physical file identity that should be recorded in the label. This required file identity will be checked automatically by the system each time a file is processed as an input or input–output file and is opened by a COBOL program, and will be inserted as part of the label written on a file opened by a COBOL program for processing as an output file. Some example FD entries follow for the files whose file-control entries were given in the previous subsection:

```
(a) FD MEMBER-DATA LABEL RECORDS OMITTED.
       01  MEMBER-RECORD     PIC X(80).
(b) FD STUDENT-FILE
       BLOCK CONTAINS 512 CHARACTERS
       LABEL RECORDS STANDARD.
       01  STUDENT-RECORD    PIC X(10).
(c) FD AN-INDEXED-FILE
       BLOCK CONTAINS 20 RECORDS
       LABEL RECORDS STANDARD
       VALUE OF ID IS "1983-DATA".
       01  RECORD-A.
         10  CODE-FIELD      PIC X.
         10  OTHER-A-FIELDS PIC X(10).
       01  RECORD-B.
         10  CODE-FIELD      PIC X.
         10  OTHER-B-FIELDS PIC X(30).
```

The file MEMBER-DATA is a punched card file and has no labels associated with it. In the latter two files labels conform to the implementation standard (LABEL RECORDS STANDARD). In the case of AN-INDEXED-FILE the identity held in the file label must have the value "1983-DATA".

Since MEMBER-DATA is a card reader file its blocks are by default one punched card record long, and so it has eighty character blocks. The file AN-INDEXED-FILE has 700 character blocks (twenty records per block; RECORD-B has the longest format, i.e., thirty-five characters including the record-length-count field, which we have assumed to be four characters long). STUDENT-FILE uses 512 character blocks (i.e., blocks with a blocking factor of 36 since each physical record will be fourteen characters long).

AN-INDEXED-FILE contains two different record types of different lengths, both of which (RECORD-A and RECORD-B) are given record descriptions.

The use of the various file handling verbs of COBOL will be introduced in this and subsequent chapters describing the processing of the various file organizations (Chapter 16, Indexed Sequential Files, Chapter 17, Relative Files).

13.2 SEQUENTIAL FILE PROCESSING IN COBOL

COBOL provides facilities for the processing of sequential files held on any common storage medium. In the FILE-CONTROL paragraph of the INPUT-OUTPUT SECTION the SELECT entry for a sequential file will specify the organization and access methods as

```
ORGANIZATION IS SEQUENTIAL
ACCESS IS SEQUENTIAL
```

although both these clauses may be omitted since the COBOL defaults for organization and access are both SEQUENTIAL. In the same paragraph the assignment of the file to a peripheral device and the degree of buffering required are also specified. The FD entry for the file in the FILE SECTION will specify the size of the file blocks or buckets (in the BLOCK CONTAINS clause) and, if the file has labels, the file identification will be defined in the LABEL RECORDS clause. Thus the physical file characteristics are declared and enable the file to be attached to the program when execution begins.

Before logical processing of a sequential file may commence it must be opened for input, output, or input–output (disk files only) processing by indicating the required processing mode in an OPEN statement.

$$\text{OPEN} \left\{ \left\{ \begin{array}{c} \text{INPUT} \\ \text{I-O} \\ \text{OUTPUT} \end{array} \right\} \textit{file-name} \quad [\,,\textit{file-name}] \quad \dots \right\} \dots$$

Input–output files are opened in I-O mode. The effect of an OPEN statement is to initialize the file window as described in Section 5.1, i.e., so that the next read operation will set the file window to contain the first record of the file.

Examples: OPEN OUTPUT FILE-1 , FILE-2.
            OPEN INPUT FILE-3.
            OPEN I-O FILE-4.

The OPEN verb carries out any label processing necessary according to the LABEL RECORDS clause in the files' FD entries (i.e., checking of labels for input and input–output files; writing of labels on output files).

When the processing of a file in a particular mode has been completed it must be closed (all files must be closed before a COBOL program terminates) using the CLOSE verb.

```
CLOSE file-name   [WITH {NO REWIND} ]
                         { LOCK    }
        [, file-name [WITH {NO REWIND} ] ]  ...
                           { LOCK    }
```

If, at the time of closure, the file window contains the end of file marker, then any trailer label processing associated with the files concerned is performed. The simple closure of a file, e.g.,

```
CLOSE FILE-1
```

allows such a file to be subsequently reopened by the file in any processing mode. Its file window (in the case of a tape or disk file) is reset to the start of the file (i.e., a magnetic tape file is rewound). A file closed WITH LOCK, e.g.,

```
CLOSE FILE-2 WITH LOCK
```

may not be used again during the program run; its peripheral unit is released (and is then available to hold some other file) and, for tape and disk files, the file window is reset to the start of the file. A (tape or disk) file closed using the WITH NO REWIND qualifier, e.g.,

```
CLOSE FILE-3 WITH NO REWIND
```

has its file window left in its current position for possible later reopening.

Thus the SELECT clause introduces the physical file into the program (and the lifetime of the file's availability within the program is effectively that of the program itself, except when the file is locked closed). A processing instance of the file has a lifetime equal to the period between matching OPEN and CLOSE operations on the file. An OPEN statement indicates the required processing mode for the particular instance.

Figure 13.1 shows the operations provided in COBOL for accessing records of files opened in the various modes (REWRITE is the COBOL record replacement operator).

Processing mode of OPEN		
INPUT	OUTPUT	I-O

	INPUT	OUTPUT	I-O
READ	x		x
WRITE		x	
REWRITE			x

Figure 13.1   COBOL file access operations

Note that COBOL does not support deletion of records from sequential files, nor does it provide the capability to write new records to a file opened as an I-O (input–output) file.

The READ, WRITE, and REWRITE verbs all involve the logical transfer of a record value between the file concerned and the record data area declared in the FD entry for the file concerned.

The READ verb may be used to obtain the next record of a sequential file opened as an INPUT or I-O file.

READ *file-name* [INTO *identifier*] AT END *imperative-statement*

The AT END clause specifies the action to be performed when the READ operation results in the file window advancing to the end of file marker, i.e., when no next logical record can be obtained from the file and the attempted READ is therefore unsuccessful. The shorter form, e.g.,

```
READ FILE-3 AT END PERFORM CLOSE-FILE-3
```

transfers the next record of FILE-3 into the record data item declared for FILE-3 in its FD entry. The longer form, e.g.,

```
READ FILE-3 INTO WORKING-RECORD
     AT END PERFORM CLOSE-FILE-3
```

not only causes the next record value to be moved into the record data item associated with FILE-3 but also assigns its value to some data item named WORKING-RECORD. However, if there is no record to be obtained from FILE-3 because it has been completely read, then the effect of the READ statement is instead to perform the paragraph CLOSE-FILE-3, and the contents of the file record area become undefined. The INTO form should not be used if the input file contains different types of records, i.e., there is more than one record description for the file.

Note that each READ may not involve a physical transfer from the file. The physical unit of transfer is a block of records which is moved into the buffer area for the file concerned — if a block contains N records then the very first READ statement will cause a block to be transferred from the file to the buffer, and the first record is then automatically extracted from the buffer (de-blocked) and assigned to the appropriate data item. The next $N-1$ READ statements executed will cause successive records of the block to be de-blocked from the buffer and assigned, after which the next READ executed will again require the physical input of the next block from the file. Hence the READ verb automatically performs the de-blocking of records.

For files opened in OUTPUT processing mode the WRITE verb is used to append a new record value as the last value in the file. For line printer files it also provides a means of advancing the line printer carriage control.

```
WRITE record-name [FROM identifier-1]
                               ( (identifier-2)  ([LINE  ])
   {BEFORE}  ADVANCING {  {  integer  }  {[LINES]} }
   {AFTER  }                (  mnemonic-name  )
                                    PAGE
```

mnemonic-name is the name of some special facility specified by the particular implementation and associated with the printer device. It must have been defined in the SPECIAL-NAMES paragraph.

The *record-name* specified in a WRITE statement must have been associated with the file in its FD entry. Notice that the WRITE verb requires to write a *record-name* whereas the READ verb reads from a *file-name*. The reason for this difference is that, at the time of reading, it may not be possible to predict which of the various possible record formats is actually about to be read from the input file.

For the simplest form, e.g.,

```
WRITE FILE-1-RECORD
```

the value to be written must have already been assigned to the record data item FILE-1-RECORD associated with the file concerned, or else it may be the value of some other data item and the longer form is used, e.g.,

```
WRITE FILE-1-RECORD FROM WORKING-RECORD
```

After successful execution of a WRITE statement the contents of the output file's record area (FILE-1-RECORD in the above examples) become undefined — however, the contents of any data item mentioned in a FROM phrase remain unaffected. Again the WRITE verb automatically performs any record blocking required.

In the case of a line printer file failure to advance the carriage control before or after each WRITE statement will result in overprinting of the previous line (which might in fact be desirable in some instances, e.g., for underlining or bold printing). The ADVANCING option provides for such vertical page formatting, e.g.,

```
WRITE FILE-2-RECORD AFTER ADVANCING 2 LINES
```

moves the carriage control two lines forward before printing the value of FILE-2-RECORD. If the ADVANCING phrase is not used for output to a printing device, the default is AFTER ADVANCING 1 LINE.

```
WRITE FILE-2-RECORD BEFORE ADVANCING PAGE
```

will print FILE-2-RECORD and then advance the printer to the start of the next page. Of course the ADVANCING option must not be used for non-printer files.

If an identifier is specified in an ADVANCING phrase its value denotes the number of lines the printer carriage control is to be advanced.

The REWRITE verb may only be executed for a file currently opened in the I-O processing mode — the record currently in the file window, which is always the last record read (since there is no delete operator for sequential files in COBOL), is replaced by the value indicated.

> REWRITE *record-name* [FROM *identifier*]

The new value must either have been assigned to the file's associated record area (say, FILE-4-RECORD), in which case the shorter form is used, e.g.,

```
REWRITE FILE-4-RECORD
```

or be the value of some other data item, in which case the longer form is used, e.g.,

```
REWRITE FILE-4-RECORD FROM WORKING-RECORD
```

After a REWRITE statement the record transferred is no longer available in the file's record area.

To illustrate the use of some of these verbs consider again the COBOL program *PROGRAM0* of Chapter 11. Two sequential files were declared in that program, a card reader file CLIENT-DATA and a printer file INTEREST-REPORT with associated record data items CLIENT-RECORD and OUTPUT-LINE, respectively. Both files were single-buffered and no block size was defined since card reader and line printer files have a standard block size equal in length to one record. Neither file had any labels associated with it. CLIENT-DATA was opened for input processing and INTEREST-REPORT for output processing (line 660).

```
OPEN INPUT CLIENT-DATA , OUTPUT INTEREST-REPORT.
```

The READ statement at line 720, viz.,

```
READ CLIENT-DATA AT END MOVE 1 TO EOF.
```

was used to transfer the next record of CLIENT-DATA into CLIENT-RECORD except when the end of file had been reached, in the event of which the value 1 was to be moved to the end of file indicator EOF. At line 790

```
WRITE OUTPUT-LINE FROM CLIENT-LINE
   AFTER ADVANCING 1 LINE.
```

causes the contents of the record CLIENT-LINE to be printed on INTEREST-REPORT (the file for which OUTPUT-LINE is the record data item) after the printer has been advanced to the next line. Likewise the WRITE statement at line 930

```
WRITE OUTPUT-LINE FROM SUMMARY-LINE
   AFTER ADVANCING 2 LINES.
```

prints the contents of SUMMARY-LINE on the same printer file but after advancing the printer carriage control two lines (i.e., causing a blank line to appear in the printed file).

Finally (line 940) the two files are both closed.

```
CLOSE CLIENT-DATA , INTEREST-REPORT.
```

13.3   CASE STUDY: SEQUENTIAL MASTER FILE INITIALIZATION

We now consider the implementation in COBOL of the program *PROGRAM1* in Chapter 5 which created an initial version of the magnetic tape sequential master file used by various other programs of the system. *PROGRAM1* read a deck of punched cards one at a time, each card containing details of a customer's account and, for each card read, wrote a corresponding record to the magnetic tape file. The format of the card file is shown again below:

1 8 9		38 39 45 46 52 53 80		
account number	client identity	current balance	minimum balance	other details

Listing 27 gives the implementation of this program in COBOL. The points to note are

1. The physical file characteristics are defined partly in the ENVIRONMENT DIVISION and partly in the DATA DIVISION of the COBOL program. Two processing instances of the master tape file are required — an output instance whose lifetime is defined by the OPEN and CLOSE statements for it in the paragraph CREATE-MASTER-FILE, and an output instance with a lifetime defined by the OPEN and CLOSE statements within LIST-MASTER-FILE.

2. The type *environment.numeric* becomes a COMP SYNC RIGHT numeric type in COBOL.

3. An input record is read directly into the data item CLIENT-RECORD by a READ statement, and the various fields are then accessible by their data names — however, there is no guarantee in COBOL that the characters read into a numeric field do not contain illegal characters and hence their correctness cannot be assumed (but may if necessary be checked using the NUMERIC condition test).

4. Special edited pictures (i.e., ZZZZ9.99) are used in the COBOL program to obtain zero suppression and decimal point insertion when printing numeric values — the *putnumeric* procedure of our extended version of Pascal is assumed to do this automatically.

5. In the COBOL program each output line is constructed in ACCOUNT-DETAIL-LINE before moving it to PRINT-LINE for printing.

6. The data item FILE-FLAG and its associated condition-name NO-RECORDS-REMAIN are used to simulate a Boolean variable.

LISTING 27 : *PROGRAM1*

```
IDENTIFICATION DIVISION.
PROGRAM-ID.        PROGRAM1.
INSTALLATION.      QUB.
AUTHOR.            JOHN ELDER.
*                  INITIALIZATION OF MASTER TAPE FILE.
DATE-WRITTEN.      FEBRUARY 1983.
DATE-COMPILED.     01/03/83.

ENVIRONMENT DIVISION.
CONFIGURATION SECTION.
SOURCE-COMPUTER.   SUPER-2000.
OBJECT-COMPUTER.   SUPER-2000.
INPUT-OUTPUT SECTION.
FILE-CONTROL.
    SELECT CLIENT-DATA ASSIGN TO CARD-READER 1 RESERVE 2 AREAS.
    SELECT MASTER-TAPE-FILE ASSIGN TO TAPE 1 RESERVE 2 AREAS.
    SELECT PRINT-FILE ASSIGN TO PRINTER 1 RESERVE 2 AREAS.

DATA DIVISION.
FILE SECTION.
FD CLIENT-DATA LABEL RECORDS OMITTED.
   01  CLIENT-RECORD.
       02   ACCOUNT-NUMBER   PIC X(8).
       02   CLIENT-IDENTITY  PIC X(30).
       02   CURRENT-BALANCE  PIC 9(5)V99.
       02   MINIMUM-BALANCE  PIC 9(5)V99.
       02   FILLER           PIC X(28).
FD MASTER-TAPE-FILE BLOCK CONTAINS 512 CHARACTERS
                    LABEL RECORDS STANDARD
                       VALUE OF ID IS "MASTER-FILE".
   01  MASTER-RECORD.
       02   ACCOUNT-NUMBER    PIC X(8).
       02   CLIENT-IDENTITY   PIC X(30).
       02   CURRENT-BALANCE   PIC 9(5)V99 COMP SYNC RIGHT.
       02   MINIMUM-BALANCE   PIC 9(5)V99 COMP SYNC RIGHT.
FD PRINT-FILE LABEL RECORDS OMITTED.
   01   PRINT-LINE           PIC X(120).
WORKING-STORAGE SECTION.
77 FILE-FLAG                 PIC 9 COMP SYNC RIGHT.
   88 NO-RECORDS-REMAIN      VALUE 1.
01 ACCOUNT-DETAIL-LINE.
   02 FILLER                 PIC X(5) VALUE SPACES.
   02 ACCOUNT-NUMBER         PIC X(8).
   02 FILLER                 PIC X(5) VALUE SPACES.
   02 CLIENT-IDENTITY        PIC X(30).
   02 FILLER                 PIC X(5) VALUE SPACES.
   02 CURRENT-BALANCE        PIC ZZZZ9.99.
   02 FILLER                 PIC X(5) VALUE SPACES.
   02 MINIMUM-BALANCE        PIC ZZZZ9.99.
PROCEDURE DIVISION.
MAIN-PARAGRAPH.
    PERFORM CREATE-MASTER-FILE.
    PERFORM LIST-MASTER-FILE.
    STOP RUN.
CREATE-MASTER-FILE.
    OPEN INPUT CLIENT-DATA, OUTPUT MASTER-TAPE-FILE.
    MOVE ZERO TO FILE-FLAG.
    PERFORM READ-NEXT-CARD-RECORD.
    PERFORM TRANSFER-RECORD UNTIL NO-RECORDS-REMAIN.
    CLOSE CLIENT-DATA, MASTER-TAPE-FILE.
READ-NEXT-CARD-RECORD.
    READ CLIENT-DATA AT END MOVE 1 TO FILE-FLAG.
TRANSFER-RECORD.
    MOVE CORRESPONDING CLIENT-RECORD TO MASTER-RECORD.
    WRITE MASTER-RECORD.
    PERFORM READ-NEXT-CARD-RECORD.
LIST-MASTER-FILE.
    OPEN INPUT MASTER-TAPE-FILE, OUTPUT PRINT-FILE.
```

```
      MOVE ZERO TO FILE-FLAG.
      PERFORM PRINT-HEADING.
      PERFORM READ-NEXT-TAPE-RECORD.
      PERFORM LIST-RECORD UNTIL NO-RECORDS-REMAIN.
      CLOSE MASTER-TAPE-FILE, PRINT-FILE.
  PRINT-HEADING.
      MOVE SPACES TO PRINT-LINE.
      WRITE PRINT-LINE AFTER ADVANCING PAGE.
  LIST-RECORD.
      MOVE CORRESPONDING MASTER-RECORD TO ACCOUNT-DETAIL-LINE.
      WRITE PRINT-LINE FROM ACCOUNT-DETAIL-LINE
          AFTER ADVANCING 1 LINES.
      PERFORM READ-NEXT-TAPE-RECORD.
  READ-NEXT-TAPE-RECORD.
      READ MASTER-TAPE-FILE AT END MOVE 1 TO FILE-FLAG.
```

Since the master file is used in subsequent programs we assume that its FD description has been placed in the library under the library text name MASTER-FD in the following form:

```
FD MASTER-FILE
   BLOCK CONTAINS 512 CHARACTERS
   LABEL RECORDS STANDARD
   VALUE OF ID IS "MASTER-FILE".
01   MASTER-RECORD.
     02   ACCOUNT-NUMBER    PIC X(8).
     02   CLIENT-IDENTITY   PIC X(30).
     02   CURRENT-BALANCE   PIC 9(5)V99
                           COMP SYNC RIGHT.
     02   MINIMUM-BALANCE   PIC 9(5)V99
                           COMP SYNC RIGHT.
```

i.e., it could have been retrieved into the text of *PROGRAM1* by the COPY statement

```
COPY MASTER-FD REPLACING MASTER-FILE
               BY MASTER-TAPE-FILE
```

in place of the FD entry for MASTER-TAPE-FILE in Listing 27.

13.4   CASE STUDY: SEQUENTIAL MASTER FILE UPDATE

In Section 5.5 the sequential file update program *PROGRAM4* (Figure 13.2) was constructed. Here we consider the implementation of *PROGRAM4* in COBOL. A file SORTED-TRANS of valid transactions sorted by date within account number is used to update the sequentially organized master file MASTER-FILE (also ordered by account number) in order to produce a new master file. This is also called MASTER-FILE and will then be used as input to the next update run.

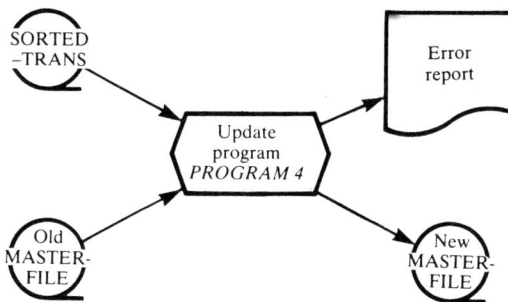

Figure 13.2   Sequential file update

Note again that only accounts with zero balances may be deleted, that accounts may not be overdrawn nor exceed an upper balance limit (currently $20 000), and minimum balances must also be recorded.

The program given in Listing 28 is the COBOL implementation of this update program. In the COBOL program the files are denoted by the identifiers OLD-MASTER, NEW-MASTER, and TRANSACTION-FILE, respectively. When the files are opened the labels of the two input files, i.e., OLD-MASTER and TRANSACTION-FILE, are automatically checked to ensure that their ID fields contain the physical file names "MASTER-FILE" and "SORTED-TRANS", respectively. Opening of the output file NEW-MASTER causes "MASTER-FILE" to be assigned to the ID field in its header label. When the files are closed, viz.,

```
CLOSE TRANSACTION-FILE,
      OLD-MASTER-FILE, NEW-MASTER-FILE.
```

all three, being tape files, are rewound.

In the paragraph READ-NEXT-TRANSACTION the statement

```
READ TRANSACTION-FILE
     AT END MOVE SENTINEL TO TRANSACTION-KEY.
```

will normally transfer the next record of the file into the record item TRANSACTION. However, if no record is available because the input file has been fully read, the AT END clause is obeyed. As discussed in Chapter 4, in order to avoid a complex termination condition when the ends of the two input files have been reached, the AT END clauses of the READ statements for both files simulate the reading of a sentinel record, i.e., one with a key higher than any

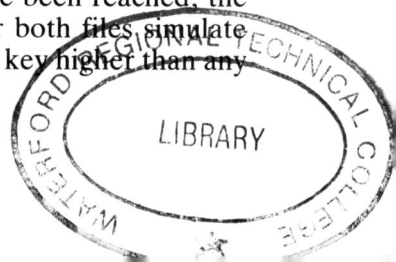

valid record key. The merging process thus terminates with a match
on the sentinel key value.

The output statement

```
WRITE NEW-RECORD.
```

of the paragraph FINAL-STATUS causes the value which has been
previously assigned to the record item NEW-RECORD to be transferred to its associated file NEW-MASTER. No ADVANCING
clause is specified since NEW-MASTER is a tape file and the value
written will simply become the last record in the file.

The following points relate to the differences between the
Pascal-based version of this program and the COBOL program.

1. The different range of types in Pascal and COBOL means that,
    whereas in Pascal we may define the transactions as an abstract
    record type, the COBOL data description of a transaction
    reflects the physical representation of the data on the original
    medium on which it was prepared. For instance, the transaction
    kind is described by an enumerated type in Pascal, but by a
    character field in COBOL.
2. We represent *boolean* variables this time by PIC 9 COMP
    SYNC RIGHT data items, and introduce data items with con-
    stant values 0 and 1 to represent the constants *false* and *true*.
3. The COBOL figurative constant HIGH-VALUES is suitable
    for use as the sentinel value, rather than some explicit account
    number value (as was used in Chapter 5).
4. The master file FD entries are copied from the library text in
    MASTER-FD with suitable file-name and record-name sub-
    stitutions.

The code for performing the listing of the new master file contents is not included in this program since it is the same as the code
included in *PROGRAM1*, Listing 27. Any error messages produced
during the update process are DISPLAYed (together with the
offending transaction record) on REPORT-DEVICE, which is
identified by the SPECIAL-NAMES paragraph as being PRINTER
1), and whose contents are shown in Listing 29.

The source text shown in Listing 28 is that presented to the
compiler. The actual compilation listing of the program produced by
the compiler will contain the actual date in the DATE-COMPILED
paragraph and the COPY statements for the master file descriptions
will be replaced by the contents of the library text concerned, with
appropriate substitution of names.

LISTING 28 : *PROGRAM4*

```
IDENTIFICATION DIVISION.
PROGRAM-ID.          PROGRAM4.
INSTALLATION.        QUB.
AUTHOR.              JOHN ELDER.
*                    SEQUENTIAL FILE UPDATE.
DATE-WRITTEN.        FEBRUARY 1983.
DATE-COMPILED.


ENVIRONMENT DIVISION.
CONFIGURATION SECTION.
SOURCE-COMPUTER.     SUPER-2000.
OBJECT-COMPUTER.     SUPER-2000.
SPECIAL-NAMES.       PRINTER 1 IS REPORT-DEVICE.
INPUT-OUTPUT SECTION.
FILE-CONTROL.
    SELECT OLD-MASTER ASSIGN TO TAPE 1 RESERVE 2 AREAS.
    SELECT NEW-MASTER ASSIGN TO TAPE 2 RESERVE 2 AREAS.
    SELECT TRANSACTION-FILE ASSIGN TO TAPE 3 RESERVE 2 AREAS.


DATA DIVISION.


FILE SECTION.
FD TRANSACTION-FILE BLOCK CONTAINS 512 CHARACTERS
                    LABEL RECORDS STANDARD
                    VALUE OF ID "SORTED-TRANS".
  01  TRANSACTION.
      02  DATE-FIELD        PIC 9(6)
      02  ACCOUNT-NUMBER    PIC X(8).
      02  KIND              PIC X.
          88  CREDIT        VALUE "C".
          88  DEBIT         VALUE "D".
          88  ADDITION      VALUE "N".
          88  DELETION      VALUE "X".
      02  AMOUNT            PIC 9(4)V99.
      02  CLIENT-IDENTITY   PIC X(30).
      02  FILLER            PIC X(29).

COPY MASTER-FD REPLACING MASTER-FILE BY OLD-MASTER
                         MASTER-RECORD BY OLD-RECORD.

COPY MASTER-FD REPLACING MASTER-FILE BY NEW-MASTER
                         MASTER-RECORD BY NEW-RECORD.

WORKING-STORAGE SECTION.
77  SENTINEL        PIC X(8) VALUE HIGH-VALUES.
77  CURRENT-KEY     PIC X(8).
77  TRANSACTION-KEY PIC X(8) VALUE LOW-VALUES.
77  OLD-MASTER-KEY  PIC X(8) VALUE LOW-VALUES.
77  TRUE            PIC 9 COMP SYNC RIGHT VALUE 1.
77  FALSE           PIC 9 COMP SYNC RIGHT VALUE ZERO.
77  INFILE          PIC 9 COMP SYNC RIGHT.
77  SAVINGS-LIMIT   PIC 9(5) COMP SYNC RIGHT VALUE 20000.
77  NEW-BALANCE     PIC S9(5)V99 COMP SYNC RIGHT.

PROCEDURE DIVISION.
UPDATE-SEQUENTIAL-FILE.
    OPEN INPUT TRANSACTION-FILE, OLD-MASTER,
         OUTPUT NEW-MASTER.
    PERFORM READ-NEXT-TRANSACTION.
    PERFORM READ-OLD-MASTER.
    PERFORM CHOOSE-NEXT-KEY.
    PERFORM PROCESS-ONE-KEY UNTIL CURRENT-KEY = SENTINEL.
    CLOSE TRANSACTION-FILE, OLD-MASTER, NEW-MASTER.
    STOP RUN.
PROCESS-ONE-KEY.
    PERFORM INITIAL-STATUS.
    PERFORM PROCESS-ONE-TRANSACTION
```

```
            UNTIL TRANSACTION-KEY NOT = CURRENT-KEY.
        PERFORM FINAL-STATUS.
        PERFORM CHOOSE-NEXT-KEY.
PROCESS-ONE-TRANSACTION.
        PERFORM APPLY-TRANSACTION-TO-MASTER.
        PERFORM READ-NEXT-TRANSACTION.
CHOOSE-NEXT-KEY.
        IF TRANSACTION-KEY < OLD-RECORD-KEY
            MOVE TRANSACTION-KEY TO CURRENT-KEY
        ELSE MOVE OLD-MASTER-KEY TO CURRENT-KEY.
INITIAL-STATUS.
        IF OLD-MASTER-KEY = CURRENT-KEY
            MOVE OLD-RECORD TO NEW-RECORD
            MOVE TRUE TO INFILE
            PERFORM READ-OLD-MASTER
        ELSE MOVE FALSE TO INFILE.
FINAL-STATUS.
        IF INFILE = TRUE WRITE NEW-RECORD.
READ-NEXT-TRANSACTION.
        READ TRANSACTION-FILE
            AT END MOVE SENTINEL TO TRANSACTION-KEY.
        IF TRANSACTION-KEY NOT = SENTINEL
            MOVE ACCOUNT-NUMBER IN TRANSACTION TO TRANSACTION-KEY.
READ-OLD-MASTER.
        READ OLD-MASTER AT END MOVE SENTINEL TO OLD-MASTER-KEY.
        IF OLD-MASTER-KEY NOT = SENTINEL
            MOVE ACCOUNT-NUMBER IN OLD-RECORD TO OLD-MASTER-KEY.
APPLY-TRANSACTION-TO-MASTER.
        IF ADDITION PERFORM APPLY-ADDITION
            ELSE IF DELETION PERFORM APPLY-DELETION
                ELSE IF DEBIT PERFORM APPLY-DEBIT
                    ELSE PERFORM APPLY-CREDIT.
APPLY-ADDITION.
        IF INFILE = TRUE
            DISPLAY "A/C NO. ALREADY ALLOCATED ",  TRANSACTION
                UPON REPORT-DEVICE
        ELSE MOVE TRUE TO INFILE
            MOVE CORRESPONDING TRANSACTION TO NEW-RECORD
            MOVE ZERO TO CURRENT-BALANCE IN NEW-RECORD,
                    MINIMUM-BALANCE IN NEW-RECORD.
APPLY-DELETION.
        IF INFILE = FALSE
            DISPLAY "A/C NO. NOT ALLOCATED      ",  TRANSACTION
                UPON REPORT-DEVICE
        ELSE IF CURRENT-BALANCE IN NEW-RECORD NOT = ZERO
                DISPLAY "BALANCE NOT ZERO            ",  TRANSACTION
                    UPON REPORT-DEVICE
            ELSE MOVE FALSE TO INFILE.
APPLY-DEBIT.
        IF INFILE = FALSE
            DISPLAY "A/C NO. NOT ALLOCATED      ",  TRANSACTION
                UPON REPORT-DEVICE
        ELSE SUBTRACT AMOUNT FROM CURRENT-BALANCE IN NEW-RECORD
                GIVING NEW-BALANCE
            IF NEW-BALANCE < ZERO
                DISPLAY "A/C OVERDRAWN               ",  TRANSACTION
                    UPON REPORT-DEVICE
            ELSE MOVE NEW-BALANCE TO CURRENT-BALANCE IN NEW-RECORD
                IF NEW-BALANCE < MINIMUM-BALANCE IN NEW-RECORD
                    MOVE NEW-BALANCE TO MINIMUM-BALANCE IN NEW-RECORD.
APPLY-CREDIT.
        IF INFILE = FALSE
            DISPLAY "A/C NO. NOT ALLOCATED      ",  TRANSACTION
                UPON REPORT-DEVICE
        ELSE ADD AMOUNT , CURRENT-BALANCE IN NEW-RECORD
                GIVING NEW-BALANCE
            IF NEW-BALANCE > SAVINGS-LIMIT
                DISPLAY "BALANCE EXCEEDS LIMIT       "  TRANSACTION
                    UPON REPORT-DEVICE
            ELSE MOVE NEW-BALANCE TO CURRENT-BALANCE IN NEW-RECORD.
```

```
LISTING 29  FILE UPDATE ERROR REPORT

BALANCE EXCEEDS LIMIT       82020210464182C400000
A/C NO. ALREADY ALLOCATED   8202012028277XN       W.COEY
A/C OVERDRAWN               82020120564880D030000
A/C NO. NOT ALLOCATED       82020230214122X
A/C NO. NOT ALLOCATED       82020230214122D000500
BALANCE NOT ZERO            82020330528232X
A/C NO. NOT ALLOCATED       82020240216640X
A/C NO. NOT ALLOCATED       82020350111116C100000
```

Since the transaction processing routine is required by other
update programs in the case study system we assume that the
library contains the following text named as TRANSACTION-
PROCESSING:

```
      IF ADDITION PERFORM APPLY-ADDITION
         ELSE IF DELETION PERFORM APPLY-DELETION
            ELSE IF DEBIT PERFORM APPLY-DEBIT
               ELSE PERFORM APPLY-CREDIT.
APPLY-ADDITION.
      IF INFILE = TRUE
         DISPLAY "A/C NO. ALREADY ALLOCATED ",
            TRANSACTION UPON REPORT-DEVICE
      ELSE MOVE TRUE TO INFILE
           MOVE CORRESPONDING TRANSACTION
              TO MASTER-RECORD
           MOVE ZERO TO CURRENT-BALANCE
                        IN MASTER-RECORD,
                        MINIMUM-BALANCE
                        IN MASTER-RECORD.
APPLY-DELETION.
      IF INFILE = FALSE
         DISPLAY "A/C NO. NOT ALLOCATED     ",
                 TRANSACTION UPON REPORT-DEVICE
      ELSE IF CURRENT-BALANCE IN MASTER-RECORD
              NOT = ZERO
              DISPLAY "BALANCE NOT ZERO          ",
                      TRANSACTION UPON REPORT-DEVICE
           ELSE MOVE FALSE TO INFILE.
APPLY-DEBIT.
      IF INFILE = FALSE
         DISPLAY "A/C NO. NOT ALLOCATED     ",
                 TRANSACTION UPON REPORT-DEVICE
      ELSE SUBTRACT AMOUNT
              FROM CURRENT-BALANCE IN MASTER-RECORD
              GIVING NEW-BALANCE
           IF NEW-BALANCE < ZERO
              DISPLAY "A/C OVERDRAWN             ",
                      TRANSACTION UPON REPORT-DEVICE
           ELSE MOVE NEW-BALANCE
                   TO CURRENT-BALANCE
                   IN MASTER-RECORD
```

```
              IF NEW-BALANCE < MINIMUM-BALANCE
                           IN MASTER-RECORD
                 MOVE NEW-BALANCE
                    TO MINIMUM-BALANCE
                       IN MASTER-RECORD.
APPLY-CREDIT.
    IF INFILE = FALSE
       DISPLAY "A/C NO. NOT ALLOCATED     ",
              TRANSACTION UPON REPORT-DEVICE
    ELSE ADD AMOUNT ,
              CURRENT-BALANCE IN MASTER-RECORD
           GIVING NEW-BALANCE
        IF NEW-BALANCE > SAVINGS-LIMIT
           DISPLAY "BALANCE EXCEEDS LIMIT     ",
                  TRANSACTION UPON REPORT-DEVICE
        ELSE MOVE NEW-BALANCE
                TO CURRENT-BALANCE
                   IN MASTER-RECORD.
```

i.e., the paragraph APPLY-TRANSACTION-TO-MASTER in Listing 28 could have taken the form

```
APPLY-TRANSACTION-TO-MASTER.
    COPY TRANSACTION-PROCESSING REPLACING
        MASTER-RECORD BY NEW-RECORD.
```

and the last four paragraphs of the program would then have been omitted as they would be incorporated as part of the retrieval from the library.

EXERCISES

1. Write COBOL file descriptions for sequential files having the following characteristics:
   (a) a card file with name ORDERS, no labels;
   (b) tape file, name PAYROLL-MASTER, standard labels with identification "MASTER-PAY-1";
   (c) disk file, name PARTS-REQUIREMENTS, 10 records per bucket, standard labels with identification "PARTS-REQUIREMENTS".

2. Implement the program of Exercise 5, Chapter 5, in COBOL.

14 DATA VALIDATION

14.1 DATA VALIDATION FEATURES IN COBOL

COBOL provides several features intended specifically for the validation of input data, while several other features may be used in data validation. In the latter category tables, REDEFINES, and indexed sequential files (see Chapter 16), can all be used to perform some of the correctness checks described in Chapter 6.

We have already described in the preceding chapter the use of file labels and how a COBOL program automatically checks the actual label contents against the expected contents.

The record-oriented input verbs of COBOL consider input data simply as a fixed-length alphanumeric data record and apply no type checks whatsoever. However, the contents of a field can be checked to ensure that they contain numeric or alphabetic characters only by means of the IS NUMERIC and IS ALPHABETIC conditions, respectively. These tests must be used wherever possible on input data to avoid the possibility (for example) of the program later applying an arithmetic operation to a supposedly numeric data item which erroneously contains non-numeric characters. The checking of numeric data items is usually preceded by use of the INSPECT verb to replace any leading spaces by zeroes, e.g.,

```
INSPECT FIELD-1
    REPLACING LEADING SPACES BY ZEROES.
```

Feasibility checks on the range of values of data items may be programmed using level 88 condition names associated with the sets of feasible and infeasible values.

Particular characters within data items may be accessed by

redefining the item as an array of single characters, e.g., suppose it is required to check that the thirteenth character of a fifty character field is a "B" and that all the characters in the string lie in the range "A".."H".

```
. . .
02  A-STRING PIC X(50).
02  INDIV-CHAR REDEFINES A-STRING PIC X
             OCCURS 50 TIMES.
. . .
    IF INDIV-CHAR (13) NOT = "B"
       DISPLAY "CHARACTER 13 NOT B".
    PERFORM CHAR-CHECK VARYING I
       FROM 1 BY 1 UNTIL I > 50.
. . .
CHAR-CHECK.
    IF INDIV-CHAR (I) "A" OR > "H"
       DISPLAY "CHARACTER", I,
               "=", INDIV-CHAR (I).
. . .
```

Redefinition is also useful for handling data that needs to be defined both as alphanumeric, for handling when it is in error, and as numeric for normal arithmetic processing. Suppose that an input data field should contain a price but that, if the input field consists of anything but digits, it is to be treated as an alphanumeric item. Hence we define

```
10 X-PRICE  PIC X(7).
10 N-PRICE  REDEFINES X-PRICE PIC 9(5)V99.
```

The PROCEDURE DIVISION may then reference the seven-character string X-PRICE or the seven-digit numeric item N-PRICE, depending upon the nature (and type requirements) of the operation to be performed.

As an example of the use of these features, the following are extracts from a COBOL program which checks whether or not a given record field ISBN contains a valid International Standard Book Number:

```
. . .
02  ISBN.
    03  ISBN-DIGITS.
        04  DIGIT PIC 9 OCCURS 9 TIMES.
    03  CHECK-DIGIT PIC X.
        88  CHECK-DIGIT-OK
                VALUES "0" THRU "9", "X".
    03  CHECK-DIGIT-VALUE
            REDEFINES CHECK-DIGIT PIC 9.
. . .
```

```
77  ISBN-ERROR PIC 9 COMP SYNC RIGHT.
  88  ISBN-OK VALUE ZERO.
. . .
CHECK-ISBN.
    MOVE ZERO TO ISBN-ERROR.
    IF ISBN-DIGITS NOT NUMERIC
        PERFORM RECORD-ERROR
    ELSE IF NOT CHECK-DIGIT-OK
            PERFORM RECORD-ERROR
        ELSE PERFORM MODULUS-11-CHECK.
    IF NOT ISBN-OK DISPLAY "ISBN ERROR", ISBN.
. . .
MODULUS-11-CHECK.
    MOVE ZERO TO SUM.    MOVE 10 TO WEIGHT.
    PERFORM WEIGHT-DIGIT VARYING I
      FROM 1 BY 1 UNTIL I > 9.
    IF CHECK-DIGIT = "X"
        ADD 10 TO SUM
    ELSE ADD CHECK-DIGIT-VALUE TO SUM.
    DIVIDE SUM BY 11 GIVING I REMAINDER J.
    IF J IS NOT ZERO PERFORM RECORD-ERROR.
WEIGHT-DIGIT.
    COMPUTE SUM = SUM + WEIGHT * DIGIT (I).
    SUBTRACT 1 FROM WEIGHT.
RECORD-ERROR.
    MOVE 1 TO ISBN-ERROR.
. . .
```

The validity of code numbers may also be checked by searching a table of valid code numbers, or by accessing an indexed-sequential file whose records are organized using the valid code numbers as key fields. Data inconsistencies may also be established by file or table look-up. The following COBOL fragments might appear in a data validation program to search a list of valid code values stored in a table CODE-TABLE and determine whether the value of SAMPLE-NUMBER represents a valid code number.

```
. . .
01  CODE-TABLE.
  02  CODE-NUMBERS OCCURS 100 TIMES
          INDEXED BY I.
    03  CODE-NUMBER PIC 9(5).
. . .
77  SAMPLE-NUMBER PIC 9(5).
77  NO-MATCH-FLAG PIC 9 COMP SYNC RIGHT.
  88  NO-MATCH VALUE ZERO.
. . .
MOVE 1 TO NO-MATCH-FLAG.
SET I TO 1.
SEARCH CODE-NUMBERS
    AT END MOVE ZERO TO NO-MATCH-FLAG
```

```
          WHEN CODE-NUMBER (I) = SAMPLE-NUMBER
              NEXT SENTENCE.
      IF NO-MATCH
          DISPLAY SAMPLE-NUMBER, "INVALID".
```

14.2 CASE STUDY: TRANSACTIONS VALIDATION PROGRAM

The implementation in COBOL of the data validation program *PROGRAM2* (previously described and constructed in Section 6.4 using our extended Pascal language) is presented in Listing 30. Note how the various structures required for the account number validation are established in the DATA DIVISION using REDEFINES, and the correctness of the characters in numeric fields is determined using the IS NUMERIC condition. Prior to checking of the AMOUNT field by means of the NUMERIC condition any leading spaces in the amount are replaced by zeroes using an INSPECT statement. Otherwise the structure of the PROCEDURE DIVISION follows closely that of the Pascal-based program except that all of the COBOL data is declared as global data (because of the absence of block structure in COBOL) and there is no parameter-passing mechanism (instead parameter values are assigned to global data items — cf., the use of ERROR-INDEX).

LISTING 30 *PROGRAM2*

```
IDENTIFICATION DIVISION.
PROGRAM-ID.          PROGRAM2.
AUTHOR.              JOHN ELDER.
INSTALLATION.        QUB.
*                    TRANSACTION VALIDATION PROGRAM.
DATE-WRITTEN.        JANUARY 1983.
DATE-COMPILED.       02/01/83.

ENVIRONMENT DIVISION.
CONFIGURATION SECTION.
SOURCE-COMPUTER.  SUPER-2000.
OBJECT-COMPUTER.  SUPER-2000.
INPUT-OUTPUT SECTION.
FILE-CONTROL.
    SELECT TRANSACTION-FILE ASSIGN TO DISK 1 RESERVE 2 AREAS.
    SELECT VALID-TRANSACTIONS-FILE ASSIGN TO TAPE 1 RESERVE 2 AREAS.
    SELECT ERROR-REPORT ASSIGN TO PRINTER 1 RESERVE 2 AREAS.

DATA DIVISION.
FILE SECTION.
FD TRANSACTION-FILE LABEL RECORDS OMITTED.
  01  TRANSACTION.
    02  DATE-FIELD.
      03  YEAR-FIELD       PIC 99.
        88  YEAR-OK        VALUE 81, 82.
      03  MONTH-FIELD      PIC 99.
        88  MONTH-OK       VALUE 1 THRU 12.
```

```
          03  DAY-FIELD          PIC 99.
      02  ACCOUNT-NUMBER.
          03  FIRST-7-DIGITS.
              04  DIGIT          PIC 9 OCCURS 7 TIMES.
          03  CHECK-DIGIT        PIC X.
              88  CHECK-DIGIT-OK VALUES ARE "0" THRU "9", "X".
          03  VALUE-OF-CHECK-DIGIT REDEFINES CHECK-DIGIT PIC 9.
      02  KIND               PIC X.
          88  KIND-OK            VALUE "C", "D", "N", "X".
          88  CREDIT             VALUE "C".
          88  DEBIT              VALUE "D".
          88  ADDITION           VALUE "N".
          88  DELETION           VALUE "X".
      02  AMOUNT             PIC 9(4)V99.
      02  CLIENT-IDENTITY    PIC X(30).
      02  FILLER             PIC X(29).

FD VALID-TRANSACTIONS-FILE BLOCK CONTAINS 512 CHARACTERS
                           LABEL RECORDS STANDARD
                                    VALUE OF ID "VALID-TRANS".
  01  VALID-TRANSACTION    PIC X(80).

FD ERROR-REPORT-FILE LABEL RECORDS OMITTED.
  01  OUTPUT-LINE.
      02  OUTPUT-DETAILS     PIC X(80).
      02  FILLER             PIC X(40).

WORKING-STORAGE SECTION.
77  TRANSACTION-COUNT       PIC 9(6) COMP SYNC RIGHT VALUE ZERO.
77  TRANSACTIONS-IN-ERROR PIC 9(6) COMP SYNC RIGHT VALUE ZERO.
77  CORRECT-TRANSACTIONS    PIC 9(6) COMP SYNC RIGHT.
77  TRANSACTION-FILE-FLAG PIC 9    COMP SYNC RIGHT VALUE ZERO.
  88  NO-TRANSACTIONS-REMAIN VALUE 1.
77  ERROR-COUNT             PIC 9    COMP SYNC RIGHT.
77  ERROR-INDEX             PIC 9    COMP SYNC RIGHT.
01  ERROR-LIST-TABLE.
  02  ERROR-LIST            PIC 9    COMP SYNC RIGHT
                                  OCCURS 5 TIMES.
77  LAST-DATE               PIC 9(6) VALUE ZEROES.
77  DATE-ERROR              PIC 9 COMP SYNC RIGHT.
  88  DATE-OK                VALUE ZERO.
77  MONTH-ERROR             PIC 9    COMP SYNC RIGHT.
  88  MONTH-VALUE-OK         VALUE ZERO.
77  SUM                     PIC 999  COMP SYNC RIGHT.
77  WEIGHT                  PIC 9    COMP SYNC RIGHT.
77  I                       PIC 99   COMP SYNC RIGHT.
77  J                       PIC 99   COMP SYNC RIGHT.
77  MAXIMUM-DEBIT           PIC 9999 COMP SYNC RIGHT VALUE 2000.
01  SUMMARY-LINE.
  02  SUMMARY-HEADER         PIC X(29).
  02  SUMMARY-COUNT          PIC ZZZZZ9.
01  MESSAGE-TABLE-1.
  02  FILLER PIC X(35) VALUE "ILLEGAL CHARACTER IN DATE".
  02  FILLER PIC X(35) VALUE "INVALID DATE".
  02  FILLER PIC X(35) VALUE "DATE OUT OF SEQUENCE".
  02  FILLER PIC X(35) VALUE "ILLEGAL CHARACTER IN A/C NUMBER".
  02  FILLER PIC X(35) VALUE "INVALID ACCOUNT NUMBER".
  02  FILLER PIC X(35) VALUE "INVALID TRANSACTION KIND".
  02  FILLER PIC X(35) VALUE "AMOUNT IS NOT NUMERIC".
  02  FILLER PIC X(35) VALUE "IDENTITY FIELD IS MISSING".
  02  FILLER PIC X(35) VALUE "DEBIT AMOUNT EXCEEDS LIMIT".
01  MESSAGE-TABLE-2 REDEFINES MESSAGE-TABLE-1.
  02  ERROR-MESSAGE PIC X(35) OCCURS 9 TIMES.
01  MONTH-TABLE-1.
  02  FILLER    PIC 99 VALUE 31.
  02  FILLER    PIC 99 VALUE 28.
  02  FILLER    PIC 99 VALUE 31.
```

```
02  FILLER    PIC 99 VALUE 30.
02  FILLER    PIC 99 VALUE 31.
02  FILLER    PIC 99 VALUE 30.
02  FILLER    PIC 99 VALUE 31.
02  FILLER    PIC 99 VALUE 31.
02  FILLER    PIC 99 VALUE 30.
02  FILLER    PIC 99 VALUE 31.
02  FILLER    PIC 99 VALUE 30.
02  FILLER    PIC 99 VALUE 31.
01  MONTH-TABLE-2 REDEFINES MONTH-TABLE-1.
02  DAYSINMONTH PIC 99 OCCURS 12 TIMES.

PROCEDURE DIVISION.
MAIN-PARAGRAPH.
    PERFORM VALIDATE-BATCH.
    PERFORM LIST-VALID-TRANSACTIONS.
    STOP RUN.

VALIDATE-BATCH.
    OPEN INPUT TRANSACTION-FILE
        OUTPUT VALID-TRANSACTIONS-FILE, ERROR-REPORT-FILE.
    PERFORM ERROR-REPORT-HEADING.
    PERFORM READ-NEXT-TRANSACTION.
    PERFORM CHECK-TRANSACTION UNTIL NO-TRANSACTIONS-REMAIN.
    PERFORM ERROR-REPORT-FOOTING.
    CLOSE TRANSACTION-FILE, VALID-TRANSACTIONS-FILE, ERROR-REPORT-FILE.

CHECK-TRANSACTION.
    ADD 1 TO TRANSACTION-COUNT.
    MOVE ZERO TO ERROR-COUNT.
    PERFORM CHECK-DATE.
    PERFORM CHECK-ACCOUNT-NUMBER.
    PERFORM CHECK-TRANSACTION-KIND.
    IF KIND-OK PERFORM CHECK-REST-OF-TRANSACTION.
    IF ERROR-COUNT > ZERO
        PERFORM ERROR-REPORT
    ELSE WRITE VALID-TRANSACTION FROM TRANSACTION.
    PERFORM READ-NEXT-TRANSACTION.

CHECK-DATE.
    MOVE ZERO TO DATE-ERROR, MONTH-ERROR.
    IF YEAR-FIELD IS NOT NUMERIC
        MOVE 1 TO ERROR-INDEX
        PERFORM RECORD-ERROR-IN-DATE
    ELSE IF NOT YEAR-OK
            MOVE 2 TO ERROR-INDEX
            PERFORM RECORD-ERROR-IN-DATE.
    IF MONTH-FIELD IS NOT NUMERIC
        MOVE 1 TO ERROR-INDEX
        PERFORM RECORD-ERROR-IN-DATE
        MOVE 1 TO MONTH-ERROR
    ELSE IF NOT MONTH-OK
            MOVE 2 TO ERROR-INDEX
            PERFORM RECORD-ERROR-IN-DATE
            MOVE 1 TO MONTH-ERROR.
    IF DAY-FIELD IS NOT NUMERIC
        MOVE 1 TO ERROR-INDEX
        PERFORM RECORD-ERROR-IN-DATE
    ELSE IF MONTH-VALUE-OK
            AND DAY-FIELD > DAYSINMONTH (MONTH-FIELD)
            MOVE 2 TO ERROR-INDEX
            PERFORM RECORD-ERROR-IN-DATE.
    IF DATE-OK PERFORM SEQUENCE-CHECK.
RECORD-ERROR-IN-DATE.
    MOVE 1 TO DATE-ERROR.
    PERFORM RECORD-ERROR.
SEQUENCE-CHECK.
```

```
    IF DATE-FIELD < LAST-DATE
        MOVE 3 TO ERROR-INDEX
        PERFORM RECORD-ERROR.
    MOVE DATE-FIELD TO LAST-DATE.

CHECK-ACCOUNT-NUMBER.
    IF FIRST-7-DIGITS IS NUMERIC AND CHECK-DIGIT-OK
        PERFORM MODULUS-11-CHECK
    ELSE MOVE 4 TO ERROR-INDEX
        PERFORM RECORD-ERROR.
MODULUS-11-CHECK.
    MOVE ZERO TO SUM.     MOVE 8 TO WEIGHT.
    PERFORM WEIGHT-DIGIT VARYING I FROM 1 BY 1 UNTIL I > 7.
    IF CHECK-DIGIT = "X"
        ADD 10 TO SUM
    ELSE ADD VALUE-OF-CHECK-DIGIT TO SUM.
    DIVIDE SUM BY 11 GIVING I REMAINDER J.
    IF J IS NOT ZERO
        MOVE 5 TO ERROR-INDEX
        PERFORM RECORD-ERROR.
WEIGHT-DIGIT.
    COMPUTE SUM = SUM + WEIGHT * DIGIT (I).
    SUBTRACT 1 FROM WEIGHT.

CHECK-TRANSACTION-KIND.
    IF NOT KIND-OK
        MOVE 6 TO ERROR-INDEX
        PERFORM RECORD-ERROR.

CHECK-REST-OF-TRANSACTION.
    IF KIND EQUALS "N"
        PERFORM CHECK-ACCOUNT-NAME
    ELSE IF KIND EQUALS "C" OR "D"
            PERFORM CHECK-AMOUNT.
CHECK-ACCOUNT-NAME.
    IF CLIENT-IDENTITY EQUALS SPACES
        MOVE 8 TO ERROR-INDEX
        PERFORM RECORD-ERROR.
CHECK-AMOUNT.
    INSPECT AMOUNT REPLACING LEADING SPACES BY ZEROES.
    IF AMOUNT IS NOT NUMERIC
        MOVE 7 TO ERROR-INDEX
        PERFORM RECORD-ERROR
    ELSE IF KIND EQUALS "D" AND AMOUNT > MAXIMUM-DEBIT
            MOVE 9 TO ERROR-INDEX
            PERFORM RECORD-ERROR.
READ-NEXT-TRANSACTION.
    READ TRANSACTION-FILE AT END MOVE 1 TO TRANSACTION-FILE-FLAG.

ERROR-REPORT-HEADING.
    MOVE "                        VALIDATION REPORT"
        TO OUTPUT-LINE.
    WRITE OUTPUT-LINE AFTER ADVANCING PAGE.
    MOVE SPACES TO OUTPUT-LINE.
    MOVE ALL "*" TO OUTPUT-DETAILS.
    WRITE OUTPUT-LINE AFTER ADVANCING 1 LINE.
ERROR-REPORT-FOOTING.
    MOVE ALL "*" TO OUTPUT-DETAILS.
    WRITE OUTPUT-LINE AFTER ADVANCING 3 LINES.
    MOVE SPACES TO OUTPUT-DETAILS.
    MOVE "TOTAL TRANSACTIONS EXAMINED =" TO SUMMARY-HEADER.
    MOVE TRANSACTION-COUNT TO SUMMARY-COUNT.
    WRITE OUTPUT-LINE FROM SUMMARY-LINE AFTER ADVANCING 2 LINES.
    MOVE "TOTAL TRANSACTIONS IN ERROR =" TO SUMMARY-HEADER.
    MOVE TRANSACTIONS-IN-ERROR TO SUMMARY-COUNT.
    WRITE OUTPUT-LINE FROM SUMMARY-LINE AFTER ADVANCING 1 LINE.
    MOVE "TOTAL CORRECT TRANSACTIONS =" TO SUMMARY-HEADER.
```

```
        SUBTRACT TRANSACTIONS-IN-ERROR FROM TRANSACTION-COUNT
           GIVING CORRECT-TRANSACTIONS.
        MOVE CORRECT-TRANSACTIONS TO SUMMARY-COUNT.
        WRITE OUTPUT-LINE FROM SUMMARY-LINE AFTER ADVANCING 1 LINE.
        MOVE ALL "*" TO OUTPUT-DETAILS.
        WRITE OUTPUT-LINE AFTER ADVANCING 2 LINES.
    RECORD-ERROR.
        ADD 1 TO ERROR-COUNT.
        MOVE ERROR-INDEX TO ERROR-LIST (ERROR-COUNT).
    ERROR-REPORT.
        ADD 1 TO TRANSACTIONS-IN-ERROR.
        MOVE "ERRORS FOUND IN TRANSACTION" TO SUMMARY-HEADER.
        MOVE TRANSACTION-COUNT TO SUMMARY-COUNT.
        WRITE OUTPUT-LINE FROM SUMMARY-LINE AFTER ADVANCING 2 LINES.
        WRITE OUTPUT-LINE FROM TRANSACTION AFTER ADVANCING 1 LINE.
        PERFORM OUTPUT-MESSAGE VARYING I FROM 1 BY 1
                            UNTIL I > ERROR-COUNT.
    OUTPUT-MESSAGE.
        MOVE ERROR-LIST (I) TO J.
        WRITE OUTPUT-LINE FROM ERROR-MESSAGE (J)
           AFTER ADVANCING 1 LINES.

    LIST-VALID-TRANSACTIONS.
        OPEN INPUT VALID-TRANSACTIONS-FILE, OUTPUT ERROR-REPORT-FILE.
        MOVE ZERO TO TRANSACTION-FILE-FLAG.
        MOVE "LISTING OF VALID TRANSACTIONS TAPE FILE" TO OUTPUT-LINE.
        WRITE OUTPUT-LINE AFTER ADVANCING PAGE.
        PERFORM READ-NEXT-RECORD.
        PERFORM LIST-RECORD UNTIL NO-TRANSACTIONS-REMAIN.
        MOVE "END OF FILE" TO OUTPUT-LINE.
        WRITE OUTPUT-LINE AFTER ADVANCING 1 LINE.
        CLOSE VALID-TRANSACTIONS-FILE, ERROR-REPORT-FILE.
    READ-NEXT-RECORD.
        READ VALID-TRANSACTIONS-FILE
           AT END MOVE 1 TO TRANSACTION-FILE-FLAG.
    LIST-RECORD.
        WRITE OUTPUT-LINE FROM VALID-TRANSACTION
           AFTER ADVANCING 1 LINES.
        PERFORM READ-NEXT-RECORD.
```

The transaction report produced by this version of *PRO-GRAM2* is the same as that shown in Listing 12, Chapter 6.

The transaction record description (but not the complete transaction file description) used in *PROGRAM4,* viz.,

```
01  TRANSACTION.
    02  DATE-FIELD.
        03  YEAR-FIELD      PIC 99.
            88  YEAR-OK      VALUE 81, 82.
        03  MONTH-FIELD     PIC 99.
            88  MONTH-OK     VALUE 1 THRU 12.
        03  DAY-FIELD       PIC 99.
    02  ACCOUNT-NUMBER.
        03  FIRST-7-DIGITS.
            04  DIGIT  PIC 9 OCCURS 7 TIMES.
        03  CHECK-DIGIT      PIC X.
            88  CHECK-DIGIT-OK
                   VALUES ARE "0" THRU "9", "X".
        03  VALUE-OF-CHECK-DIGIT
               REDEFINES CHECK-DIGIT PIC 9.
```

```
02  KIND                  PIC X.
    88  KIND-OK   VALUE "C", "D", "N", "X".
    88  CREDIT    VALUE "C".
    88  DEBIT     VALUE "D".
    88  ADDITION  VALUE "N".
    88  DELETION  VALUE "X".
02  AMOUNT                PIC 9(4)V99.
02  CLIENT-IDENTITY       PIC X(30).
02  FILLER                PIC X(29).
```

is now assumed to be held in the library as the text named
TRANSACTION-DESCRIPTION, and so the file description
entry in *PROGRAM2* could have taken the form

```
FD TRANSACTION-FILE LABEL RECORDS OMITTED.
   COPY TRANSACTION-DESCRIPTION.
```

This library text could have been used in the sequential file update
program of the previous chapter.

EXERCISES

1. Write a fragment of COBOL program to validate a code number composed of
   six digits in the range 0 to 6; one of the digits is a Modulus 7 check digit and the
   weights assigned to the digits are 1 to 6, starting at the left.

2. Three common types of data error are:
   (i)   mispunching of numeric data;
   (ii) loss of one or more records of a batch of data;
   (iii) use of the wrong data file.

   (a) What precautions can be taken to prevent such errors from happening?
   (b) What checks should a data validation program perform to detect such errors?
   (c) How does COBOL help the programmer perform such checks?

3. Implement the enhancements to the COBOL version of *PROGRAM2* as
   described in Exercise 6, Chapter 6.

4. Each record in a file has the following format
   character 1   : sales code (either *A*, *I*, *X*, or *D*)
   characters 3–4   : salesman number (>10 and <70)
   characters 5–14   : customer number (a Modulus 11 number)
   characters 15–21   : sales amount (in pence)
   Given a file of such records, write a COBOL data validation program that produces a listing of the records that contain invalid data. In addition to checking
   that the data satisfies the requirements described above, the program should
   check the sales amount for reasonableness — the first digit in the customer
   number indicates what amount is reasonable. If it is greater than 3 then the
   sales amount should not exceed $50 000, otherwise it should not exceed
   $10 000.

15 SORTING IN COBOL

15.1 THE SORT VERB

COBOL provides a special SORT verb which is used to sort a sequence of records which may be either obtained from a sequential file or generated by the program itself. The records to be sorted must first be transferred to a special *sort-file*, which is then sorted (by means of a SORT statement), after which the records will either be written to a sequential output file or made available to the program, in key order.

```
SORT file-name-1   ON {DESCENDING}   data-name-1
                      {ASCENDING }
                                      [, data-name-2] ...
             [ ON {DESCENDING}   data-name-3
                  {ASCENDING }
                                      [, data-name-4] ... ]
         {USING      file-name-2              }
         {INPUT PROCEDURE IS section-1}
         {GIVING     file-name-3               }
         {OUTPUT PROCEDURE IS section-2}
```

file-name-1 is known as the *sort-file* and must be described in a SELECT entry and also in a sort-file (SD) description entry in the FILE SECTION.

For example, assume that it is required to sort 60 character records whose first six characters form a numeric key field. The sort-file required might be named SORT-FILE and assigned to, say, disk drive 1 (this device assignment is usually specified by the particular COBOL implementation)

```
SELECT SORT-FILE ASSIGN TO DISK 1.
```

Sort-files must be assigned to tape or disk devices, depending upon the medium required for the auxiliary work files employed during the execution of the SORT verb. No other properties are associated with the sort-file in its SELECT clause other than its peripheral device. The SD entry might then be

```
SD SORT-FILE.
   01   SORT-RECORD.
      02   KEY-FIELD              PIC 9(6).
      02   OTHER-DATA-FIELDS      PIC X(54).
```

SORT-RECORD is referred to as the *sort-file-record*. This SD entry is similar to an FD entry and the record description must give the format of the records to be sorted. In particular the key field(s) must be given names, which are then cited in the ASCENDING/ DESCENDING clause(s) of the SORT statement, in order of decreasing significance.

The source of the records to be sorted must be identified in the SORT statement by the use of either the USING clause or the INPUT PROCEDURE clause. The USING clause specifies the name of a sequential organization file (*file-name-2*) containing the records to be sorted — in which case the file contents are automatically transferred to the sort-file by the SORT statement before the actual sorting takes place. *file-name-2* must denote a file which uses the same storage medium as the sort-file.

The destination of the sorted records after the sorting of the sort-file has been completed must be specified either by a GIVING clause or an OUTPUT PROCEDURE clause. If the GIVING clause is used, then the (sorted) contents of the sort-file are written to the sequential file *file-name-3*, which must again reside on the same medium as the sort-file.

Hence, if a disk file of records FILE-1 with the same format as given earlier in the declaration of SORT-FILE is to be sorted into ascending order of the field KEY-FIELD, the SORT statement required to produce a sorted file on another disk file FILE-2 would be

```
SORT SORT-FILE ON ASCENDING KEY-FIELD
     USING FILE-1 GIVING FILE-2.
```

FILE-1 and FILE-2 must be given suitable FD entries (in particular the record sizes for FILE-1, FILE-2, and SORT-FILE must be identical) — however, the opening and closing of these files is carried out automatically by the SORT statement. In the above example FILE-1 is first opened, then its contents are transferred to SORT-FILE, and finally it is closed. SORT-FILE is then sorted, FILE-2 opened and the sorted records written to it, after which it is closed.

However, it may be necessary for the program to generate the records itself, in which case the INPUT PROCEDURE clause specifies the name of a section which is to be executed by the SORT statement to produce the records to be sorted and to write them to the sort-file. This section will be in the form of a loop which generates the records one-by-one; as each record is generated it is transferred to the sort-file by assigning its value to the sort-file-record and executing a RELEASE statement (analogous to a WRITE statement).

RELEASE *sort-file-record-name* [FROM *identifier*]

Once the records have all been transferred to the sort-file, i.e., execution of the input procedure has been completed, it is then sorted.

If it is intended that the progam should process the sorted records in order, then the OUTPUT PROCEDURE clause names a section which will be executed, after the sorting has been completed, to perform the required processing. *section-2* is again in the form of a loop which obtains the records in sorted sequence from the sort-file by means of a RETURN statement.

RETURN *sort-file-name* [INTO *identifier*]
   AT END *imperative-statement*

This is similar to a READ statement and places the value of the next record of the sort-file in the sort-file-record item, or some other data item identified by an INTO phrase. The AT END clause enables *section-2* to determine when the end of the sorted record sequence has been reached. Note the similarities in both format and effect between the RETURN and RELEASE verbs and the READ and WRITE verbs, respectively.

If input or output procedures are used, then these must be self-contained, i.e., control must transfer into or out of them by means of the SORT verb only and they must not attempt to pass control to other sections. If it is desired to generate records of the above format within a program (possibly by reading them from a file and pre-processing them in some way), sort them, and then to process the sorted records in key order (possibly then writing them to some file), sections named GENERATE-RECORDS and PROCESS-RECORDS, say, could be written and the SORT verb used in the form

```
SORT SORT-FILE ON ASCENDING KEY-FIELD
    INPUT PROCEDURE IS GENERATE-RECORDS
    OUTPUT PROCEDURE IS PROCESS-RECORDS.
```

The input procedure GENERATE-RECORDS will contain a loop which produces one record per iteration, assigns its value to SORT-RECORD, and then transfers it to SORT-FILE using a RELEASE statement:

```
RELEASE SORT-RECORD
```

The output procedure PROCESS-RECORDS will also contain a loop which obtains records, one per iteration, from SORT-FILE by means of a RETURN statement, e.g.,

```
RETURN SORT-FILE AT END PERFORM EXIT-FROM-LOOP
```

which will leave the next record value in SORT-RECORD. The AT END clause enables the loop to be terminated when all the sorted records have been processed.

The use of these COBOL sorting features is illustrated by the implementation of the Model Savings Bank transaction sorting program *PROGRAM3* in the next section.

15.2   CASE STUDY: SORTING THE VALID TRANSACTIONS FILE

The validated transactions stored on the magnetic tape file TRANS-ACTIONS by the validation program *PROGRAM2* have to be sorted into date within account number order in preparation for their input to the sequential master file update program *PROGRAM4* of Chapter 13 (Figure 15.1).

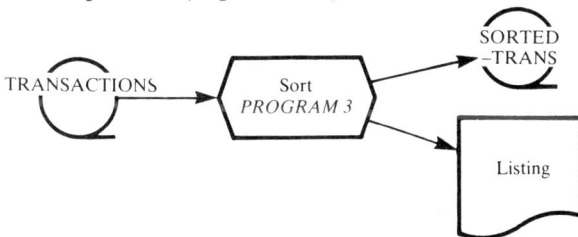

Figure 15.1   Sort program

The sorted records are to be written to a tape file labelled
SORTED-TRANS and a listing of the sorted records is to be produced on line printer unit 1 for verification purposes. The input file
is held on magnetic tape unit 1, the sorted file on magnetic tape unit
2.

In the COBOL program the physical file TRANSACTIONS is
given the file identifier VALID-TRANSACTIONS-FILE and the
physical file SORTED-TRANS is identified as SORTED-
TRANSACTIONS-FILE.

The sort-file is assigned to tape drive 99 — this device assignment is assumed to be required by the utility program used by our
COBOL implementation to perform the actual sorting (control is
transferred automatically to this program by the SORT verb). Its
SD entry identifies the fields upon which the sort is based, and the
remaining fields are just described as a single FILLER.

```
SD   SORT-FILE.
   01   SORT-RECORD.
      02   DATE-FIELD        PIC 9(6).
      02   ACCOUNT-NUMBER    PIC X(8).
      02   FILLER            PIC X(66).
```

We have chosen to call the sort-file SORT-FILE and its record size
(80 characters) is equal to that of the two tape files. The records to
be sorted will be generated by a section GET-TRANSACTIONS,
and processing of the records will be performed by an output procedure PRINT-AND-WRITE-TO-TAPE. The introduction of
input or output procedures means that the PROCEDURE
DIVISION must be written in sections. Hence the main program
section (MAIN-PROGRAM) contains a sort statement

```
SORT SORT-FILE
   ON ASCENDING ACCOUNT-NUMBER,
              DATE-FIELD
   INPUT PROCEDURE IS
      GET-TRANSACTIONS
   OUTPUT PROCEDURE IS
      PRINT-AND-WRITE-TO-TAPE.
```

ACCOUNT-NUMBER is the major file sorting key and is thus
specified before the minor sorting key DATE-FIELD.

GET-TRANSACTIONS reads records one at a time from the
input file VALID-TRANSACTIONS-FILE and transfers them to
SORT-FILE by means of a RELEASE statement

```
RELEASE SORT-RECORD FROM TRANSACTION
```

and PRINT-AND-WRITE-TO-TAPE obtains the next record in

sorted order from SORT-FILE by means of the RETURN statement

```
RETURN SORT-FILE INTO SORTED-TRANSACTION
AT END MOVE 1 TO FILE-FLAG
```

after which it lists the record on the line printer file and also transfers it to the tape file SORTED-TRANSACTIONS-FILE.

The full text of the COBOL program *PROGRAM3* is presented in Listing 31.

LISTING 31 PROGRAM3

```
IDENTIFICATION  DIVISION.
PROGRAM-ID.        PROGRAM3.
INSTALLATION.      QUB.
AUTHOR.            JOHN ELDER.
*                  USE OF COBOL SORT VERB.
DATE-WRITTEN.      JANUARY 1983.
DATE-COMPILED.     01/17/83.

ENVIRONMENT DIVISION.
CONFIGURATION SECTION.
SOURCE-COMPUTER.  SUPER-2000.
OBJECT-COMPUTER.  SUPER-2000.
INPUT-OUTPUT  SECTION.
FILE-CONTROL.
    SELECT VALID-TRANSACTIONS-FILE ASSIGN TO TAPE 1 RESERVE 2 AREAS.
    SELECT SORTED-TRANSACTIONS-FILE ASSIGN TO TAPE 2 RESERVE 2 AREAS.
    SELECT PRINT-FILE ASSIGN TO PRINTER 1 RESERVE 2 AREAS.
    SELECT SORT-FILE ASSIGN TO TAPE 99.

DATA DIVISION.

FILE SECTION.
FD  VALID-TRANSACTIONS-FILE BLOCK CONTAINS 512 CHARACTERS
                            LABEL RECORDS STANDARD
                                 VALUE OF ID "TRANSACTIONS".
    01  TRANSACTION PIC X(80).
FD  SORTED-TRANSACTIONS-FILE BLOCK CONTAINS 512 CHARACTERS
                            LABEL RECORDS STANDARD
                                 VALUE OF ID "SORTED-TRANS".
    01  SORTED-TRANSACTION PIC X(80).

FD  PRINT-FILE LABEL RECORDS OMITTED.
    01  PRINT-LINE PIC X(120).

SD  SORT-FILE.
    01  SORT-RECORD.
        02  DATE-FIELD       PIC 9(6).
        02  ACCOUNT-NUMBER    PIC X(8).
        02  FILLER            PIC X(66).

WORKING-STORAGE SECTION.
77  FILE-FLAG PIC 9 COMP SYNC RIGHT.
    88  NO-RECORDS-REMAIN VALUE 1.

PROCEDURE DIVISION.

MAIN-PROGRAM SECTION.
MAIN-PARAGRAPH.
    SORT SORT-FILE ON ASCENDING ACCOUNT-NUMBER, DATE-FIELD
        INPUT PROCEDURE IS GET-TRANSACTIONS
```

```
            OUTPUT PROCEDURE IS PRINT-AND-WRITE-TO-TAPE.
        STOP "SORT COMPLETED".

GET-TRANSACTIONS SECTION.
MAIN-INPUT-PARAGRAPH.
    OPEN INPUT VALID-TRANSACTIONS-FILE.
    MOVE ZERO TO FILE-FLAG.
    PERFORM READ-NEXT-TRANSACTION.
    PERFORM TRANSFER-TRANSACTION UNTIL NO-RECORDS-REMAIN.
    CLOSE VALID-TRANSACTIONS-FILE.
    GO TO EXIT-1.
TRANSFER-TRANSACTION.
    RELEASE SORT-RECORD FROM TRANSACTION.
    PERFORM READ-NEXT-TRANSACTION.
READ-NEXT-TRANSACTION.
    READ VALID-TRANSACTIONS-FILE AT END MOVE 1 TO FILE-FLAG.
EXIT-1.
    EXIT.

PRINT-AND-WRITE-TO-TAPE SECTION.
MAIN-OUTPUT-PARAGRAPH.
    OPEN OUTPUT SORTED-TRANSACTIONS-FILE, PRINT-FILE.
    PERFORM PRINT-HEADING.
    MOVE ZERO TO FILE-FLAG.
    PERFORM RETURN-A-RECORD.
    PERFORM TRANSFER-AND-LIST-A-RECORD UNTIL NO-RECORDS-REMAIN.
    PERFORM PRINT-FOOTING.
    CLOSE SORTED-TRANSACTIONS-FILE, PRINT-FILE.
    GO TO EXIT-2.
PRINT-HEADING.
    MOVE "LISTING OF SORTED TRANSACTIONS FILE" TO PRINT-LINE.
    WRITE PRINT-LINE AFTER ADVANCING PAGE.
TRANSFER-AND-LIST-A-RECORD.
    WRITE PRINT-LINE FROM SORTED-TRANSACTION
        AFTER ADVANCING 1 LINE.
    WRITE SORTED-TRANSACTION.
    PERFORM RETURN-A-RECORD.
PRINT-FOOTING.
    MOVE "END OF FILE" TO PRINT-LINE.
    WRITE PRINT-LINE AFTER ADVANCING 1 LINE.
RETURN-A-RECORD.
    RETURN SORT-FILE INTO SORTED-TRANSACTION
        AT END MOVE 1 TO FILE-FLAG.
EXIT-2.
    EXIT.
```

Although the program uses an input procedure (the section GET-TRANSACTIONS), this has been introduced merely to illustrate the use of the RELEASE verb and is not really necessary. Instead this section might be omitted altogether and the SORT statement changed to

```
SORT SORT-FILE
    ON ASCENDING ACCOUNT-NUMBER,
                 DATE-FIELD
    USING
        VALID-TRANSACTIONS-FILE
    OUTPUT PROCEDURE IS
        PRINT-AND-WRITE-TO-TAPE.
```

EXERCISE

1. Write a COBOL program which generates 30 pseudo-random numbers, sorts them into ascending sequence, and displays the sorted numbers upon the operator console. Use a simple technique for the generation of the pseudo-random numbers.

16 INDEXED SEQUENTIAL FILES

16.1 INDEXED SEQUENTIAL FILE PROCESSING IN COBOL

16.1.1 File Descriptions

In its SELECT entry the organization for an indexed sequential file is given as

```
ORGANIZATION INDEXED
```

and the ACCESS clause specifies which of the three access methods is to be used

$$\text{ACCESS} \begin{Bmatrix} \text{SEQUENTIAL} \\ \text{RANDOM} \\ \text{DYNAMIC} \end{Bmatrix}$$

where RANDOM access is equivalent to what we have described in Chapter 8 as indexed access.

The file must have a RECORD KEY data item associated with it in its SELECT entry — this data item must be a field of a record associated with the file in its FD description and its value is always used as the key value by any access operation which attempts to locate (via the index tables) the record thus specified. For example, an indexed sequential file might be declared with the following SELECT entry

```
SELECT AN-INDEXED-FILE
    ASSIGN TO DISK 1
    ORGANIZATION INDEXED
    ACCESS RANDOM
    RECORD KEY IS CODE-NUMBER.
```

This indicates that random access is to be employed for this file and that the key of any record to be accessed will be given by the value of the field CODE-NUMBER in the file records. The file description entry for this file might then be

```
FD   AN-INDEXED-FILE
     BLOCK CONTAINS 512 CHARACTERS
     LABEL RECORDS STANDARD
         VALUE OF ID "EXAMPLE-FILE".
01   RECORD-FIELD.
   02    CODE-NUMBER    PIC 999.
   02    DATA-FIELDS    PIC X(17).
```

The OPEN verb takes the same form for indexed sequential files as for sequential files and its effect is the same. The CLOSE verb permits only simple or locked closure of a file.

> CLOSE *file-name-1* [WITH LOCK]
>
>   [, *file-name-2* [WITH LOCK]] ...

16.1.2 Sequential Access

The four sequential access verbs take the forms:

> READ *file-name* [INTO *identifier*]
>   AT END *imperative-statement*
>
> DELETE *record-name*
>
> WRITE *record-name* [FROM *identifier*]
>   INVALID KEY *imperative-statement*
>
> REWRITE *record-name* [FROM *identifier*]
>   INVALID KEY *imperative-statement*

The verbs which may be used in each of the processing modes defined by an OPEN statement for a sequential access file are indicated in Figure 16.1.

	Processing modes		
	INPUT	OUTPUT	I-O
READ	x		x
DELETE			x
WRITE		x	
REWRITE			x

Figure 16.1   Verbs permitted for sequential access

The operation of the READ, WRITE, and REWRITE verbs is as for sequential organization file processing, with two exceptions. In the case of a file opened for OUTPUT processing a new record value written to a file by a WRITE statement must maintain the key ordering of the records in the file and always becomes the last record on the file — since this addition must maintain the key ordering of the file records its value must therefore be such that its key value is the greatest in the file. If this is not the case, then an INVALID KEY condition exists, the WRITE statement is unsuccessful, and control passes to the *imperative-statement* of the INVALID KEY clause in the WRITE statement. This means that records must be written in ascending key order to any indexed sequential file which is accessed sequentially. Similarly, a REWRITE statement should not attempt to change the key of the record being replaced, otherwise an INVALID KEY condition exists, and control again passes to the *imperative-statement* of the INVALID KEY clause.

The DELETE verb is provided for the removal of records from a sequentially accessed file processed as an input–output file.

16.1.3   Random Access

The random access verbs are

```
READ file-name [ INTO identifier ]
     INVALID KEY imperative-statement

DELETE record-name INVALID KEY imperative-statement

WRITE record-name [ FROM identifier ]
      INVALID KEY imperative-statement

REWRITE record-name [ FROM identifier ]
        INVALID KEY imperative-statement
```

Figure 16.2 shows the verbs which may be used in each of the three processing modes.

	Processing modes		
	INPUT	OUTPUT	I-O
READ	x		x
DELETE			x
WRITE		x	x
REWRITE			x

Figure 16.2   Verbs permitted for random access

Any random access operation first involves moving the key of the record concerned to the RECORD KEY field in the file's record data item, e.g.,

```
MOVE 123 TO CODE-NUMBER
```

If the record with this key value is to be read from the file, a READ statement, e.g.,

```
READ AN-INDEXED-FILE
    INVALID KEY PERFORM NO-RECORD-IN-FILE
```

is then executed, with the INVALID KEY clause specifying the alternative action to be taken in the event of there not being any record in the file with the required key value.

For a record deletion, e.g.,

```
DELETE RECORD-FIELD
    INVALID KEY PERFORM NO-RECORD-IN-FILE
```

the record whose key value is equal to the value of the RECORD KEY field is removed from the file. However, if no such record exists in the file an INVALID KEY condition exists and the alternative action specified in the INVALID KEY clause is executed instead.

Records may be replaced by a REWRITE statement, e.g.,

```
REWRITE RECORD-FIELD
    INVALID KEY PERFORM NO-RECORD-IN-FILE
```

The REWRITE may be unsuccessful due to the specified record key being absent from the file, in which case the INVALID KEY condition again exists.

For insertion of new record values the WRITE verb is used, e.g.,

```
WRITE RECORD-FIELD
    INVALID KEY PERFORM DUPLICATE-RECORD
```

inserts the record whose value is in RECORD-FIELD at its correct (key-ordered) position in the file as defined by the RECORD KEY value — this insertion may fail if the specified key is already in the file and the INVALID KEY clause specifies the alternative action to be taken in that case.

16.1.4 Dynamic Access

For dynamic access the permitted verbs in each processing mode are the same as for random (indexed) access; see Figure 16.2. Any sequential access or random access verb may be executed except that, for dynamic access, the sequential READ verb takes the form

> READ *file-name* NEXT [INTO *identifier*]
>   AT END *imperative-statement*

Note also that the WRITE and REWRITE verbs for sequential and random access are such that they are equivalent both in form and effect. A switch from random access to sequential access is achieved by execution of a sequential

```
READ ... NEXT AT END ...
```

statement. Hence a group of successive records may be accessed by using a random access

```
READ ... INVALID KEY ...
```

statement to access the first record, and a sequence of sequential access

```
READ ... NEXT AT END ...
```

statements to access the subsequent records. Records in this sequence may be replaced using REWRITE, deleted by DELETE, or new records inserted into the sequence by WRITE. To switch to random access again a

```
READ ... INVALID KEY ...
```

statement is executed.

16.2 CASE STUDY: INDEXED SEQUENTIAL MASTER FILE INITIALIZATION

We now consider the implementation in COBOL of the indexed sequential master file, previously constructed as *PROGRAM6* in Chapter 8. The indexed sequential master file to be used in the Model Savings Bank system was created by copying the records of the sequential master file held on magnetic tape to the disk file, as shown in Figure 16.3.

In the COBOL file initialization program *PROGRAM6*, given as Listing 32, the master disk file (on disk drive 1) is named MASTER-IS-FILE and defined to be an indexed sequential organization file. Since its records will be accessed purely in key sequence order, its access mode is declared to be SEQUENTIAL. The primary record

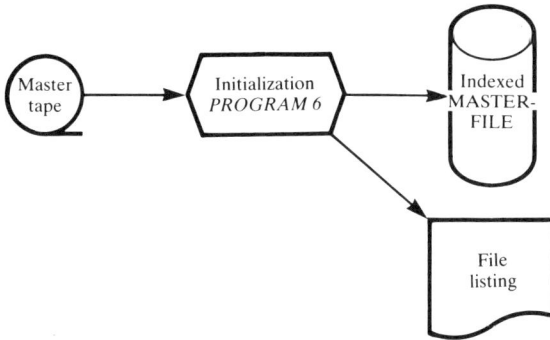

Figure 16.3   Initialization of indexed sequential master file

key is declared to be the field ACCOUNT-NUMBER of NEW-MASTER-RECORD (the record item associated with MASTER-IS-FILE). The FD entries for the master tape and disk files are obtained from the library by suitable COPY statements which retrieve the library text MASTER-FD and specify appropriate name replacements.

The sequential access READ and WRITE verbs are used for the indexed sequential file (see the paragraphs TRANSFER-RECORD and READ-NEXT-DISK-RECORD) with the WRITE statement's INVALID KEY clause reporting any key sequence errors (which, of course, there should not be in this program, since the tape file records are known to be in ascending account number order).

```
                         LISTING  32  PROGRAM6
IDENTIFICATION DIVISION.
PROGRAM-ID.        PROGRAM6.
INSTALLATION.      QUB.
AUTHOR.            JOHN ELDER.
*                  INITIALIZATION OF INDEXED SEQUENTIAL MASTER FILE.
DATE-WRITTEN.      FEBRUARY 1983.
DATE-COMPILED.

ENVIRONMENT DIVISION.
CONFIGURATION SECTION.
SOURCE-COMPUTER.   SUPER-2000.
OBJECT-COMPUTER.   SUPER-2000.
INPUT-OUTPUT SECTION.
FILE-CONTROL.
    SELECT MASTER-TAPE-FILE ASSIGN TO TAPE 1 RESERVE 2 AREAS.
    SELECT MASTER-IS-FILE ASSIGN TO DISK 1 RESERVE 2 AREAS
        ORGANIZATION INDEXED
        ACCESS SEQUENTIAL
        RECORD KEY IS ACCOUNT-NUMBER OF NEW-MASTER-RECORD.
    SELECT PRINT-FILE ASSIGN TO PRINTER 1 RESERVE 2 AREAS.

DATA DIVISION.
FILE SECTION.
COPY MASTER-FD REPLACING MASTER-FILE BY MASTER-TAPE-FILE
                         MASTER-RECORD BY OLD-MASTER-RECORD.
```

```
COPY MASTER-FD REPLACING MASTER-FILE BY MASTER-IS-FILE
                        MASTER-RECORD BY NEW-MASTER-RECORD.
FD  PRINT-FILE LABEL RECORDS OMITTED.
    01  PRINT-LINE              PIC X(120).
WORKING-STORAGE SECTION.
77  FILE-FLAG                   PIC 9 COMP SYNC RIGHT.
    88  NO-RECORDS-REMAIN       VALUE 1.
01  ACCOUNT-DETAIL-LINE.
    02  FILLER                  PIC X(5) VALUE SPACES.
    02  ACCOUNT-NUMBER          PIC X(8).
    02  FILLER                  PIC X(5) VALUE SPACES.
    02  CLIENT-IDENTITY         PIC X(30).
    02  FILLER                  PIC X(5) VALUE SPACES.
    02  CURRENT-BALANCE         PIC ZZZZ9.99.
    02  FILLER                  PIC X(5) VALUE SPACES.
    02  MINIMUM-BALANCE         PIC ZZZZ9.99.
PROCEDURE DIVISION.
MAIN-PARAGRAPH.
    PERFORM CREATE-IS-FILE.
    PERFORM LIST-IS-FILE.
    STOP RUN.
CREATE-IS-FILE.
    OPEN INPUT MASTER-TAPE-FILE, OUTPUT MASTER-IS-FILE.
    MOVE ZERO TO FILE-FLAG.
    PERFORM READ-NEXT-TAPE-RECORD.
    PERFORM TRANSFER-RECORD UNTIL NO-RECORDS-REMAIN.
    CLOSE MASTER-TAPE-FILE, MASTER-IS-FILE.
READ-NEXT-TAPE-RECORD.
    READ MASTER-TAPE-FILE AT END MOVE 1 TO FILE-FLAG.
TRANSFER-RECORD.
    WRITE NEW-MASTER-RECORD FROM OLD-MASTER-RECORD
        INVALID KEY PERFORM REPORT-ERROR.
    PERFORM READ-NEXT-TAPE-RECORD.
REPORT-ERROR.
    DISPLAY ACCOUNT-NUMBER OF OLD-MASTER-RECORD, " SEQUENCE ERROR".
LIST-IS-FILE.
    OPEN INPUT MASTER-IS-FILE, OUTPUT PRINT-FILE.
    MOVE ZERO TO FILE-FLAG.
    PERFORM PRINT-HEADING.
    PERFORM READ-NEXT-DISK-RECORD.
    PERFORM LIST-RECORD UNTIL NO-RECORDS-REMAIN.
    CLOSE MASTER-IS-FILE, PRINT-FILE.
PRINT-HEADING.
    MOVE SPACES TO PRINT-LINE.
    WRITE PRINT-LINE AFTER ADVANCING PAGE.
LIST-RECORD.
    MOVE CORRESPONDING NEW-MASTER-RECORD TO ACCOUNT-DETAIL-LINE.
    WRITE PRINT-LINE FROM ACCOUNT-DETAIL-LINE
        AFTER ADVANCING 1 LINES.
    PERFORM READ-NEXT-DISK-RECORD.
READ-NEXT-DISK RECORD.
    READ MASTER-IS-FILE AT END MOVE 1 TO FILE-FLAG.
```

16.3 CASE STUDY: INDEXED SEQUENTIAL MASTER FILE UPDATE

The indexed sequential master file update program *PROGRAM7* of Chapter 8 used the file TRANSACTIONS of validated but unsorted transactions to update the file MASTER-FILE initialized by the previous case study program (Figure 16.4). We shall now construct that program using COBOL as the implementation language.

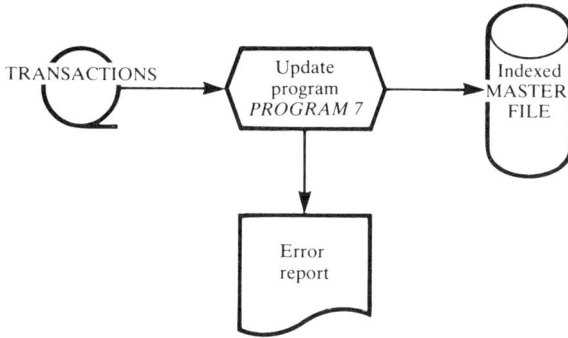

Figure 16.4   Indexed sequential master file update

The updating of the indexed sequential master file using the sorted transactions file produced by the validation program *PROGRAM2* is performed by the program *PROGRAM7* whose text as presented to the compiler is given in Listing 33.

The SELECT clause for the file MASTER-FILE identifies it as an indexed sequential file which is to be accessed randomly and its RECORD KEY item is identified as the field ACCOUNT-NUMBER of its file record data item MASTER. The FD entry for MASTER-FILE is copied from the library text MASTER-FD with the record name specified as MASTER (the file-name is not specified since it is also MASTER-FILE in the library text).

The paragraph INITIAL-STATUS attempts to determine whether there is an account record or not for a given account number (the current-value of CURRENT-KEY) by assigning this value to ACCOUNT-NUMBER OF MASTER, and then performing a READ. The INVALID KEY clause of the READ statement specifies that FALSE is to be assigned to ORIGINALLYINFILE should the READ statement be unable to locate a record with the specified key. The transaction processing routine is the same as for the sequential file update and is copied from the library text TRANSACTION-PROCESSING with the master file record name again specified as MASTER.

The FINAL-STATUS paragraph determines what information is to be written back to the file. If an account record is to be replaced (i.e., account number currently and initially allocated) a REWRITE is required to replace the record previously READ. If a new account record is to be written (i.e., the account number is now allocated, but initially was not) then a random access WRITE operation is required. If the account number was initially allocated but is no longer in use, the account record previously READ must be deleted. These statements allow for possible INVALID KEY conditions and take appropriate reporting actions. The logic of this program, however, is such that INVALID KEY conditions should never occur.

LISTING 33 *PROGRAM7*

```
IDENTIFICATION DIVISION.
PROGRAM-ID.     PROGRAM7.
INSTALLATION.   QUB.
AUTHOR.         JOHN ELDER.
*               INDEXED-SEQUENTIAL MASTER FILE UPDATE.
DATE-WRITTEN.   JANUARY 1983.
DATE-COMPILED.

ENVIRONMENT DIVISION.
CONFIGURATION SECTION.
SOURCE-COMPUTER.   SUPER-2000.
OBJECT-COMPUTER.   SUPER-2000.
SPECIAL-NAMES.     PRINTER 1 IS REPORT-DEVICE.
INPUT-OUTPUT SECTION.
FILE-CONTROL.
    SELECT TRANSACTION-FILE ASSIGN TO TAPE 1 RESERVE 2 AREAS.
    SELECT MASTER-FILE ASSIGN TO DISK 1
        ORGANIZATION INDEXED
        ACCESS RANDOM
        RECORD KEY IS ACCOUNT-NUMBER IN MASTER.

DATA DIVISION.
FILE SECTION.
FD TRANSACTION-FILE BLOCK CONTAINS 512 CHARACTERS
                    LABEL RECORDS STANDARD
                        VALUE OF ID "TRANSACTIONS".
   COPY TRANSACTION-DESCRIPTION.

COPY MASTER-FD REPLACING MASTER-RECORD BY MASTER.

WORKING-STORAGE SECTION.
77 SENTINEL         PIC X(8) VALUE HIGH-VALUES.
77 CURRENT-KEY      PIC X(8).
77 TRANSACTION-KEY  PIC X(8) VALUE LOW-VALUES.
77 TRUE             PIC 9 COMP SYNC RIGHT VALUE 1.
77 FALSE            PIC 9 COMP SYNC RIGHT VALUE 0.
77 INFILE           PIC 9 COMP SYNC RIGHT.
77 ORIGINALLYINFILE PIC 9 COMP SYNC RIGHT.
77 SAVINGS-LIMIT    PIC 9(5) COMP SYNC RIGHT VALUE 20000.
77 NEW-BALANCE      PIC S9(5)V99 COMP SYNC RIGHT.

PROCEDURE DIVISION.
UPDATE-INDEXED-FILE.
    OPEN INPUT TRANSACTION-FILE , I-O MASTER-FILE.
    PERFORM READ-NEXT-TRANSACTION.
    PERFORM CHOOSE-NEXT-KEY.
    PERFORM PROCESS-ONE-KEY UNTIL CURRENT-KEY = SENTINEL.
    CLOSE TRANSACTION-FILE , MASTER-FILE.
    STOP RUN.
PROCESS-ONE-KEY.
    PERFORM INITIAL-STATUS.
    PERFORM PROCESS-ONE-TRANSACTION
       UNTIL TRANSACTION-KEY NOT = CURRENT-KEY.
    PERFORM FINAL-STATUS.
    PERFORM CHOOSE-NEXT-KEY.
PROCESS-ONE-TRANSACTION.
    PERFORM APPLY-TRANSACTION-TO-MASTER.
    PERFORM READ-NEXT-TRANSACTION.
```

```
CHOOSE-NEXT-KEY.
    MOVE TRANSACTION-KEY TO CURRENT-KEY.
READ-NEXT-TRANSACTION.
    READ TRANSACTION-FILE
        AT END MOVE SENTINEL TO TRANSACTION-KEY.
    IF TRANSACTION-KEY NOT = SENTINEL
        MOVE ACCOUNT-NUMBER IN TRANSACTION TO TRANSACTION-KEY.
INITIAL-STATUS.
    MOVE CURRENT-KEY TO ACCOUNT-NUMBER IN MASTER.
    MOVE TRUE TO ORIGINALLYINFILE.
    READ MASTER-FILE
        INVALID KEY MOVE FALSE TO ORIGINALLYINFILE.
    MOVE ORIGINALLYINFILE TO INFILE.
FINAL-STATUS.
    IF INFILE = TRUE
        IF ORIGINALLYINFILE = TRUE
            REWRITE MASTER
                INVALID KEY DISPLAY "KEY CHANGED  ", TRANSACTION
                            UPON REPORT-DEVICE
        ELSE WRITE MASTER
                INVALID KEY DISPLAY "DUPLICATE KEY", TRANSACTION
                            UPON REPORT-DEVICE
    ELSE IF ORIGINALLYINFILE = TRUE
            DELETE MASTER
                INVALID KEY DISPLAY "MISSING KEY  ", TRANSACTION
                            UPON REPORT-DEVICE.
APPLY-TRANSACTION-TO-MASTER.
    COPY TRANSACTION-PROCESSING REPLACING MASTER-RECORD BY MASTER.
```

EXERCISES

1. Outline the sequence of actions to be performed in a standard COBOL pro-
    gram which accesses a record of an indexed sequential file with a certain key
    value, updates it, and returns it to the file in its original position. How would
    your program check that any records it attempts to read are actually in the file?

2. Implement Exercise 2, Chapter 8, using COBOL.

3. An indexed sequential master file is to be updated from amendments in a text
    file. There is at most one amendment per master file record and the hit ratio is
    very low. The identification contained in the master file's label is *ISMASTER-
    FILE*, its bucket size is two sectors and its record format is
    characters 1–4   : key field
    characters 5–8   : four digit numeric quantity
    characters 9–36 : other details
    The amendment file contains one amendment per line, each with the following
    format:
    characters 1–4   : key value
    characters 5–8   : quantity
    character 9   : amendment type
    characters 10–37 : other details
    Write the FILE-CONTROL and FD entries for these two files, for use in a
    COBOL program which performs the master file update. Assume a sector is
    512 characters long.

17 RELATIVE FILES

17.1 RANDOM FILES IN COBOL

In COBOL random files are provided as *relative* files. A relative file consists of an ordered sequence of N records, each of which is uniquely identified by an integer value in the range $1..N$. Records are stored and retrieved by specifying their ordinal position, or *relative record number*, within the sequence.

17.1.1 Relative File Descriptions

In its SELECT entry the organization for a relative file is given as

```
ORGANIZATION RELATIVE
```

and the ACCESS clause specifies which of the three access methods is to be used

```
         (SEQUENTIAL)
ACCESS  {  RANDOM    }
         ( DYNAMIC   )
```

where RANDOM access is equivalent to what we have described in Chapter 9 as direct access.

For sequential access the records are read in ascending order of the relative record numbers of all records currently in the file (i.e., unoccupied record areas are ignored) and written to each record position in turn, starting with the first. For direct (RANDOM) access the order of access is determined by the programmer — to access a record its relative record number must first be determined (using the addressing function appropriate to the file) and assigned to a data item known as the RELATIVE KEY data item for the file, before the required input or output operation is performed.

A file's RELATIVE KEY data item is associated with its SELECT entry — this data item must be declared in the WORKING-STORAGE SECTION or be a field of some other file's records, and its current value is always used as the relative record number by any access operation which attempts to locate a particular record. For example, a relative organization file might be declared with the following SELECT entry

```
SELECT A-RELATIVE-FILE
    ASSIGN TO DISK 1
    ORGANIZATION RELATIVE
    ACCESS RANDOM
    RELATIVE KEY IS RECORD-NUMBER.
```

This indicates that random (direct) access is to be employed for this file and that the relative record number of any record to be accessed will be given by the value of the data item RECORD-NUMBER. If the file is to contain, say, 47 record areas, then this item might be declared in the WORKING-STORAGE SECTION as

```
77 RECORD-NUMBER PIC 99 COMP SYNC RIGHT.
```

The file description entry for the file might then be

```
FD A-RELATIVE-FILE
    BLOCK CONTAINS 512 CHARACTERS
    LABEL RECORDS STANDARD
        VALUE OF ID "EXAMPLE-FILE".
01  RECORD-FIELD.
  02   CODE-NUMBER     PIC 999.
  02   DATA-FIELDS     PIC X(17).
```

The OPEN and CLOSE verbs have the same form and effect for relative organization files as for indexed sequential files.

17.1.2 Sequential Access

The four sequential access verbs take the forms:

> READ *file-name* [INTO *identifier*]
>   AT END *imperative-statement*
>
> DELETE *record-name*
>
> WRITE *record-name* [FROM *identifier*]
>   INVALID KEY *imperative-statement*
>
> REWRITE *record-name* [FROM *identifier*]

The verbs which may be used in each of the processing modes defined by an OPEN statement for a sequentially accessed file are as indicated in Figure 16.1 for indexed sequential files.

The READ verb accesses the record stored in the next occupied record area of the file following the previous record read, and assigns its relative record number to the file's RELATIVE KEY data item. The first READ statement executed for a relative file obtains the record in the first occupied record area and the AT END condition arises when a READ statement is unable to find any occupied record area. The WRITE verb causes records to be written to the file so that the first record written will have a relative record number of 1 and subsequent records written will have relative record numbers of 2,3,4,... Following upon execution of either of these verbs the RELATIVE KEY item for the file concerned will contain the relative record number of the last record read or written. The INVALID KEY condition exists for a WRITE statement when an attempt is made to write to a record area outside the range of relative record numbers defined for the file (this range is established when the physical file is first created).

The DELETE and REWRITE statements operate on the record accessed by the previous READ statement, which must have been the last input or output statement executed for the file.

17.1.3   Random Access

The random access verbs are the same as for indexed sequential files accessed randomly

```
READ file-name [ INTO identifier ]
    INVALID KEY imperative-statement

DELETE record-name INVALID KEY imperative-statement

WRITE record-name [ FROM identifier ]
    INVALID KEY imperative-statement

REWRITE record-name [ FROM identifier ]
    INVALID KEY imperative-statement
```

Figure 16.2 shows the verbs which may be used in each of the three processing modes.

Any random access operation first involves determining the relative record number of the record concerned and assigning it to the file's RELATIVE KEY item, e.g., for our file A-RELATIVE-

FILE, assuming it to contain 47 record areas, we might locate the records using prime division by 47. If the key of a required record is given by the value of a data item CODE-REQUIRED then

```
DIVIDE CODE-REQUIRED BY 47
   GIVING I REMAINDER RECORD-NUMBER.
ADD 1 TO RECORD-NUMBER.
```

The appropriate input–output verb is then executed and will use the value of the RELATIVE KEY item as the relative record number of the record area to be accessed. For a random access READ, DELETE, or REWRITE statement the INVALID KEY condition will exist if the specified record area is unoccupied. In the case of a WRITE statement the INVALID KEY condition exists if the record area specified is already occupied. For any of the verbs an INVALID KEY condition will also arise whenever the value of the RELATIVE KEY item lies outside the defined range of record numbers for the file.

   Synonyms, i.e., record keys mapping onto the same relative record number, will cause problems when inserting new records and subsequently retrieving them. Thus an attempt to write a record to a file may result in the preferred record area being found to be already occupied, and hence a rehashing strategy will have to be employed to determine the alternative position to be used.

17.1.4   Dynamic Access

For dynamic access the permitted verbs in each processing mode are the same as for random access; see Figure 16.2. Any sequential access or random access verb may be executed except that, for dynamic access, the sequential READ verb again takes the form

> READ *file-name* NEXT [INTO *identifier*]
>   AT END *imperative-statement*

   The use of the dynamic access verbs is the same for relative files as for indexed sequential files.

17.2   CASE STUDY: RELATIVE MASTER FILE INITIALIZATION

   We now consider the initialization of a relative organization master file (Figure 17.1) for our Model Savings Bank system — the

Figure 17.1   Initialization of random organization master file

initialization of a random file was described in Chapter 9. This process will involve copying the records of the sequential master file to appropriate record locations of a relative file.

Before executing a COBOL program to initialize the relative organization master file, this file must first be physically created and initialized to the required structure using the facilities provided by the local operating system — this physical file initialization was handled automatically by our random file abstraction in Chapter 9.

What addressing algorithm should we use for access to the records of this file? Since the first seven digits of each account number uniquely identify the account concerned (remember that the final character is simply a redundant check digit) the use of self-indexing requires that the file should contain 10 000 000 records. The first digit of each account number identifies the area in which the account holder's branch is located, the next two digits identify the branch in that area, and the next four digits are the local account number. Hence there are no more than 10 000 accounts in each branch. From Listing 22, Chapter 10, we can deduce that, currently, there are only six areas making up the bank (i.e., at most 60% of the total range of account numbers are allocated) and that no area contains more than five branches (i.e., at most 50% of the possible account numbers in each area are allocated) — thus at most 30% of the possible account numbers are potentially allocated. Since each branch contains at most 10 000 accounts, and each area contains at most 50 000 accounts, the bank itself has at most 300 000 account holders.

Therefore we shall set up a relative file of 300 000 record areas and use the following address algorithm for calculating the relative record number R for an account with local account number c in branch b of area a

$$R = (a-1)*50\ 000 + (b-1)*10\ 000 + c$$

i.e., the first area's accounts occupy the first 50 000 record positions, the second area's accounts occupy the next 50 000 positions in the file, and so on; within the record positions for each area the first branch uses the first 10 000 positions, the second branch the next 10 000, and so on; within the positions for each branch the records are located according to self-indexing using the local account number. Thus the account for account number 20231997 will be located at relative record position 63199.

The SELECT clause for the master file takes the form

```
SELECT MASTER-RELATIVE-FILE
    ASSIGN TO DISK 1
    ORGANIZATION RELATIVE
    ACCESS RANDOM
    RELATIVE KEY IS RECORD-NUMBER.
```

where the RELATIVE KEY item which we name RECORD-NUMBER is declared in the WORKING-STORAGE SECTION as

```
77 RECORD-NUMBER PIC 9(6) COMP SYNC RIGHT.
```

Since the file is processed as an output file it is opened thus:

```
OPEN OUTPUT MASTER-RELATIVE-FILE
```

The only input–output record access operation applied to the master file is a WRITE operation which attempts to write a record to its correct file position as determined by the addressing function, viz.,

```
COMPUTE RECORD-NUMBER =
    (AREA-NUMBER - 1) * AREA-SIZE +
    (BRANCH-NUMBER - 1) * BRANCH-SIZE +
    LOCAL-NUMBER
```

which is assumed to be stored in the library as the text named ADDRESS-ROUTINE. If this preferred position is already occupied (which it should not be if the program is functioning correctly, since the addressing function is such that each account number maps onto a distinct relative record number) the INVALID KEY condition will arise in the execution of the WRITE statement. The full text of the COBOL program *PROGRAM9* to perform the relative file initialization is given in Listing 34.

```
                    LISTING 34  PROGRAM9
IDENTIFICATION DIVISION.
PROGRAM-ID.       PROGRAM9.
INSTALLATION.     QUB.
AUTHOR.           JOHN ELDER.
*                 INITIALIZATION OF RELATIVE ORGANIZATION MASTER FILE.
DATE-WRITTEN.     FEBRUARY 1983.
DATE-COMPILED.

ENVIRONMENT DIVISION.
CONFIGURATION SECTION.
SOURCE-COMPUTER.  SUPER-2000.
```

```
OBJECT-COMPUTER.  SUPER-2000.
INPUT-OUTPUT SECTION.
FILE-CONTROL.
    SELECT MASTER-TAPE-FILE ASSIGN TO TAPE 1 RESERVE 2 AREAS.
    SELECT MASTER-RELATIVE-FILE ASSIGN TO DISK 1
        ORGANIZATION RELATIVE
        ACCESS RANDOM
        RELATIVE KEY IS RECORD-NUMBER.

DATA DIVISION.
FILE SECTION.
FD MASTER-TAPE-FILE BLOCK CONTAINS 512 CHARACTERS
                    LABEL RECORDS STANDARD
                        VALUE OF ID IS "MASTER-FILE".
  01  OLD-MASTER-RECORD.
      02  ACCOUNT-NUMBER.
          03  AREA-NUMBER     PIC 9.
          03  BRANCH-NUMBER   PIC 99.
          03  LOCAL-NUMBER    PIC 9999.
          03  CHECK-DIGIT     PIC X.
      02  CLIENT-IDENTITY     PIC X(30).
      02  CURRENT-BALANCE     PIC 9(5)V99 COMP SYNC RIGHT.
      02  MINIMUM-BALANCE     PIC 9(5)V99 COMP SYNC RIGHT.
COPY MASTER-FD REPLACING MASTER-FILE BY MASTER-RELATIVE-FILE
                         MASTER-RECORD BY NEW-MASTER-RECORD.

WORKING-STORAGE SECTION.
77  FILE-FLAG           PIC 9 COMP SYNC RIGHT.
  88  NO-RECORDS-REMAIN  VALUE 1.
77  RECORD-NUMBER      PIC 9(6) COMP SYNC RIGHT.
77  AREA-SIZE          PIC 9(5) COMP SYNC RIGHT VALUE 60000.
77  BRANCH-SIZE        PIC 9(5) COMP SYNC RIGHT VALUE 10000.

PROCEDURE DIVISION.
MAIN-PARAGRAPH.
    PERFORM CREATE-RELATIVE-FILE.
    STOP RUN.
CREATE-RELATIVE-FILE.
    OPEN INPUT MASTER-TAPE-FILE, OUTPUT MASTER-RELATIVE-FILE.
    MOVE ZERO TO FILE-FLAG.
    PERFORM READ-NEXT-TAPE-RECORD.
    PERFORM TRANSFER-RECORD UNTIL NO-RECORDS-REMAIN.
    CLOSE MASTER-TAPE-FILE, MASTER-RELATIVE-FILE.
READ-NEXT-TAPE-RECORD.
    READ MASTER-TAPE-FILE AT END MOVE 1 TO FILE-FLAG.
TRANSFER-RECORD.
    COPY ADDRESS-ROUTINE.
    MOVE OLD-MASTER-RECORD TO NEW-MASTER-RECORD.
    WRITE NEW-MASTER-RECORD
        INVALID KEY DISPLAY "FILE ERROR ??", ACCOUNT-NUMBER.
    PERFORM READ-NEXT-TAPE-RECORD.
```

17.3 CASE STUDY: RELATIVE MASTER FILE UPDATE

Figure 17.2 shows the files involved in the updating of the relative organization master file, which is performed by the program *PROGRAM10* presented in Listing 35, using the unsorted transactions file TRANSACTIONS produced by the validation program *PROGRAM2* in Chapter 14. The same master file is used as in *PROGRAM9* as well, obviously, as the same addressing algorithm for determining the correct file position for any record.

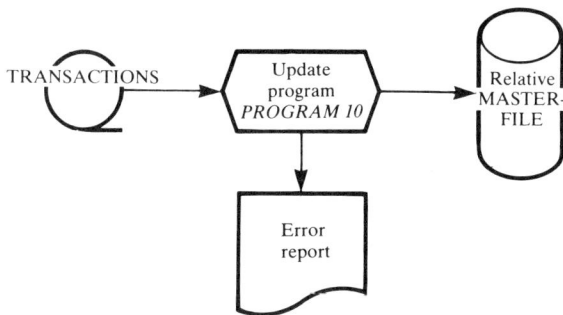

Figure 17.2   Relative organization master file update

The paragraph INITIAL-STATUS attempts to find a required master file record by performing a READ operation on the master file. If the record position given by the addressing function is unoccupied, then the INVALID KEY clause specifies the appropriate action to indicate that the record is not in the file.

The FINAL-STATUS paragraph is exactly as in the indexed sequential file update program. If a new record is written to the file, the position at which it is to be inserted is the (empty) file position located previously by the READ operation in INITIAL-STATUS.

Once again the transaction processing routine is the same as for the sequential and indexed sequential master file updates.

```
                  LISTING  35  PROGRAM10

IDENTIFICATION DIVISION.
PROGRAM-ID.        PROGRAM10.
INSTALLATION.      QUB.
AUTHOR.            JOHN ELDER.
*                  RELATIVE ORGANIZATION MASTER FILE UPDATE.
DATE-WRITTEN.      JANUARY 1983.
DATE-COMPILED.

ENVIRONMENT DIVISION.
CONFIGURATION SECTION.
SOURCE-COMPUTER.   SUPER-2000.
OBJECT-COMPUTER.   SUPER-2000.
SPECIAL-NAMES.     PRINTER 1 IS REPORT-DEVICE.
INPUT-OUTPUT SECTION.
FILE-CONTROL.
    SELECT TRANSACTION-FILE ASSIGN TO TAPE 1 RESERVE 2 AREAS.
    SELECT MASTER-FILE ASSIGN TO DISK 1
        ORGANIZATION RELATIVE
        ACCESS RANDOM
        RELATIVE KEY IS RECORD-NUMBER.

DATA DIVISION.
FILE SECTION.
FD TRANSACTION-FILE BLOCK CONTAINS 512 CHARACTERS
                    LABEL RECORDS STANDARD
                    VALUE OF ID "TRANSACTIONS".
```

```
01  TRANSACTION.
    02  DATE-FIELD              PIC 9(6).
    02  ACCOUNT-NUMBER.
        03  AREA-NUMBER         PIC 9.
        03  BRANCH-NUMBER       PIC 99.
        03  LOCAL-NUMBER        PIC 9999.
        03  CHECK-DIGIT         PIC X.
    02  KIND                    PIC X.
        88  CREDIT              VALUE "C".
        88  DEBIT               VALUE "D".
        88  ADDITION            VALUE "N".
        88  DELETION            VALUE "X".
    02  AMOUNT                  PIC 9(4)V99.
    02  CLIENT-IDENTITY         PIC X(30).
    02  FILLER                  PIC X(29).

COPY MASTER-FD REPLACING MASTER-RECORD BY MASTER.

WORKING-STORAGE SECTION.
77  SENTINEL        PIC X(8) VALUE HIGH-VALUES.
77  CURRENT-KEY     PIC X(8).
77  TRANSACTION-KEY PIC X(8) VALUE LOW-VALUES.
77  TRUE            PIC 9 COMP SYNC RIGHT VALUE 1.
77  FALSE           PIC 9 COMP SYNC RIGHT VALUE 0.
77  INFILE          PIC 9 COMP SYNC RIGHT.
77  ORIGINALLYINFILE PIC 9 COMP SYNC RIGHT.
77  SAVINGS-LIMIT   PIC 9(5) COMP SYNC RIGHT VALUE 20000.
77  NEW-BALANCE     PIC S9(5)V99 COMP SYNC RIGHT.
77  RECORD-NUMBER   PIC 9(6) COMP SYNC RIGHT.
77  AREA-SIZE       PIC 9(5) COMP SYNC RIGHT VALUE 60000.
77  BRANCH-SIZE     PIC 9(5) COMP SYNC RIGHT VALUE 10000.

PROCEDURE DIVISION.
UPDATE-RELATIVE-FILE.
    OPEN INPUT TRANSACTION-FILE , I-O MASTER-FILE.
    PERFORM READ-NEXT-TRANSACTION.
    PERFORM CHOOSE-NEXT-KEY.
    PERFORM PROCESS-ONE-KEY UNTIL CURRENT-KEY = SENTINEL.
    CLOSE TRANSACTION-FILE , MASTER-FILE.
    STOP RUN.
PROCESS-ONE-KEY.
    PERFORM INITIAL-STATUS.
    PROCESS-ONE-TRANSACTION.
    PERFORM FINAL-STATUS.
    PERFORM CHOOSE-NEXT-KEY.
PROCESS-ONE-TRANSACTION.
    PERFORM APPLY-TRANSACTION-TO-MASTER.
    PERFORM READ-NEXT-TRANSACTION.
CHOOSE-NEXT-KEY.
    MOVE TRANSACTION-KEY TO CURRENT-KEY.
READ-NEXT-TRANSACTION.
    READ TRANSACTION-FILE
        AT END MOVE SENTINEL TO TRANSACTION-KEY.
    IF TRANSACTION-KEY NOT = SENTINEL
        MOVE ACCOUNT-NUMBER IN TRANSACTION TO TRANSACTION-KEY.
INITIAL-STATUS.
    COPY ADDRESS-ROUTINE.
    MOVE TRUE TO ORIGINALLYINFILE.
    READ MASTER-FILE
        INVALID KEY MOVE FALSE TO ORIGINALLYINFILE.
    MOVE ORIGINALLYINFILE TO INFILE.
FINAL-STATUS.
    IF INFILE = TRUE
        IF ORIGINALLYINFILE = TRUE
            REWRITE MASTER
                INVALID KEY DISPLAY "KEY CHANGED   ", TRANSACTION
                            UPON REPORT-DEVICE
```

```
      ELSE WRITE MASTER
              INVALID KEY DISPLAY "DUPLICATE KEY ", TRANSACTION
                       UPON REPORT-DEVICE
      ELSE IF ORIGINALLYINFILE = TRUE
              DELETE MASTER
              INVALID KEY DISPLAY "MISSING KEY  ", TRANSACTION
                       UPON REPORT-DEVICE.
APPLY-TRANSACTION-TO-MASTER.
      COPY TRANSACTION-PROCESSING REPLACING MASTER-RECORD BY MASTER.
```

EXERCISES

1. Outline the sequence of actions to be performed in a standard COBOL program which accesses a record of a relative organization file with a certain key value, updates it, and returns it to the file in its original position. How would your program check that any record it attempts to read is actually in the file?

2. Extend the relative file update program *PROGRAM10* so that it also validates incoming transactions.

3. Implement *PROGRAM9* and *PROGRAM10* using one of the addressing algorithms described in Chapter 9.

4. Write a library text entry containing the record description of a transaction record such that this description may be retrieved with suitable textual replacement into any of the case study programs of Chapters 13 to 17.

5. A relative organization file named RANDOMFILE contains 512 character blocks and has standard labels. The format of the records in the file is
   characters 1–4   : record length count
   characters 5–8   : a four-digit item code
   characters 9–12   : the unit price of an item
   characters 13–44 : a description of the item
   The preferred record position for each record is calculated by dividing the product code by 47 and adding 1. The file is updated by amendments with the following format
   characters 1–4   : item code
   characters 5–8   : new unit price
   characters 9–40   : updated description
   Write a COBOL program which reads a file of amendment records and updates the master file. If any errors occur during an input or output operation the program should be abandoned with a suitable message displayed on the operator's console.

18 REPORT WRITING IN COBOL

18.1 CASE STUDY: IMPLEMENTING THE REPORT PROGRAM IN COBOL

The COBOL program *PROGRAM5* given in Listing 36 demonstrates the use of the program inversion technique (described in Section 10.3) to implement the report construction program previously developed in Section 10.2, by inverting the logical structure process *generatelogicalreportgroups* with respect to the physical structure process *printpagedreport*. However, this program generates only a summary report — the detail lines, i.e., individual customer's balances, are omitted, as are branch control headings, and the report therefore only contains summaries of the branch, area, and bank totals. The form of its output will be that illustrated in Listing 23.

In this program *printpagedreport* and *generatelogicalreportgroups* are implemented as appropriately named sections. In addition, the body of GENERATE-LOGICAL-REPORT-GROUP has been further subdivided into a number of other sections. The section GENERATE-LOGICAL-REPORT-GROUP remembers (using a data item SWITCH) where its next invocation is to begin. This involves assigning SWITCH a suitable value prior to each exit from GENERATE-LOGICAL-REPORT-GROUP, and a GO TO DEPENDING ON statement at the start of GENERATE-LOGICAL-REPORT-GROUP switches control to the appropriate point each time that GENERATE-LOGICAL-REPORT-GROUP is called from PRINT-PAGED-REPORT.

GENERATE-LOGICAL-REPORT-GROUP passes the next report group to be printed as the value of the field REPORT-

402

GROUP of the record item LOGICAL-REPORT-GROUP, the number of lines to be skipped before this report group is printed is assigned as the value of another field LINES-TO-SKIP, and the number of lines comprising the report group is assigned to the field NUMBEROFLINES.

Each addition to the buffer in the original process *generatelogicalreportgroup* becomes a sequence of assignments to REPORT-GROUP, LINES-TO-SKIP, NUMBEROFLINES and SWITCH followed by an exit from GENERATE-LOGICAL-REPORT-GROUP (by means of a transfer of control to the final END-GENERATE paragraph of GENERATE-LOGICAL-REPORT-GROUP). Each attempt to obtain a report group from the buffer by the original *printpagedreport* process simply becomes PERFORM GENERATE-LOGICAL-REPORT-GROUP.

The indexed sequential master file (accessed sequentially) is used in this program.

LISTING 36 *PROGRAM5*

```
IDENTIFICATION DIVISION.
PROGRAM-ID.        PROGRAM5.
INSTALLATION.      QUB.
AUTHOR.            J ELDER.
*                  IMPLEMENTATION OF REPORT PROGRAM
*                  USING PROGRAM INVERSION.
DATE-WRITTEN.      MARCH 1983.
DATE-COMPILED.     MARCH 1983.

ENVIRONMENT DIVISION.
CONFIGURATION SECTION.
SOURCE-COMPUTER.   SUPER-2000.
OBJECT-COMPUTER.   SUPER-2000.
INPUT-OUTPUT SECTION.
FILE-CONTROL.
   SELECT MASTER-FILE ASSIGN TO DISK 1 RESERVE 2 AREAS
                      ORGANIZATION INDEXED
                      ACCESS SEQUENTIAL
                      RECORD KEY IS ACCOUNT-NUMBER OF MASTER.
   SELECT SAVINGS-PRINTOUT ASSIGN TO PRINTER 1 RESERVE 2   AREAS.

DATA DIVISION.
FILE SECTION.
FD MASTER-FILE BLOCK CONTAINS 512 CHARACTERS
               LABEL RECORDS STANDARD
               VALUE OF ID "MASTER-FILE".
01  MASTER.
   02  ACCOUNT-NUMBER.
      03  AREA-NUMBER   PIC 9.
      03  BRANCH-NUMBER PIC 99.
      03  CLIENT-NUMBER PIC X(5).
   02  CLIENT-IDENTITY PIC X(30).
   02  CURRENT-BALANCE PIC 9(5)V99 COMP SYNC RIGHT.
   02  MINIMUM-BALANCE PIC 9(5)V99 COMP SYNC RIGHT.

FD SAVINGS-PRINTOUT LABEL RECORDS OMITTED.
01  REPORT-HEADING          PIC B(19)X(101).
01  REPORT-FOOTING          PIC B(28)X(92).
```

```
01  PAGE-HEADING-OR-FOOTING    PIC B(38)ZZ9B(79).
01  REPORT-LINE                PIC X(120).

WORKING-STORAGE SECTION.
*   COMMUNICATION DATA ITEMS
01  LOGICAL-REPORT-GROUP.
    02  REPORT-FLAG            PIC 9 COMP SYNC RIGHT VALUE ZERO.
        88  END-OF-REPORT-GROUP-SEQUENCE VALUE 1.
    02  LINES-TO-SKIP          PIC 99 COMP SYNC RIGHT.
    02  NUMBEROFLINES          PIC 99 COMP SYNC RIGHT.
    02  REPORT-GROUP           PIC X(120) OCCURS 2 TIMES.
*   DATA ITEMS USED TO CONSTRUCT PAGED REPORT
77  REPORT-HEADING-LINES       PIC 99 COMP SYNC RIGHT VALUE 19.
77  REPORT-FOOTING-LINES       PIC 99 COMP SYNC RIGHT VALUE 19.
77  PAGE-HEADING-LINE          PIC 99 COMP SYNC RIGHT VALUE 1.
77  PAGE-FOOTING-LINE          PIC 99 COMP SYNC RIGHT VALUE 62.
77  FIRST-DETAIL-LINE          PIC 99 COMP SYNC RIGHT VALUE 2.
77  LAST-DETAIL-LINE           PIC 99 COMP SYNC RIGHT VALUE 56.
77  REPORT-HEADING-CONTENT     PIC X(39)
            VALUE "SAVINGS SUMMARY BY AREA AND BRANCH".
77  REPORT-FOOTING-CONTENT     PIC X(15)
            VALUE "END OF REPORT".
77  PAGE-COUNT                 PIC 999 COMP SYNC RIGHT VALUE ZERO.
77  LINE-COUNT                 PIC 99 COMP SYNC RIGHT.
77  END-OF-GROUP               PIC 99 COMP SYNC RIGHT.
77  I                          PIC 99 COMP SYNC RIGHT.
*   DATA ITEMS USED IN GENERATING LOGICAL REPORT GROUPS
77  SWITCH                     PIC 9 COMP SYNC RIGHT VALUE 1.
77  FILE-FLAG                  PIC 9 COMP SYNC RIGHT VALUE ZERO.
        88  END-OF-FILE VALUE 1.
77  BANK-TOTAL                 PIC 9(8)V99 COMP SYNC RIGHT VALUE ZERO.
77  AREA-TOTAL                 PIC 9(8)V99 COMP SYNC RIGHT.
77  BRANCH-TOTAL               PIC 9(8)V99 COMP SYNC RIGHT.
77  BANK-INTEREST              PIC 9(6)V99 COMP SYNC RIGHT VALUE ZERO.
77  AREA-INTEREST              PIC 9(6)V99 COMP SYNC RIGHT.
77  BRANCH-INTEREST            PIC 9(6)V99 COMP SYNC RIGHT.
77  INTEREST                   PIC 9(6)V99 COMP SYNC RIGHT.
77  LOWER-RATE                 PIC V9999 VALUE 0.0075.
77  UPPER-RATE                 PIC V9999 VALUE 0.01.
77  THRESHOLD                  PIC 99999 VALUE 5000.
77  THIS-AREA-NUMBER           PIC 9 COMP SYNC RIGHT.
77  THIS-BRANCH-NUMBER         PIC 99 COMP SYNC RIGHT.
01  FINAL-HEADING.
    02  FILLER                 PIC X(36) VALUE SPACES.
    02  FILLER                 PIC X(12) VALUE "BANK   REPORT".
01  FINAL-FOOTING-1.
    02  FILLER                 PIC X(20) VALUE "BANK   TOTAL   SAVINGS".
    02  BANK-FINAL-TOTAL       PIC B(45)$$$,$$$,$$9.99.
01  FINAL-FOOTING-2.
    02  FILLER                 PIC X(21) VALUE "              INTEREST".
    02  BANK-FINAL-INTEREST    PIC B(44)$$$,$$$,$$9.99.
01  AREA-HEADING.
    02  FILLER                 PIC X(5) VALUE "AREA ".
    02  AREA-NO                PIC 9.
01  AREA-FOOTING-1.
    02  FILLER                 PIC X(5) VALUE "AREA ".
    02  AREA-NO                PIC 9.
    02  FILLER                 PIC X(8) VALUE " SAVINGS".
    02  AREA-FINAL-TOTAL       PIC B(51)$$$,$$$,$$9.99.
01  AREA-FOOTING-2.
    02  FILLER                 PIC X(15) VALUE "     INTEREST".
    02  AREA-FINAL-INTEREST    PIC B(50)$$$,$$$,$$9.99.
01  BRANCH-FOOTING-1.
    02  FILLER                 PIC X(10) VALUE "    BRANCH".
    02  BRANCH-NO              PIC ZZZZ9.
    02  FILLER                 PIC X(8) VALUE " SAVINGS".
    02  BRANCH-FINAL-TOTAL     PIC B(30)$$$,$$$,$$9.99.
```

```
01  BRANCH-FOOTING-2.
    02  FILLER                  PIC X(23) VALUE "            INTEREST".
    02  BRANCH-FINAL-INTEREST PIC B(50)$$$,$$$,$$9.99.


PROCEDURE DIVISION.

MAIN-PROGRAM SECTION.
BEGIN-MAIN-PROGRAM.
    PERFORM PRINT-PAGED-REPORT.
    STOP RUN.

PRINT-PAGED-REPORT SECTION.
BEGIN-PRINT-PAGED-REPORT.
    OPEN OUTPUT SAVINGS-PRINTOUT.
    PERFORM PRINT-REPORT-HEADING.
    PERFORM GENERATE-LOGICAL-REPORT-GROUP.
    PERFORM NEXT-PAGE UNTIL END-OF-REPORT-GROUP-SEQUENCE.
    PERFORM PRINT-REPORT-FOOTING.
    CLOSE SAVINGS-PRINTOUT.
    GO TO END-PRINT-PAGED-REPORT.
NEXT-PAGE.
    PERFORM TAKE-NEW-PAGE.
    ADD 1 TO PAGE-COUNT.
    MOVE 1 TO LINE-COUNT.
    PERFORM PRINT-PAGE-HEADING.
    ADD LINES-TO-SKIP, NUMBEROFLINES, LINE-COUNT
        GIVING END-OF-GROUP.
    PERFORM PRINT-NEXT-GROUP UNTIL END-OF-REPORT-GROUP-SEQUENCE
                    OR END-OF-GROUP > LAST-DETAIL-LINE.
    PERFORM PRINT-PAGE-FOOTING.
PRINT-REPORT-HEADING.
    PERFORM TAKE-NEW-PAGE.
    WRITE REPORT-HEADING FROM REPORT-HEADING-CONTENT
        AFTER ADVANCING REPORT-HEADING-LINES.
PRINT-REPORT-FOOTING.
    PERFORM TAKE-NEW-PAGE.
    WRITE REPORT-FOOTING FROM REPORT-FOOTING-CONTENT
        AFTER ADVANCING REPORT-HEADING-LINES.
PRINT-PAGE-HEADING.
    MOVE PAGE-COUNT TO PAGE-HEADING-OR-FOOTING.
    WRITE PAGE-HEADING-OR-FOOTING
        AFTER ADVANCING PAGE-HEADING-LINE  LINES.
    ADD PAGE-HEADING-LINE TO LINE-COUNT.
    MOVE SPACES TO REPORT-LINE.
    WRITE REPORT-LINE AFTER ADVANCING FIRST-DETAIL-LINE LINES.
    ADD FIRST-DETAIL-LINE TO LINE-COUNT.
PRINT-PAGE-FOOTING.
    SUBTRACT LINE-COUNT FROM PAGE-FOOTING-LINE GIVING LINE-COUNT.
    MOVE PAGE-COUNT TO PAGE-HEADING-OR-FOOTING.
    WRITE PAGE-HEADING-OR-FOOTING AFTER ADVANCING LINE-COUNT  LINES.
PRINT-NEXT-GROUP.
    MOVE SPACES TO REPORT-LINE.
    WRITE REPORT-LINE AFTER ADVANCING LINES-TO-SKIP LINES.
    MOVE 1 TO I.
    PERFORM PRINT-LINE UNTIL I > NUMBEROFLINES.
    MOVE END-OF-GROUP TO LINE-COUNT.
    PERFORM GENERATE-LOGICAL-REPORT-GROUP.
    ADD LINES-TO-SKIP , NUMBEROFLINES, LINE-COUNT
        GIVING END-OF-GROUP.
TAKE-NEW-PAGE.
    MOVE SPACES TO REPORT-LINE.
    WRITE REPORT-LINE AFTER ADVANCING PAGE.
END-PRINT-PAGED-REPORT.
    EXIT.

GENERATE-LOGICAL-REPORT-GROUP SECTION.
```

```
BEGIN-GENERATE.
    GO TO 1, 2, 3, 4, 5, 6 DEPENDING ON SWITCH.
1.
    OPEN INPUT MASTER-FILE.
    MOVE 3 TO LINES-TO-SKIP. MOVE 1 TO NUMBEROFLINES.
    MOVE FINAL-HEADING TO REPORT-GROUP (1).
    MOVE 2 TO SWITCH. GO TO END-GENERATE.
2.
    PERFORM READ-MASTER.
    PERFORM NEXT-AREA UNTIL END-OF-FILE.
    MOVE 3 TO LINES-TO-SKIP. MOVE 2 TO NUMBEROFLINES.
    MOVE BANK-TOTAL TO BANK-FINAL-TOTAL.
    MOVE FINAL-FOOTING-1 TO REPORT-GROUP (1).
    MOVE BANK-FINAL-INTEREST TO BANK-FINAL-INTEREST.
    MOVE FINAL-FOOTING-2 TO REPORT-GROUP (2).
    MOVE 3 TO SWITCH. GO TO END-GENERATE.
3.
    CLOSE MASTER-FILE.
    MOVE 1 TO REPORT-FLAG.
END-GENERATE.
    EXIT.


NEXT-AREA SECTION.
BEGIN-NEXT-AREA.
    MOVE AREA-NUMBER TO THIS-AREA-NUMBER, AREA-NO IN AREA-HEADING.
    MOVE 2 TO LINES-TO-SKIP. MOVE 1 TO NUMBEROFLINES.
    MOVE AREA-HEADING TO REPORT-GROUP (1).
    MOVE 4 TO SWITCH. GO TO END-GENERATE.
4.
    MOVE ZERO TO AREA-TOTAL, AREA-INTEREST.
    PERFORM NEXT-BRANCH UNTIL END-OF-FILE
                        OR AREA-NUMBER NOT = THIS-AREA-NUMBER.
    ADD AREA-TOTAL TO BANK-TOTAL.
    ADD AREA-INTEREST TO BANK-INTEREST.
    MOVE 1 TO LINES-TO-SKIP. MOVE 2 TO NUMBEROFLINES.
    MOVE THIS-AREA-NUMBER TO AREA-NO IN AREA-FOOTING-1.
    MOVE AREA-TOTAL TO AREA-FINAL-TOTAL.
    MOVE AREA-FOOTING-1 TO REPORT-GROUP (1).
    MOVE AREA-INTEREST TO AREA-FINAL-INTEREST.
    MOVE AREA-FOOTING-2 TO REPORT-GROUP (2).
    MOVE 5 TO SWITCH. GO TO END-GENERATE.
5.
    EXIT.


NEXT-BRANCH SECTION.
BEGIN-NEXT-BRANCH.
    MOVE BRANCH-NUMBER TO THIS-BRANCH-NUMBER.
    MOVE ZERO TO BRANCH-TOTAL, BRANCH-INTEREST.
    PERFORM NEXT-ACCOUNT UNTIL END-OF-FILE
                        OR AREA-NUMBER NOT = THIS-AREA-NUMBER
                        OR BRANCH-NUMBER NOT = THIS-BRANCH-NUMBER.
    ADD BRANCH-TOTAL TO AREA-TOTAL.
    ADD BRANCH-INTEREST TO AREA-INTEREST.
    MOVE 1 TO LINES-TO-SKIP.  MOVE 2 TO NUMBEROFLINES.
    MOVE THIS-BRANCH-NUMBER TO BRANCH-NO.
    MOVE BRANCH-TOTAL TO BRANCH-FINAL-TOTAL.
    MOVE BRANCH-FOOTING-1 TO REPORT-GROUP (1).
    MOVE BRANCH-INTEREST TO BRANCH-FINAL-INTEREST.
    MOVE BRANCH-FOOTING-2 TO REPORT-GROUP (2).
    MOVE 6 TO SWITCH. GO TO END-GENERATE.
6.
    EXIT.


NEXT-ACCOUNT SECTION.
BEGIN-NEXT-CLIENT.
    PERFORM CALCULATE-INTEREST.
```

```
    ADD INTEREST TO CURRENT-BALANCE, BRANCH-INTEREST.
    ADD CURRENT-BALANCE TO BRANCH-TOTAL.
    MOVE CURRENT-BALANCE TO MINIMUM-BALANCE.
    REWRITE MASTER.
    PERFORM READ-MASTER.
CALCULATE-INTEREST.
    IF MINIMUM-BALANCE > THRESHOLD
        COMPUTE INTEREST = THRESHOLD * LOWER-RATE
                         + (MINIMUM-BALANCE -THRESHOLD) * UPPER-RATE
    ELSE
        COMPUTE INTEREST = MINIMUM-BALANCE * LOWER-RATE.

READ-MASTER SECTION.
BEGIN-READ-MASTER.
    READ MASTER-FILE AT END MOVE 1 TO FILE-FLAG.
```

Other points to note:

1. The taking of a new page involves printing a blank line at the start of that page — to simplify the subsequent computation of the line numbers at which the page heading and first detail lines are to be printed the values of the data items PAGE-HEADING-LINE and FIRST-DETAIL-LINE are specified not as absolute line numbers but instead as values relative to this first blank line and the page heading line, respectively.

2. It is not necessary to use REDEFINES for the definitions of the various output line formats in the SAVINGS-PRINTOUT file since it is possible to give more than one definition of an output file record.

3. Each section opens and closes only the files which it uses.

4. The program inversion technique results in the use of some highly undesirable programming practices — the program jumps into and out of the middle of sections, leading to a program which is difficult to understand and even more difficult to debug — indeed, such switches of control would be almost impossible to program in a language such as Pascal which has stricter rules regarding the use of goto statements (thus we conclude that the use of parallelism or coroutines provides a better implementation of this report program and other programs whose designs are similar).

18.2 THE COBOL REPORT WRITER

As can be seen from the programs in Chapter 10 and in this chapter, the control structure of a report generation program depends only upon the number of key fields in the records of the file being processed. The differences between one report generation program and another are the definitions of the input file and report contents —

the control key fields, the contents of the headings, footings and details, and the layout of data on a page. Since the control structure is largely fixed, it was possible for the designers of COBOL to introduce a semi-automatic report generation facility into the language (although not all COBOL implementations provide it).

The COBOL Report Writer is an event-driven program to which the programmer supplies, as data definitions in the REPORT SECTION of the DATA DIVISION, a list of the control fields in the input file from which the report is to be generated, and the source and formats of the information to be printed for each detail, heading, and footing, as well as at each page break. Other details such as the physical format of the report, e.g., page sizes and various printing limit positions for the various report groups, are also specified. Special data items to be used as counter items in association with control groups may be declared.

The detail report groups are then generated one-by-one by the COBOL program (using GENERATE statements) and the detection of control and page breaks, printing of the various report groups, and incrementing and resetting of counter data items, are all handled automatically by the *Report Writer Control System.*

Some of the features of the Report Writer facility are illustrated here by demonstrating how they may be used to construct the same summary report as was generated by the program *PROGRAM5.*

The file on which the report is to be produced is named as usual in a SELECT entry, e.g.,

```
SELECT SAVINGS-PRINTOUT ASSIGN TO PRINTER 1.
```

In the DATA DIVISION SAVINGS-PRINTOUT is given an FD entry (but no record description) and a REPORT clause names the report which it is to hold

```
FD SAVINGS-PRINTOUT
   LABEL RECORDS OMITTED
   REPORT IS SAVINGS-REPORT.
```

Hence the report is introduced with the name SAVINGS-REPORT. Declaration of the report name automatically introduces two built-in data items, PAGE-COUNTER (OF SAVINGS-REPORT) and LINE-COUNTER (OF SAVINGS-REPORT). The value of PAGE-COUNTER is always the number of the page currently being printed; that of LINE-COUNTER is the line currently being printed on that page. Both are assigned initial value zero, and are automatically incremented and reset as necessary during the production of the report.

A description of SAVINGS-REPORT then follows in the REPORT SECTION — this declares the characteristics of the report such as the data items to be used as control keys, the number of lines to be printed on each page, the lines on which particular report groups are to appear, the contents of these report groups, and details of any items used as counters (and when they are to be incremented and reset).

The report definition begins with a header whose simplest form is usually

> RD *report-name*
> [*controls-clause*]
> [*page-limit-clause*] .

The *controls-clause* identifies the data items used as control keys in the input file, and thus control breaks can be identified by the system when the program is executed. These keys must be listed in order of decreasing significance. If the end of file is to be treated as a control break, then FINAL must appear as the first control key, viz.,

```
CONTROLS ARE FINAL, AREA-NUMBER, BRANCH-NUMBER
```

The *page-limit-clause* defines how the report is printed on a page. For our example the appropriate clause is

```
PAGE LIMIT IS 66 LINES
HEADING 2
FIRST DETAIL 4
LAST DETAIL 56
FOOTING 62
```

The LINES phrase indicates that the page is 66 lines long and the remaining phrases determine where on the page the various report groups may appear when printed. The HEADING phrase indicates that report and page headings may begin as from line 2. The FIRST DETAIL phrase indicates that no detail lines or control headings may begin before line 4, while the LAST DETAIL phrase confines details and control footings to begin before or on line 56. The FOOTING phrase states that no control footing may extend below line 62; this restriction is not applicable to report and page footings. The report heading may thus start anywhere between lines 2 and 62, the page footing anywhere between lines 57 and 62. Figure 18.1 shows the relationship between the above set of values and the positions on a page at which the printing of the various report groups may take place.

| Report
heading/
footing | Page
heading | Details &
control
heading | Control
footing | Page
footing |

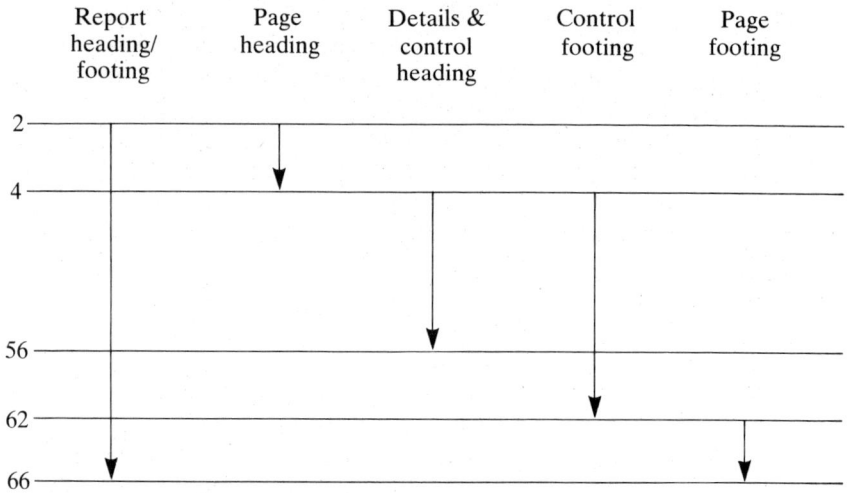

Figure 18.1   Placement of report groups according to PAGE LIMIT clause

Now we consider the definitions of the report groups that make up the report itself. Each of these defines the type of the report group concerned, when it is to be printed, where it is to be printed, the values making up the report group and their placement. Each report group is given a level 01 description and may be made up of several fields defining the elementary items of the report group. For example, the final control heading report group requires the following description

```
01   TYPE IS CONTROL HEADING FINAL LINE PLUS 4.
     02   COLUMN 37 PIC X(12) VALUE "BANK   REPORT".
```

The TYPE clause defines the nature of the report group and has the following alternative forms

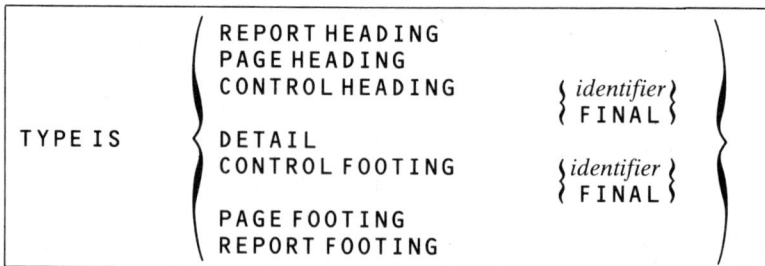

```
                  ⎧ REPORT HEADING                        ⎫
                  ⎪ PAGE HEADING                          ⎪
                  ⎪ CONTROL HEADING   ⎧ identifier ⎫      ⎪
                  ⎪                   ⎨ FINAL      ⎬       ⎪
  TYPE IS         ⎨ DETAIL                                ⎬
                  ⎪ CONTROL FOOTING   ⎧ identifier ⎫      ⎪
                  ⎪                   ⎨ FINAL      ⎬       ⎪
                  ⎪ PAGE FOOTING                          ⎪
                  ⎩ REPORT FOOTING                        ⎭
```

The CONTROL HEADING and CONTROL FOOTING report groups must specify the control key from the report definition header with which they are associated (e.g., FINAL in the above example). Each of the various report groups is printed automatically by the system whenever the condition associated with it (as defined by its TYPE) arises.

The LINE clause gives the absolute or relative line number on which the printing of a report group is to take place. In the previous example the final control heading is printed four lines after the previous report group. For

```
01   TYPE IS PAGE HEADING.
   02   LINE 2 COLUMN 39 PIC ZZ9
          SOURCE PAGE-COUNTER.
```

the printing of the page heading takes place on line 2 of a page. For

```
01   TYPE IS REPORT FOOTING LINE NEXT PAGE.
   02   LINE 20 COLUMN 29 PIC X(15)
          VALUE "END OF REPORT".
```

the printing of a report footing takes place on line 20 of the next page (any subfield of a report group may specify additional line spacing). The general format for the LINE clause is

$$
\text{LINE} \begin{Bmatrix} integer\text{-}1 \\ \text{PLUS } integer\text{-}2 \\ \text{NEXT PAGE} \end{Bmatrix}
$$

The NEXT GROUP clause indicates the line spacing to take place *after* printing of a report group, e.g., the report heading report group

```
01   TYPE IS REPORT HEADING NEXT GROUP NEXT PAGE.
   02   LINE 20 COLUMN 20
          PIC X(39) VALUE
          "SAVINGS SUMMARY BY AREA AND BRANCH".
```

specifies that the report group following this report heading is to be printed on the next page of the report.

The COLUMN clause indicates where printing of a field is to begin on a line, e.g., the report footing is printed starting at column 29. Each elementary data item in a report group description must contain a COLUMN clause.

The SOURCE clause specifies the data item whose value is to be printed at a particular position, e.g., the page heading consists of the value of the built-in data item PAGE-COUNTER printed in columns 39 to 41.

If a literal is to be printed out, then its value is given by a VALUE clause, as in the report heading and report footing.

In the report we are generating we wish to sum the balances for each branch, each area, and the whole bank. A SUM clause may appear in an elementary item in a control footing and causes automatic summation of the values of the data item named, e.g.

```
01   TYPE IS CONTROL FOOTING BRANCH-NUMBER
   02   LINE PLUS 4.
      03   COLUMN 5 PIC X(6) VALUE "BRANCH".
      03   COLUMN 12 PIC ZZ9 SOURCE BRANCH-NUMBER.
      03   COLUMN 16 PIC X(7) VALUE "SAVINGS".
      03   BRANCH-TOTAL COLUMN 53
                    PIC $$$,$$$,$$9.99
                    SUM CURRENT-BALANCE.
```

The field BRANCH-TOTAL (note that this field has been given a name) is declared as a SUM counter in which the values of the individual CURRENT-BALANCE fields (in the input file records) will be accumulated each time a detail record is processed (known as *sub-totalling*). Following the printing of the footings associated with a branch-number control break the counter BRANCH-TOTAL will have its value automatically reset to zero. In the area control footing another counter AREA-TOTAL is introduced which is incremented by the value of BRANCH-TOTAL each time that a branch control break occurs, i.e., it accumulates the total balances for the area (this is known as *rolling forward*). After the printing of the area control footing the value of AREA-TOTAL is reset to zero. Likewise the final control footing SUM counter BANK-TOTAL rolls forward the area balances at each area control break. All SUM counters are automatically initialized to zero.

Since our report is a summary report we need only name the detail report group, viz.,

```
01 CLIENT-RECORD TYPE IS DETAIL.
```

without giving any details of line printing and group contents.

However, if it had been required that the detail lines were to be printed (as in Listing 22, Chapter 10) the detail report group might have been specified as

```
01   CLIENT-RECORD TYPE IS DETAIL LINE PLUS 1.
   02   COLUMN 10 PIC X(8)
        SOURCE ACCOUNT-NUMBER.
   02   COLUMN 28 PIC X(30)
        SOURCE CLIENT-IDENTITY.
   02   COLUMN 60 PIC ZZZZ9.99
        SOURCE CURRENT-BALANCE.
```

If an elementary data item within a detail report group description is qualified with a GROUP INDICATE clause, then the value

of that item is only printed out after a control or page break. This
facility is useful for printing running headers whenever all the values
of a field in the detail records of a control group are the same (as are
the area and branch fields in our example report).

How is the report actually generated? To initialize generation
of a report the INITIATE *report-name* statement is used, e.g.,

```
INITIATE SAVINGS-REPORT
```

This has the effect of initializing all the various counters.

To generate the report itself the GENERATE statement is
used, each execution of which generates a detail report group, i.e.,
makes it available to the Report Writer System. If the GENERATE
statement refers to the report name, then this indicates that a summary report is being produced and the detail lines are not actually to
be printed, otherwise the GENERATE statement should name the
detail report group. Since, in our example, the detail report group
CLIENT-RECORD has no contents and is therefore not printed, it
need not have been introduced. Thus the statement

```
GENERATE SAVINGS-REPORT
```

has exactly the same effect as

```
GENERATE CLIENT-RECORD
```

and both generate the next detail report group of our example
report. The Report Writer System automatically checks for any control or page breaks that have occurred as a result and prints any
necessary headings and footings, as well as automatically incrementing and resetting any counters involved. Thus the body of the report
program is essentially a loop containing a GENERATE statement,
and the loop body is executed once per record of the input file. The
first GENERATE executed will cause the report heading, first page
heading, final control heading, and the first control heading to be
generated.

In our program the body of the loop (i.e., the paragraph
GENERATE-CLIENT-RECORD) first computes the interest to
be awarded to the account, then makes the detail record available to
the Report Writer System via a GENERATE statement, and finally
writes the updated account record back to the master file.

To complete generation of the report a TERMINATE *report-
name* statement must be executed — this generates a final control
break and hence triggers the processing associated with the end of
the report, i.e., the production of the last branch and area footings,
followed by the final control and report footings. For our report, its
execution is completed by

TERMINATE SAVINGS-REPORT

Hence we have the following Report Writer COBOL program (Listing 37) which has the same effect as the earlier program *PROGRAM5* (Listing 36).

LISTING 37 REPORT WRITER PROGRAM

```
IDENTIFICATION DIVISION.
PROGRAM-ID.        REPORT-EXAMPLE.
AUTHOR.            J ELDER.
*                  USE OF COBOL REPORT WRITER.
DATE-WRITTEN.      MARCH 1983.
DATE-COMPILED.     03/03/83.

ENVIRONMENT DIVISION.
CONFIGURATION SECTION.
SOURCE-COMPUTER.  SUPER-2000.
OBJECT-COMPUTER.  SUPER-2000.
INPUT-OUTPUT SECTION.
FILE-CONTROL.
    SELECT MASTER-FILE ASSIGN TO DISK 1 RESERVE 2 AREAS
                       ORGANIZATION INDEXED
                       ACCESS SEQUENTIAL
                       RECORD KEY IS ACCOUNT-NUMBER IN MASTER.
    SELECT SAVINGS-PRINTOUT ASSIGN TO PRINTER 2 RESERVE 2 AREAS.

DATA DIVISION.
FILE SECTION.
FD MASTER-FILE BLOCK CONTAINS 512 CHARACTERS
               LABEL RECORDS STANDARD
               VALUE OF ID "MASTER-FILE".
01  MASTER.
    02  ACCOUNT-NUMBER.
        03  AREA-NUMBER    PIC 9.
        03  BRANCH-NUMBER  PIC 99.
        03  CLIENT-NUMBER  PIC X(5).
    02  CLIENT-IDENTITY    PIC X(30).
    02  CURRENT-BALANCE    PIC 9(5)V99 COMP SYNC RIGHT.
    02  MINIMUM-BALANCE    PIC 9(5)V99 COMP SYNC RIGHT.

FD SAVINGS-PRINTOUT LABEL RECORDS OMITTED
                    REPORT IS SAVINGS-REPORT.

WORKING-STORAGE SECTION.
77  FILE-FLAG        PIC 9 COMP SYNC RIGHT VALUE ZERO.
    88  END-OF-FILE      VALUE 1.
77  LOWER-RATE       PIC V9999 COMP SYNC RIGHT VALUE 0.0075.
77  UPPER-RATE       PIC V9999 COMP SYNC RIGHT VALUE 0.0100.
77  THRESHOLD        PIC 99999 COMP SYNC RIGHT VALUE 5000.
77  INTEREST         PIC 9(3)V99 COMP SYNC RIGHT.
REPORT SECTION.
RD SAVINGS-REPORT CONTROLS ARE FINAL, AREA-NUMBER, BRANCH-NUMBER
                  PAGE LIMIT IS 66 LINES
                  HEADING 2
                  FIRST DETAIL 4
                  LAST DETAIL 56
                  FOOTING 62.
01  TYPE IS REPORT HEADING NEXT GROUP NEXT PAGE.
    02  LINE 20 COLUMN 20 PIC X(39)
        VALUE "SAVINGS SUMMARY BY AREA AND BRANCH".
01  TYPE IS REPORT FOOTING LINE NUMBER NEXT PAGE.
    02  LINE 20 COLUMN 29 PIC X(15) VALUE "END OF REPORT".
01  TYPE IS PAGE HEADING.
    02  LINE 2 COLUMN 39 PIC ZZ9 SOURCE PAGE-COUNTER.
```

```
01  TYPE IS PAGE FOOTING.
   02  LINE 62 COLUMN 39 PIC ZZ9 SOURCE PAGE-COUNTER.
01  TYPE IS CONTROL HEADING FINAL LINE PLUS 4.
   02  COLUMN 37 PIC X(12) VALUE "BANK REPORT".
01  TYPE IS CONTROL FOOTING FINAL.
   02  LINE PLUS 4.
      03  COLUMN 1 PIC X(20) VALUE "BANK TOTAL SAVINGS".
      03  BANK-TOTAL COLUMN 66 PIC $$$,$$$,$$9.99 SUM AREA-TOTAL.
   02  LINE PLUS 1.
      03  COLUMN 14 PIC X(8) VALUE "INTEREST".
      03  BANK-INTEREST COLUMN 66 PIC $$$,$$$,$$9.99 SUM AREA-INTEREST.
01  TYPE IS CONTROL HEADING AREA-NUMBER.
   02  LINE PLUS 3.
      03  COLUMN 1 PIC X(4) VALUE "AREA".
      03  COLUMN 6 PIC 9 SOURCE AREA-NUMBER.
01  TYPE IS CONTROL FOOTING AREA-NUMBER.
   02  LINE PLUS 2.
      03  COLUMN 1 PIC X(4) VALUE "AREA".
      03  COLUMN 6 PIC 9 SOURCE AREA-NUMBER.
      03  COLUMN 8 PIC X(7) VALUE "SAVINGS".
      03  AREA-TOTAL COLUMN 66 PIC $$$,$$$,$$9.99 SUM BRANCH-TOTAL.
   02  LINE PLUS 1.
      03  COLUMN 8 PIC X(8) VALUE "INTEREST".
      03  AREA-INTEREST COLUMN 66 PIC $$$,$$$,$$9.99 SUM BRANCH-INTEREST.
01  TYPE IS CONTROL FOOTING BRANCH-NUMBER.
   02  LINE PLUS 2.
      03  COLUMN 5 PIC X(6) VALUE "BRANCH".
      03  COLUMN 12 PIC ZZ9 SOURCE BRANCH-NUMBER.
      03  COLUMN 16 PIC X(7) VALUE "SAVINGS".
      03  BRANCH-TOTAL COLUMN 53 PIC $$$,$$$,$$9.99 SUM CURRENT-BALANCE.
   02  LINE PLUS 1.
      03  COLUMN 16 PIC X(8) VALUE "INTEREST".
      03  BRANCH-INTEREST COLUMN 53 PIC $$$,$$$,$$9.99 SUM INTEREST.
01  CLIENT-RECORD TYPE IS DETAIL.

PROCEDURE DIVISION.
START-PARAGRAPH.
    OPEN I-O MASTER-FILE, OUTPUT SAVINGS-PRINTOUT.
    INITIATE SAVINGS-REPORT.
    PERFORM READ-MASTER-FILE.
    PERFORM GENERATE-CLIENT-RECORD UNTIL END-OF-FILE.
    TERMINATE SAVINGS-REPORT.
    CLOSE MASTER-FILE, SAVINGS-PRINTOUT.
    STOP RUN.
READ-MASTER-FILE.
    READ MASTER-FILE AT END MOVE 1 TO FILE-FLAG.
GENERATE-CLIENT-RECORD.
    PERFORM CALCULATE-INTEREST.
    ADD INTEREST TO CURRENT-BALANCE.
    MOVE CURRENT-BALANCE TO MINIMUM-BALANCE.
    GENERATE SAVINGS-REPORT.
    REWRITE MASTER.
    PERFORM READ-MASTER-FILE.
CALCULATE-INTEREST.
    IF MINIMUM-BALANCE > THRESHOLD
       COMPUTE INTEREST = THRESHOLD * LOWER-RATE
                        + (MINIMUM-BALANCE — THRESHOLD) * UPPER-RATE
       ELSE COMPUTE INTEREST = MINIMUM-BALANCE * LOWER-RATE.
```

Although the COBOL Report Writer is a powerful tool for the generation of report programs, several precautionary comments should be noted:

(a) it is not as flexible as RPGII, the report generation language whose facilities the Report Writer appears to try to emulate;

(b) its definition takes as many as 56 pages in the COBOL-74 definition and some of its more subtle aspects are quite difficult to understand;

(c) it is not widely implemented, and rarely in conformance with the standard.

18.3 REPORT WRITER DECLARATIVES

Declaratives are sections of statements which appear in the DECLARATIVES part at the start of the PROCEDURE DIVISION of a COBOL program and which define actions to be carried out whenever certain special conditions arise in the execution of a program. Report programs may include declaratives specifying actions to be taken immediately prior to the production of any heading or footing report group named in the Report Section. Such a declarative will have the form

> *section-name* SECTION.
>   USE BEFORE REPORTING *report-group-name*.
>   .
>   .
>   .

This section will then be executed before the printing of the named report group.

As an example consider the problem of printing the page numbers in the page headings of our report using Roman rather than Arabic numerals. The definition of the page heading report group would then be

```
01   PAGE-HEADING TYPE IS PAGE HEADING.
   02   LINE 2 COLUMN 36 PIC X(8)
            SOURCE ROMAN-PAGE-NUMBER.
```

where the page heading report group has now been given the name PAGE-HEADING and ROMAN-PAGE-NUMBER is a PIC X(8) data item declared in the Working-Storage Section. A suitable declarative would then be declared at the start of the PROCEDURE DIVISION.

```
PROCEDURE DIVISION.
DECLARATIVES.
ROMAN SECTION.
```

```
             USE BEFORE REPORTING PAGE-HEADING.
    *        THIS SECTION CONVERTS THE VALUE
    *        OF PAGE-COUNTER TO A STRING OF
    *        ROMAN NUMERALS WHICH IS ASSIGNED
    *        TO THE DATA ITEM ROMAN-PAGE-NUMBER
         .
         .
         .
    END DECLARATIVES.
```

Each time that the Report Writer system is about to print a page heading the section ROMAN will be executed, converting the current value of PAGE-COUNTER to a string of Roman numerals and assigning this string to ROMAN-PAGE-NUMBER, which is the SOURCE of the value to be printed in the page heading.

If page footings also were to contain Roman numerals, then a second section would be required, identical to ROMAN except with a different name and a USE statement specifying the page footing name, e.g.,

```
ROMAN-2 SECTION.
    USE BEFORE REPORTING PAGE-FOOTING.
```

where PAGE-FOOTING would be declared in the Report Section as the name of the PAGE FOOTING report group.

BIBLIOGRAPHY

Two excellent texts describing data processing activities and file structures are

M.J.R. Shave and K.N. Bhaskar, *Computer Science applied to Business Systems,* Addison-Wesley, 1982.
H.D. Clifton, *Business Data Systems* (2nd Edition), Prentice-Hall International, 1983.

A popular introductory text on programming in Pascal is

J. Welsh and J. Elder, *Introduction to Pascal* (2nd Edition), Prentice-Hall International, 1982.

For an introduction to abstract data types and concurrent programming in Ada consult

J.G.P. Barnes, *Programming in Ada,* Addison-Wesley, 1982.

The development and use of a software library of abstract data types is illustrated in

J. Welsh, J. Elder, D. Bustard, *Sequential Program Structures,* Prentice-Hall International, 1984.

A comprehensive overview of file organization and access methods is given in

O. Hanson, *Design of Computer Files,* Pitman, 1982.

The paper on file updating used as the basis of Chapter 4 is

B. Dwyer, One more time — how to update a master file, *Communications of the A.C.M.,* **24**(1) 1981.

Two of the main texts on searching and sorting algorithms are

N. Wirth, *Algorithms + Data Structures = Programs,* Prentice-Hall, 1976.
D.E. Knuth, *The Art of Computer Programming Vol. 3 : Sorting and Searching,* Addison-Wesley, 1973.

A discussion of addressing algorithms appears in the paper

R. Morris, Scatter storage techniques, *Communications of the A.C.M.,* **11**(1) 1968.

Michael Jackson's programming methodology for the construction of data processing applications programs is discussed in his book

M.A. Jackson, *Principles of Program Design*, Academic Press, 1975.

SIMULA is a language which provides coroutines. These facilities and those provided in other languages are examined in

C.D. Marlin, *Coroutines,* Lecture Notes in Computer Science 95, Springer-Verlag, 1980.

The official definition of COBOL-74 is

American National Standard Programming Language COBOL (ANSI X3.23 – 1974), American National Standard Institute, 1974.

There is an abundance of text books on COBOL. Two of the more complete and readable are

N. Lyons, *Structured COBOL for Data Processing*, Glencoe, 1980.
D. McCracken, *A Simplified Guide to Structured COBOL Programming*, Wiley, 1976.

APPENDIX: SOLUTIONS
TO SELECTED EXERCISES

EXERCISES 3

1. From the formula on page 43 :

Block size	input time
100	350 secs
1000	80 secs
2000	65 secs
10000	53 secs

4. (a) Since the input is serial, there are 200 arm movements in all
    (one per cylinder) each across one cylinder, i.e., the total arm
    movement time is 200*25 msecs. There is an average half-
    revolution of rotational delay per bucket read (2000 buckets in
    all), i.e., a total of 20 seconds latency. Each bucket transfer
    takes one revolution, and hence the total transfer time is 40
    seconds, giving a total serial input time of 65 seconds.

   (b) For random input the total latency and transfer times are as
    above.   However, reading each bucket involves an arm movement
    across an average of 100 cylinders, which takes 25 + (0.5*100)
    msecs per movement, i.e., 75 msecs.   Hence the total arm
    movement time increases to 150 seconds, and the total input time
    to 210 seconds.

5. From the formulae on pages 42-43, and the square-root rule :

	file length (M chars)	block size (chars)	reels	file transfer time (secs)
transactions file	64	3200	4	1267
old master file	36	2400	2	750
new master file	36	2400	2	750

6. The size of the product file is 50 cylinders.
    For random access the average arm movement time is thus
    25+(0.5*25) msecs, i.e., 37.5 msecs.   There are 100 000 product
    references, each requiring one such arm movement, 10 msecs
    latency, and 5 msecs transfer time (since there are four buckets
    per track). Hence the total access time is 87.5 minutes.
    If the product lines of each customer order are first sorted to the
    same sequence as the file (e.g., product code sequence) then the
    five "hit" cylinders will normally be equi-spaced over the file -
    average arm movement per order then is one movement from end to
    start of the 50 cylinder file, plus four movements of 10
    cylinders, i.e., 170 msecs.   Thus the total arm movement time is
    reduced from 3750 seconds to 3400 seconds, and the total access
    time becomes 81 minutes 40 secs.
    Further, by sorting the product references to alternate ascending
    and descending product code sequence, the 25 msecs return arm
    movements can be eliminated and the total disk access time
    is reduced to 65 minutes.

7. The file will occupy 100 cylinders.   The hit ratio indicates an
    average of 100 references to the file per run.   The arm movement
    per reference is over an average of 50 cylinders, hence taking 50
    msecs.   The latency per reference is 10 msecs and the transfer
    time is 5 msecs (four buckets per track). The total file access
    time is thus 65 seconds.

8. The file will occupy 125 cylinders.   The hit ratio indicates an
    average of 5000 record updates per run, i.e., 40 per cylinder.
    Since processing is in key sequence there will be a total of 125
    single-cylinder arm movements, each taking 25 msecs, i.e., 3.125
    seconds in all.   There will be 125 half-revolution latencies in
    reading the track index prior to accessing each cylinder, i.e.,
    1.25 seconds.   For each bucket accessed there will be a half-
    revolution latency prior to both reading and rewriting (100
    seconds total) and the total transfer time for both reading and
    rewriting a bucket will be 25 seconds (since a bucket transfer
    will take 2.5 msecs). The total disk access time is therefore
    129.375 seconds.

9. The file will occupy 100 cylinders and each run will, on average,
    update 4000 records.   For random order processing, each update
    will involve an average arm movement across 50 cylinders, taking
    50 msecs.   For each update there will be a half-revolution
    latency in reading the track index and before reading and writing
    the bucket concerned, i.e., 30 msecs per update.   Transferring a
    bucket takes 5 msecs, so the total transfer time per update is 10
    msecs. Hence the total disk access time for 4000 updates is 360
    seconds.

EXERCISES 6

1.(a)   0000001643   0000275980   003062584X
  (b)   only 0220668647 is valid

EXERCISES 7

2. By tracing the heapsort program for a heap size of 8, we find
    that the following three initial strings will be generated :
        1 7 17 19 29 37 41 47 53 54 61 67 92
        3 5 6 11 13 19 20 22 23 24 31 36 43 44 59
        4 8
    If this program is used to distribute the initial strings in a Von
    Neumann sort then only one merge of the files is required to
    complete the sort.

7. program Sortnumbers ;

        const max = 50 ;

        class integerfile = sequentialfile in library
                            (where type itemtype = integer) ;
        instance sortedfile : integerfile (' ', true) ;
        instance unsortedfile : integerfile (' ', true) ;

        class console operator = console in library ;

        function ltequal (i1, i2 : integer) : Boolean ;
          begin ltequal := (i1 <= i2) end ;

```
procedure filesort in library
  (where class seqfile = integerfile ;
         type recordtype = integer) ;

procedure generatenumbers ;
  var i : 3.. maxint ;
      n1, n2, n3 : 0..999 ;
  begin
    with unsortedfile do
      begin
        open (output) ;
        operator.read (n1) ; write (n1) ;
        operator.read (n2) ; write (n2) ;
        for i := 3 to max do
          begin
            n3 := (n1 + n2) mod 1000 ; write (n3) ;
            n1 := n2 ; n2 := n3
          end ;
        close
      end
  end {generatenumbers} ;

procedure list ;
  var i : integer ; endofdata : Boolean ;
  begin
    with sortedfile do
      begin
        open (input) ; read (i, endofdata) ;
        while not endofdata do
          begin operator.write (i) ; read (i, endofdata) end ;
        operator.message ('Sort complete') ;
        close
      end
  end {list} ;

begin {main program}
  generatenumbers ;
  filesort (unsortedfile, sortedfile, ltequal) ;
  list
end.
```

EXERCISES 9

1.(i) self-addressing gives record position of 4321
      file address = cylinder 43, track 2
      actual address = cylinder 51, track 2
  (ii) prime division - required prime is 9973
      record position = 1624
      actual address = cylinder 24, track 2
(iii) using mid square method
      record position = 758327(9989)971041 = 9989
      actual address = cylinder 107, track 8
  (iv) folding algorithm using sum of first 4 and last 4 digits
      record position = (1)3086
      actual address = cylinder 38, track 8
   (v) 87654321 to base 11 transforms to decimal 1863788176
      record position = (186378)8176
      actual address = cylinder 89, track 7

5.   {solution using prime division by 9973}
     const prime = 9973 ;
     type accountnumber = 0..999999 ;
          addressrange = 1..9973 ;
```
```

```
          customer = record
                         key : accountnumber ;
                         rating : integer
                     end ;

   procedure getnumber (c : customer ; var k : accountnumber) ;
     begin k := c.key end ;

   function samenumber (k1, k2 : accountnumber) : Boolean ;
     begin samenumber := (k1 = k2) end ;

   function primedivision (k : accountnumber) : addressrange ;
     begin primedivision := k mod prime + 1 end ;

   class randomfile in library
     (where type elementtype = customer ;
            type keytype = accountnumber ;
            function address = primedivision ;
            procedure getkey = getnumber ;
            function samekey = samenumber) ;

   instance masterfile = randomfile ('RATINGS') ;
```

EXERCISES 11

1.
```
     IDENTIFICATION DIVISION.
     PROGRAM-ID.      EXERCISE-11-1.
     *    THIS PROGRAM REPRODUCES A COBOL SOURCE PROGRAM AND INSERTS
     *    (1) A PROGRAM IDENTIFICATION
     *    (2) SEQUENCE NUMBERS (IN MULTIPLES OF 10)
     *
     *    INPUT : A COBOL SOURCE PROGRAM,
     *            PRECEDED BY A CONTROL LINE CONTAINING
     *               COLS  1 - 6    999999
     *               COLS 73 -80    REQUIRED PROGRAM IDENTIFICATION
     *    OUTPUT : A NEW VERSION OF THE SOURCE PROGRAM WITH
     *               COLS  1 - 6    NEW SEQUENCE NUMBERS
     *               COLS  7 -72    TEXT AS IN ORIGINAL PROGRAM
     *               COLS 73 -80    PROGRAM IDENTIFICATION

     ENVIRONMENT DIVISION.
     CONFIGURATION SECTION.
     SOURCE-COMPUTER.      SUPER-2000.
     OBJECT-COMPUTER.      SUPER-2000.
     INPUT-OUTPUT SECTION.
     FILE-CONTROL.
         SELECT INPUT-FILE ASSIGN TO CARD-READER 1.
         SELECT OUTPUT-FILE ASSIGN TO CARD-PUNCH 1.
     DATA DIVISION.
     FILE SECTION.
     FD INPUT-FILE LABEL RECORDS OMITTED.
         01  A-LINE.
             05  SEQUENCE-FIELD   PIC X(6).
             05  TEXT-FIELD       PIC X(66).
             05  NAME-FIELD       PIC X(8).
     FD OUTPUT-FILE LABEL RECORDS OMITTED.
         01  NEW-SOURCE-LINE     PIC X(80).
     WORKING-STORAGE SECTION.
         01  NEW-LINE.
             05  NEW-SEQUENCE     PIC 9(6) VALUE 10.
             05  NEW-TEXT         PIC X(66).
             05  NEW-NAME         PIC X(8).
         77  FILE-FLAG PIC 9 COMP SYNC RIGHT VALUE ZERO.
             88  END-OF-FILE      VALUE 1.
```

```
PROCEDURE DIVISION.
START-PARAGRAPH.
    OPEN INPUT INPUT-FILE, OUTPUT OUTPUT-FILE.
    PERFORM READ-A-LINE.
    IF END-OF-FILE
       DISPLAY "NO DATA FOR PROGRAM"
       PERFORM END-OF-PROGRAM.
    IF SEQUENCE-FIELD NOT EQUAL TO "999999"
       DISPLAY "CONTROL LINE MISSING"
       PERFORM END-OF-PROGRAM.
    MOVE NAME-FIELD TO NEW-NAME.
    PERFORM READ-A-LINE.
    PERFORM PROCESS-NEXT-LINE UNTIL END-OF-FILE.
    PERFORM END-OF-PROGRAM.
READ-A-LINE.
    READ INPUT-FILE AT END MOVE 1 TO FILE-FLAG.
PROCESS-NEXT-LINE.
    MOVE TEXT-FIELD TO NEW-TEXT.
    WRITE NEW-SOURCE-LINE FROM NEW-LINE.
    ADD 10 TO NEW-SEQUENCE.
    PERFORM READ-A-LINE.
END-OF-PROGRAM.
    CLOSE INPUT-FILE AND OUTPUT-FILE.
    STOP RUN.
```

EXERCISES 12

1.
DATA-ITEM-1	1 byte	
DATA-ITEM-2	1 byte	(sign stored in one of the unused bits)
DATA-ITEM-3	5 bits	(sign bit + 4 bits for value)
DATA-ITEM-4	18 bits	(sign bit + 17 bits)
DATA-ITEM-5	9 bytes	

3.(a)
```
01  WORK-STORE.
    02  FIRST-4    PIC XXXX.
    02  LAST-4     PIC XXXX.
01  STORE-WORK REDEFINES WORK-STORE.
    02  FILLER     PIC XX.
    02  MIDDLE-4   PIC XXXX.
    02  FILLER     PIC XX.
```

   (b)
```
01  AMOUNT          PIC 9999V99.
01  AMOUNT-1 REDEFINES  AMOUNT.
    02  INT-PART    PIC 9999.
    02  FRAC-PART   PIC 99.
```

4.(a)   INSPECT SAMPLE-ITEM REPLACING ALL SPACES BY "-".
   (b)   INSPECT SAMPLE-ITEM TALLYING SOME-COUNT-ITEM
                            FOR LEADING ZEROES.
   (c)   INSPECT SAMPLE-ITEM TALLYING SOME-COUNT-ITEM
                            FOR LEADING SPACES
                            REPLACING LEADING SPACES BY ".".
   (d)   INSPECT SAMPLE-ITEM REPLACING CHARACTERS
                            BEFORE INITIAL "X" BY "X".

5.

SAMPLE	COUNT-ITEM
$128,064.32	4
$?????12.69	undefined
535 22 1583	2
9A6X77X.,XX	undefined
JOHN SMITH	2
1.23	7

6.   MOVE ZEROES TO BLANK-COUNT, COMMA-COUNT, PERIOD-COUNT.
     INSPECT TEXT-FRAGMENT TALLYING
          BLANK-COUNT FOR ALL SPACES
          COMMA-COUNT FOR ALL ","
          PERIOD-COUNT FOR ALL ".".
     COMPUTE WORD-COUNT
            = BLANK-COUNT - COMMA-COUNT - 2 * PERIOD-COUNT.

8.   Using working-storage items
          77 PRINT-COUNT PIC 9 COMP SYNC RIGHT VALUE 0.
           88 READY-TO-PRINT VALUE 2.
          77 END-FLAG   PIC 9 COMP SYNC RIGHT VALUE ZERO.
           88 END-OF-DATA VALUE 1.

     PROCEDURE DIVISION.
     MAIN-PROGRAM.
        OPEN INPUT CARD-FILE, OUTPUT PRINT-FILE.
        MOVE SPACES TO PRINT-RECORD.
        WRITE PRINT-RECORD BEFORE ADVANCING PAGE.
        PERFORM GET-CARD.
        PERFORM PRINT-TWO-UP UNTIL END-OF-DATA.
        CLOSE CARD-FILE, PRINT-FILE.
        STOP RUN.
     GET-CARD.
        READ CARD-FILE AT END MOVE 1 TO END-FLAG ;
                              MOVE 2 TO PRINT-COUNT.
     PRINT-TWO-UP.
        ADD 1 TO PRINT-COUNT.
        MOVE CARD-DETAILS TO CARD-PLACES (PRINT-COUNT).
        PERFORM GET-CARD.
        IF READY-TO-PRINT WRITE PRINT-RECORD AFTER 1 LINE ;
                          MOVE SPACES TO PRINT-RECORD ;
                          MOVE ZERO TO PRINT-COUNT.

     The moving of 2 into PRINT-COUNT by the AT END clause ensures
     that, if there is an odd number of cards in the deck, the last
     card will still be printed.

11.   Receiving Field

		Z9	+9	-9	S9	+++	$*.**
	0	0	+0	0	0		$****
Source	3.4	3	+3	3	3	+3	$3.40
Value	0.07	0	+0	0	0		$*.07
	-7.24	7	-7	-7	!7	-7	$7.24

     ! - sign stored in leading byte

12.
SOURCE ITEM		RECEIVING ITEM	
PICTURE	CONTENTS	PICTURE	EDITED RESULT
9(6)	000197	ZZZ999	197
9(6)	290866	999B99B99	029 08 66
9(6)	019113	Z(6)00	1911300
9999V99	148143	ZZZ,ZZZ.Z	1,481.4
S9(6)	543210	-999,999	543,210
S9(6)	543210	+999,999	+543,210
99V999	03456	ZZV999	3456
X(6)	ABCDEF	X(7)	ABCDEF
X(6)	ABCDEF	XBXXXBBXX	A BCD EF
S9(6)	000312	ZZZ,ZZ9CR	312

13. A   10 bytes $000123.45
    B   10 bytes $123.45
    C   10 bytes $ 123.45
    D   13 bytes $****123.45DB
    E   10 bits   0001111011   (123 in binary)
    F   2 bytes   23   (sign stored with the 2)
    G   4 bytes   2345   (sign stored with the 2)
    H   1 byte   5   (sign stored with the 5)

EXERCISES 13

1.(a) FD ORDERS
         LABEL RECORDS OMITTED.
  (b) FD PAYROLL-MASTER
         LABEL RECORDS STANDARD
         VALUE OF ID IS "MASTER-PAY-1".
  (c) FD PARTS-REQUIREMENTS
         BLOCK CONTAINS 10 RECORDS
         LABEL RECORDS STANDARD
            VALUE OF ID IS "PARTS-REQUIREMENTS".

EXERCISES 15

1.
    IDENTIFICATION DIVISION.
    PROGRAM-ID.   RANDOM-NUMBER-SORT.

    ENVIRONMENT DIVISION.
    CONFIGURATION SECTION.
    SOURCE-COMPUTER.   SUPER-2000.
    OBJECT-COMPUTER.   SUPER-2000.
    INPUT-OUTPUT SECTION.
    FILE-CONTROL.
       SELECT WORK-FILE ASSIGN TO DISK 1.

    DATA DIVISION.
    FILE SECTION.
    SD WORK-FILE.
       01   RANDOM-NUMBER.
          02   KEY-VALUE   PIC 99999.
    WORKING-STORAGE SECTION.
    77   N-1 PIC 9(5) COMP SYNC RIGHT.
    77   N-2 PIC 9(5) COMP SYNC RIGHT.
    77   N-3 PIC 9(6) COMP SYNC RIGHT.
    77   TOTAL-GENERATED   PIC 99 COMP SYNC RIGHT VALUE ZERO.
      88   ALL-GENERATED   VALUE 30.
    77   FILE-FLAG   PIC 9 COMP SYNC RIGHT VALUE ZERO.
      88   END-OF-FILE   VALUE 1.

    PROCEDURE DIVISION.

    MAIN-PROGRAM SECTION.
    MAIN-PARAGRAPH.
    *   OBTAIN TWO INTEGERS FROM TERMINAL.
         DISPLAY "INPUT TWO FIVE-DIGIT NUMBERS".
         ACCEPT N-1, N-2.
         SORT WORK-FILE ON ASCENDING KEY-VALUE
                          INPUT PROCEDURE IS GENERATE-NUMBERS
                          OUTPUT PROCEDURE IS DISPLAY-NUMBERS.
         DISPLAY "END OF NUMBER SORTING".
         STOP RUN.

```
GENERATE NUMBERS SECTION.
G-N-MAIN.
   PERFORM GENERATE-NEXT-NUMBER UNTIL ALL-GENERATED.
   GO TO G-N-EXIT.
GENERATE-NEXT-NUMBER.
   ADD N-1, N-2 GIVING N-3.
   IF N-3 > 99999 SUBTRACT 100000 FROM N-3.
   MOVE N-2 TO N-1.
   MOVE N-3 TO N-2.
   RELEASE RANDOM-NUMBER FROM N-3.
   ADD 1 TO TOTAL-GENERATED.
G-N-EXIT.
   EXIT.

DISPLAY-NUMBERS SECTION.
D-N-MAIN.
   PERFORM DISPLAY-NEXT-NUMBER UNTIL END-OF-FILE.
   GO TO D-N-EXIT.
DISPLAY-NEXT-NUMBER.
   RETURN WORK-FILE INTO N-3 AT END MOVE 1 TO FILE-FLAG.
   DISPLAY N-3.
D-N-EXIT.
   EXIT.
```

INDEX